SharePoint 2010 Development
with Silverlight

SharePoint 2010 Development with Silverlight

Bob German
Paul Stubbs

✦ Addison-Wesley

Upper Saddle River, NJ • Boston • Indianapolis • San Francisco
New York • Toronto • Montreal • London • Munich • Paris • Madrid
Cape Town • Sydney • Tokyo • Singapore • Mexico City

The publisher offers excellent discounts on this book when ordered in quantity for bulk purchases or special sales, which may include electronic versions and/or custom covers and content particular to your business, training goals, marketing focus, and branding interests. For more information, please contact:

U.S. Corporate and Government Sales
(800) 382-3419
corpsales@pearsontechgroup.com

For sales outside the United States please contact:

International Sales
international@pearson.com

Visit us on the Web: informit.com/aw

Library of Congress Cataloging-in-Publication Data:

German, Bob.

Sharepoint 2010 development with Silverlight / Bob German, Paul Stubbs. — 1st ed.

p. cm.

ISBN 978-0-321-76959-6 (paperwork)

1. Microsoft SharePoint (Electronic resource) 2. Silverlight (Electronic resource) 3. Intranets (Computer networks) 4. Web servers. I. Stubbs, Paul R., 1969- II. Title.

TK5105.875.I6G46 2012

004'.36—dc23

2011036853

ISBN-13: 978-0-321-76959-6
ISBN-10: 0-321-76959-7

Text printed in the United States on recycled paper at Edwards Brothers in Ann Arbor, Michigan.

First printing November 2011

I dedicate this book to my parents, Don German and Joan German-Grapes, who inspired and encouraged me to write.
—Bob

This book is dedicated to my brilliant friends and colleagues in the Share-Point community who inspire and encourage me every day.
—Paul

Contents at a Glance

Contents

Index

Foreword

As Microsoft developed Silverlight versions 3 and 4, it enabled developers to create compelling business applications that were distributed and run in the browser with a rich, refreshing, and engaging experience. This technology was a natural addition to the SharePoint developer's toolbox, as so many companies store business data within intranets and extranets on the SharePoint platform. With the release of SharePoint 2010, Microsoft made it easier to consume and integrate data stored within SharePoint into Silverlight applications with the client object model and a new RESTful service.

While many technologies (such as HTML 5) promise and deliver, to varying degrees of success, the ability to build rich business applications in the browser, Silverlight has a proven and mature track record. It is an obvious choice when building a new business application. SharePoint serves not only as a fantastic delivery mechanism, but the application can also leverage the vast amounts of business data that is stored in corporate SharePoint deployments.

Over the years, I've been fortunate enough to know and work with both Bob German and Paul Stubbs. Bob and I have worked on other book projects, and I've worked on numerous development projects with Paul. Both have solid, real-world experience and perspectives on the SharePoint platform and both also spent a considerable amount of time with Silverlight. They have presented many informative and engaging presentations at conferences and user groups, as well as written numerous articles on the subject. Who better to collaborate on the topic!

Most SharePoint development books only touch on the client object model and how to use the Silverlight implementation or the new List-Data.svc RESTful service. If you are building a Silverlight business application, you need a good resource from some trusted names to deliver solid guidance on working with both Silverlight and SharePoint together.

The authors break the learning experience into three parts. Part 1 of the book focuses on getting you up-to-speed quickly on SharePoint and Silverlight development. Part 2 dives into the fundamentals and basics you need to know, such as working with the client object model, the REST service, web services, and external data (that which SharePoint is aware of but lives in another system). Part 3 kicks into high gear, teaching you how to leverage Silverlight to create sophisticated navigation controls, utilize the emerging and ever more important cloud, and even create custom field controls.

I can't imagine two better people to collaborate and deliver a fantastic book on the subject of SharePoint 2010 and Silverlight. Consider this a must-have for your bookshelf...I do!

Andrew Connell
Co-Founder, Developer, Instructor, Speaker
Critical Path Training, LLC
www.CriticalPathTraining.com
August 2011

Preface

IN EARLY VERSIONS OF SHAREPOINT, the developer experience was an afterthought at best. Microsoft finally opened up a supported way for developers to create SharePoint features in 2007. Although the tooling was still primitive, this led to an interest in developing applications on top of SharePoint. These solutions are generally cheaper and faster to build and more flexible for business users because they build on all the capabilities included in SharePoint.

Around the same time, the Internet was offering a richer user experience. Page refreshes became passé in favor of pages that were interactive. This drove a number of client-side technologies for bringing pages to life right within a web page. Silverlight was making a name for itself as a very productive way to build compelling business applications that run in a web browser.

The authors both noticed that more and more customers were asking how they could develop rich business applications on SharePoint, the kind of applications that lend themselves to a Silverlight user interface. Paul co-authored a book about SharePoint and Silverlight, which shows how to build solutions using the tools that were available at the time.

The advent of SharePoint 2010 and Visual Studio 2010 changed everything. Suddenly SharePoint wasn't just allowing applications, but it was encouraging them. Features like sandboxed solutions and client object models enabled a whole new class of light-weight applications. And the tooling in Visual Studio 2010 removed the tedious and arcane aspects of SharePoint development and seamlessly knitted in Silverlight as well.

Bob and Paul started speaking on SharePoint and Silverlight development and developed collections of sample applications. And both wanted someday to write a book (or another book!) on the topic. At one of the conferences after speaking in adjacent rooms, they decided to coauthor this book.

This book is for any .NET, SharePoint, or Silverlight developer who wants to learn how to build a new, richer class of applications. SharePoint provides a data layer, a hosting platform, and a suite of collaboration and publishing features to build on. Silverlight makes the experience richer and easier to use.

Late one night last winter, Bob's wife Kate wandered into his home office and observed how much time he was putting into this book. "But," she added, "you seem to be having fun!" It's true, programming with SharePoint and Silverlight is actually fun!

Whether you read it during your day job or late at night, may this book bring some of that fun to you, too.

Acknowledgments

ALTHOUGH THERE ARE ONLY TWO NAMES on the cover, this book is the result of many people who contributed their time, energy and expertise to the project.

First of all, we want to thank Matt Burnett, who wrote Chapter 14 on Office 365 and Windows Azure. Matt works for Microsoft Consulting Services and has a wealth of experience making SharePoint and Silverlight work with Microsoft's cloud offerings. We were really glad he agreed to bring his knowledge and expertise to the book.

The technical review team was a cast of SharePoint luminaries, and we were very fortunate and honored to have them. The team members were: Andrew Connell and Ted Pattison, co-founders of Critical Path training; Scott Jamison, CEO of Jornata; Matt Jackson, Director at BlueMetal Architects; and Ed Hild, Architect at the Microsoft Technology Center in Reston, Virginia. Their perspectives and guidance greatly improved the quality of this book.

We'd also like to thank everyone from Addison-Wesley who contributed to this book, many of whom we never had the opportunity to meet. We'd especially like to thank Joan Murray for the opportunity to write the book, for her constant feedback and encouragement, and for deftly guiding us throughout the publishing process.

Bob German

I want to thank my parents, who wrote more than 35 books, for inspiring me to write and exposing me to the writing process at a young age. I remember proofreading galleys with them as soon as I learned to read.

I also want to thank my teachers: John Campbell, for introducing me to programming as a child, and my many excellent college professors, especially Mark Seiden and the late Anita Goldner. I thank Scott Jamison for my first serious education in SharePoint on a project in 2002 and Ted Pattison for sharing his development wizardry and exposing the magic that makes it all work.

I'm thankful to Paul Stubbs for being a great and experienced coauthor and helping me with this, my first book project, with lots of ongoing technical and writing advice. Also his chapters are great!

Andrew Connell has been a great friend and mentor throughout the project. He gave me the opportunity to write two chapters in his Web Content Management book, which was an extremely valuable experience. He also gave me a huge amount of encouragement and guidance.

Ed Hild was also an invaluable advisor and sounding board. He shared a great deal of helpful experience from his own book writing and was equally helpful in working out technical problems and digging deeply into issues while reviewing the book.

My most heartfelt thanks goes to my wife, Kate Severinsen, who supported and encouraged me throughout the project. She cut me endless slack while I was working nights and weekends on the book, and she reminded me to stop and laugh along the way.

Paul Stubbs

First I want to thank Bob German for being a great coauthor. This may be Bob's first book, but he was the one that held it all together and went above and beyond to see this book to completion. Bob is going to have a bright future in writing more books, and I look forward to doing more projects with Bob in the future.

I want to thank Matt Burnett for being a good friend to me over the years and listening to all of my crazy ideas. Matt is always ready to help me solve the tough problems that come up when developing SharePoint solutions.

I also want to thank Steve Fox. Steve has been a good friend and was the co-author of my first SharePoint and Silverlight book years ago. Steve has also been a real motivation for me in writing. He is a writing machine, cranking out multiple books a year. This has driven me to try and keep up and finish projects that I never would have even started in the past.

Last, but certainly not least, I want to thank my wife Rosa for allowing me the time required to write yet another book.

About the Authors

Bob German is an architect at the Microsoft Technology Center (MTC) near Boston, Massachusetts, where he helps customers create and prove out solutions that fit their business and technology needs. Bob works on SharePoint solutions for customers in a wide range of industries and technology environments. He also advises independent software vendors who are looking to build products on, or integrate them with, SharePoint technologies.

Bob's career began as a systems programmer in the minicomputer industry. Eventually he became a project leader and architect specializing in network protocols and distributed systems. In 1995, he took his networking and development experience to Microsoft Consulting Services. This soon led to web development engagements, including a knowledge management web site for a major industry analyst. The site was based on Site Server 3.0, a precursor to SharePoint.

In 2000, Bob joined the very first Microsoft Technology Center and provided consulting services in an incubation environment to the burgeoning dot-com industry. This involved quite a bit of performance and scalability testing and plenty of troubleshooting because most of the applications crashed under load testing. It also involved helping out with some pretty cool web sites, although not all of them saw the light of day.

Bob has specialized in SharePoint technologies since a major project in 2002 threw him head-first into the SharePoint 2003 beta. He's helped many customers get started and regularly develops SharePoint and Silverlight solutions for proof of concept and demonstrations. Bob is a frequent speaker at conferences such as TechEd North America, the Microsoft Share-Point Conference, and MIX, as well as at user groups and SharePoint Saturdays.

Paul Stubbs is a Microsoft Technical Evangelist for SharePoint and Office, where he focuses on information worker development community around SharePoint and Office, Silverlight, and Web 2.0 social networking. He has authored several books on solution development using Microsoft Office, SharePoint, and Silverlight, several articles for *MSDN Magazine*, and has also spoken at Microsoft Tech-Ed, PDC, SharePoint Conference, DevConnections and MIX conferences.

Paul has also worked as a Senior Program Manager on Visual Studio in Redmond, Washington. Paul is a Microsoft Certified Trainer (MCT) and frequently participates in the developer community on the Microsoft forums. Visit Paul's blog at blogs.msdn.com/pstubbs for deep SharePoint developer information.

PART I

Getting Started

1

Getting Started with SharePoint and Silverlight

SHAREPOINT AND SILVERLIGHT are a great combination of technologies for building great web applications. Users can create and configure their own web-based collaboration and publishing solutions with SharePoint and can incorporate richer user interface components with Silverlight. Further, Silverlight extends the things that SharePoint's user-installable "sandboxed solutions" can do, such as reaching across SharePoint site collections and line of business systems and integrating multi-media features.

For developers, SharePoint provides an easily-packaged data layer, and Silverlight allows rich display and interaction with that data. SharePoint and Silverlight offer a unified development experience based on Visual Studio 2010, a consistent runtime environment (.NET) on both client and server, and extensive client-side APIs for accessing SharePoint in Silverlight.

This book began at Microsoft technology conferences such as TechEd, the Microsoft SharePoint Conference, MIX, and other venues where the authors delivered a variety of talks on the subject of SharePoint and Silverlight. Attendance was high, and feedback was positive, revealing a lot of interest in this combination of technologies. The authors of this book dive much more deeply than a conference talk or boot camp would allow, however, showing you all the tricks and techniques for being successful with this strong combination of technologies.

Why SharePoint?

A great struggle for control has been underway since the first business-oriented personal computer, the IBM model 5150, was introduced in 1981. Finally business managers could thumb their noses at lengthy IT backlogs and take direct control over computing tasks by purchasing a PC and using the simple word processors, spreadsheets, and other applications that were available at the time.

Although this independence led to business innovation and empowerment, it also led to a number of unanticipated problems. The IT people, despite their backlogs and sometimes conflicting priorities, had been securing and backing up their software and data, ensuring it complied with relevant laws and policies, and planning for contingencies in case anything went wrong. The newly empowered PC users often skipped over such concerns, unwittingly adding huge business risks. Meanwhile, data proliferated in companies, leading to confusion when a dozen variations of the same spreadsheet all yielded different results, with no way to know which was the right one.

Over time, personal computing has become ubiquitous, and IT has found ways to manage their companies' personal computers. Although some of these risks can be mitigated by, for example, a group policy that forces everyone to encrypt their data, other risks still remain.

SharePoint is one of a new breed of application environments that balances the needs of business users and those of IT. With SharePoint, business users can innovate and build simple solutions on their own while IT ensures that the environment is secure and backed up. The central idea of "sharing" eliminates or reduces the proliferation problem, so users all work on one common set of data, conflicts don't arise, and IT can govern the environment to encourage business users to comply with legal and company policies.

All this has led to SharePoint being a huge success in the marketplace. It's a platform that allows business and IT to work together rather than at cross purposes.

To a business user, SharePoint is a place to collaborate and publish information. Many simple business solutions can be created directly by savvy business users, with no need to involve IT in the details. It is mainly browser based; however, rich applications also integrate with SharePoint so users can share directly from tools such as Microsoft Word and Microsoft Outlook.

One of SharePoint's strengths is its extensibility. A developer can add functionality to the palette of available features, and business users can then use these extensions to build richer solutions. The most common extension by far is to add custom "web parts," which are small application components that appear on the screen as part of a SharePoint solution. (Web parts are similar to "portlets" or "widgets" used by other portal platforms.) However this is really only the beginning, as developers can also extend SharePoint workflows, add custom application and administrative pages, connect to line-of-business data, and more.

SharePoint's popularity, along with this extensibility, has led to a whole marketplace of independent software vendors who provide add-ons to SharePoint. SharePoint integration has become a critical component of many business applications, which can then be combined in the SharePoint user interface for simple, one-stop access by business users.

From a technical point of view, SharePoint has another strong advantage, which really amounts to code re-use. Why reinvent site provisioning or document management when SharePoint has both? Why create a new security model or rendering framework when you can build on an already established one? Why spend resources figuring out how to package your application or host your workflows when the SharePoint team already made the same investment? The list goes on and on, and since the entry level product, SharePoint Foundation, is free with the Windows Server operating system, it need not add to your cost of entry.

All in all, SharePoint saves developers work and comes with a large marketplace of customers who have already adopted SharePoint and want to extend its capabilities. This is why so many developers have gone beyond ASP.NET and are developing on SharePoint as a platform.

> **■ TIP**
>
> Shocking as it might seem, there is no product called SharePoint! SharePoint is a family of products that build on one another, each adding more capabilities and features. Throughout this book, the word "SharePoint" refers to the family of products because it's a lot shorter than spelling out "Microsoft SharePoint 2010 Products and Technologies."
>
> The base product, Microsoft SharePoint Foundation 2010, is a free download and includes basic document management and collaboration. Microsoft Share-Point Server 2010 comes in Standard and Enterprise editions, each adding more features.

Why Silverlight?

It wasn't long after the introduction of NCSA Mosaic, the first graphical web browser, that it was dubbed a "killer application." Instead of a hodgepodge of tools such as WAIS, FTP, and Gopher, the web browser provided universal access to Internet resources in a way that was easy enough for any computer user.

Yet the standardization that made the World Wide Web possible has also been a limiting factor. Standardization takes time, and interoperability is tricky. To this day, web developers need to test on a variety of target web browsers to ensure their sites look right, and they need to be aware of quirks that can affect the behavior and rendering in one browser versus another. This makes web development inherently more difficult and less flexible than other development environments.

There are at least two ways to address these issues. Runtime environments such as JQuery on the client side or ASP.NET on the server try to hide the browser-specific quirks from developers so they can focus on their applications. These environments work pretty well, but cross-browser testing is still advised, and the applications are still functionally limited to rendering what the target browsers can support.

Another approach is to use a browser plug-in, such as Oracle Java, Adobe Flash, or Microsoft Silverlight. With this approach, a trusted third-party builds a plug-in that runs in multiple browsers, and applications run inside the plug-in. These applications may appear to be part of a web page, yet the plug-in can go beyond what the web browser can do. For example, a plug-in can display streaming video even in browsers that don't have any video features by bypassing the browser and accessing the native operating system.

This architecture generally includes some kind of "sandbox" to protect end-users from malicious or poorly constructed applications. If the user trusts the plug-in, which comes from a major, established software vendor, he knows that the plug-in will limit what applications can do to his computer when they run.

Silverlight is a .NET-based plug-in that runs in Firefox, Internet Explorer, and Safari on Windows, Macintosh, and on Linux desktops as well through the "Moonlight" project. Silverlight adds a lot of functionality to the browsers it supports, including

- Consistent rendering on all supported platforms, using an extensive set of reusable controls from Microsoft and other software vendors
- A strongly-typed object-oriented development environment based on the popular .NET framework
- Effective separation of visual design and code, which, along with advanced data binding technology, allows designers and developers to work more independently and greatly facilitates automated testing
- 2D and 3D vector animation and graphics
- Video (up to 720p high definition) and audio streaming in a number of standard formats
- Isolated storage for saving state on the client
- Easy access to web services and network sockets, with support for advanced scenarios such as multicast networking
- Access to client devices such as webcam and microphone

- Access to the web browser for tight integration with JavaScript and dynamic HTML
- Support for theming, localization, visual state management, multi-threading, accessibility, and other attributes that are useful in many applications

At this writing, the RIA (Rich Internet Application) Statistics web site at http://riastats.com/ reports that Silverlight is installed on about 70% of client computers on the public Internet. Most SharePoint sites, however, are not on the public Internet but are used within enterprises as "intranets" for employee use or as "extranets" for working with business partners. In these environments it's easier to ensure the Silverlight plug-in is available; indeed, installation across an enterprise can be automated using Windows Update Services. This means that Silverlight is likely to be available or could be made available to users of most SharePoint sites.

There's been a lot of excitement in the industry lately about the forth-coming HTML 5 standard, which will provide a number of features such as 2D vector graphics and video support that were previously only avail-able using browser plug-ins. At the time of this writing, HTML 5 is in Work-ing Draft stage, and features based on the draft are beginning to show up in new versions of web browsers such as Internet Explorer, Mozilla Firefox, and Google Chrome.

When the new standard is complete, it will be implemented in incre-mental releases by browser vendors, continuing to complicate compatibil-ity testing. Script libraries like JQuery and KnockOut can help by offering features such as cross-browser consistency and data binding to the browser programming experience. Other libraries like Modernizr can check to see what browser features are available so the developer can adapt the user interface accordingly. Many web developers hope that these advances will finally make developing browser-based code as easy and productive as other modern development environments.

In the meantime, developers need to choose between a browser plug-in such as Silverlight, grappling with the emerging HTML 5 draft implemen-tations, or sticking with more mature but functionally limited web standards such as HTML 4. There is no one-size-fits-all answer to this decision, and in some cases it can be a tough one to make.

The key is to focus, as developers have always done, on the target for the application. If the application must run on devices that don't run Silverlight, then clearly it's not an option. But if the application is targeted toward computers running Windows or Mac OS, or mobile devices running Windows Phone 7 (which runs Silverlight natively), then developers can take advantage of all that Silverlight offers. In addition to providing a richer user experience, Silverlight can reduce development and testing time by providing a strongly-typed object-oriented development environment that works consistently across platforms. It's also a good approach for developers who know .NET because they will be able to leverage their knowledge in Silverlight.

HTML has a rich future for sure, and Silverlight will be there as well. Browser technology will continue to advance, reducing the need for plug-ins, and plug-ins will advance as well to fill gaps in the new browsers. If you're working in an environment where you can ensure Silverlight is available, and want to take advantage of its consistency, productivity, and features, then go for it! If you're not sure but want some of the advantages of Silverlight anyway, then selective use of Silverlight within an otherwise HTML UI might be advised. It's a balancing act that everyone needs to be aware of as the technology evolves. This may not make the decision obvious, but hopefully it can help with the thought process.

Why SharePoint and Silverlight Together?

The phrase "better together" has become almost a cliché at Microsoft, as it engineers its products for easier integration with one another. SharePoint and Silverlight are indeed better together for a number of reasons.

First and foremost, both are based on the .NET framework, and both share a common development tool (Visual Studio 2010), which in addition to reducing the learning curve for developers, generally simplifies development. A Visual Studio 2010 solution can contain both SharePoint and Silverlight projects, and the output of the Silverlight projects can be automatically included in the SharePoint deployment package. Debugging is also a unified experience; a developer can set and hit breakpoints in both the client and server-side code when troubleshooting code.

In addition, SharePoint provides a client object model for Silverlight to allow easy access to SharePoint content. This is also true for JavaScript, but not for other browser plug-ins such as Adobe Flash. Developers for Flash or Java could consume SharePoint's SOAP web services or RESTful OData interface, but the level of difficulty could increase dramatically.

Another important consideration is the emergence of sandboxed solutions in SharePoint 2010. Many people think of a development or testing environment when they hear the term "sandboxed solutions" but this is something different.

Sandboxed solutions provide an isolated environment for running applications that are only partially trusted, whether in development, testing, or in production. This allows end-users to upload SharePoint web solution packages they have written and purchased and run them without putting the SharePoint installation at risk. The sandbox means that whoever is hosting SharePoint, be it the local IT department or an online service such as Microsoft Office 365, can allow the code to run without worrying about security breaches, memory leaks, or other issues that could affect the overall SharePoint environment.

Sandboxed solutions are, by necessity, limited in nature. They can declare workflows, lists and library structures, and they can include .NET code, but the code runs with very restricted privileges. It cannot, for example, make any kind of network or database call, nor can it access the SharePoint object model outside of the site collection where it is installed.

Silverlight is a natural complement to sandboxed solutions because it can access resources directly from the client that would be outside of the reach of the SharePoint sandbox. For example, Silverlight can easily call a web service or another SharePoint site collection using the client object model. Because the Silverlight application can be deployed right in the SharePoint web solution package, end users can install it like any other SharePoint solution and need not be bothered with the details of deploying the Silverlight application or embedding the Silverlight plug-in on the page.

Finally, using SharePoint with Silverlight can simplify Silverlight applications while giving the user more flexibility. Rather than using a framework such as the Microsoft Extensibility Framework (MEF) or PRISM, SharePoint and Silverlight follow a similar pattern by allowing users to dynamically add web parts without recompiling the application. The assemblies just reside in a library as .xap files.

All in all, Silverlight can make SharePoint solutions richer and more powerful for end users while making the development experience simpler as well.

Who Should Read This Book

This book is written for developers, architects, and application designers who want to build solutions using SharePoint and Silverlight. It assumes you have a working knowledge of .NET programming, especially ASP.NET, which is the basis for SharePoint.

The book is focused on where SharePoint and Silverlight meet and shows you how to use the two technologies in concert. Although it doesn't offer comprehensive coverage of either SharePoint or Silverlight, it does provide a sufficient introduction to allow someone new to either or both technologies to understand what's in the book.

There is a code download to accompany the book, which is located at www.informit.com/title/0321769597. Most chapters include code samples to illustrate the concepts, and all the code is available at this location so you can try it out in your own environment. The code listings in the book are intended to illustrate concepts, but supporting code and packaging isn't always shown. If you want the complete solutions, they're in the download.

How to Use This Book

This book is organized so you can read it from end-to-end or in pieces according to your needs and interests.

The first few chapters are introductory in nature, and you might choose to skip over them. If you already have a SharePoint and Silverlight development environment set up, you don't need to read "Creating a Development Environment" later in this chapter. Chapter 2, "Introduction to SharePoint Development," provides an introduction to SharePoint development targeted at the ASP.NET developer; Chapter 3, "Introduction to Silverlight Development," does the same for Silverlight. If you already know the basics, you can skip over these chapters.

Chapters 4 through 11 form the core of SharePoint and Silverlight development. Although each chapter can stand on its own, any given chapter might refer back to concepts from an earlier one. Chapter 4, "A First Look at Silverlight in SharePoint," explains the Silverlight features that are built into SharePoint 2010, and Chapter 5, "Web Part Development," gets you started developing Silverlight web parts for SharePoint. Chapter 6, "Expression Blend, Data Binding, and Sample Data," explains how to use Expression Blend with SharePoint and Silverlight. Expression Blend is a design tool for Silverlight that makes it easy to prototype and visually design Silverlight applications. Then Chapters 7 through 11 focus on various ways of accessing SharePoint content in Silverlight, ranging from the new client object model to web services and OData access.

The last four chapters focus on specific situations. You learn how to work with SharePoint in Windows Phone 7 applications and how to develop for the new hosted Office 365. You also learn how to use Silverlight in site navigation and how to create field controls that use Silverlight to render and edit new kinds of data in SharePoint.

■ SILVERLIGHT VERSIONS IN THIS BOOK

Silverlight 5 was in beta testing while this book was being written. Although most of the programming examples work with Silverlight 4 or 5, some chapters include special sections to show how you can take the solutions a step further with new Silverlight features. These sections are shaded for easy identification.

Creating a Development Environment

SharePoint development took a big leap forward in the 2010 version due to greatly improved tooling built into Visual Studio 2010. All you have to do is press the F5 key, and Visual Studio will build your projects, package them, and deploy them to a local SharePoint server for debugging. However, this experience assumes that there is a local SharePoint server running on the same computer as Visual Studio. So for practical purposes, every developer will need his own copy of SharePoint in his development environment.

Most of the material in this book works with the free SharePoint Foundation 2010; the examples in Chapters 10, 13, and 15 require the full SharePoint Server 2010 product.

For development purposes, SharePoint 2010 will run on the following operating systems:

- Windows Server 2008 R2 x64
- Windows Server 2008 x64
- Windows 7 x64
- Windows Vista SP3 or greater, x64

Notice that all the choices are x64 because SharePoint can't run in a 32-bit environment. This can present a challenge if your development environment is 32-bit today. Virtualization can help, as can the new boot to VHD option in Windows 7. Some SharePoint development shops host virtual servers and allow developers to connect with remote desktops. There are several options, but they all lead to the same place: x64 is mandatory.

Table 1.1 shows an inventory of tools to be installed in a SharePoint and Silverlight development environment. All of these are available either for free or as trial versions; those that aren't free are available under some MSDN subscriptions. Please note that the download links were current as of this writing but could change over time; the URL shortening service bit.ly does not allow updating the links.

TABLE 1.1: Tools for a SharePoint and Silverlight Development Environment

Needed for	Tool	Download
Both	**Visual Studio 2010** Visual Studio is the common development tool for both SharePoint and Silverlight. Be sure to install at least Service Pack 1 as well.	http://bit.ly/SPSL_VS2010
SharePoint	**SharePoint Server 2010 or SharePoint Foundation 2010** Note that SharePoint Foundation is a subset of SharePoint server. The examples in Chapters 10, 13, and 15 depend on the full SharePoint Server.	http://bit.ly/SPSL_SharePoint
SharePoint	**Visual Studio 2010 SharePoint Power Tools** These tools make it easier to develop sandboxed solutions for SharePoint. Some of the examples in this book make use of the Visual Web Part (Sandboxed) template that is included.	http://bit.ly/SPSL_PowerTools
Both	**Silverlight Web Parts for SharePoint (VSIX)** This adds two templates for building Silverlight web parts and requires the Visual Studio 2010 SharePoint Power Tools. Some of the examples in this book make use of the Silverlight Web Parts for SharePoint.	http://bit.ly/SPSL_VSIX_WebParts
Silverlight	**Silverlight 4.0 Tools for Visual Studio or Silverlight 5.0 Tools for Visual Studio** Visual Studio 2010 ships with Silverlight 3.0 support; the Silverlight Tools add support for later versions and are required to run the examples in this book.	http://bit.ly/SPSL_GettingStarted

Needed for	Tool	Download
Silverlight	**Expression Blend 4.0 or Expression Blend 5.0** Expression Blend is a visual designer for Silverlight and is used in several chapters. Blend makes some tasks much easier in Silverlight and is well worth using.	http://bit.ly/SPSL_GettingStarted
SharePoint	**SharePoint Designer 2010** SharePoint Designer is a tool for editing SharePoint content and is a free download. Some chapters assume you have SharePoint Designer available, although strictly speaking it doesn't need to run on your development machine.	http://bit.ly/SPSL_SPDesigner64
SharePoint	**ADO.NET Data Services Update for .NET 3.5** This add-on is required to access SharePoint's RESTful interface as explained in Chapter 9.	http://bit.ly/SPSL_DataServicesUpdate
(optional)	A web tracing tool such as the "F12" developer tool included with Internet Explorer 9, or a download such as Fiddler or Nikhil's Web Development Helper. These tools allow tracing all requests coming from a web browser, including Silverlight network calls. Having one of them handy can help with troubleshooting.	http://bit.ly/SPSL_Fiddler or http://bit.ly/SPSL_WebDevHelper

Setting Up Your Environment

There are a few strategies for setting all this up in a development environment.

The first and surely the easiest approach is to simply download the whole environment with everything preinstalled as trial versions, which can be updated with your product keys from MSDN or elsewhere to allow them to run indefinitely. This is available at http://bit.ly/SPSL_2010VM. With this approach, all you need is the ability to run a Hyper-V virtual machine image. All the examples in this book have been tested on this virtual machine.

If you're interested in doing your development on a Windows 7 machine, you might want to start with the SharePoint 2010 Easy Setup Script, which can be downloaded at http://bit.ly/SPSL_EasySetup. This amazing script will download and install on a Windows 7 machine trial versions of nearly everything on the list just provided; the only missing items are the Silverlight Web Parts, ADO.NET Data Services, and a network tracing tool such as Fiddler or Nikhil's Web Development Helper. It's easy to configure the script to plug in your license keys if you don't want to run trial versions, and it can be adapted to crank out custom developer workstations for your shop.

The Easy Setup Script can install these tools directly on a Windows 7 x64 machine, or it will set up a Boot to VHD environment for you. Windows 7 is capable of booting directly to a virtual hard disk (.vhd) file; if you provide a .vhd with Windows 7 x64 installed, the script will install all the developer tools on that as an option.

Please note that the Easy Setup Script expects a clean and fully patched version of Windows 7. Before running the script, ensure none of the tools it installs are already installed and that you've run Windows Update to install all service packs and updates for Windows.

Installing SharePoint "From Scratch"

If you want to build a SharePoint development environment on your own, it can be a helpful learning experience and give you complete control over the configuration. For example, you might want to run SharePoint as part of an Active Directory domain; this should be done before installing SharePoint. This is helpful for working with user profiles, which can be synchronized with Active Directory, and is the most secure and easiest way to set up a multi-server environment. The virtual machine download mentioned earlier is already configured as its own domain controller; you can do this as well or join an existing domain prior to installing SharePoint.

All the products in Table 1.1 are easy to install and require no special instructions, except one, and that's SharePoint itself. This section shows you how to set up SharePoint 2010 on a clean Windows Server 2008 R2 machine as a single-server SharePoint "farm." Your production and staging environments may well have several servers, but that's beyond the scope of this book.

Begin with a clean Windows Server 2008 R2 computer and install all available service packs and Windows updates. It is not necessary to configure any roles on the server; SharePoint's Prerequisite Installer will take care of that and will correctly set up Internet Information Services (IIS) and other dependencies for you.

It's best to set up at least one service account to run SharePoint services; many developers run SharePoint under the Administrator account, which can lead to problems in production if they write code that depends on administrative privileges. If your SharePoint server will be part of a Windows domain, make the service account be an ordinary domain user. In production and staging, many service accounts can be used to create a "least privilege" set-up; here we are content to avoid running everything under administrator privileges.

In addition to a service account, you also need an installation account that has administrator rights on the SharePoint server. This can be the same as your developer account, which needs server administrator rights to run the debugger.

SharePoint 2010 needs SQL Server 2005 SP3 or later in order to run, and the SharePoint installer will set up SQL Server Express for you unless you install your own SQL server. If you prefer the improved management features and storage capacity of real SQL Server, the developer edition is a better choice. So before installing SharePoint, install SQL Server yourself, ideally running under its own service account (which can be another ordinary domain user). You also have the option to use an existing SQL Server instance on another server in your environment—just remember that you need to give the SharePoint service account some pretty high privileges, and that SharePoint creates a number of databases, so a separate SQL instance for each developer is often preferred.

Open SQL Server Management Studio to give the SharePoint service account the permissions it needs. Under Security right-click Logins and add a new user. The new login dialog box is displayed, as shown in Figure 1.1.

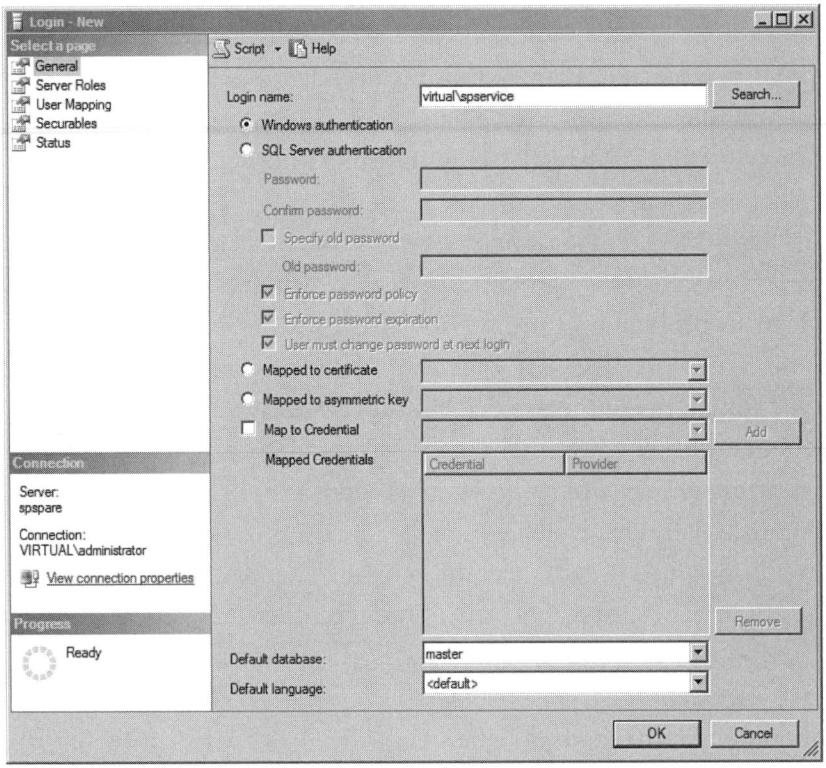

FIGURE 1.1: Adding a login for the SharePoint Service account in SQL Server

In the screen shots, the service account is called SPService and is in the Virtual domain. Before clicking OK to create the new login, click the Server Roles option on the left and grant your service account the dbcreator and securityadmin roles so it can create and secure new databases when the configuration runs, and when running the SharePoint Central Administration web site. This is shown in Figure 1.2.

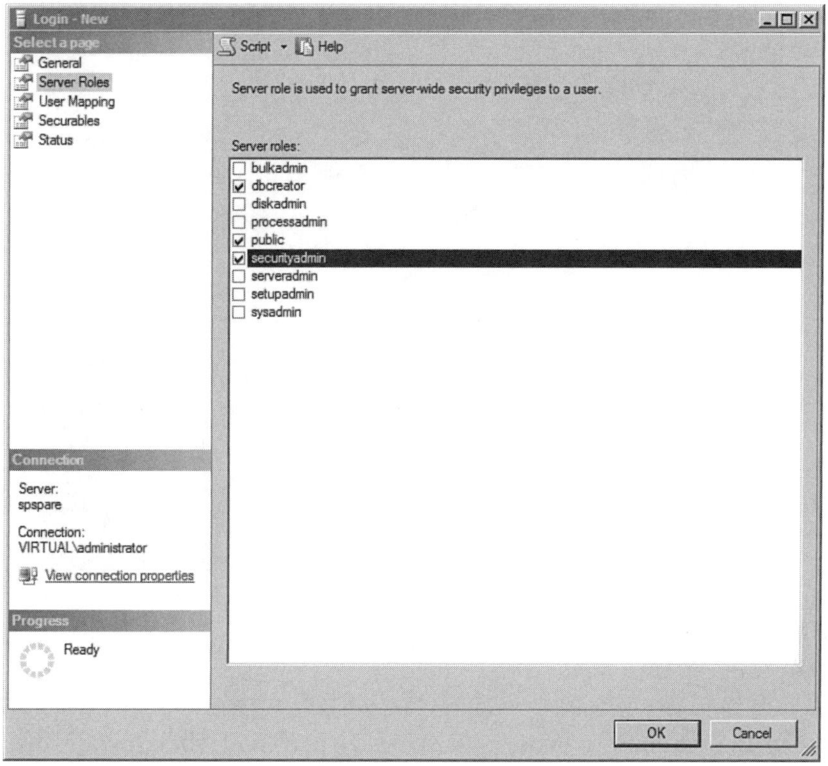

FIGURE 1.2: Granting server roles to a SharePoint service account

With SQL Server set up, it's time to install SharePoint. When you install (or virtually mount) the installation DVD, you see the splash screen shown in Figure 1.3. The screen shots are for full SharePoint Server 2010; the Share-Point Foundation installation is similar.

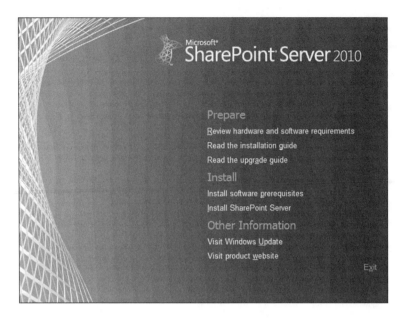

FIGURE 1.3: The SharePoint installation splash screen

If you like, you can review the links under Prepare to learn more about SharePoint installation. When you're ready to install, click Install software prerequisites under the Install heading. This leads you through a wizard that shuts down any conflicting services, asks you to agree to license terms, and then installs SharePoint's prerequisites. In addition to server roles, this includes the Windows Identity Foundation (for claims security), chart controls (for rendering reports), and even the Microsoft Speech Server runtime (for phonetic name searching). There isn't much you have to do here except provide an Internet connection because the prerequisite installer will download the latest versions of the prerequisites as it runs.

When the prerequisite installer completes, reboot the server if you're directed to do so and then begin the installation again. This time click Install SharePoint Server.

You are then prompted for a product key. The product key determines whether you're using the trial or full version of the product and also whether you have the Standard or Enterprise edition. The Standard edition is enough for the examples in this book, but the Enterprise edition unlocks several great features you might want to try. You can always change to the Enterprise edition or graduate from trial to full product by entering a new key later in SharePoint Central Administration. If you need a trial product key, it's given right on the SharePoint download page.

After accepting license terms, you are offered a choice of a Standalone or Server Farm installation as shown in Figure 1.4.

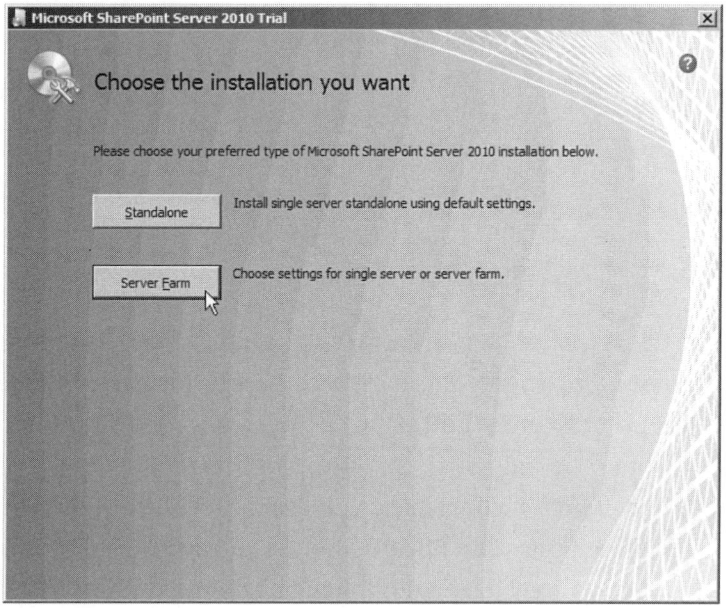

FIGURE 1.4: Choosing the SharePoint installation

Although you might be tempted to click the Standalone option, this will install SQL Server Express for you. If you want to use full SQL Server, either on your development machine or elsewhere, you need to select the Server Farm option. When you do this, you are asked to select the Server Type as shown in Figure 1.5.

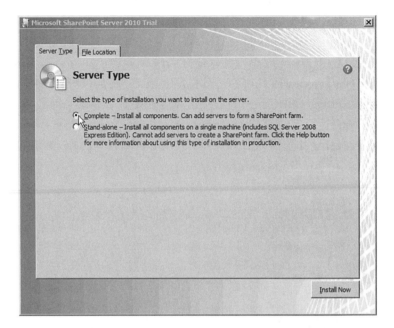

FIGURE 1.5: Selecting the Server Type

Because this is a single server farm, you need to select Complete so all of the SharePoint components are installed. Again, the Stand-alone option installs SQL Server Express Edition. Click the Install Now button and wait while SharePoint is installed.

When the installation completes, you see a checkbox to Run the SharePoint Products Configuration Wizard now. Go ahead and let it run, or if you want to do it later, you can find it on the Start menu.

The SharePoint Products Configuration Wizard creates the SharePoint databases and configures the server to run SharePoint. After a warning about restarting services, you are presented with the opportunity to connect to an existing server farm or to create a new one, as shown in Figure 1.6. For a single-server farm, of course, you want to create a new server farm.

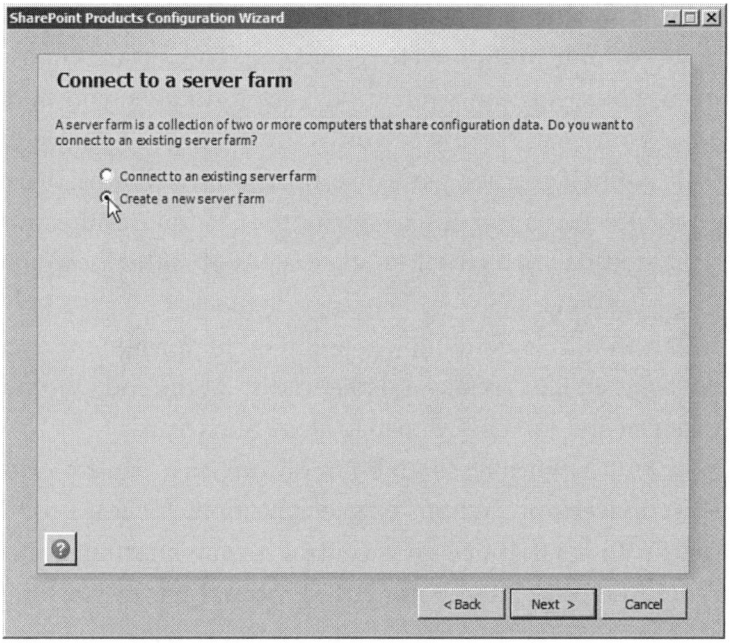

FIGURE 1.6: Creating a new server farm

Next, you are prompted to enter the database server name and the name and access accounts for the configuration database. The configuration database is at the center of the SharePoint configuration and contains information about all the other farm databases, server roles, web application, and other farm settings. Enter your SharePoint service account name and password as the access account; because you already gave it dbcreate and security admin rights on the database server, it is able to create the configuration and other databases. It is not easy to change the location of the configuration database after it's been set up.

Next you are asked to choose a Passphrase. This phrase is used to unlock configuration information, including service account passwords. Select a secure phrase you can remember.

After this, you are invited to create the web application for the Share-Point Central Administration web application. The wizard chooses a random port number; you can override it with a number you find easy to remember if you wish. Normally you want the default choice of NTLM authentication, but if you need to authenticate with Kerberos, that option is also available. Keep in mind this is only for the Central Administration web application and that you can select other types of authentication for your own web applications.

The wizard confirms your choices and then performs a number of configuration tasks, which can take a while to run. At the end, you should see a success screen and can click Finish to close the wizard.

You now have a working SharePoint farm with a Central Administration site but no web applications or site collections for users (or development testing). To set that up, visit Central Administration; a link can be found under Microsoft SharePoint 2010 Products on the start menu. The first time you visit Central Administration another wizard runs and offers to walk you through setting up the farm. Decide if you want to send feedback to Microsoft, and then click the Start the Wizard button to begin this last phase of setup.

Figure 1.7 shows the next screen, which allows you to set up the available SharePoint services. If you don't want to use a separate account, click the Use existing managed account radio button and select the same service account you've been using. If for some reason you don't want to run some services, uncheck them and click the Next button.

This might take a while; eventually the wizard offers to set up a site collection for you, which is your farm's first SharePoint site (other than Central Administration)! Give the site a name and description and select a site template. The standard Team Site template is fine for most tasks; Chapters 13 and 15 require the Publishing Portal template on the Publishing tab.

Your reward, as shown in Figure 1.8 is a working SharePoint site, ready for you to start testing your development work!

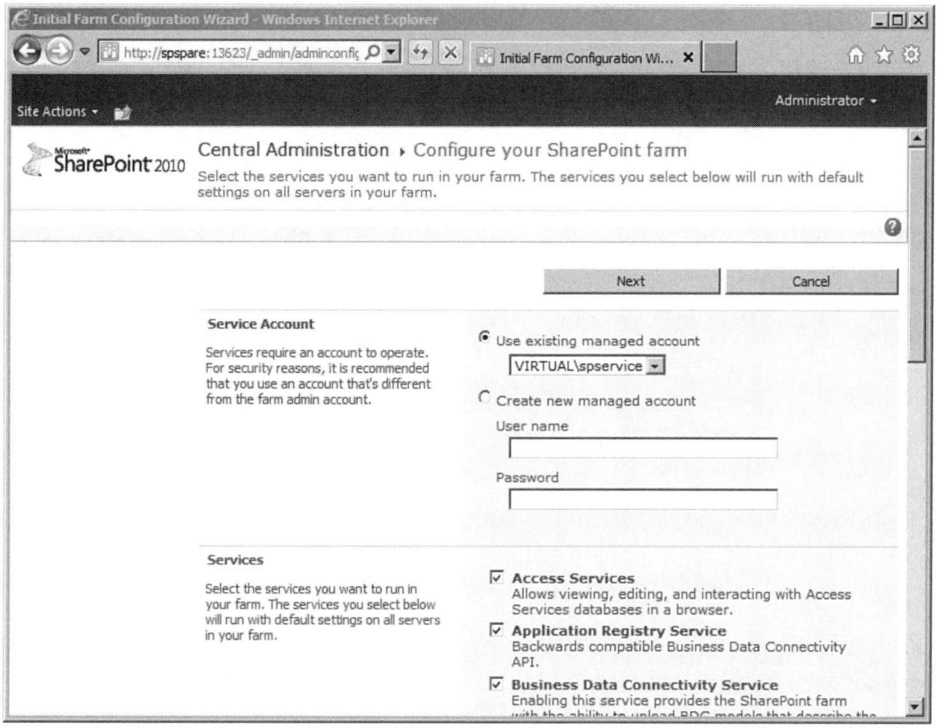

Figure 1.7: The Central Administration Wizard configures SharePoint services

Now that SharePoint is set up, go down the list in Table 1.1 and install everything else. The other product installations are straight-forward; just be sure you include the SharePoint and Silverlight portions of Visual Studio 2010 when you set it up.

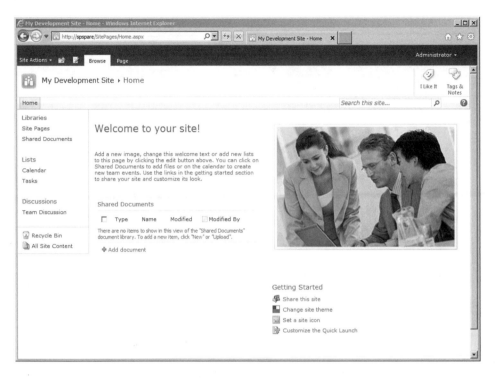

Figure 1.8: Your SharePoint farm's first team site

Summary

Whether you downloaded the pre-built virtual machine, used the Easy Setup Script, or built it all by hand, you should now be ready to begin developing SharePoint solutions. The chapters that follow show you how to do quite a lot with SharePoint and Silverlight in your new development environment.

Have fun with it!

▪ 2 ▪

Introduction to SharePoint Development

With the introduction of SharePoint 2010 and Visual Studio 2010, SharePoint development is easier than ever. This chapter introduces the concepts you need to get started with SharePoint development and leads you through creating your first SharePoint web part in Visual Studio. It is intended to help new SharePoint developers be successful with this book, rather than as a comprehensive guide to SharePoint development.

This chapter shows you

- How content is organized in SharePoint and how SharePoint combines web server files with content and customizations stored in SharePoint content databases
- How to build and deploy SharePoint web parts, both as "Visual" Web Parts which are based on an ASP.NET User Control, and code-based web parts based on ASP.NET Web Part objects
- How to create SharePoint lists and libraries in Visual Studio for use in your project

- How to access lists and libraries using the SharePoint API and LINQ to SharePoint

- How to intercept changes to lists and libraries using event receivers

- How to package your projects with SharePoint Solutions and Features

The first thing to remember is that SharePoint is an ASP.NET application. The web parts you see on the page are ASP.NET web parts, and they are part of an .aspx page just like any other ASP.NET application. The biggest difference is that whereas an ASP.NET site stores its pages in the web server file system, SharePoint stores pages in content databases.

Understanding SharePoint Content

Figure 2.1 shows a SharePoint content database. One or more *site collections* are inside, each with a top-level *site* and possibly a hierarchy of child sites, grandchild sites, and so on. As the name suggests, a site collection is a collection of SharePoint sites that are stored and managed together. Each site contains *lists* and *libraries* which hold all sorts of information. SharePoint announcements, blog entries, contacts, and tasks are all stored as lists. A threaded discussion is a list of postings, and a calendar is a list of events. Libraries are lists that include a binary file integrated with each item, so for example there are document libraries, picture libraries, and media asset libraries. The web pages you see are stored as content too, either in a Pages or SitePages library or as free-floating .aspx files, depending on the features enabled in your site.

Placing all the content in databases makes it easier to manage and update and to share the content among a group of web servers. SharePoint supports flexible "farms" of servers working together, and traffic is often load balanced across multiple web servers.

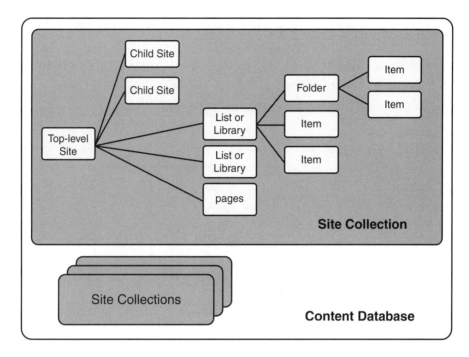

FIGURE 2.1: SharePoint content

There's a problem, however, with simply storing all the pages and files in every SharePoint site within a content database: Much of the content in each site is redundant, such as the pages used for site administration, to display and manipulate lists, and so on. Storing all this duplicate data for every site would be wasteful and would make it hard to update the pages globally. On the other hand, if a single set of pages were shared by all sites, it would be hard to customize them for any individual site.

SharePoint manages to balance both of these, sharing central copies of page and file templates among many sites unless they are customized using SharePoint Designer 2010, a free SharePoint editing tool. You might hear this sharing called *ghosting*, a term that dates back to earlier versions of SharePoint. A physical file was "ghosted" into the site URL space until it was "unghosted" (or "customized"). This haunting terminology was deemed confusing to end-users, so now we say that a file is uncustomized until it is customized; you can decide which is clearer!

Figure 2.2 shows page and file templates stored on the file system of each web server. SharePoint ghosts them into an apparent file structure accessible by a URL within each site. For example, given two newly created sites from the same site definition, http://server1/sites/site1/default.aspx is the same file as http://server1/sites/site2/default.aspx.

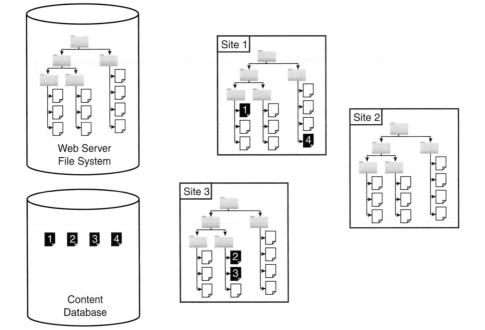

FIGURE 2.2: SharePoint customization

When users edit SharePoint pages in the web browser, they don't really edit the pages but only the content in the pages' web part zones, wiki fields, or other page fields. This avoids having to edit the original pages all together but doesn't allow changing their structure or editing their HTML.

To do that, SharePoint Designer 2010 is needed. In this case, the file is customized, and the changed copy is saved in the site collection's content database. The customized pages are shown as numbered pages in Figure 2.2. You can tell if a page has been customized in SharePoint Designer by the blue i icon that appears next to customized files as shown in Figure 2.3 and the Customization Status shown on the file information summary. If you want to revert to the initial file contents, simply right-click and select

Reset to Site Definition to uncustomize the file. A site definition is a set of files that is used to create new sites; this is where the original page templates are stored. Uncustomizing a file removes the customizations and allows the original template to show through.

By overlaying customized files from the content database over the baseline files on the web servers, SharePoint achieves the best of both worlds: It's possible to customize pages as needed without repeatedly storing the boilerplate files that are used most of the time.

FIGURE 2.3: A customized file in SharePoint Designer 2010

TIP

The best way to inspect the content in SharePoint is to use SharePoint Designer 2010, which is a free download available from http://bit.ly/SPSL_SPDesigner64. Use the file menu to open a SharePoint site. You will see more content if you choose the top-level site at the root of a SharePoint site collection, considering these sites store shared content that is used by all the sites in the collection, such as the Master Page Gallery.

SharePoint Designer presents you with a site summary page showing the name and location of the site, site permissions, and a list of child or subsites (if any). To the left of this, you can see a Navigation panel with shortcuts to the content most frequently edited with SharePoint designer. Click the All Files shortcut at the bottom of the list to see all the content in the site, with shared content from the file system seamlessly overlaid with content from the content database. Many of the files are set to use SharePoint's versioning system, with checkouts turned on and sometimes approvals as well.

This is the same content that your code sees when it runs in SharePoint and uses the SharePoint API. SharePoint Designer only works at the content layer; it never changes the file system.

A SharePoint developer needs to be aware of these two layers: the files installed on each web server and database contents that overlay them. In many cases, a given change can be made on either layer, with different consequences.

For example, suppose a developer wants to create a new master page to brand SharePoint's look and feel. Master pages in SharePoint are just like they are in other ASP.NET applications: they provide a common outer HTML structure used to brand a site, and they include elements that are common to all web pages. Master pages are stored in the Master Page Gallery, which is a document library in every SharePoint top-level site.

If the developer creates the master page in SharePoint Designer or uploads it into the Master Page Gallery using a web browser, it is created directly in the content database and is only visible to the site collection where it was created. If another site collection wants to use the master page, it needs to be copied into place, and two independent copies will be stored in the content database.

On the other hand, the master page could be created in Visual Studio 2010 as part of a SharePoint web solution package (.wsp file). Web solution packages are the vehicle for deploying customizations to SharePoint, and they correspond one-to-one with Visual Studio solutions. If the master page is in a farm-level web solution package, it can be installed on each web server's file system so all site collections share the same copy of the master page. Those copies can all be changed by updating the solution package—except in sites where someone used SharePoint designer to customize the master page (and thus saved a one-off copy in the content database).

Similarly, web page content is layered in SharePoint. Special pages, such as web part pages, wiki pages, and page layouts used in web publishing, are files ending in .aspx in SharePoint's content system. Whether ghosted from the file system or retrieved from a SharePoint content database, they are passed to ASP.NET for rendering.

These pages contain special ASP.NET controls that emit dynamic content on the page, such as the placement of web parts, text, and other elements that are edited in the web browser. The web part settings can be personalized by each user; for example, if it's enabled in a web part zone, users can rearrange and reconfigure web parts to personalize their view of a SharePoint site. Thus, when you look at a typical SharePoint page, you're actually seeing the web page (including its master page), overlaid with web parts and other content residing in the content database. Although the web part code might be installed on each web server, the web part placement and metadata are treated as content. The user sees a seamless blend of web pages and controls that are installed on the web server, overlaid with controls placed on the page as content, possibly with customizations, as shown in Figure 2.4.

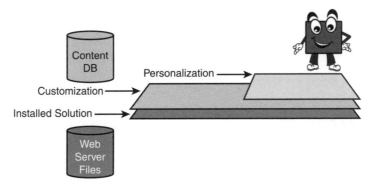

FIGURE 2.4: Customization and personalization in SharePoint

For more detail on SharePoint customization see http://bit.ly/ SPSL_SPCustomization.

Building a Web Part

A good first project for SharePoint development is to build a web part. Begin by setting up your development environment as described in Chapter 1, "Getting Started with SharePoint and Silverlight." Log in to your development machine as a server and SharePoint administrator and then open a web browser and visit the test SharePoint site you created at the end of the SharePoint installation. Then open Visual Studio 2010 and be sure to give it administrative privileges by right-clicking the icon and selecting Run as Administrator.

You might want to download the finished solution from http://code.msdn.com/SPSL/. If you're starting from scratch, click New Project ... in the Visual Studio 2010 start screen, and the New Project dialog box presents itself as in Figure 2.5. On the left, under Installed Templates click the SharePoint project template.

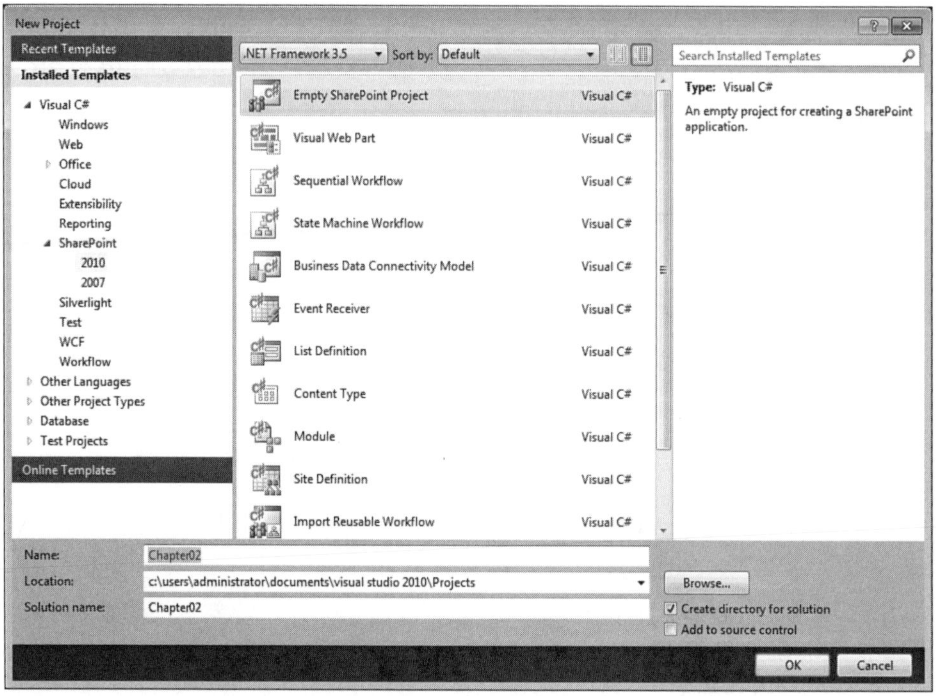

FIGURE 2.5: Visual Studio 2010 New Project dialog box

SharePoint 2010 uses .NET Framework 3.5, so be sure that's the version that's selected. For this project, start with an Empty SharePoint Project and enter a project name before pressing the OK button.

The next dialog box, shown in Figure 2.6, asks for the site you wish to use for debugging; enter your test site URL. It also asks you if you want a sandboxed or farm solution. This web part is a sandboxed solution, which means the entire solution is to be installed into the content database, and in many situations it can be installed by a business user. Because they're so easy to deploy and don't require the approval of a high-level administrator, sandboxed solutions run with limited trust. They can only use a subset of the SharePoint API within the site collection where they are installed, and they can't call out over the network or gain access to the servers where they run.

Farm solutions, on the other hand, require the full trust of the Share-Point farm administrator because they can place files on the web server file systems and can install .dlls into the web application's bin directory or the global assembly cache.

Sandboxed solutions are the recommended choice when it's possible to work within their limitations. They can be deployed by a larger audience, and developers will appreciate that the debugger starts much faster after each build of your project, given Visual Studio only has to restart the sand-boxed solution service rather than the whole web application as in a farm solution. After ensuring the Deploy as a Sandboxed Solution radio button is selected, click Finish to close the wizard.

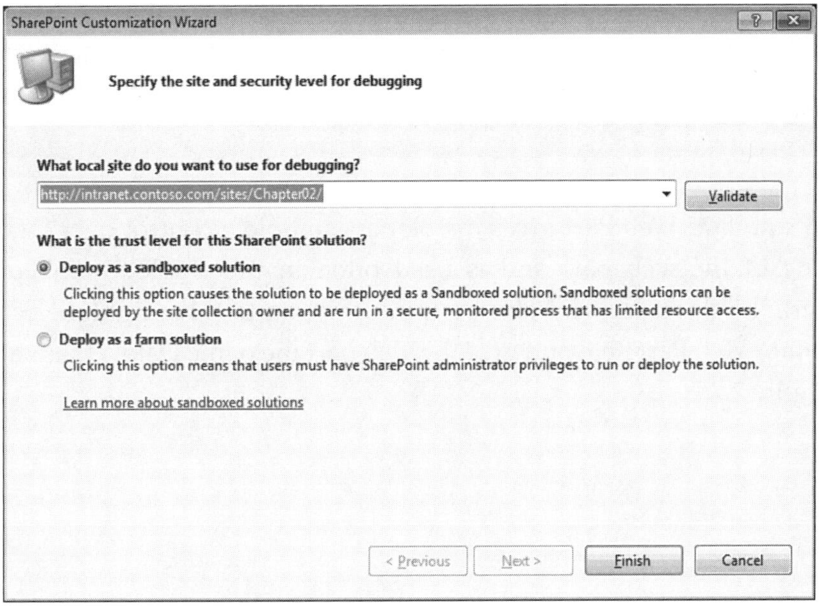

FIGURE 2.6: SharePoint Customization Wizard

With the project selected in Solution Explorer on the right, use the Project menu to Add New Item. For this first project, select a Web Part option; this is the traditional web part, which is entirely implemented in code, rather than an .ascx file with ASP.NET markup.

■ TIP

Use Visual Web Parts when you want a design surface for laying out ASP.NET controls. Use the standard Web Part when you want to control rendering in your code.

Both techniques are used in this book; because Silverlight is doing most of the rendering, the Visual Web Part is most useful when you want to edit the Silverlight object tag or other markup or Javascript on the page.

You might also notice two kinds of Visual Web Parts: Visual Web Part and Visual Web Part (Sandboxed). Standard Visual Web Parts won't work in sandboxed solutions, but the Sandboxed ones will. They were added after SharePoint 2010 was released and are part of the Visual Studio 2010 SharePoint Power Tools, which can be downloaded at http://bit.ly/SPSL_PowerTools.

A standard Web Part gives developers complete control over the rendering of the web part and is used often in this book to embed the Silverlight object tag and also pass information to Silverlight. Select the standard Web Part item and give the web part the name DateWP, as shown in Figure 2.7.

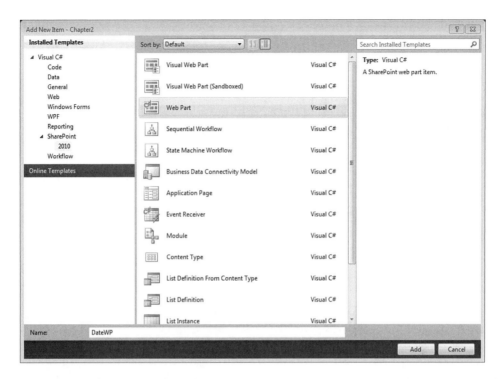

FIGURE 2.7: Add New Item Web Part

Visual Studio presents you with a web part class containing a single method, `CreateChildControls()`. Like all web controls, a web part is basically a .NET object that spits out HTML; because it's a web part, it also knows how to be edited and can be placed on the page using a web browser. To display the current date in the web part, add to `CreateChildControls()` as shown in Listing 2.1.

LISTING 2.1: CreateChildControls()

```
private Label messageLabel;

protected override void CreateChildControls()
{
    Label messageLabel = new Label();
    messageLabel.Text = DateTime.Now.ToLongDateString();
    messageLabel.Style.Add("Font-Weight", "Bold");
    messageLabel.Style.Add("Font-Size", "18pt");

    this.Controls.Add(messageLabel);
}
```

This code creates a new web control, a `Label` that simply renders whatever text you place in its `Text` property. After setting the text property to the current date, it adds a couple of CSS styles to the label and adds it to the web part's `Controls` collection, making the `Label` a child of the `WebPart`. The web part automatically renders all the child controls in order, and the date is displayed.

To build and deploy your solution, select Deploy Solution under the Build menu. Visual Studio packages up the solution and deploys it to your debugging web site. If you prefer to simply start the debugger by pressing F5, Visual Studio also attaches the debugger and launches a web browser to the debugging site URL.

■. TIP

To run a sandboxed solution, the sandboxed code service must be running on the SharePoint server. To check this, start SharePoint Central Administration in the start menu of your SharePoint server. Click the Application Management heading and then under Service Applications, click Manage services on server. Ensure the Microsoft SharePoint Foundation Sandboxed Code Service is started in order to run a sandboxed solution.

Within the web browser, place your new web part on the page to test the new web part. Begin by clicking the Page tab and then the Edit button on the Ribbon. This should switch the page into edit mode, enabling two additional editing tabs. Click the spot where you wish to add the new web part and then go to the Insert tab and click Web Part. Below the Ribbon, the web part insertion tool appears; click the Custom category and select DemoWP, which is your web part, as shown in Figure 2.8. Finally, click Add to place the web part on the page. If it looks OK, return to the Page tab and click Save to close the page editor.

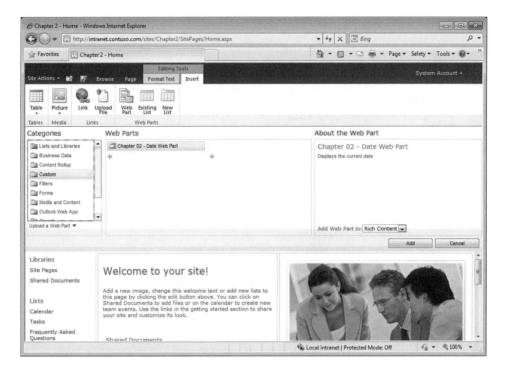

FIGURE 2.8: Inserting a Web Part

The web part should display today's date in large, bold letters.

Using this simple technique, it's possible to render most anything with a web part. ASP.net provides a wide range of controls to choose from, but like the Label in this example, they are created and set up in procedural code instead of in a declarative .aspx or .ascx file. This makes the web part a composite control, which means that rather than generating its own HTML, it creates a composite of child controls to do the HTML generation.

You can make the web part more flexible by adding some properties that users can set. The easiest way to do this is to create some public properties in your web part and decorate them with attributes to let SharePoint know that it should save the properties and allow the user to edit them. For example, add the code in Listing 2.2 to your DateWP class.

LISTING 2.2: Adding Editable Properties to a Web Part

```
public enum color { Black, Red, Blue, Green, Gold };

private color _messageColor = color.Black;
[Personalizable(PersonalizationScope.Shared),
 WebBrowsable(true),
 WebDisplayName("Date Color"),
 System.ComponentModel.Category("Configuration")]
public color MessageColor
{
    get { return _messageColor; }
    set { _messageColor = value; }
}

private int _messageSize = 18;
[Personalizable(PersonalizationScope.Shared),
 WebBrowsable(true),
 WebDisplayName("Font Size"),
 System.ComponentModel.Category("Configuration")]
public int MessageSize
{
    get { return _messageSize; }
    set { _messageSize = value; }
}

private bool _messageIsBold = true;
[Personalizable(PersonalizationScope.Shared),
 WebBrowsable(true),
 WebDisplayName("Bold"),
 System.ComponentModel.Category("Configuration")]
public bool MessageIsBold
{
    get { return _messageIsBold; }
    set { _messageIsBold = value; }
}
```

If the property is a string or integer, SharePoint displays a text box; if it's a bool, SharePoint shows a checkbox, and for an enum, SharePoint shows a drop-down list of options. Now when editing the web part, the user sees a Configuration section as shown in Figure 2.9.

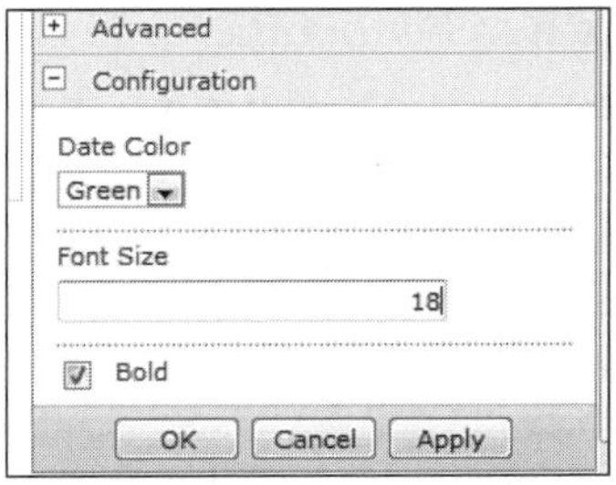

FIGURE 2.9: Web part editing

The values can then be used to change the web part rendering and logic, as shown in Listing 2.3.

LISTING 2.3: Updating CreateChildControls() to Use Custom Properties

```
private Label messageLabel;

protected override void CreateChildControls()
{
    messageLabel = new Label();
    messageLabel.Text = DateTime.Now.ToLongDateString();
    messageLabel.Style.Add("Color", MessageColor.ToString());
    if (MessageIsBold) messageLabel.Style.Add("Font-Weight", "Bold");
    messageLabel.Style.Add("Font-Size", MessageSize.ToString() + "pt");

    this.Controls.Add(messageLabel);
}
```

To test these changes, re-deploy and edit the web part. On the right under Configuration, you should see the options as shown in Figure 2.9. If you apply the changes, you see your selected color, font size, and weight in your web part display.

This approach works well for simple property settings. In some cases, however, you might want to put your own custom controls in the editing panel instead of one that SharePoint generates for you. For example, you might want to populate a drop-down list with options that are determined at runtime or even include a Silverlight user interface to capture more complex data sets. Chapter 7, "Accessing SharePoint Using the HTML Bridge," shows how to do this.

Notice that there are a number of other web part settings available. For example, if you want to suppress the title above the web part, under Appearance change the Chrome Type to None and click OK. Now the title only appears when you are editing the page. It's useful to know how to set these built-in properties in your web part as well as custom ones. The easiest way to do this is to export your web part and view its web part template file, which ends in a .webpart file name extension. A web part template file is an XML configuration file that describes the web part to SharePoint, along with all its settings.

To export your modified web part, the first step is to edit it again, and under the Advanced category change the Export Mode to Export All Data and press Apply. This allows you to go the web part's drop-down menu (to the right of its title as seen in Figure 2.10) and select Export.

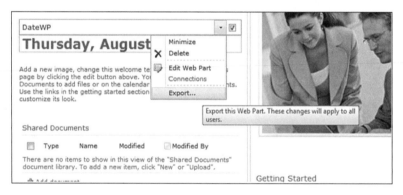

FIGURE 2.10: Exporting a web part

Save the web part template to your desktop and open it in Notepad or another text editor. Here you can see the web part properties such as the one that hid the title earlier, the ChromeType property in Listing 2.4.

There is also a web part template file in your Visual Studio 2010 project, under the DateWP folder, and it's called DateWP.webpart. Paste the property element from the exported web part into the one in Visual Studio. You also can add your custom properties and clean up the out-of-the-box properties to reflect what's shown in Listing 2.4.

LISTING 2.4: Properties in the Web Part Template File

```
<properties>
  <property name="Title" type="string">Date Web Part</property>
  <property name="Description"
           type="string">Displays the current date</property>
  <property name="ChromeType" type="chrometype">None</property>
  <property name="ExportMode" type="exportmode">All</property>
  <property name="MessageColor"
           type="Chapter2.DateWP.DateWP.color">Blue</property>
  <property name="MessageSize" type="int">48</property>
</properties>
```

Deploy the solution in Visual Studio and then return to the web browser. Delete the web part and place a new one on the page. If you changed the web part title, the new title now appears on the list of custom web parts, and the new web part is preloaded with the default settings you have specified in the .webpart file.

Lists and Libraries

One way to view SharePoint is as a colossal list manager. SharePoint uses lists to store many kinds of data, including obvious things like contacts and tasks and less obvious things like calendars (a list of events) and threaded discussions (a list of postings). A list is similar to a database table: it has columns with specific data types and rows containing data items. Business users with site administrator permission can add and remove columns to capture whatever data they wish, and SharePoint displays these columns in forms and views. Views are similar to database views and can expose specific columns, sort orders, and groupings to end users.

A library in SharePoint is simply a list with an integrated binary component, such as a document or image, in each row. In libraries the binary component is a file corresponding to the library type, such as a document, web page, image, or multimedia file.

Figure 2.11 shows a diagram of *content types* and lists in SharePoint. A content type defines the schema for a list or library and is primarily made up of a set of *site columns*, which are also called *fields* in the SharePoint API.

Each field has a type and can be from any of the myriad *field types* that ship with SharePoint. In Chapter 15, "Creating a Silverlight Field Control," you learn how to create your own field type that uses Silverlight to edit and display its content, but that's for another day.

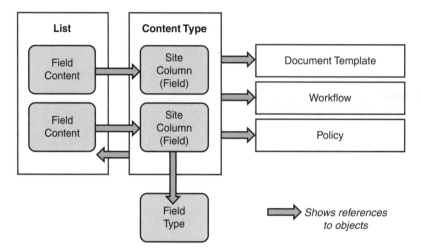

FIGURE 2.11: Content types and lists in SharePoint

In addition to referencing a field type, each site column stores information about the field such as its default value, options for choice fields, and validation settings.

Content types store a set of site columns and can also include a *document template* such as an Office document template or InfoPath form template. In addition, they can reference SharePoint *workflows* and *policies* that are related to the content type. So for example, a Press Release content type can include its own standard Microsoft Word template, an approval workflow, and a disposition policy for how long to retain each Press Release.

Content types also support inheritance. For example, a Press Release could inherit from a Public Document content type, which inherits from the out-of-the-box Document content type. Site columns can be added, and other settings can be overridden at each level.

Content types can be scoped at the site collection, site, or list level. Content types at the site collection level are stored in the top-level site; you can see them by going to Site Administration for the top-level site and clicking the Site Content Types link. From there, they can propagate down into child sites, grandchild sites, and so on—and also into lists. This defines the storage and user interface for the list.

All lists have list content types; however, they might not be visible in the user interface. A list that appears to not have a content type actually has a hidden list content type that is presented in the SharePoint User Interface as the list's own columns and settings. List content types usually reference out-of-the-box content types from the site and can be customized to change the columns and other settings within a particular list.

Lists and libraries begin their lives as list definitions; this is a set of XML files that describes the list, the list content type, and other details. You can include list definitions in your solution by creating them in Visual Studio and packaging them in your web solution package. In general, to ensure that your code knows what data to expect in a list, you should either use the out-of-the-box list definitions or create your own and include them with your solution.

A list definition describes the columns and other list settings and can be used to create list instances where users can store and work with data. When an end user creates a list or library, she selects a list definition that might have been included with SharePoint by a solution package that is installed or by a list template that another user saved as a starting point for making new lists. In each case, a list instance is created, and the user can then begin entering data or uploading documents. Again, your visual studio solution can include list instances to provide a location to store content.

The next programming example is a web part that displays Frequently Asked Questions (FAQs) and allows users to submit new questions. The FAQs are kept in a SharePoint list. If end-users were expected to create the FAQ list manually, the solution would be fragile because a mistakenly named column would break the code. To avoid this, the first step is to create the FAQ list definition and instance in Visual Studio and to package the list along with the code that uses it.

To do this, right-click the project in Visual Studio and select Add and then New Item…. In the Add New Item dialog box, select List Definition and name the list definition FAQ, as shown in Figure 2.12.

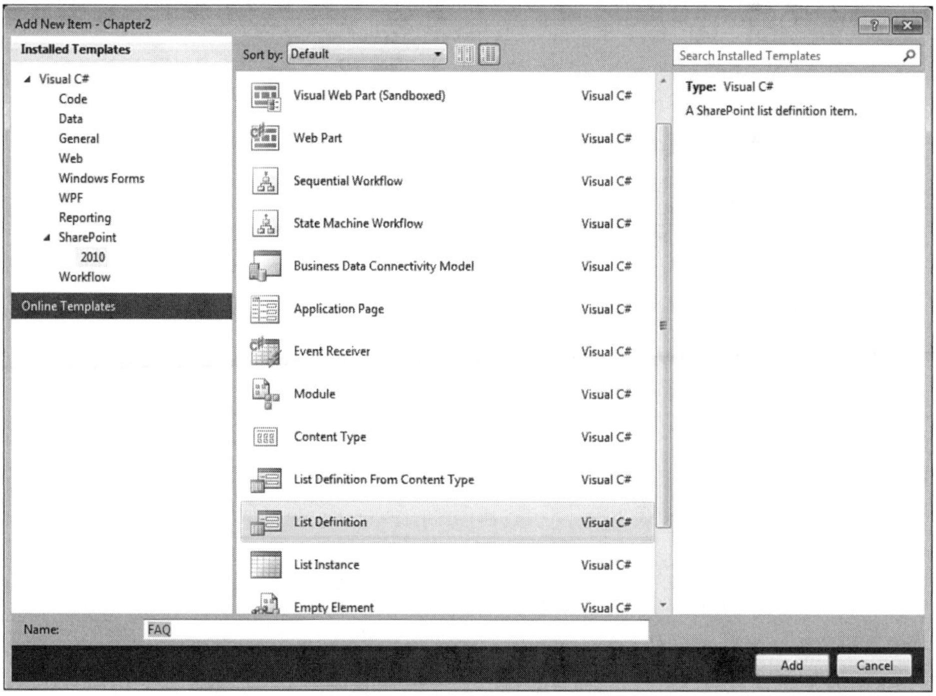

FIGURE 2.12: Adding a list definition

The SharePoint Customization Wizard then runs and captures the display name of the new list definition as well as the type of list to start with; in this case select Custom List and be sure to check the checkbox next to Add a List Instance for This List Definition, as shown in Figure 2.13.

Visual Studio creates a new folder in your project called FAQ, which is populated with some XML files to declare the list definition and instance. The next step is to add the columns and other settings for the FAQ list. The schema for the list definition is in a file called Schema.xml. First, you need to add new fields to the list, so add to the `<Fields>` XML element as shown in Listing 2.5 to the Schema.xml file.

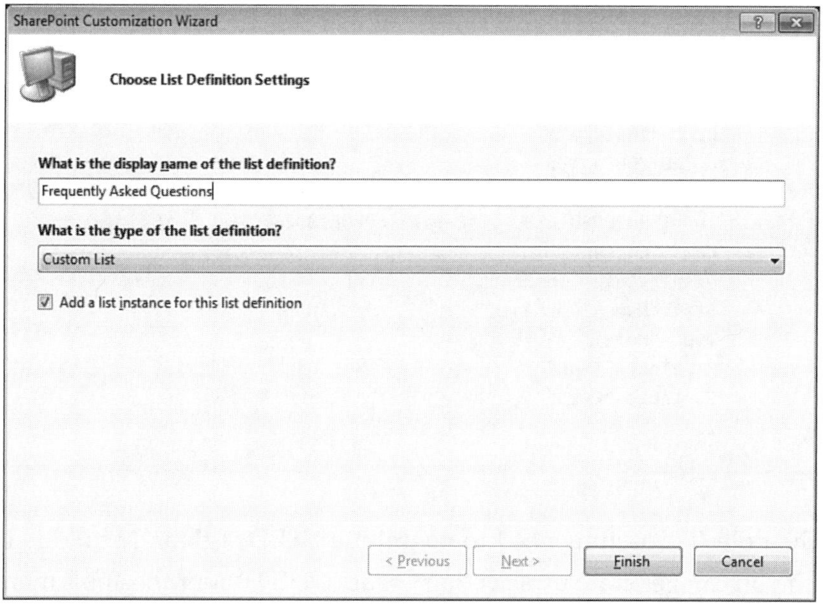

FIGURE 2.13: Choosing list definition settings

LISTING 2.5: FAQ List Definition

```
<Fields>
  <Field ID="{129883A2-82F4-4B32-86D2-8541DE9715CD}"
         Name="Answer"
         DisplayName="Answer"
         StaticName="Answer"
         Type="Note"
         RichText="TRUE"
         RichTextMode="FullHtml"
         IsolateStyles="TRUE"
         NumLines="15"
         Sortable="FALSE"
         />
  <Field ID="{86057F1F-D120-4BB1-8055-2E75025733FC}"
         Name="WebPage"
         DisplayName="Related Web Page"
         StaticName="WebPage"
         Type="URL"
         />
  <Field ID="{3f6c8ca4-d576-45d1-8fe8-452a2d37ef80}"
         Name="Answered"
         DisplayName="Answered"
         StaticName="Answered"
```

```
                Type="Boolean"
                EnforceUniqueValues="FALSE"
                Indexed="FALSE"
                ColName="bit1"
                RowOrdinal="0">
          <Default>0</Default>
        </Field>
        <Field ID="{E94EDB6D-EE39-4C4E-9F9F-6D8DE1882C8C}"
                Name="Comments"
                DisplayName="Comments"
                StaticName="Comments"
                Type="Note"
                RichText="TRUE"
                Sortable="FALSE"
                />
      </Fields>
```

The field ID columns need to be unique GUIDs (globally unique IDs), which you can generate by selecting Create GUID under the Tools menu in Visual Studio. The FAQ list uses the built-in Title field for the question; the Title field is inherited from the `Custom List` definition that was specified as the base for this list. To this, the solution adds a rich-text column for the answer, a hyperlink to a related web page, a Boolean to indicate if the question has been answered, and a comments field. Many other types of fields are possible and are documented in the SharePoint Software Developer's Kit List Schema reference at http://bit.ly/SPSL_ListSchemaRef.

Next, you can add these new fields to the list Content Type. Content types can be defined at a site or site collection level, where they can be used by multiple lists. In this case, you just want to add the new fields to the single content type for an FAQ list, so you just need to add some `FieldRef` elements to the list content type in Schema.xml, as shown in Listing 2.6. The remainder of the content type remains unchanged from the initial Schema.xml.

LISTING 2.6: FAQ Content Type

```
<ContentType ID="0x01" Name="Item"
             Group="List Content Types"
             Description="Create a new list item."
             FeatureId="{695b6570-a48b-4a8e-8ea5-26ea7fc1d162}">
  <FieldRefs>
    <FieldRef ID="{c042a256-787d-4a6f-8a8a-cf6ab767f12d}"
              Name="ContentType" />
    <FieldRef ID="{fa564e0f-0c70-4ab9-b863-0177e6ddd247}"
              Name="Title" Required="TRUE" />
    <FieldRef ID="{129883A2-82F4-4B32-86D2-8541DE9715CD}"
              Name="Answer" ShowInNewForm="TRUE" ShowInEditForm="TRUE"
              ShowInDisplayForm="TRUE" />
    <FieldRef ID="{86057F1F-D120-4BB1-8055-2E75025733FC}"
              Name="WebPage" ShowInNewForm="TRUE" ShowInEditForm="TRUE"
              ShowInDisplayForm="TRUE" />
    <FieldRef ID="{3f6c8ca4-d576-45d1-8fe8-452a2d37ef80}"
              Name="Answered" ShowInNewForm="TRUE" ShowInEditForm="TRUE"
              ShowInDisplayForm="TRUE" />
    <FieldRef ID="{E94EDB6D-EE39-4C4E-9F9F-6D8DE1882C8C}"
              Name="Comments" ShowInNewForm="TRUE" ShowInEditForm="TRUE"
              ShowInDisplayForm="TRUE" />
  </FieldRefs>
...
```

Notice that in addition to adding our new fields, we also tell SharePoint to show these fields in the forms it automatically generates to create, modify, and view list items.

Finally, add the new fields to the default view for the list, so they show up when a user displays the whole list. To do this, add more `FieldRef` elements, this time to `ViewFields` at the bottom of Schema.xml for the default view, as shown in Listing 2.7.

LISTING 2.7: Defining a View for the FAQ List

```
<ViewFields>
  <FieldRef Name="LinkTitleNoMenu"></FieldRef>
  <FieldRef Name="Answered"></FieldRef>
  <FieldRef Name="Answer"></FieldRef>
  <FieldRef Name="WebPage"></FieldRef>
  <FieldRef Name="Comments"></FieldRef>
</ViewFields>
```

When the Schema.xml file is complete, expand the `FAQListInstance` item and edit the Elements.xml file inside (not the Elements.xml file under `FAQList`). Ensure the list title is Frequently Asked Questions. If you want the list to be displayed on the Quick Launch (left navigation) bar, add an attribute to the `ListInstance` for `OnQuickLaunch="True"`, as shown in Listing 2.8.

LISTING 2.8: Elements.xml under FAQListInstance

```
<?xml version="1.0" encoding="utf-8"?>
<Elements xmlns="http://schemas.microsoft.com/sharepoint/">
  <ListInstance Title="Frequently Asked Questions"
              OnQuickLaunch="TRUE"
              TemplateType="10000"
              Url="Lists/FAQ"
              Description="Frequently asked questions and answers">
  </ListInstance>
</Elements>
```

Having made all these changes, deploy the solution. The site should now create both a definition for an FAQ and an instance of the list called Frequently Asked Questions. This is a fully functioning list, and SharePoint creates the views, editing forms, and even a built-in web part to display it. Like all SharePoint lists, it can support versioning, approval, workflow, item-level security, folders, RSS feeds, and more. Some of these capabilities aren't enabled by default; you could turn them on by visiting the List Settings screen for your list instance or by changing the code in your Visual Studio project.

For more details about lists and content types, see http://bit.ly/ SPSL_ListDataModel.

> ## ■ TIP
>
> The second time you successfully deploy your solution, you can expect a Deployment Conflict notice from Visual Studio as shown in the following figure. This conflict occurs because the list instance you are deploying already exists. If you click Resolve Automatically, Visual Studio deletes the list instance in SharePoint and creates a new one; this makes sense if you've changed the list schema, but it removes any test data you have placed in the list. Therefore, if you haven't changed the list definition, you might want to click Cancel to allow the list to remain unchanged in SharePoint.
>
>
> To eliminate the prompt, select the list instance (in this case FAQInstance) in Visual Studio and edit the Deployment Conflict property. Selecting Automatic replaces the list instance every time the solution is deployed; selecting None leaves the list in place; and Prompt brings up the dialog box to allow you to choose each time.

Accessing Lists and Libraries with the SharePoint Server API

SharePoint provides server- and client-side APIs; this chapter introduces the server-side object model. Chapter 8, "Accessing SharePoint Data with the Client Object Model," explains how to access SharePoint's client API from Silverlight.

On the server, the SharePoint API for manipulating lists and libraries, as well as the sites that contain them, is in the `Microsoft.SharePoint` namespace. Going back to Figure 2.1, recall that sites are grouped into site collections with a single top-level site and a hierarchy of subsites; lists and libraries reside within these sites. The SharePoint API includes object classes to represent each of these as shown in Table 2.1.

TABLE 2.1: SharePoint Object Classes

SharePoint Content	SharePoint Object Class
Site Collection	SPSite
Site	SPWeb
List or Library	SPList
Folder	SPFolder
Item	SPListItem
File	SPFile

For historical reasons, the object for a site collection is called an `SPSite`, and the object for a site is an `SPWeb`. This is somewhat confusing and leads to ambiguity when referring to a "site." This book calls an `SPSite` a "site collection" and an `SPWeb` a "site" to be consistent with common usage. Recall that a site collection is a hierarchy of sites containing a top-level site, which might or might not have descendent sites. The site collection and its top-level site are represented by two different objects in the SharePoint API: `SPSite` is the site collection, and its top-level site is the `SPWeb` object at the root of the site collection, accessed using the `RootWeb` property of the `SPSite` object.

The next step is to create an FAQ web part to display the answered frequently asked questions and to allow users to add new questions. This time it will be a Visual Web Part, which is based on an ASP.NET user control. Out of the box, a Visual Web Part can't run in a sandboxed solution, but this limitation is removed by the Visual Studio 2010 SharePoint Power Tools, which can be downloaded from http://bit.ly/SPSL_PowerTools. Later you learn how to build the same FAQ web part using a traditional web part with no .ascx file.

∎ TIP

Some of the key objects in the SharePoint API are *disposable*, which means that they consume resources outside of the .NET object system and must be formally disposed of using the IDisposable interface. If these objects were just left for the .NET garbage collector, only the .NET resources would be released, and a memory leak would result from the abandoned external resources. The most notable of these disposable objects are SPSite and SPWeb, both of which are used frequently, as well as the DataContext object used in LINQ to SharePoint. To correctly dispose of these objects, use either the Dispose() method or the C# using statement. The following example shows both methods:

```
using (SPSite mySiteCollection = new SPSite("http://myserver/"))
{
    SPWeb myWeb = null;
    try
    {
        myWeb = mySiteCollection.RootWeb;
        // Do something with the SPWeb ...
    }
    finally
    {
        // Now formally dispose of the SPWeb object
        if (myWeb != null) myWeb.Dispose();
    }
} // Closing the using statement will dispose of the SPSite object
```

Notice that the try/finally block is needed to ensure the SPWeb object doesn't leak if an exception is thrown. The using statement takes care of this for you automatically and streamlines the code.

To add to the fun, there's another rule about disposing of SPSite and SPWeb objects: if you got the objects from the SharePoint context object, they shouldn't be disposed of after all! The SharePoint context keeps a couple of these objects around, and if you dispose of them the API will begin to behave unpredictably. For example, here the SPSite object does not need to be disposed of because it came from SPContext.Current, but the SPWeb object is a copy obtained from SPSite.RootWeb and therefore must be disposed of.

```
SPSite mySiteCollection = SPContext.Current.Site;
using (SPWeb myWeb = mySiteCollection.RootWeb)
{
    // Do something with the SPWeb
}
```

continues

> ■
>
> SharePoint Dispose Check is a great tool that will check your code for these problems. It includes a Visual Studio 2010 add-in that automatically checks every project after it is built. SharePoint Dispose Check is available on MSDN code gallery at http://code.msdn.microsoft.com/SPDisposeCheck.

Begin by adding a new SharePoint 2010 item to your Visual Studio project and select Visual Web Part (Sandboxed), giving the web part a name such as FaqVisualWP. Visual studio creates an .ascx file for your web part, which can be edited using the Visual Studio design surface or in text. Below the pregenerated directives in the .ascx file, add the user control markup shown in Listing 2.9.

Listing 2.9: Markup in a Visual Web Part

```
<asp:DataList ID="FaqDataList" runat="server">
  <HeaderTemplate>
    <ul>
  </HeaderTemplate>
  <FooterTemplate>
    </ul>
  </FooterTemplate>
  <ItemTemplate>
    <li>
      <asp:HyperLink ID="HyperLink1" runat="server"
        NavigateUrl='<%# DisplayUrl( DataBinder.Eval(Container.DataItem,
                "ID")) %>'
        Text='<%# DataBinder.Eval(Container.DataItem, "Title") %>'>
      </asp:HyperLink>
    </li>
  </ItemTemplate>
</asp:DataList>
<br />Ask a question: <br />
<asp:TextBox ID="QuestionTextBox" Width="320px"
            runat="server"></asp:TextBox>
<asp:Button ID="QuestionButton" runat="server" Text="Ask"
            OnClick="QuestionButton_Click" />
<asp:Label ID="MessageLabel" runat="server" Text="" />
```

The design view of the web part is shown in Figure 2.14. A `DataList` was used instead of a `BulletedList` to allow more flexibility; in this case the flexibility is needed because there's no way to directly bind the list item's URL, given that the `SPListItem` object doesn't have a useful URL property to bind to. Instead, the URL is built from the item's unique ID by a function called `DisplayURL`, which you see later in this chapter in Listing 2.10. The `DataList` is also more flexible in that the rendering can be changed using ASP.NET Templates for the header, footer, item, and so on.

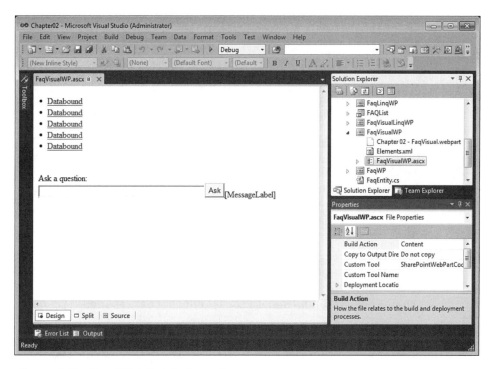

FIGURE 2.14: Visual Web Part design surface

Next, add some code behind the web part to retrieve the list of FAQs and bind them to `FaqDataList`. It's best to do the binding late in the page rendering cycle in case the list has changed in response to some user input elsewhere on the page; therefore a good place to retrieve the SharePoint data and connect it to the data list is during the PreRender stage. This is accomplished by overriding the `OnPreRender` event in the FaqVisualWP.ascx.cs file, as shown in Listing 2.10.

LISTING 2.10: Querying and Binding List Data

```
private string listFormUrl;

protected override void OnPreRender(EventArgs e)
{
    base.OnPreRender(e);
    try
    {
        SPWeb myWeb = SPContext.Current.Web;
        SPList faqList = myWeb.Lists["Frequently Asked Ques-
tions"];

        this.listFormUrl = myWeb.Url + "/" +
                faqList.Forms[0].Url + "?ID=";

        SPQuery q = new SPQuery();
        q.Query = "<Where><Eq><FieldRef Name='Answered' />" +
                "<Value
Type='Bool'>True</Value></Eq></Where>" +
                "<OrderBy><FieldRef Ascending=\"TRUE\" " +
                "Name=\"Title\" /></OrderBy>";

        SPListItemCollection answeredQuestions =
            faqList.GetItems(q);

        this.FaqDataList.DataSource = answeredQuestions;
        this.FaqDataList.DataBind();
    }
    catch (Exception ex)
    {
        this.Controls.Clear();
        this.Controls.Add(new LiteralControl(ex.Message));
    }
}
```

The work is done in a Try/Catch block in case SharePoint throws an exception; in that case, the code throws away all the child controls that were generated from the .ascx code and adds a new one to show the error message. In a production application, it would be bad form to show the error message directly to an end-user because it might contain sensitive information; instead you would want to log the error and display a generic message, but for debugging purposes this is fine.

When in the Try block, the code begins by obtaining an SPWeb object for the current site in the statement:

```
SPWeb myWeb = SPContext.Current.Web;
```

SPContext represents a SharePoint context such as which site collection and site are currently in use; the SPContext.Current static method always returns the current SharePoint context, which is the SharePoint site where the web part is running. The using statement ensures that the SPWeb object will be properly disposed of.

At this point you can store away a piece of information you will need later, which is the URL to display the FAQ list item when a user clicks. SharePoint maintains a number of forms for displaying and editing list items, so there is no one obvious URL, and the SPListItem's URL property is of little help. The statement

```
this.listFormUrl = myWeb.Url + "/" +
            faqList.Forms[0].Url +
            "?ID=";
```

saves the URL of the default form (the display form) for the list. This is used during data binding; as you can see in Listing 2.9, the binding to the HyperLink object's NavigationUrl property calls a function called DisplayUrl(), shown in Listing 2.11. DisplayUrl concatenates the list form URL with the item's unique ID, which is passed as an argument in the data binding expression.

LISTING 2.11: DisplayUrl() Function

```
public string DisplayUrl(object id)
{
    return this.listFormUrl + id.ToString();
}
```

Note that the code uses Hyperlink objects rather than link buttons because there is no way to redirect after a post-back in a sandboxed solution. This makes sense if you think about it: You're running in the sandbox, so you can't touch the HTTP context.

Next, you want to select just the FAQ items that have been answered. Getting to the FAQ list instance is simple:

```
SPList faqList = myWeb.Lists["Frequently Asked Questions"];
```

At this point, you could just enumerate faqList.Items and only display the FAQ items that have been answered, but this is inefficient because you might have to loop through a lot of unanswered items. Instead, the code builds a query to retrieve only the answered questions and to retrieve them in alphabetical order. This query does not use the SharePoint search engine, which provides full-text search across many lists and sites; think of it more like a database query against the SharePoint list. The query is written in SharePoint's internal language called CAML, which stands for Collaboration Application Markup Language; this is the same language that was used in the list definition. In this case, a query is created in CAML, as shown in Listing 2.12. This query is already in the code, which you might have noticed in Listing 2.10.

LISTING 2.12: CAML Query for Answered FAQ Items

```
<Where>
    <Eq>
        <FieldRef Name='Answered' />
        <Value Type='Bool'>True</Value>
    </Eq>
</Where>
<OrderBy>
    <FieldRef Ascending="True" Name="Title" />
</OrderBy>
```

As you can see, CAML uses an XML element hierarchy to structure the query; although this is easily parsed by computers, it can seem cumbersome to humans. The query is placed in an SPQuery object, which can then be used to get the desired list items, already sorted and ready for binding to the DataList.

If you want to give the web part a try, add a stubbed-out event handler to the code-behind for the QuestionButton_Click event so the project will compile:

```
void QuestionButton_Click(object sender, EventArgs e)
{
}
```

Given some answered questions in the FAQ list, which can easily be created within the SharePoint user interface, the resulting web part displays them as shown in Figure 2.15. Be sure to edit the items and check the Answered column so they match the CAML query and are shown in the web part display.

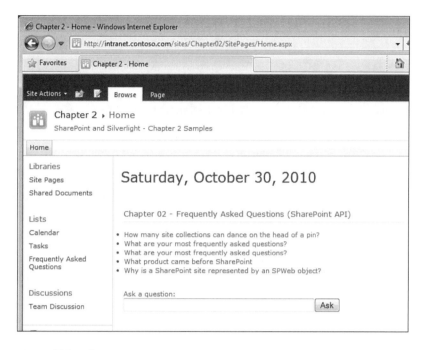

FIGURE 2.15: FAQ web part

Updating List Data with the SharePoint API

Next up is to add the ability for a user to enter a new FAQ question into the list. To do this, a text box for the user to type in and a button to post the question in the .ascx file are already included, so all that remains is to create the code to update the list, as shown in Listing 2.13.

LISTING 2.13: QuestionButton Click Event Handler

```
void QuestionButton_Click(object sender, EventArgs e)
{
    try
    {
        SPWeb myWeb = SPContext.Current.Web;
        SPList faqList = myWeb.Lists["Frequently Asked Questions"];
        SPListItem li = faqList.AddItem();
        li["Title"] = this.QuestionTextBox.Text;

        li.Update();

        this.QuestionTextBox.Text = "";
```

```
            this.MessageLabel.Text = "<br />Thank you for submitting a " +
                                "new question.";
        }
        catch (Exception ex)
        {
         // TODO: In production, log the error and show a generic message
            this.MessageLabel.Text = "Error saving your question: " +
                ex.Message;
        }
    }
}
```

Notice that the new list item is obtained from the `SPList` object's `AddItem()` method and is then filled in with its property values. A call to the list item's `Update()` method persists the changes to SharePoint. In general the SharePoint API expects an `Update()` method to be called when updating data, allowing you to make several changes to an object before persisting it.

LINQ to SharePoint

You might notice that the SharePoint API is not strongly typed with respect to SharePoint data, and runtime errors can occur if a list name, field name, or CAML query doesn't match the underlying SharePoint content. To address this, as well as to remove the need to write queries in the arcane CAML syntax, SharePoint 2010 introduces support for LINQ to SharePoint. LINQ stands for Language Integrated Query and allows your code to include strongly typed data references and queries that interact with Share-Point data.

The problem of loose typing is not entirely solved by LINQ; rather it is moved from the human developer to a tool. For LINQ to SharePoint, this tool is called SPMetal.exe, and it is installed along with all editions of Share-Point. The developer captures a snapshot of site content using SPMetal, which generates strongly-typed wrapper classes for the lists in the site. This code is then imported into Visual Studio where it can be accessed by your code.

Presumably SPMetal is less error-prone than a human programmer, and any errors are more likely to be caught by Visual Studio as the developer is typing rather than at runtime. It's still the developer's responsibility to ensure that the lists and libraries the code is accessing are identical in structure to the ones passed to SPMetal during development. In this case, because the code and list structure are defined within the same solution, SPMetal can be safely run on the developer's test SharePoint site with confidence that an identical list will be there in production.

SPMetal can be found in the SharePoint Root, which is where most of the SharePoint files are installed. Its default location is C:\Program Files\Microsoft Shared\Web Server Extensions\14; SPMETAL is in the bin directory within. Enter **spmetal /?** for help; an example command might be

```
spmetal /web:http://myserver /code:"C:\SomePath\FaqEntity.cs"
```

Use SPMetal to generate an entity file for your development site where the FAQ list instance is installed and import it into your Visual Studio project. The code allows you to query and update the FAQ list using LINQ to SharePoint.

> **■ TIP**
>
> Take care when choosing which user account to use when running the SPMetal utility, as it only generates code for objects that a user has permission to see.

A second web part called FaqVisualLINQWP is included in the code download to show the same web part using LINQ to SharePoint instead of the SharePoint API. The two web parts are very similar, except of course in how the SharePoint data is accessed. As you can see in Listing 2.14, the OnPreRender method now uses LINQ instead of a CAML query to show the answered questions, sorted by title.

LISTING 2.14: LINQ Code for FAQL Web Part

```
protected override void OnPreRender(EventArgs e)
{
    base.OnPreRender(e);
    try
```

```
{
    using (FaqEntityDataContext dc =
                new FaqEntityDataContext(SPContext.Current.Web.Url))
    {
        EntityList<FrequentlyAskedQuestionsItem> faqs =
                    dc.GetList<FrequentlyAskedQuestionsItem>
                    ("Frequently Asked Questions");

        if (faqs.Any<FrequentlyAskedQuestionsItem>())
        {
            var faqEnumerable = from item in faqs
                                where (item.Answered == true)
                                orderby item.Title
                                select item;

            this.FaqDataList.DataSource = faqEnumerable;
            this.FaqDataList.DataBind();
        }
    }
}
catch (Exception ex)
{
    this.Controls.Clear();
    this.Controls.Add(new LiteralControl(ex.Message));
}
}
```

The `FaqEntityDataContext` class was generated by SPMetal and is derived from the LINQ to SharePoint `DataContext` class. This class is used whenever SharePoint data is queried or updated using LINQ to SharePoint. Because `DataContext` is `IDisposable`, a `using` statement is included to ensure there is no memory leak. The query itself is now easier to read and is validated by the compiler.

One difference between the LINQ and SharePoint API code is that where the `SPQuery` returned its results in an `SPListItemCollection`, LINQ returns them in a generic collection—specifically an `IEnumerable` `<FrequentlyAskedQuestionsItem>` where the `FrequentlyAskedQuestions` `Item` is defined in the code generated by SPMetal. `FrequentlyAsked` `QuestionsItem` is strongly typed, so the code can access its properties with compile-time checking to make certain they're used correctly.

New questions can also be added to the list using LINQ to SharePoint, as shown in Listing 2.15. Notice that the `DataContext` can manage changes to the site data and updates them when its `SubmitChanges()` method is invoked.

LISTING 2.15: Updating the List with LINQ

```
void QuestionButton_Click(object sender, EventArgs e)
{
    try
    {
        using (FaqEntityDataContext dc = new
                FaqEntityDataContext(SPContext.Current.Web.Url))
        {
            EntityList<FrequentlyAskedQuestionsItem> faqList =
                dc.GetList<FrequentlyAskedQuestionsItem>
                ("Frequently Asked Questions");

            FrequentlyAskedQuestionsItem i =
                new FrequentlyAskedQuestionsItem()
                {
                    Title=this.QuestionTextBox.Text
                };
            faqList.InsertOnSubmit(i);

            dc.SubmitChanges();
        }

        this.QuestionTextBox.Text = "";
        this.MessageLabel.Text = "<br />Thank you for the question.";
    }
    catch (Exception ex)
    {
        // TODO: In production, log the error and show a generic message
        this.MessageLabel.Text = "Error saving your question: " +
            ex.Message;
    }
}
```

Web Parts as Composite Controls

As a SharePoint developer, you don't want to be confined to developing Visual Web Parts. Sometimes it's easier to write web parts in procedural code, especially if the goal is to simply place a Silverlight object tag on the page and pass in some data. The reusability of a simple `WebControl` allows the Silverlight tag rendering and application details to be encapsulated into separate classes. Many of the other kinds of SharePoint customizations, such as editor parts and field controls, are only possible as composite controls. This section shows you how to build the same web parts as composite controls so you can take advantage of these scenarios later in the book.

A composite control is an ASP.NET control that, rather than spitting out its own HTML, renders its contents by creating and manipulating a set of child controls. The child controls are created in code by overriding the CreateChildControls() method instead of declaring the controls in an .ascx file as in the Visual Web Part. Listing 2.16 shows the code to create the exact same controls declared in the previous example's .ascx file.

LISTING 2.16: The Web Part as a Composite Control

```
// Fields to hold child controls
private DataList FaqDataList = new DataList();
private TextBox QuestionTextBox = new TextBox();
private Label MessageLabel = new Label();

protected override void CreateChildControls()
{
    try
    {
        // Add the data list that will display the FAQ
        this.FaqDataList.HeaderTemplate = new FaqWP_HeaderTemplate();
        this.FaqDataList.ItemTemplate = new FaqWP_ItemTemplate();
        this.FaqDataList.FooterTemplate = new FaqWP_FooterTemplate();
        this.Controls.Add(this.FaqDataList);

        // Add a literal instructing the user to ask a question
        this.Controls.Add
            (new LiteralControl("<br />Ask a question:<br />"));

        // Add a text box to capture a new question
        this.QuestionTextBox.Width = Unit.Pixel(320);
        this.Controls.Add(this.QuestionTextBox);

        // Add a button for the user to click to enter a new question
        Button QuestionButton = new Button();
        QuestionButton.Text = "Ask";
        QuestionButton.Click += new EventHandler(QuestionButton_Click);
        this.Controls.Add(QuestionButton);
```

```
        // Add a label to display a message to the user
        this.Controls.Add(this.MessageLabel);
    }
    catch (Exception ex)
    {
        this.Controls.Clear();
        this.Controls.Add(new LiteralControl("Error: " + ex.Message));
    }
}
```

As you can see, some of the controls are saved as private fields so other code in the web part such as the OnPreRender override and the button click event handler can find them. All the controls are created and configured in CreateChildControls() just as they were in the .ascx file, and each control is added to the web part's Controls collection. The click event handler on the QuestionButton is connected in code, as are the DataList templates.

The DataList templates need to be objects that implement the ITemplate interface, so you need to add a class for each template to replace the template code in the .ascx file. The code is shown in Listing 2.17. ITemplate requires a single method, InstantiateIn(), which adds the template's child controls into a container during data binding much as in CreateChildControls().

LISTING 2.17: Code for Data Binding Templates

```
public class FaqWP_HeaderTemplate : ITemplate
{
    public void InstantiateIn(Control container)
    {
        container.Controls.Add(new LiteralControl("<ul>"));
    }
}

public class FaqWP_ItemTemplate : ITemplate
{
    public void InstantiateIn(Control container)
    {
        container.Controls.Add(new LiteralControl("<li>"));

        HyperLink h = new HyperLink();
        h.DataBinding += new EventHandler(h_DataBinding);
        container.Controls.Add(h);
```

```
            container.Controls.Add(new LiteralControl("</li>"));
        }

        void h_DataBinding(object sender, EventArgs e)
        {
            HyperLink h = (HyperLink)sender;
            DataListItem container = (DataListItem)h.NamingContainer;
            SPListItem li = (SPListItem)container.DataItem;
            h.Text = li.Title;
            h.NavigateUrl = li.Web.Url + "/" +
                            li.ParentList.Forms[0].Url +
                            "?ID=" + li.ID;
        }
    }

    public class FaqWP_FooterTemplate : ITemplate
    {
        public void InstantiateIn(Control container)
        {
            container.Controls.Add(new LiteralControl("</ul>"));
        }
    }
}
```

The code approach removed the need to save the display form URL for use in data binding; instead the h_DataBinding event handler is able to fill in the properties of the bound control directly. The LINQ to SharePoint version varies slightly because the data binding is with a FrequentlyAskedQuestionsItem instead of a SPListItem; in this case the display form is hard-coded to simplify the code, as shown in Listing 2.18.

LISTING 2.18: LINQ Version of Data Binding Code

```
void h_DataBinding(object sender, EventArgs e)
{
    HyperLink h = (HyperLink)sender;
    DataListItem container = (DataListItem)h.NamingContainer;
    FrequentlyAskedQuestionsItem li =
        (FrequentlyAskedQuestionsItem)container.DataItem;
    h.Text = li.Title;
    h.NavigateUrl = li.Path + "/DispForm.aspx?ID=" + li.Id;
}
```

Event Receivers

Another arrow in the SharePoint developer's quiver is the event receiver. Event receivers are components that execute code on the server in response to various events in SharePoint, such as a list item being created or a feature being activated. SharePoint 2010 provides an extensive list of events, as shown in Table 2.2.

TABLE 2.2: SharePoint Foundation Site and List Events

Scope	Event Source(s)	Events
Site Collection	SPSite	SiteDeleting, SiteDeleted
Site	SPWeb or SPSite	WebAdding, WebProvisioned, WebDeleting, WebDeleted, WebMoving, WebMoved
List	SPSite or SPWeb	ListAdding, ListAdded, ListDeleting, ListDeleted
List Field	SPSite, SPWeb, SPList or SPContentType	FieldAdding, FieldAdded, FieldDeleting, FieldDeleted, FieldUpdating, FieldUpdated
List Item	SPSite, SPWeb, SPList or SPContentType	ItemAdding, ItemAdded, ItemDeleting, ItemUpdating, ItemUpdated, ItemFileConverted, ItemFileMoving, ItemFileMoved, ItemCheckingIn, ItemCheckedIn, ItemCheckingOut, ItemCheckedOut, ItemAttachment Adding, ItemAttachmentAdded, ItemAttachmentDeleting, ItemAttachmentDeleted

For example, if a new list is added to a SharePoint site, the ListAdding and ListAdded events run. The events with names ending in ing are "before" events that run synchronously, before the actual event takes place. In this case, your code could cancel the operation if, for example, it contained business logic that determined the item should not be added. The events with names ending in ed are "after" events that run asynchronously, after the event has completed. This is useful for auditing or other activities that run after the action takes place.

To extend on the previous examples, let's add an event receiver to enforce a business rule that stipulates that no FAQ question should be deleted until it has been answered. To do this, hook the `ItemDeleting` event and check to be sure the question has been answered; if not, the deletion is aborted, and an error is reported back to the user.

To begin, add a new item to your project in Visual Studio. This time select the SharePoint 2010 Event Receiver item. As shown in Figure 2.16, the SharePoint Customization Wizard prompts you for the type of event receiver to create, the event source, and the events to be handled. You want a List Item event receiver, and for the source you want to select the Frequently Asked Questions list that is created in your own Visual Studio project. You only need to handle the situation of an item being deleted and need the synchronous version to abort it if necessary; therefore you should select An Item Is Being Deleted for the event.

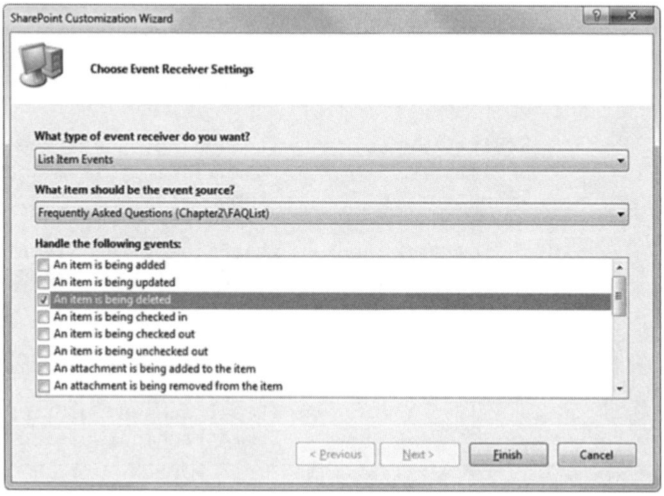

FIGURE 2.16: Adding an event receiver

At this point, Visual Studio creates your event receiver along with its class file and an Elements.xml file to declare the event receiver. The class file is set up with an override of the `ItemDeleting()` method, so add the event logic as shown in Listing 2.19.

LISTING 2.19: ItemDeleting Event Receiver

```
public override void ItemDeleting(SPItemEventProperties properties)
{
    base.ItemDeleting(properties);

    bool isAnswered = Boolean.Parse
                      (properties.ListItem["Answered"].ToString());
    if (!isAnswered)
    {
        properties.ErrorMessage =
            "You cannot delete an unanswered question.";
        properties.Cancel = true;
    }
}
```

Solutions and Features

When creating this simple web part, you have created a SharePoint solution. It's not only a solution in Visual Studio, it's also a SharePoint *Solution*, which is an installable package stored in a single file with the extension .wsp. The letters "wsp" stand for Web Solution Package; just to add to the confusion about sites and webs, they are installed at the SharePoint farm or site collection levels.

A .wsp file is simply a cabinet file; you can rename one to end in .cab and open it up if you want to look inside. A .wsp file must contain a root file called manifest.xml, which tells SharePoint how to install the package. The .wsp also includes all the files that need to be installed including executable .dlls, supporting files such as images and style sheets, and a variety of .xml files that tell SharePoint how to stitch your content into the content system. SharePoint administrators generally expect to install .wsp files rather than run scripts or proprietary setup programs when adding new extensions to their SharePoint installations. This has the advantage of providing a single point of control and knowing that SharePoint takes care of provisioning the package as needed to new SharePoint servers as they are added to the farm.

To view the solution in the web browser, open the Site Actions menu and select Site Settings. Sandboxed solutions are managed at the site collection level, so if you are in a child site, click Go to Top Level Site Settings under Site Collection Administration. Here you see a number of options under the Galleries heading. The .webpart file you just edited is in the Web Part Gallery, and the solution is in the Solution Gallery. Click into the Solution Gallery and you see your solution, along with resource usage statistics, as shown in Figure 2.17.

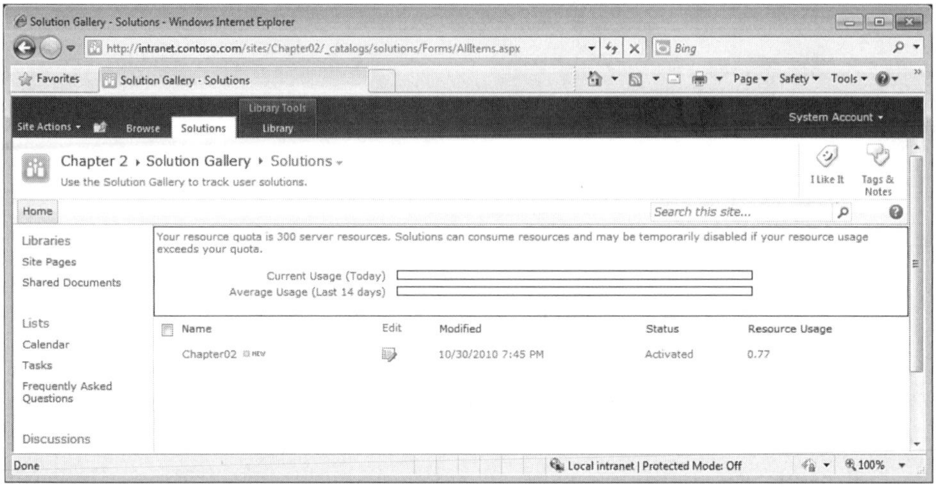

FIGURE 2.17:   Site Collection Solution Gallery

The Solution Gallery is a SharePoint library containing .wsp files. The Solutions tab allows sandboxed solutions to be uploaded and managed. If this was a farm solution instead of a sandboxed one, it would be managed in Central Administration. To see this, open Central Administration and click System Settings; then under Farm Management, click Manage Farm Solutions.

Within a solution there are *features* that administrators can selectively enable to make functionality "light up" in SharePoint. Features can be scoped at the farm, web application, site collection, or site level, giving administrators at all these levels the ability to enable or disable functionality. In addition to web parts, features can contain SharePoint content types, list definitions, list instances, application pages, Ribbon items, and more.

The solution created so far in this chapter has two features. One contains all the web parts and is scoped at the site collection (SPSite) level. This is because all web parts depend on the Web Part Gallery to hold their

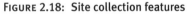

.webpart files, and the Web Part Gallery is always shared by all sites in a site collection. The other feature is scoped at the site (SPWeb) level and contains the FAQ list definition along with its list instance and the event handler.

To view the web part feature, open Site Settings, and under Site Collection Administration, click Site Collection Features. To view the site scoped feature, click Site Features in the settings of your debug site. In the code download, the feature is called "Chapter 02 - Web Parts," as in the Figure 2.18; in your project it might be different. You can change the name in the Feature Designer, which is explained later in this section.

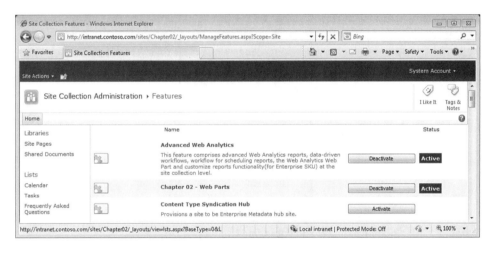

FIGURE 2.18: Site collection features

Each Visual Studio 2010 solution is always one SharePoint solution that produces a single .wsp file. Within that solution, Visual Studio can associate SharePoint Items with one or more SharePoint features. Each of the things you created in Visual Studio—the web parts, the list and the event handler—appears in Visual Studio as a SharePoint Item or SPI. SPIs act like folders with special icons to indicate their types, properties to configure them, and the source code and declarative XML inside the folder.

The Visual Studio Solution Explorer shows the Visual Studio hierarchy: a solution containing one or more projects with SharePoint Items inside at least one of the projects. To view the SharePoint hierarchy, you need to look at the Packaging Explorer instead. To enable this in Visual Studio 2010, open the View menu, and under Other Windows, click Packaging Explorer.

Now you can see the SharePoint solution with its two features and the SharePoint items within each feature. Figure 2.19 shows both displays as they appear for the sample project developed in this chapter.

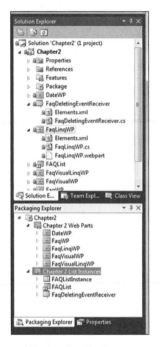

FIGURE 2.19: Solution Explorer and Packaging Explorer

To see more detail, right-click the solution (top node) in the Packaging Explorer and select View Designer. The Solution Designer opens, as shown in Figure 2.20. Here you can move Visual Studio project items in and out of the .wsp package; by clicking the Advanced tab at the bottom of the designer, you can also add additional .dll files that you need to deploy. The Manifest tab shows the solution's Manifest.xml file, which is at the core of the solution. Notice that the manifest refers to your compiled .dll file and also includes a SafeControl setting that is placed in the ASP.NET web.config file to mark your assembly as safe to run. If you ever need to edit solution and feature files manually, always do so in the Visual Studio 2010 packaging designer so it can correctly merge your changes with the XML generated by Visual Studio.

FIGURE 2.20: The SharePoint Solution Designer

■ TIP

If you developed your solution in the "top-level" site, your list definition and instance might be in the same site collection feature as the
web part. This causes your solution to break if it's used in a child site
because the FAQ list appears in the top-level site! It's a good practice
to test your solutions in top-level and child sites, as this sort of mistake
is easy to make.

To correct it, on the Visual Studio View menu, select Other Windows
and then Packaging Explorer. The top item in the Packaging Explorer
is the SharePoint solution, and the feature(s) are immediately below
this. Right-click the solution name and select Add Feature. Give your
feature a name and ensure its scope is set to Web. Then in the panel on
the lower left, select the FAQ list definition, list, and deleting event
handlers and click the >> button to move them to your new feature.

Click the Edit link on either feature to open the Feature Designer. Figure
2.21 shows the Feature Designer for the web part feature; as you can see, the
scope is set to Site, and all the web part SPIs are included in the feature.
Using the Feature Designer, you can easily consolidate or rearrange
features as desired to allow administrators to turn your functionality on
and off.

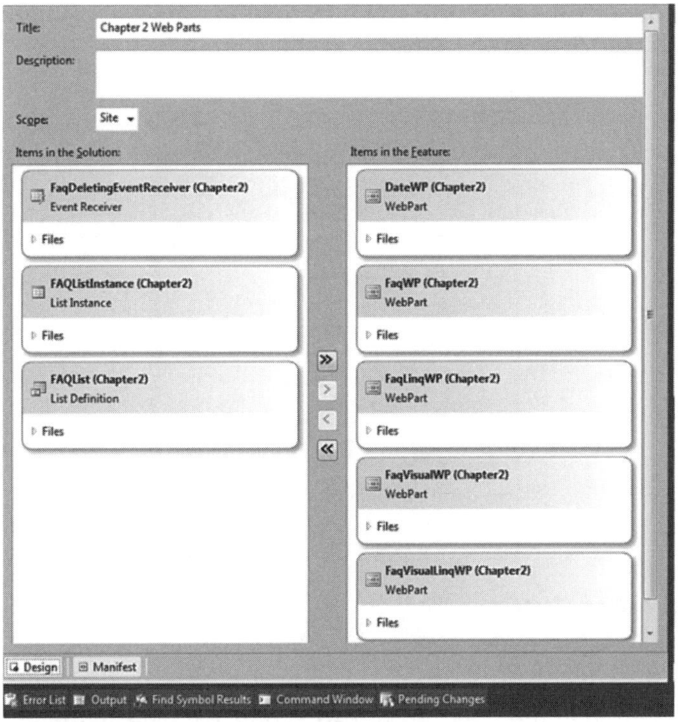

FIGURE 2.21: Feature Designer

Feature Receivers

Another kind of event receiver you may find helpful is a feature receiver, which runs your code when a SharePoint feature is activated, deactivated, installed, or updated (with the same ing variations available as well). This allows you to do any kind of setup or cleanup that can't be handled in the declarative feature.xml and other files associated with your project.

To show this, add a simple feature receiver to the FAQ solution to add an initial question to the list when it is provisioned. To create the feature receiver, go to Solution Explorer in Visual Studio, and under the Features folder, find the web level feature that contains the FAQ list instance (probably Feature2 if you did the project in the same order as the chapter). Right-click the feature and click Add Event Receiver as shown in Figure 2.22.

Visual Studio creates a class derived from SPFeatureReceiver, which you can edit to add your event code.

FIGURE 2.22: Adding a feature receiver

In this case, we want to hook the FeatureActivated event, so uncomment the method in the class file and add code to create an initial FAQ entry, as shown in Listing 2.20.

LISTING 2.20: FeatureActivated Event Receiver

```
public override void FeatureActivated
            (SPFeatureReceiverProperties properties)
{
    using (SPWeb web = properties.Feature.Parent as SPWeb)
    {
        if (web != null)
        {
            SPList faqList = web.Lists["Frequently Asked Questions"];
            SPListItem li = faqList.AddItem();
            li["Title"] = "What are your most frequent questions?";
            li["Answer"] = "Use this list to capture and answer them!";
            li["Answered"] = true;
            li.Update();
        }
    }
}
```

Now, whenever your feature is activated, the initial FAQ question is added; this is done by default every time you deploy your solution in Visual Studio, so you can end up with quite a lot of them if you continue working on the project and have disabled deployment conflicts on the FAQ List Instance.

Summary

You now are equipped with a baseline of SharePoint development knowledge to tackle the rest of this book. You have been exposed to the core concepts needed to build lists to hold content, event receivers to extend list behavior, and solutions and features to package your work. Although web parts are rendered in Silverlight after this chapter, they are still based on the SharePoint web part or Visual Web Part project items introduced here. Becoming adept at composite control development helps as well, especially when tackling more advanced projects such as field controls and connected web parts.

3.

Introduction to Silverlight Development

M ICROSOFT SILVERLIGHT APPLICATIONS are flexible and have many forms and can have different appearances. Often it's video or a dynamic user experience that drives interest in web sites and gives developers good reason to construct these applications. These applications are frequently called rich Internet applications (RIA).

Although rich Internet applications often take over the entire user interface, including navigation and all layout elements, in SharePoint users generally expect to use SharePoint as a basis for the user interface. This allows users to compose their own web user interfaces using web parts, page layouts, and navigation settings and to reuse the many assets included in SharePoint. Therefore, Silverlight solutions in SharePoint are generally small islands of RIA residing on a SharePoint page in a web part or elsewhere in the SharePoint user interface. This is the approach taken in this book.

In the sections that follow, you learn how to create your own Silverlight applications and test them in a local web site in Visual Studio 2010. First, however, you learn how to put a Silverlight application on a web page.

Placing Silverlight on a Web Page

Placing a Silverlight application on a web page begins by creating a Silverlight application package in a file ending with the .xap extension, which is commonly pronounced "zap." A .xap file is really a Zip archive, and if you rename one to end with a .zip filename extension, you can open it and look inside. This can be helpful in learning Silverlight, as well as to understand what's taking up space in an overly large .xap file. Web browsers download .xap files from web sites just like any other file, and they are cached just like other web files. The .xap file can be deployed to a web site just like any other.

■ TIP

Typically, other than external data, everything a Silverlight application needs to run is contained within its .xap file. However, this isn't necessary: The application can load additional code and resources (also in .xap files) after it has started running. This can reduce startup time and also allow the browser to cache libraries that are used by multiple solutions.

Dynamic .xap loading is covered in Chapter 8, "Accessing SharePoint Data with the Client Object Model," where you learn to load the SharePoint client object model dynamically after your application has started up.

After the .xap file has been created and placed on a web site for download, the next step is to place the Silverlight browser plug-in on a web page and pass it the location of the .xap file to be rendered. An HTML `<object>` tag, as shown in Listing 3.1, is used to instruct the browser to display Silverlight.

LISTING 3.1: Placing Silverlight on an HTML Page

```
<div id="silverlightControlHost">
    <object data="data:application/x-silverlight-2,"
type="application/x-silverlight-2" width="100%" height="100%">
                <param name="source" value="ClientBin/Chapter03.xap"/>
                <param name="onError" value="onSilverlightError" />
                <param name="background" value="white" />
                <param name="minRuntimeVersion" value="4.0.50826.0" />
                <param name="autoUpgrade" value="true" />
                <a
href="http://go.microsoft.com/fwlink/?LinkID=149156&v=4.0.50826.0"
style="text-decoration:none">
                    <img
src="http://go.microsoft.com/fwlink/?LinkId=161376" alt="Get Microsoft
Silverlight" style="border-style:none"/>
                </a>
        </object><iframe id="_sl_historyFrame"
style="visibility:hidden;height:0px;width:0px;border:0px"></iframe></div>
```

This example is taken from the code download for this chapter, in the file Chapter03TestPage.aspx. When you create a new Silverlight project, Visual Studio 2010 offers to create a test web project, and this is from the test web page from the test project. The .xap file itself is placed in the Silverlight project's bin directory and is copied to the ClientBin directory in the test project to make it accessible on the test web site.

It's a best practice to use the test page that ships with Silverlight as a basis for placing Silverlight on a web page, given there are many nuances in the HTML that can affect rendering in specific browsers. It's safe to change the Silverlight parameters (the <param> elements), the <object> tag's height and width attributes, and the <div> attributes, but the rest of the markup should be copied exactly to ensure your solution works properly in all web browsers. For example, the hidden <iframe> tag ensures that navigation works in Safari.

Notice the <a> tag and the image within it; this is what is rendered when Silverlight is not installed. This default content shows an image, asking the user to download Silverlight and links to the download page. If you want to override this logic, you can replace this with some other HTML. For example, rather than asking the user to download Silverlight, you could provide a simple HTML rendering of your solution.

You can pass parameters into Silverlight using `<param>` elements in the `<object>` tag. Table 3.1 explains the most commonly used parameters, including the ones shown in Listing 3.1.

TABLE 3.1: Common Silverlight Parameters

Parameter	Meaning
autoUpgrade	If true, Silverlight automatically upgrades to a newer version if the currently installed plug-in is older than the minRuntimeVersion.
background	The background color to show behind the Silverlight application.
initparams	Allows the developer to pass a set of name/value pairs to the Silverlight application in the format, name1=value1, name2=value2.
minRuntimeVersion	The minimum Silverlight runtime version required to run the application.
onError	A Javascript function to run if an unhandled exception is thrown in Silverlight. The Silverlight test application includes a good implementation of this.
source	The location of the Silverlight application .xap file.

Building a Simple Silverlight Application with Visual Studio 2010

From a developer's point of view, Silverlight is a subset of Microsoft's Windows Presentation Foundation (WPF); indeed Silverlight began its life as "WPFe," which is an acronym for "WPF Everywhere." The idea was to build a simpler subset of WPF that would run in web browsers across platforms with the ambitious goal of eventually running everywhere. There are many advantages in this strategy, including significant reuse of code, tools (such as Visual Studio and Expression Blend), and developer expertise.

Like WPF, a Silverlight application contains a combination of procedural code and a user interface markup in a language called *XAML*. XAML stands for *Extensible Application Markup Language* and is an XML syntax for defining a WPF or Silverlight user interface. This approach is similar to

HTML on a web page and has the advantage of providing a clean break between user interface and procedural code. XAML is considerably richer than HTML, however, and is also designed to allow very exact control over rendering.

Like many other application development environments, Silverlight has "controls" ranging from buttons to data grids, which are arranged on a design surface to create a user interface. Visual Studio 2010 provides a control toolbox and designer for adding drag-n-drop controls, as well as a properties grid to change them. The underlying code page describes the controls as XAML.

XAML defines controls using XML tags. Each control is a .NET object, and XAML is actually a way to serialize these objects using XML.

To begin building a simple application, open Visual Studio 2010 and select New Project; you are presented with the New Project dialog box as shown in Figure 3.1. Choose the Silverlight template and update the project name to Chapter03. Select Silverlight Application and click OK to create the project.

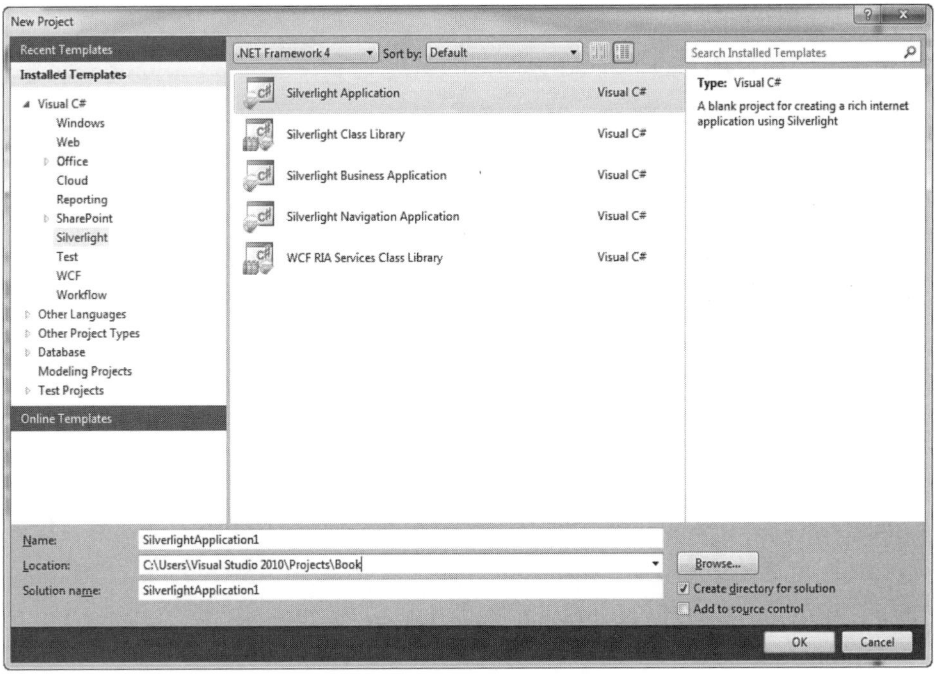

FIGURE 3.1: Creating a new Silverlight project

The projects in this book use the Silverlight Application project template, which creates a simple, single-page Silverlight application. A Silverlight Class Library might be useful as well if you want to break your application up into multiple .xap files that can be downloaded at runtime. The Silverlight Navigation Application and Silverlight Business Application templates add navigation and login code within the Silverlight application; when SharePoint is involved, it generally handles these functions. WCF RIA Services Class Libraries are briefly discussed later in this chapter but are not otherwise used in this book.

When the application type has been selected, you are prompted to choose the Silverlight version you want to target and asked if you want to Host the Silverlight application in a new web site. If you check this option, Silverlight generates a test web site to host your application during development. For this example, select Silverlight 4 or 5 and go ahead and let Visual Studio create the test web site.

After creating the Silverlight project, you are presented with a blank design surface. This starting XAML looks like the markup in Listing 3.2.

LISTING 3.2: The XAML Markup for a New Silverlight Project

```
<UserControl x:Class="Chapter3.MainPage"
    xmlns="http://schemas.microsoft.com/winfx/2006/xaml/presentation"
    xmlns:x="http://schemas.microsoft.com/winfx/2006/xaml"
    xmlns:d="http://schemas.microsoft.com/expression/blend/2008"
    xmlns:mc="http://schemas.openxmlformats.org/markup-compatibility/2006"
    mc:Ignorable="d"
    d:DesignHeight="300" d:DesignWidth="400">

    <Grid x:Name="LayoutRoot" Background="White">
    </Grid>
</UserControl>
```

At the root of the XAML is a `UserControl`, which is the base class for the main page, as implemented in MainPage.xaml and MainPage.xaml.cs. User controls in Silverlight are similar to user controls in ASP.NET in that they host a number of other controls that define all or part of your application's user interface. The `UserControl` also contains the namespaces for other controls that are used on the page.

The user control contains one child element, which is a `Grid` control. A grid can have one or more children, including child grids that can create their own children. The grid control is one of a handful of "layout controls" that arrange other controls on its surface; in the case of a grid, its children are arranged in rows and columns.

To begin building the user interface, ensure the toolbox is visible by selecting Toolbox on the View menu. Then drag a Button control onto the design surface from the toolbox. When placed on the surface, the controls are added to the XAML for you. Single click the button and drag the square on its right to the right so the button is larger. In the XAML, set the button's content to Please Do Not Push This Button. Your UI should now be similar to what's shown in Figure 3.2.

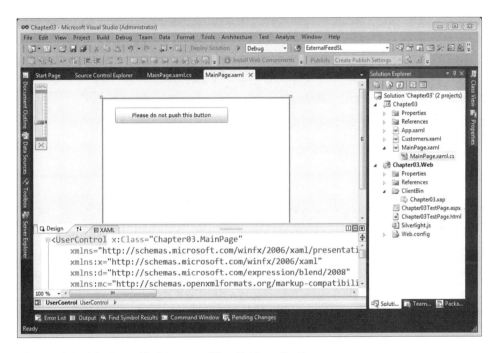

FIGURE 3.2: A button added to a new Silverlight application

Listing 3.3 shows the generated XAML for the application. When you dropped the button control on the design surface, Visual Studio captured the exact location in the Margin attribute of each element, so your values will probably be different depending on where you dropped it.

LISTING 3.3: The TextBox and Button in XAML

```
<UserControl x:Class="Chapter03.MainPage"
 xmlns="http://schemas.microsoft.com/winfx/2006/xaml/presentation"
 xmlns:x="http://schemas.microsoft.com/winfx/2006/xaml"
 xmlns:d="http://schemas.microsoft.com/expression/blend/2008"
 xmlns:mc="http://schemas.openxmlformats.org/markup-compatibility/2006"
 mc:Ignorable="d"
 d:DesignHeight="300" d:DesignWidth="400">

  <Grid x:Name="LayoutRoot" Background="White">
    <Button Name="button1" Click="button1_Click" Margin="5"
          Content="Please do not push this button" Height="32" />
  </Grid>
</UserControl>
```

Adding a click event handler to the button is as simple as double-clicking on the button in the Visual Studio design surface to generate the method stub. Listing 3.4 shows an example that changes the text on the button control.

LISTING 3.4: The Button Click Event Handler

```
        private void button1_Click(object sender, RoutedEventArgs e)
        {
            button1.Content = "Please do not push this button again!";
        }
```

Add the line of code assigning new text to button1.Content and press the F5 key to run the application. Visual Studio builds the Silverlight project, deploys its .xap file to the test project, and then starts the test project to display the Silverlight application in Internet Explorer. Click the button, and the text box displays the message as defined in the event handler. Figure 3.3 shows the application running in the test web site.

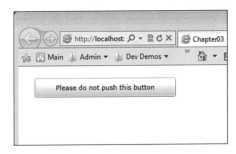

FIGURE 3.3: Running the application

▪ TIP

Expression Blend provides a richer design experience for Silverlight and WPF than Visual Studio and is the tool of choice for Silverlight UI designers. You might want to switch to Expression Blend for complex UI manipulation such as managing layout controls, setting up navigations, and using styles.

Fortunately, Visual Studio 2010 plays nicely with Expression Blend 3.0 or greater. If you've installed Expression Blend on your development machine, simply right-click any .xaml file and select Open in Expression Blend. Blend opens and allows you to edit the file, even if it's also open in Visual Studio. Blend also respects source control, and if a file was open in Visual Studio when you close Blend, Visual Studio offers to reload the new version of the file.

Chapter 6, "Expression Blend, Data Binding, and Sample Data," provides details on using Expression Blend and its prototyping tool, SketchFlow, in conjunction with SharePoint 2010.

Toolbox and Layout Controls

To familiarize yourself with the full suite of controls, open up the toolbox again and take a look at its contents, as shown in Figure 3.4. Scroll down to look over the whole list.

FIGURE 3.4: The Silverlight toolbox in Visual Studio 2010

Some of these controls render content such as text and images, but many of them are responsible for managing and arranging other controls on the display. Table 3.2 shows the basic types of controls with examples.

TABLE 3.2: Types of Silverlight Controls

Control Type	Examples
Text and Media Controls: Controls that render text only	`TextBlock, TextBox, PasswordBox, Image, MediaElement`
Content Controls: Controls that render a single element or a single element and a header	`Button, CheckBox, ListBoxItem, ComboBoxItem, DataGridCell`
Collection Controls: Controls that render a collection of items, possibly including a header	`ListBox, ComboBox, DataGrid`
Layout Controls: Controls that lay out an arrangement of other controls in the UI	`Grid, Canvas, StackPanel`

This allows for a lot of flexibility: For example, because a Button can contain another element, it could include an image to make an image button. To take it a step further, the button could contain a `Grid` layout control, which could contain an `Image` and a `TextBlock` to provide a button with an image and text arranged in a grid. By limiting the content controls to a single child, developers are forced to use layout controls such as a `Grid` throughout the user interface to arrange multiple child controls. This is a good thing as it ensures consistency in how controls are arranged whether they're in the top-level user control or in a tiny button deep within.

The Layout controls are important because they are used to lay out other controls in the user interface. The earlier example didn't really make use of the `Grid` control; it only contained one row and cell, and its children were laid out based on their Margin attributes. The `Grid` control is designed to present its child elements in rows and columns. Table 3.3 shows the layout controls and their general use.

TABLE 3.3: Silverlight Layout Controls

Layout	Description
StackPanel	Elements are arranged in sequence, either horizontally or vertically.
Grid	Elements are arranged in rows and columns.
Canvas	Elements are arranged using explicit x,y coordinates.
WrapPanel (part of the Silverlight Toolkit)	Elements are wrapped in lines, similar to the way HTML flows elements on a page.
DockPanel (part of the Silverlight Toolkit)	Elements are aligned along the top, bottom, left, and right edges.

Listing 3.5 shows an updated user interface button from the earlier example arranged using layout controls. The grid now has two rows, and the second row contains a StackPanel with two child objects, a TextBlock and another Button. The two grid rows are defined in the Grid.RowDefinitions element; the top one has a fixed height of 70 pixels, and the bottom one is given the default height of "auto," meaning it takes up as much room as is available.

LISTING 3.5: Using Layout Controls in XAML

```
<UserControl x:Class="Chapter03.MainPage"
 xmlns="http://schemas.microsoft.com/winfx/2006/xaml/presentation"
 xmlns:x="http://schemas.microsoft.com/winfx/2006/xaml"
 xmlns:d="http://schemas.microsoft.com/expression/blend/2008"
 xmlns:mc="http://schemas.openxmlformats.org/markup-compatibility/2006"
 mc:Ignorable="d"
 d:DesignHeight="300" d:DesignWidth="400">

  <Grid x:Name="LayoutRoot" Background="White">
    <Grid.RowDefinitions>
      <RowDefinition Height="70" />
      <RowDefinition Height="*" />
    </Grid.RowDefinitions>
```

```
        <Button Name="button1" Click="button1_Click" Margin="5"
                Content="Please do not push this button" Height="32"
                Grid.Row="0" />
        <StackPanel Grid.Row="1" Height="230" HorizontalAlignment="Left"
                    Name="stackPanel1" VerticalAlignment="Top" Width="400">
          <TextBlock Name="textBlock1" Margin="10"
                     Text="Press this button to show a customer list:" />
          <Button Content="Customers" Name="button2"
                  Height="23" Width="75" />
        </StackPanel>
      </Grid>
</UserControl>
```

When you're working with layout controls, you're likely to run into *attached properties*, which bear a little explanation. The first <Button> and the <StackPanel> in Listing 3.4 include an attached property, Grid.Row, to specify the grid row that will hold the stack panel. The Grid.Row attribute is attached to the grid control, and tells it which row to place the Stack-Panel in. Although this new concept might seem a bit confusing at first, it is a lot easier to work with than the row and column counting endemic in HTML tables, and it allows you to specify the position of each child control directly in the child rather than in the parent.

The new user interface should resemble the design shown in Figure 3.5. You can either enter the XAML from Listing 3.4 or drag the controls in from the toolbox and configure them in the designer in Visual Studio 2010.

Later in this chapter you implement a show customers feature to display customer information when the second button is pressed. For now the application should run, but the Customers button won't do anything.

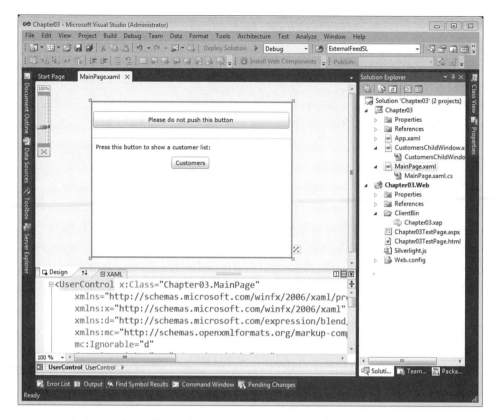

FIGURE 3.5: The updated Silverlight application in Visual Studio 2010

Setting Control Properties

Control properties specify the appearance and content of controls and can be set in the Properties window, in XAML or in code. For example, to display text in a text box, simply set the control's Text property. This can easily be done in code, but you can also do it at design time. Figure 3.6 shows how to change the text in a text box using the property grid in Visual Studio. Another option would be to edit the XAML directly and include a Text property in the <TextBox> element. By using Visual Studio's property grid, however, you have the advantage that Visual Studio helps you select a valid property setting, in many cases providing pick lists and other facilities for selecting a value.

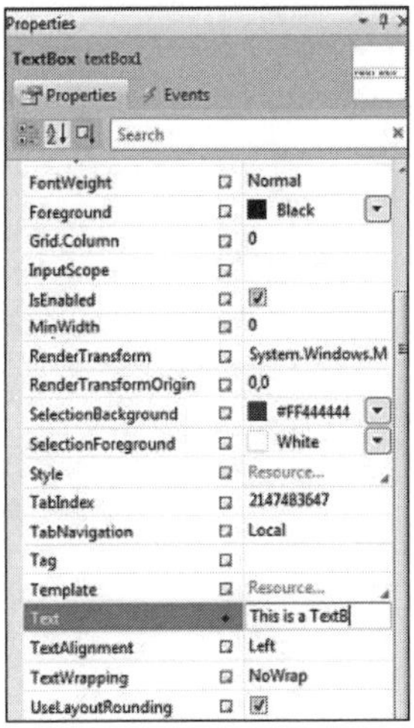

FIGURE 3.6: Property grid for a text box control

Creating and Showing Child Windows

A UserControl element is at the root of the simple example just shown; the user control is displayed as the Silverlight application's user interface. User controls always have a single child control, which is a layout control named LayoutRoot by convention. An application could easily have more than one user control to offer different displays. In this case the MainPage user control is displayed by code in the Application_Startup event handler in App.Xaml.cs.

Sometimes, however, you might want to display a pop-up or child window, and this is easily accomplished as well. A child window is similar to a user control except that it pops up over the rest of the user interface like a dialog box. To begin, right-click your Silverlight project and select Add New Item, as shown in Figure 3.7.

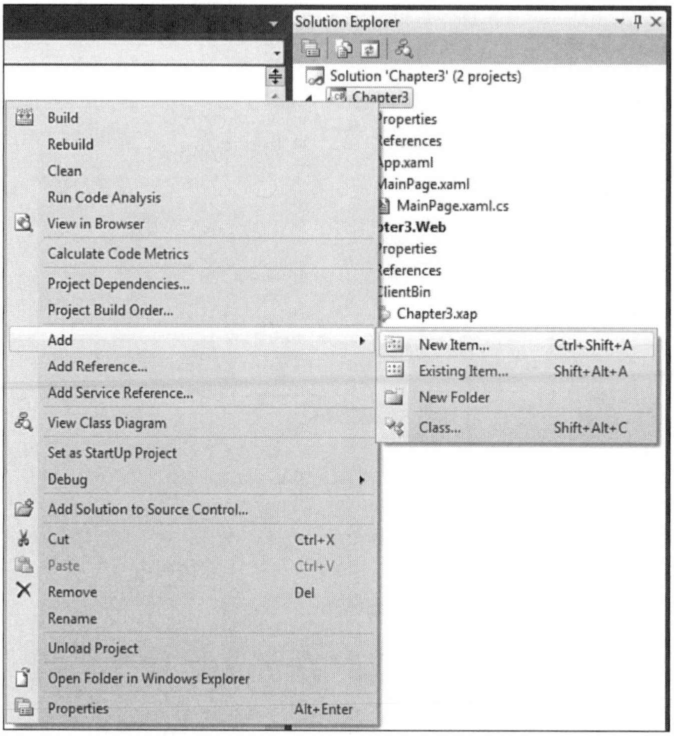

FIGURE 3.7: Adding a child window to the Silverlight project

Add a new Silverlight Child Window and name the window
CustomersChildWindow.xaml, as shown in Figure 3.8. Click OK to create
the child window.

When created, the child window has button controls ready to use, as
shown in Figure 3.9.

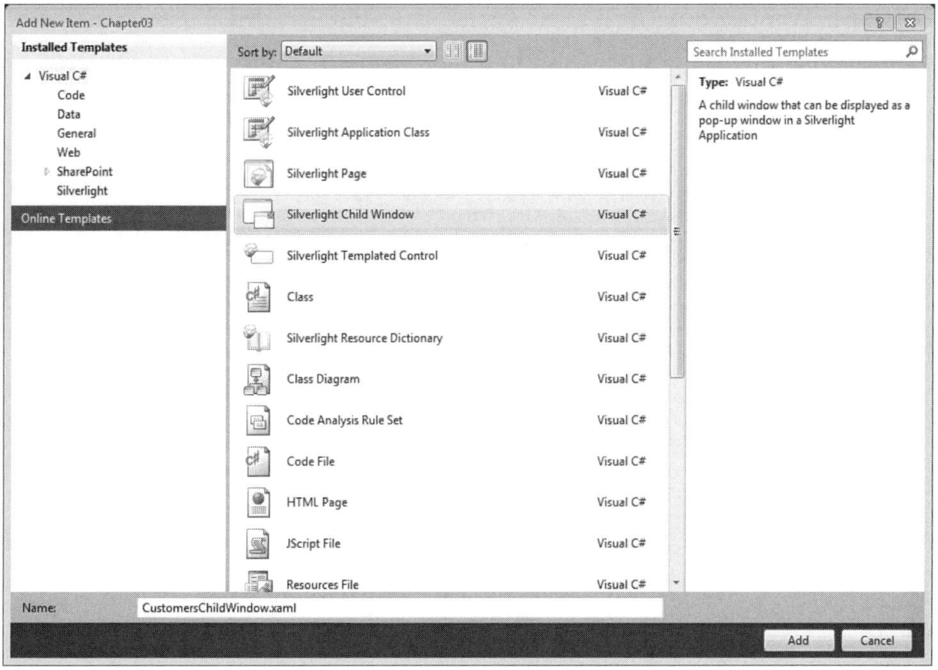

FIGURE 3.8: Adding a child window to the Silverlight project

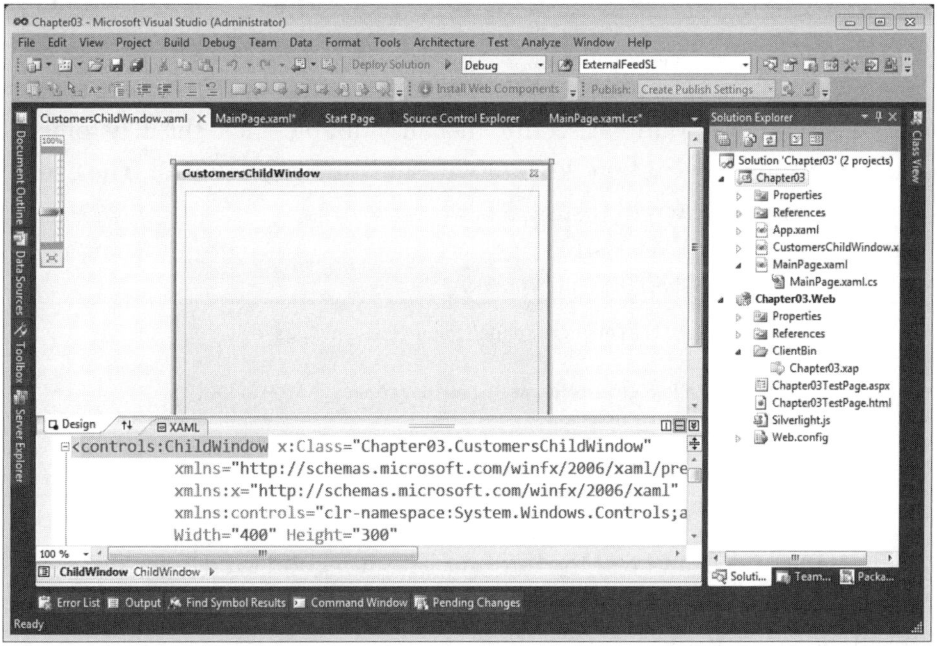

FIGURE 3.9: A new child window

Add combo box and data grid controls to the CustomersChild Window.xaml designer by dragging them from the toolbox onto the design surface. Then resize them to fit, as shown in Figure 3.10.

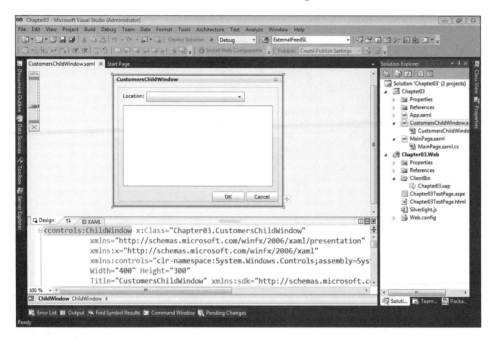

FIGURE 3.10: Updated child window

Return to the MainPage.xaml file and double-click the Customers button to add an event handler that will show the child control. The event handler code is shown in Listing 3.6.

LISTING 3.6: Method to Show the Child Window

```
private void button2_Click(object sender, RoutedEventArgs e)
{
    CustomersChildWindow childWindow = new CustomersChildWindow();
    childWindow.Title = "Customers";
    childWindow.Show();
}
```

Run the project and test the buttons. This is a good time to try out more of the controls to familiarize yourself with the palette of controls you use throughout this book.

Advanced Features of .NET in Silverlight

Silverlight does not support the entire .NET framework, but only a subset. Experienced .NET developers might be distressed to see some of their old friends have been omitted from Silverlight. For example, the `ArrayList` is nowhere to be found, `XmlDocument` has been banished, and the familiar ADO.NET is gone as well. Fortunately, all of these have been replaced by new and improved alternatives, and this section provides an overview of them.

Generic Collections

Generics in .NET have been around since .NET 2.0; if you haven't started using them, now is the time to start. Generic classes act on types that aren't specified until the classes are used, when the type is specified in angle brackets. This allows classes that are general in nature and still act in a strongly-typed way on objects whose types aren't known until later.

Generic collections are generic classes that manage various kinds of collections on any type specified. Compare this to a construct such as an `ArrayList`, which operates on .NET Object types which then need to be cast to their specific type at runtime. Generic collections provide a type-safe way to separate the collection logic from the items in the collection. Generic collections come from the `System.Collections.Generic` namespace. For example, consider the `Customer` class shown in Listing 3.7.

LISTING 3.7: Customer Class

```
public class Customer  {
    public string Name { get; set; }
    public string Address { get; set; }
}
```

Given this example, a list of customers would be coded as `List<Customer>`, and an enumerable collection of customers as `IEnumerable<Customer>`.

Automatic Properties

Listing 3.7 shows two *automatic properties*. These are properties that simply get and set an automatically generated field within the class. Automatic properties allow short-hand property declarations, and the compiler emits getters and setters behind the scenes.

Anonymous Methods

An *anonymous method* is code that is declared inline without naming an actual method. Generally this is useful when the method is used only once as a call-back or event handler. The method's code is defined inline, as shown in Listing 3.8. In this example, the `delegate` keyword is used to define the inline code to handle an event. To use a full event receiver, which is passed a reference to the sender object and event arguments, the code can be extended as shown in Listing 3.9.

LISTING 3.8: An Anonymous Method

```
button2.Click += delegate {
    textBox1.Text = "We can make this the Cancel button.";
};
```

LISTING 3.9: An Anonymous Event Handler

```
button1.Click += new RoutedEventHandler(
    delegate(Object s, RoutedEventArgs e)
    {
        textBox1.Text = "Hello, world";
    });
```

A shorthand for the delegate keyword is called a *lambda expression* and is shown in Listing 3.10. The => symbol is used instead of the delegate keyword, and the argument types are inferred, in this case from the definition of `RoutedEventHandler`.

LISTING 3.10: Using a Lambda Expression to Define an Anonymous Function

```
button1.Click += new RoutedEventHandler((s, e) =>
{
    textBox1.Text = "Hello, world";
});
```

Although placing short anonymous methods inline can improve readability, especially when handling asynchronous network calls, overuse of anonymous methods leads to code complexity and more difficult troubleshooting. The effect is especially visible when single-stepping in the debugger, where the anonymous function is run when the event fires rather than inline with the rest of the code. In general, if you have more than a few lines of code in an event handler or call-back function, you should spell out the function separately.

■ TIP

Silverlight and WPF have a single User Interface thread. It's only possible to update the UI from that specific thread. If the thread is busy, the UI becomes unresponsive. That's why network calls in Silverlight are asynchronous—so the UI thread won't be tied up while waiting for a response from the network.

When an event handler fires, if it's not a UI event such as a button click, you might not be running on the UI thread, and therefore you can't touch the UI directly. This is generally the case when a network request completes.

Silverlight provides a Dispatcher for this purpose; it's like a message loop that runs on the UI thread. All you need to do is put your code in a function and pass a delegate to the `Dispatcher.BeginInvoke()`method. Anonymous functions can make this seem much easier, as in

```
private void SomeEventHandler object sender, EventArgs e)
{
    Dispatcher.BeginInvoke(() =>
    {
        MessageBox.Show("The event fired!");
    });
}
```

Anonymous Types

Listing 3.11 shows two variable declarations. In the first, the variable's type is clearly spelled out, and in the second the variable uses an *anonymous type*. The C# `var` keyword declares that the type of an object is anonymous and should be inferred from the expression to the right of the assignment statement. This allows developers to use variables without declaring their types.

LISTING 3.11: Anonymous Types

```
List<Customer> list1 = new List<Customer>();
var list2 = new List<Customer>();
```

The var keyword in C# should not be confused with the one in JavaScript in which the type is evaluated at runtime; this is handled in C# by the dynamic type. Instead, the data type of a var is inferred at compile time, and normal type checking occurs when it's used. Just as an anonymous person is a real person whose name is unknown, an anonymous type is a real type, and the compiler knows its name even if you don't.

Examining the code in Listing 3.11, both list1 and list2 are of the type List<Customer>. The benefit of this is easier to see in the example in Listing 3.12.

LISTING 3.12: An Anonymous Type with LINQ Query

```
var query = from c in Customers
            where c.Name == "Matt"
            select new { Name = c.Name };
```

This code contains a Language Integrated Query (LINQ) that queries a collection called Customers for customers with the name "Matt" and generates a collection of anonymous objects that contain a single Name property. There are two anonymous types here: The first one is selected for each customer named "Matt," and the second is a collection of the first. In this situation there is no way to explicitly define the type, and the var keyword saves the day.

Language Integrated Query (LINQ)

Whole books have been written on .NET's new Language Integrated Query (LINQ) capability and this section only scratches the surface. LINQ allows strongly-typed queries directly in code, and can query .NET objects, XML structures, SharePoint content, or any other data source that has a LINQ provider.

LINQ to XML provides a rich alternative to XmlDocument, and is capable of building as well as querying XML structures in memory. In general the code is more readable than XmlDocument code.

It's time to go back to the coding example to demonstrate some typical uses of LINQ queries in Silverlight. The code provides the customer display in the child window created earlier in this chapter.

To begin with, you need some customers to display. For the sake of demonstration the customers are hard coded as simple .NET objects. Declare the customer class as shown in Listing 3.13, either in its own class file or in the CustomersChildWindow.xaml.cs file (outside of the CustomersChildWindow partial class, of course).

LISTING 3.13: Customer Class

```
public class Customer
{
    public string Name { get; set; }
    public string Location { get; set; }
}
```

Next, inside the CustomerChildWindow partial class, declare and initialize a customer list as shown in Listing 3.14.

LISTING 3.14: Initializing the Customer List

```
List<Customer> xx = new List<Customer>();

// Fortunately the customer list is short and never changes.
List<Customer> customers = new List<Customer>
    {
        new Customer { Name = "Paul", Location = "Washington" },
        new Customer { Name = "Matt", Location = "Arkansas" },
        new Customer { Name = "Bob", Location = "Massachusetts" },
        new Customer { Name = "Andrew", Location = "Florida" },
        new Customer { Name = "Ed", Location = "Virginia" },
        new Customer { Name = "Matt", Location = "Massachusetts" },
        new Customer { Name = "Scott", Location = "Massachusetts" },
        new Customer { Name = "Ted", Location = "Florida" }
    };
```

Next, add code to the `CustomersChildWindow` constructor to initialize the combo box with a list of locations. The code is shown in Listing 3.15, and it uses a LINQ query to create a collection of strings to bind to the combo box.

LISTING 3.15: CustomersChildWindow Constructor

```
public CustomersChildWindow()
{
    InitializeComponent();

    // Set the combo box to show the locations in ascending
    // order with no duplicates
    var locations = from c in this.customers
                    orderby c.Location
                    select c.Location;
    comboBox1.ItemsSource = locations.Distinct();
}
```

The LINQ code is querying a collection of .NET objects; this is possible as long as the collection implements the `IEnumerable<>` or `IQueryable<>` interface. In the case of `IEnumerable<>`, the interface only provides the ability to enumerate the collection, and LINQ must grovel through the whole thing in order to execute the query. `IQueryable<>` extends `IEnumerable<>` to provide an interface that can evaluate and run LINQ queries itself and is implemented by query providers such as LINQ to SQL or LINQ to XML.

Reading the query expression from the beginning,

```
from c in this.customers
```

specifies that the query is over the customers list and that the symbol c is used to represent customer items in the query. The next line,

```
orderby c.location
```

sorts the query results in order by the customer location field. Finally,

```
select c.location;
```

tells the compiler what you want the query to produce. In this case, the customer's location is a string, so the query produces an `IEnumerable<string>`. If the statement were changed to

```
select c;
```

then it would produce an IEnumerable<Customer>, given that c on its own represents a Customer object from the list. If it were

```
select new { Who = c.Name, Where = "at " + c.Location };
```

then the query would return an IEnumerable of some anonymous type with two string properties called Who and Where, and the word at would be inserted in front of each location. As you can see, this is very flexible!

Following the query, the combo box is bound to the collection of locations in the statement:

```
comboBox1.ItemsSource = locations.Distinct();
```

If the locations collection had been assigned directly to the combo box's ItemsSource property, it would work, but there would be duplicates on the list because some locations are present in more than one customer. The Distinct() method eliminates the duplicates and is called a *method-based query*. For more details, see http://bit.ly/SPSL_LinqIntro.

The final step to complete the sample application is to show the customers in the data grid when a location is chosen in the combo box. To do this, return to the CustomerChildWindow.xaml file and double-click the combo box to add an event handler for its SelectionChanged event. Fill in the event handler as shown in Listing 3.16.

LISTING 3.16: Combo Box SelectionChanged Event Handler

```
private void comboBox1_SelectionChanged(object sender,
                                SelectionChangedEventArgs e)
{
    // A new location was selected; show the customers in that location
    var cust = from c in this.customers
               where c.Location == comboBox1.SelectedValue.ToString()
               orderby c.Name
               select c;
    dataGrid1.ItemsSource = cust;
}
```

This time the LINQ query includes a where clause, which is a simple comparison in C#. Because the SelectedValue combo box property is an Object, it needs to be converted to a string before it can be compared to the c.Location property.

At this point the sample application should work. When the Customers button on the main page is pressed, the child window should launch as shown in Figure 3.11. Selecting a location in the combo box should display the customers from that location.

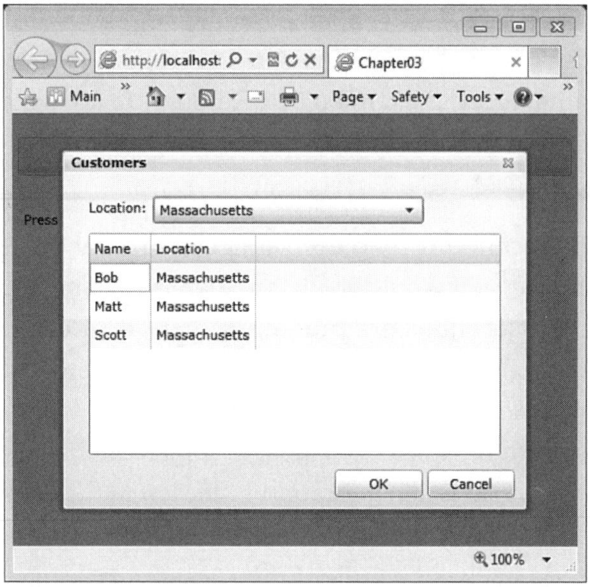

FIGURE 3.11: Customers child window

Networking and Web Services in Silverlight

Silverlight doesn't have a way to directly call a database like SQL Server or Oracle, but it does have strong support networking and web services so you can access services that provide data. For example, a common pattern is to develop a web service to access a database using ADO.NET Entity Framework and then to consume the web service in Silverlight.

This section summarizes the options for network access in Silverlight.

Networking Options in Silverlight

Silverlight provides a number of ways to access networked resources and web services. This section lists the major options.

WebClient Class

Silverlight provides a WebClient class for accessing HTTP resources. It can be used to request a simple page or newsfeed or to build custom web service proxies.

Web Services

Calling web services could be a complex affair, but Visual Studio makes it easy by generating a local proxy class to do all the nitty-gritty work. Your code can simply call the proxy service locally, and it takes care of all the networking details. WCF supports a number of protocols such as HTTP and TCP/IP and data formats such as Atom, SOAP, and XML.

Chapter 10, "Accessing SharePoint with Web Services," shows you how to create WCF services in SharePoint and consume them in Silverlight.

WCF Data Services

WCF Data Services is a framework for working with data using the Open Data Protocol (OData). Like WCF web services, WCF Data Services handles all the serialization and networking for you.

OData is a REST style protocol for accessing tables of data, including full Create, Read, Update, and Delete operations. There are a number of products, including Microsoft SharePoint 2010, Microsoft SQL Server Reporting Services, and IBM Websphere, that provide OData interfaces. In addition, public services such as eBay and Netflix provide OData feeds.

Chapter 9, "Accessing SharePoint Data with WCF Data Services," shows how to access Silverlight data using SharePoint 2010's OData feed.

WCF RIA Services

WCF rich Internet application (RIA) services is a tool for developing n-tier enterprise solutions. WCF RIA Services builds matching client- and server-side projects, and Visual Studio automates, keeping the data model in sync across both projects. This is a wonderful thing, but because it requires .NET 4.0, and SharePoint uses .NET 3.5, it's not particularly useful in SharePoint solutions unless the server component can be hosted on a separate ASP.NET 4.0 web server.

Sockets and Multicast

If all else fails you can access the network directly by using the System.Net.Sockets namespace. With direct access to TCP and UDP and advanced features such as full-duplex and multicast operation, this is the right choice if you want to build your own streaming media client or any time you need complete control over the networking stack.

Asynchronous Response Handling

In Silverlight, all network calls are asynchronous. That means that when you call a web service or request something on the network, the next line of code that runs will *not* contain the result from the server! A successful return only means that the local networking stack successfully made a request; the response (if any) from the server is returned using a call-back function or event. This leads to having lots of event handlers and delegates in your code and explains why anonymous functions are so popular among Silverlight developers.

For example, Listing 3.17 shows some code from Chapter 10 to read an ATOM feed. As you can see, there is a method to request the feed and an event handler to handle the response. When the response is received, it's loaded into a SyndicationFeed object and transformed into a collection of objects that are bound to the user interface.

LISTING 3.17: Code to Read an RSS or ATOM Feed in Silverlight

```
// RequestActivityFeed - Kick off the request for an activity (ATOM) feed
private void RequestActivityFeed(string userName)
{
    // Transform the person's my site URL into an activity feed URL
    string feedUrl = this.userUrl.Substring(0,
        this.userUrl.IndexOf("Person.aspx")) +
        "_layouts/activityfeed.aspx?consolidated=false&publisher=" +
        System.Windows.Browser.HttpUtility.UrlEncode(userName);

    // Request the feed
    WebClient wc = new WebClient();
    wc.OpenReadCompleted +=
      new OpenReadCompletedEventHandler(RequestActivityFeedCompleted);
    wc.OpenReadAsync(new Uri(feedUrl));
}
```

```
// Handle the activity feed when it comes back
void RequestActivityFeedCompleted(object sender,
        OpenReadCompletedEventArgs e)
{
    // Transform the result stream into a SyndicationFeed for easy
    // ATOM parsing
    XmlReader feedReader = XmlReader.Create(e.Result);
    SyndicationFeed feed = SyndicationFeed.Load(feedReader);

    // Project a collection of ActivityItems for binding to the View
    this.Activities = from item in feed.Items
                      select new ActivityItem
                      {
                          Title = item.Title.Text,
                          Description = FixHtml (item.Summary.Text),
                          PubDate = item.PublishDate.LocalDateTime
                      };
}
```

In some cases, anonymous functions can make the code easier to read. Listing 3.18 shows an example from Chapter 9 of reading an OData source. In this case, the request is made when the code calls `BeginExecute()`, but instead of passing in a separate delegate, the function is specified inline. In this case, it's a call to `Dispatcher.BeginInvoke()`to move processing over to the Silverlight UI thread. The dispatcher calls yet another anonymous function to actually handle the completion and bind the data to the UI.

LISTING 3.18: Handling Asynchronous Completion with Anonymous Functions

```
// Create a query of all contacts, sorted by name
DataServiceQuery<SharePointContent.ContactsItem> q =
    (DataServiceQuery<SharePointContent.ContactsItem>)
    (
        from contact in dataContext.Contacts
        orderby contact.FullName
        select contact
    );

// Execute the query asynchronously, and when it completes,
q.BeginExecute((IAsyncResult result) =>
{
    // Schedule some work on the UI thread, and when we get there,
    // bind the feed data to the data grid
    Dispatcher.BeginInvoke(() =>
    {
        // Get result as IEnumerable
```

```
    q = result.AsyncState as
        DataServiceQuery<SharePointContent.ContactsItem>;
    IEnumerable<SharePointContent.ContactsItem> items =
        q.EndExecute(result);

    // Place result in an observable collection and bind to the grid
    dataServiceCollection = new
        DataServiceCollection<SharePointContent.ContactsItem>(items);
    listDataGrid.ItemsSource = dataServiceCollection;

    needsRefresh = false;
    });
}, q);
```

Introducing Silverlight 5

Silverlight 5 was in Beta testing while this book was being written. Although most of the programming examples work with Silverlight 4 or 5, some chapters include special sections to show how you can take the solutions a step further with new Silverlight 5 features as detailed in Table 3.4.

TABLE 3.4: Silverlight 5 Examples in This Book

Example	Details
Debugging Data Binding	Chapter 9 shows you how to debug your data binding expressions. Although this is a Silverlight 5 feature, it works with solutions targeted for Silverlight 4 if the Silverlight 5 tools are installed.
Binding Data to Style Setters	Chapter 9 shows you how to bind data to Silverlight style setters so the display style is driven by bound data. In this example, data items with key values are highlighted.
Implicit Data Templates	Chapter 10 shows you how to use more than one template during data binding, where templates are selected implicitly based on the class of each data item. In this example, document and people search results are rendered with different data templates to give them different visual treatment.

Example	Details
Using the Browser Control	In earlier versions of Silverlight, rendering an HTML page via the WebBrowser control was only possible in out of browser applications. Silverlight 5 allows this with in-browser applications, as long as the security is set up correctly. In this example, an HTML preview of RSS feed entries is shown.

Silverlight 5 includes a number of additional features which, although not specifically applicable to SharePoint development, can be useful in any Silverlight application. These include

- Improved Media Support, including GPU acceleration of H.264 decoding and TrickPlay to play video at different speeds and to support fast forward and rewind
- Text improvements to allow text to flow across columns and linked text containers and to improve text rendering
- Data binding and MVVM enhancements such as the ones shown in Chapters 9 and 10, plus Markup Extensions,which allow you to write your own code to parse properties and event handlers in XAML, and `Ancestor RelativeSource` to allow a `DataTemplate` to bind to a property on the control that contains it
- Extended "Trusted Appliction" model to allow full desktop access if a Silverlight application is trusted
- Many other performance and graphics improvements

Summary

Silverlight is powerful and a lot of fun to work with. As you go through this book, you'll learn more, yet that's still only the beginning. There are many aspects of Silverlight such as media streaming and animation that don't especially relate to SharePoint and therefore aren't in this book, but all of them are useful in your projects wherever you choose to host Silverlight.

PART II

SharePoint and Silverlight Development

■ 4 ■

A First Look at Silverlight in SharePoint

SHAREPOINT HAS A NUMBER OF OUT-OF-THE-BOX FEATURES that take advantage of Silverlight if it is available. This greatly improves the usability of SharePoint in a few key areas. This chapter demonstrates how you use Silverlight in SharePoint without writing any SharePoint code in Visual Studio. The goal is to understand how the SharePoint team thinks about Silverlight in the product and demonstrate techniques that you can use to quickly leverage Silverlight on SharePoint.

When learning about building Silverlight applications for SharePoint, it is helpful to learn from those who have come before you. In this case looking at the work that the SharePoint team has done and how they overcame their issues helps you understand some of the issues you will face. The first control you see is the Create Content dialog. This dialog solves a number of interesting problems such as how to have a pluggable provider model to support new items in the dialog in the future at runtime. It solves the problem of having a down-level experience for users who do not have Silverlight installed. It demonstrates how to do diagnostic logging to the SharePoint Unified Logging Service (ULS) logs. And most importantly, it is a great user experience for completing a very common task in SharePoint, adding new content to your SharePoint sites.

Next you see how SharePoint leverages the media capabilities of Silverlight to deliver video and audio content to users. Looking at the media features that ship with SharePoint from a developer's perspective demonstrates another interesting pattern. It demonstrates how to build a JavaScript accessible API into your Silverlight solutions. Having a JavaScript API makes your Silverlight applications programmable by other parts of the SharePoint page. In this case you can control the Media Web Part from other web parts on the page to do things like starting and stopping the videos. The Media Web Part also demonstrates how to integrate the Ribbon with your Silverlight Web Parts. Another interesting feature of the Media Web Part is the ability to provide different skins to completely change the look and feel of the web part. You also see more examples of Silverlight in SharePoint such as workflow visualizations and an Organizational Browser.

Finally the last part of the chapter demonstrates various techniques you can use to easily add your own Silverlight applications. SharePoint ships with a Silverlight Web Part that is designed to add Silverlight applications without your having to write any code. You also see some additional ways to use SharePoint to host your Silverlight applications using the Content Editor Web Part and IFrame.

Create Content

The Create Content dialog, also known as Add Gallery, is the most prominent use of Silverlight in SharePoint. This is used by every developer and content creator when they add new items to SharePoint. The Create Content dialog allows you to browse a gallery of various items that you want to add to your SharePoint site. The look and feel of the Create Content dialog is very similar to the Backstage feature in many of the Office client applications such as Word and Excel, making it familiar for Office users, as shown in Figure 4.1.

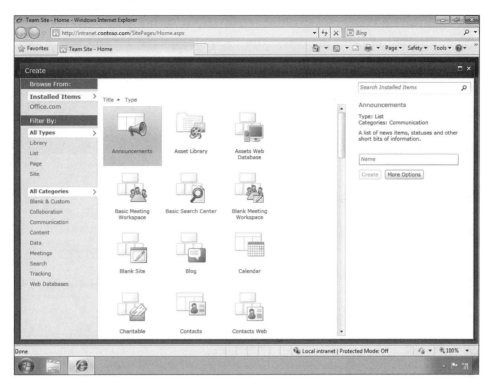

FIGURE 4.1: Create Content dialog

The Create Content dialog can create Libraries, Lists, Pages, and Sites and has two very important features that are not found in the down-level experience—filtering and searching. Filtering and searching enable you to quickly locate the item you are looking to create. This is more important as the number of templates or types of items you can create grows. In large organizations with many developers creating solutions, the number of templates can expand quickly.

Filtering

This dialog allows you to filter by four types: Libraries, Lists, Pages, and Sites. It also enables you to browse by 10 categories—All Categories, Blank and Custom, Collaboration, Communication, Content, Data, Meetings, Search, Tracking, and Web Databases. Selecting a type and a category displays the intersection of these two filters to give you a focused result.

For example in Figure 4.2, if you select List from the types section and select Communication from the categories section, you see a result set of four items: Announcements, Contacts, Discussion Board, and Links.

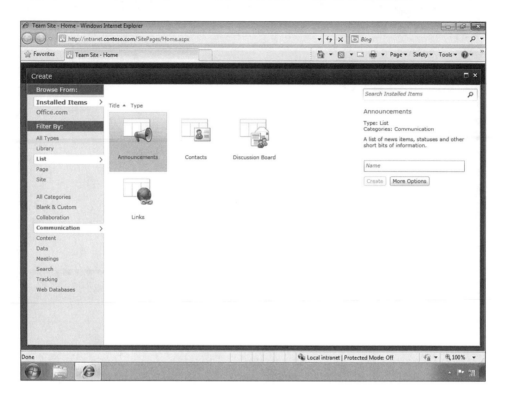

FIGURE 4.2: Filter by List and Communication

Search

The Create Content dialog also has a search box in the top right that you can use to search the titles of all of the installed items by keyword. The search feature searches the Display Name, Type, and Categories fields of the content items, looking for keywords you enter. The search feature is not very sophisticated and does a simple text match for the search string you enter as shown in Figure 4.3. Wildcards are not used. Select an item to see the properties on the right side of the dialog in the details pane. You can see the three properties, Display Name, Type, and Categories, which are searched by the dialog. This should help you understand why a particular item was returned by the search string you entered.

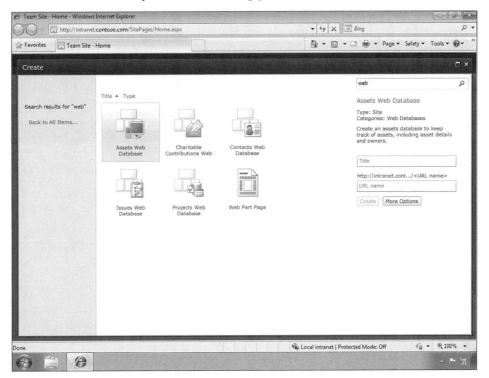

FIGURE 4.3: Search by keyword web

More Options

Selecting any item in the Create Content dialog enables you to create Libraries, Lists, and Pages using only a name. Sites require you to provide a title and a URL name to the new site. But many of the various item types have additional properties that you can set when you create the item. To access these additional properties, you need to click the More Options button. This displays the additional properties in the dialog, as shown in Figure 4.4. The additional properties for each item type look similar to the create page in the down-level experience. For example if you select the Picture Library and then press the More Options button, you can set additional properties such as enabling version support for the images. Keep in mind that this is a XAML representation of the down-level properties page as Silverlight 3, which the SharePoint controls are written in, does not support HTML displayed inside of the control. Any changes you make to the down-level property pages or custom types are not represented in the Silverlight Create Content dialog.

FIGURE 4.4: More options

Down-level

The use of Silverlight is optional in many features of SharePoint. This is true for the Create dialog as well. If you do not have Silverlight installed or have it disabled, you get the down-level experience, as shown in Figure 4.5. This is a similar experience to that of SharePoint 2007. The create page is located in the layouts directory at /_layouts/create.aspx. The down-level experience does have a little interactivity. Hovering over an item changes the header area to display the name and description of the item. But beyond that, this is it. There are no filtering or searching capabilities with the down-level page. The number of categories is also reduced to five (Libraries, Communications, Tracking, Custom Lists, and Pages and Sites).

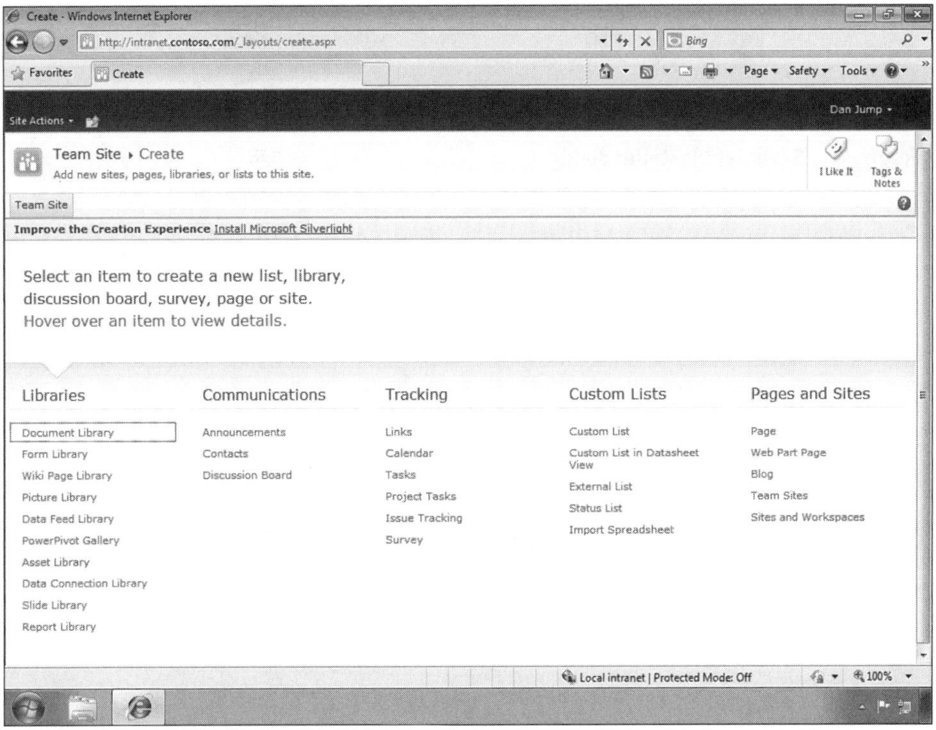

FIGURE 4.5: A down-level creation experience

At the top of the page you see a yellow status bar informing you that you can improve the creation experience by installing Silverlight. A link called Install Microsoft Silverlight, which takes you to http://go.microsoft.com/fwlink/?LinkID=149156, is found there. This link redirects you to the current version of the Silverlight.exe installer, as shown in Figure 4.6. You have the option to save or open the executable.

FIGURE 4.6: Silverlight Installer dialog

Clicking an item, for example, the Picture Library, opens the Create New Item page, shown in Figure 4.7, which has the properties that apply to the specific item type being created. Creating a Picture Library has one additional property, aside from the standard Name, Description, and Quick Launch properties, for setting the versioning of the images.

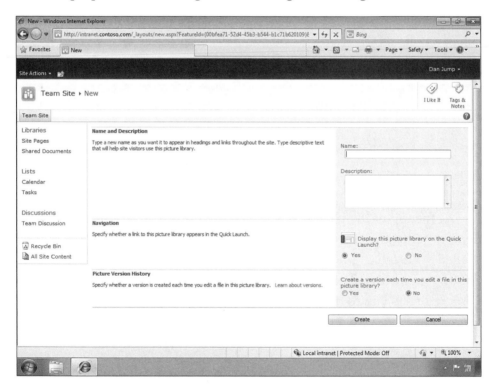

FIGURE 4.7: Create a new Picture Library

The Create Content dialog packs many features into a simple dialog that is easy for new users to use and for experienced users to have the power to access the advanced features.

Pluggable Providers

The Create Content dialog also supports a pluggable provider model. This means you can add additional items to the dialog at runtime by building a provider that returns items from your own custom store. SharePoint ships with one custom provider out-of-the-box for Office.com. You can see a list of all of the providers in the top left on the Create Content dialog under the Browse From section. The first and default provider is the built-in one for the local SharePoint instance. The second is for Office.com. Providers are loaded from the _Layouts\AddGalleryProviders folder. By default the Office.com provider, AddGallery.OfficeOnlineProvider.dll, is the only file in this folder. Although this feature of connecting to Office.com for templates never fully shipped with the server-side components of this provider, it is still a good example of a design pattern you should follow. You might see a warning message, or it might even be removed all together in future updates. The next most common Silverlight control in SharePoint is the Media Web Part for playing video and audio content, which you learn about in the next section.

Media Web Part

SharePoint ships with a Media Web Part that plays video and audio content. The Media Web Part is implemented as a Silverlight control that uses the media element to play the media. The type of content is restricted to media supported by Silverlight. The Media Web Part supports .wmv, .wma, .avi, .mpg, .mp3, and .mp4 audio and video content. The Media Web Part does not support true streaming content. SharePoint supports a progressive download model that has been optimized for a very responsive experience, but to have a true streaming solution, you would need to use Microsoft Media Services. But with that said, the Media Web Part is tightly integrated into SharePoint and makes it easy for site builders to quickly add rich media to their sites.

Let's add a video to the home page of the site to understand what is involved and the various available options. Just like adding any web part, put the page in Edit mode. Click the page to set the cursor to the location where the web part will be inserted. When in Edit mode, click the Insert tab of the Editing Tools context Ribbon, as shown in Figure 4.8. On the Insert Ribbon you can add the Media Web Part by clicking the Web Part button, which opens the insert Web Part Gallery. Under the Categories section click the Media and Content item. Click the Media Web Part to insert it into the page. This is the same process you would use to insert any web part on the page, but there is a shortcut for the Media Web Part. It has its own Ribbon group called Media. The Media group has two items, Picture button and the Video and Audio button. The Video and Audio button inserts the Media Web Part.

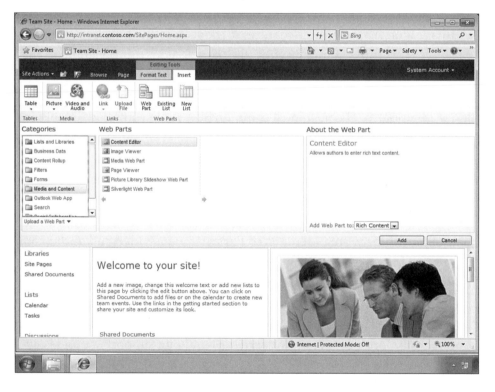

FIGURE 4.8: Insert Media Web Part

After the Media Web Part has been added to the page, you need to set the content source. For most web parts you set the properties using the web part's edit tool, but for the Media Web Part, you use the Ribbon. The Media Web Part has a context-sensitive Ribbon associated to the Edit mode of the Web Part. While the page is in Edit mode, click the Media Web Part to select it. When it is selected you see a new tab on the Ribbon called Media, which has an Options tab and has a single split button called Change Media. The Change Media button has four options. The first three allow you to pick media from your computer's file system, from an existing SharePoint library, or from an Internet URL. The last option clears the source property for the Media Web Part. Picking a video from your computer prompts you to browse to the video and pick an existing SharePoint Library to upload the video to. The second option to select a video from SharePoint opens the Asset Picker Dialog, which allows you to browse your SharePoint site to select an existing video or audio file. The last option to select a video by address enables you to enter a URL of a video or audio file.

I have an existing video called Bear.wmv that I wish to run on the home page. To do so, I select the second option to load the video from my computer. The video is located in my Videos Library, and I upload it to the existing Site Assets Library. At this point the video source is set and ready to play. Save the page and click the Play button on the Media Web Part to play the video, as shown in Figure 4.9.

You might have noticed that the video does not show a preview image if the video is not playing. Instead it shows a default thumbnail image. SharePoint does not automatically extract and display a thumbnail preview image—you must do this manually. To set the preview image, put the page back in Edit mode and click the Media Web Part to set focus, which enables the context menu. The second group on the Media Web Part context menu is the Preview group. The Preview group has one split button called Change Image. The Change Image button has the same options as the Change Media button—From Computer, From SharePoint, From Address, and Remove. Select From Computer to browse to an image on your local computer; in this case I pick the Bear.png image and upload it to the Site Assets folder as well. When you have set the preview image, you see this image when the video is not playing.

FIGURE 4.9: Media Player Web Part

The Properties group contains three properties. The first is the Title for the Media Web Part; this is the same as you can set in the Web Part Edit Tools pane. The second controls whether the video automatically starts when the page is loaded, and the third option sets the looping behavior of the video if it is playing.

The Player Styles group enables you to pick the Media Web Part's skin. The Media Web Part ships with two skins called Light and Dark (Dark being the default). You can design and add your own skins as well. More details on skinning are discussed later in this chapter.

The last group of the Media Web Part's context menu is the Size group. The Size group enables you to set the height and width of the video in pixels. You can also select if the video is stretched to fit or maintains its original aspect ratio.

JavaScript API

Many times you want to be able to programmatically control the Media Web Part from other parts of your page. The Media Web Part contains a JavaScript API that allows you to manipulate the media from JavaScript. The JavaScript API is implemented as a class in the Silverlight control itself, which is located in the _layouts/clientbin/mediaplayer.xap file. Silverlight contains a feature called the HTML Bridge, which allows you to access the HTML DOM from managed code and allows JavaScript to access managed code. You can also handle and throw events from either JavaScript or managed code. The Media Web Part exposes a subset of its API through the HTML Bridge. The Media Web Part JavaScript API has three methods: `Pause()`, `Play()`, and `Stop()`. The API also enables you to set the media source and other properties. These are generally the same ones you can set from the Ribbon, including setting the looping and startup behaviors.

Including a JavaScript API in your Silverlight applications, like the Media Web Part does, is a good best practice to follow. You want your Silverlight applications to fit seamlessly into the SharePoint user experience. Allowing developers to control your Silverlight controls as if they are native SharePoint controls provides the best end-user experiences.

Ribbon

Earlier you saw how the Ribbon was used to help you set the properties of the Media Web Part. There is not much more to add about how to use the Ribbon. But it is worth calling attention to the fact that, just like providing a JavaScript API is a best practice, providing a great Ribbon experience is also a best practice. The Ribbon is a new user interface component in Share-Point and provides the same experience as those of the Office client applications, such as Word, Excel, Outlook, and PowerPoint. Users expect that actions related to the object selected appear on the Ribbon. As you look at the Media Web Part, think about how you can provide a great Ribbon experience to your users similar to Figure 4.10.

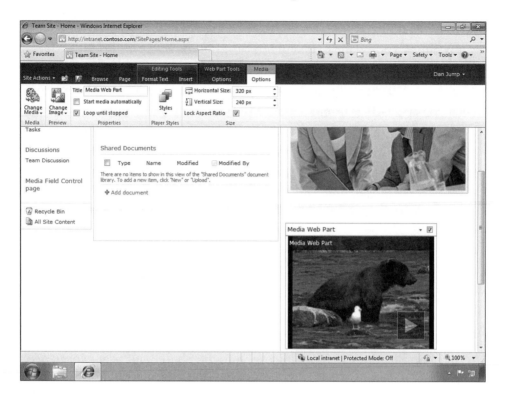

FIGURE 4.10: Media Player Web Part context Ribbon

Skinning

The Media Web Part also supports creating custom skins. As described earlier, SharePoint ships with two skins, Dark and Light, with Dark being the default. The Light skin is located in the sitecollection/StyleLibrary/ MediaPlayer/AlternateMediaPlayer.xaml file. The Media Player Web Part looks to the ~sitecollection/Style Library/Media Player folder when you are in Design mode and displays the files in the Player Styles group of the Ribbon. You can put additional custom skins in this folder as XAML files. The file names display in the drop-down, and users can select the skin at design time. You can also set the skin at runtime using the JavaScript API by setting the TemplateSource property.

Skinning is another way to make your Silverlight applications feel like they are part of the SharePoint site and allows users to customize the application to suit their needs and tastes.

Media Field Control

SharePoint includes a custom field control called the Media Field Control, which behaves the same as the Media Web Part. It allows you to play audio and video media assets, except that it is implemented as a field control and not a web part. This gives you the ability to embed a video into a publishing page or on a list, as shown in Figure 4.11. Adding the Media Field Control to a page layout is no different than adding other non-Silverlight field controls to a page. At a high level, to add the Media Field Control to a publishing page, create a new site column of type Rich Media Data for Publishing. Add the new site column to a page layout using SharePoint Designer. You can now create an instance of your new page layout that contains the Media Field Control. Users can set the properties of the Media Field Control in the same way they did with the Media Web Part, by selecting the Media Field Control while in Edit mode and setting the properties on the Ribbon.

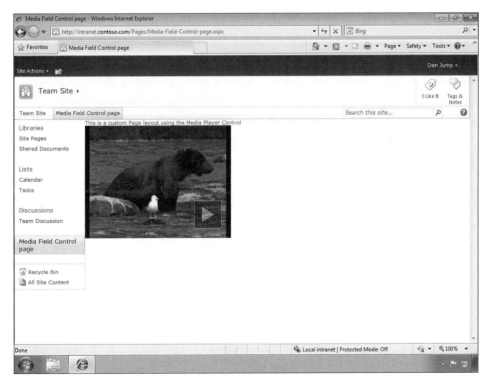

FIGURE 4.11: Media Field Control in a custom page layout

You can provide custom skins for the Media Field Control just as you can with the Media Web Part. The Media Field Control demonstrates an important concept to keep in mind as you develop Silverlight applications for SharePoint. It demonstrates that you can integrate your Silverlight applications wherever SharePoint allows you to put HTML code. Most tend to think about Silverlight in SharePoint in the context of web parts, but as you have seen with the Media Field Control, it can play a much larger role in your SharePoint solutions.

Organizational Chart

SharePoint has a concept similar to your Facebook page called a My Site. A My Site in SharePoint is your own personal space to display information about you and the activities you are working on. My Sites have both a public and private side so you can store documents just for yourself or share them with the rest of your team or your company. Another social aspect to My Sites is the ability to associate yourself with your corporate "friends," which SharePoint calls colleagues. Many times your colleagues are already set up for you by your company and are based on employees in Active Directory. This is good because it allows you to use SharePoint to browse the organizational structure of your company out-of-the-box with no custom coding required.

Organizational charts are hierarchical diagrams based on who works for whom. The hierarchy is determined from the Manager field in Active Directory. Silverlight is great at representing and visualizing data. SharePoint ships a Silverlight organizational chart out-of-the-box and is part of the My Site template. Simply browse to your My Site and click the Organization tab to view the Silverlight organizational chart. It displays the Name, Title, About Me, and Image of each user. You can browse horizontally and vertically through your colleagues, as shown in Figure 4.12. Although talking about it in a book doesn't do it justice, the organizational chart is very intuitive, and the animations are smooth and responsive.

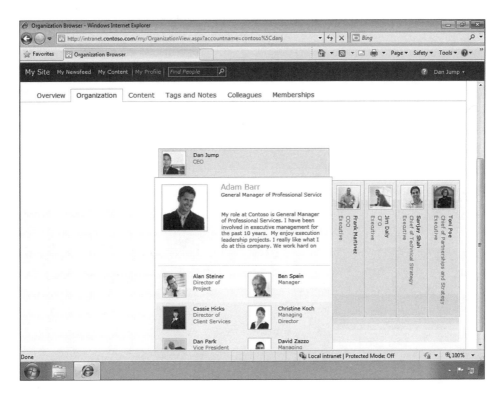

FIGURE 4.12: Silverlight-based Organization Browser

Down-level

The organizational chart provides a down-level experience just like the Create Content dialog did. As with the Create Content dialog, the Organization Browser's down-level experience is very basic and is simply an HTML tree control. Clicking each node expands the branch, showing you hierarchy of colleagues. One thing to note that is different from the Create Content dialog is how you get to the down-level experience. The Create Content dialog doesn't really provide any way to get to the down-level experience unless you turn off Silverlight or browse directly to the /_layouts/create.aspx page. The Organizational Browser has a small text link at the very bottom of the page called HTML View. Click the HTML View to go to the down-level organizational page, as shown in Figure 4.13.s

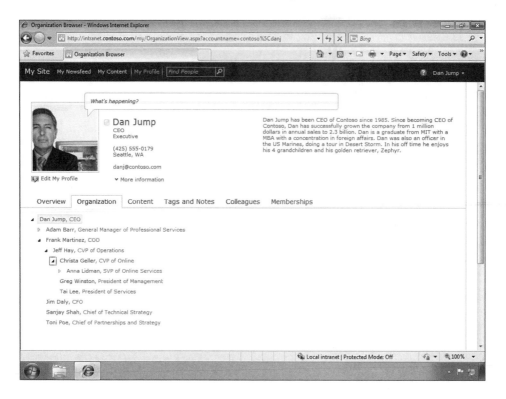

FIGURE 4.13: HTML-based Organizational Browser

Workflow Visualization

SharePoint uses Visio to visualize workflows. This is not only helpful for users to understand the overall process and steps within a workflow, but it also shows them what steps have been completed and the path that was taken. For example you can see in Figure 4.14 the visualization of an approval workflow attached to a document library. When a document is added to the library, a new approval workflow is started. In this particular example the workflow has a step called compare data source. If the compare data source is true, it sets a value in the document properties to approved and if it is false, it sets the value to denied. In the Visio workfslow diagram you can see the path that the workflow has taken. In Figure 4.14, the steps that have been completed have a green check mark over the step.

Although rendering workflows is a great use of Silverlight in Visio, it also demonstrates another technique you can use within your own Share-Point applications. The green check marks are implemented as XAML overlays onto the base Visio workflow diagram. Visio Web Applications contain a JavaScript API to program the Visio diagrams, including handling events and reading and writing shape data. One of the more interesting features of the Visio Web Application model is the ability to render overlays on top of your diagrams. In this case the green check marks are rendered as a canvas element with the check mark drawn as a vector image. Using the JavaScript API, the check marks are dynamically drawn on top of the diagram based on the status. What is important to understand is that this can be done for any Visio diagram and hosted as a web part in SharePoint. You then can overlay any XAML object onto the diagram at runtime using the Visio JavaScript API.

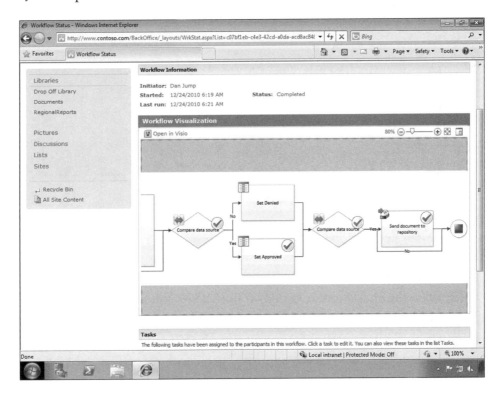

FIGURE 4.14: Visio Workflow Visualization

Down-level

The Visio Web Applications also have a down-level experience. If Silverlight is not installed or not enabled, then the Visio diagram is rendered using a .png image file. This doesn't result in the best user experience. For example, you can see in Figure 4.15 that the quality of the rendering is not clear at any zoom level other than 100%. In this case the zoom level is 80%, which is the same as the zoom level in Figure 4.14 and which is using Silverlight. The status indicators are also implemented as individual .png images that overlay the base diagram .png using a div element.

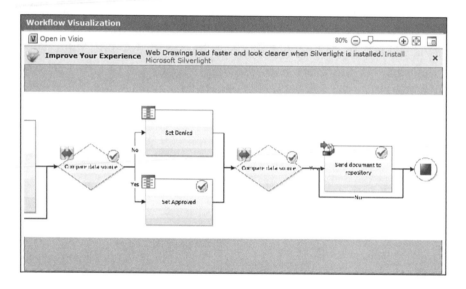

FIGURE 4.15: Down-level Workflow Visualization

The Visio Web Application also displays a yellow status bar informing the user that the diagram will load faster and look clearer when Silverlight is installed and a link to install Silverlight, as shown in Figure 4.14. This link, unlike the SharePoint down-level link, takes you to an Office landing page that has a link to download Silverlight but also has other general information about Silverlight. You can find the Silverlight landing page at the URL, http://www.microsoft.com/getsilverlight/office/?scenario= visio&loc=en-US.

Silverlight Web Part

Up to this point you have seen how SharePoint uses Silverlight out-of-the-box. One of the best new features of SharePoint 2010 is that it also ships a Silverlight Web Part. The Silverlight Web Part enables you to add Silverlight applications to SharePoint without writing any code. Users and Developers can easily leverage the web part to quickly add rich functionality to any site.

Let's walk through an example of using the Silverlight Web Part to add functionality to the home page. In this example you add an existing Silverlight application to the right side bar of the home page. The application calls a service on NetFlix and displays a list of movies released on or after 2010. As you work through the book you see that there are two fundamental questions you need to answer in order to run Silverlight in SharePoint. The first is where the Silverlight application file is located, which is normally a single file with an .xap extension. The second question is how is the Silverlight application hosted? For this first walkthrough the answer to the first question is that the Silverlight application is located in the Shared Documents library. The answer to the second question is that you use the built-in Silverlight Web Part to host the Silverlight application.

Uploading the Silverlight Application

Start by uploading the Silverlight application to the Shared Documents library as you would any other document type. To SharePoint, the Silverlight application is just another document. It doesn't know anything about the file type and treats it just like any other binary file. You can see in Figure 4.16 that that application is called SPNetFlix, and hovering over the file shows the path in the status bar of http://intranet.contoso.com/Shared%20Documents/SPNetFlix.xap. Copy this path to the clipboard because you will need it in the next step.

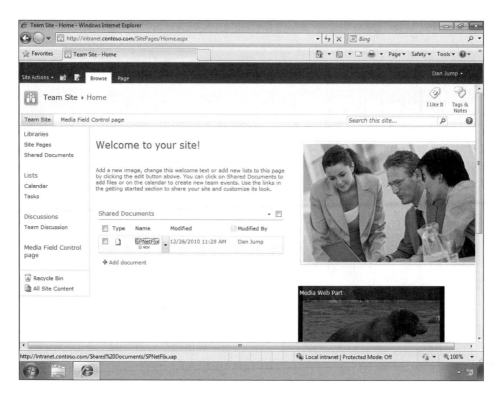

FIGURE 4.16: Upload Silverlight application package file (.xap) to SharePoint

Adding the Silverlight Web Part

Now that you have uploaded the Silverlight application to the Shared Documents Library, you can add a Silverlight Web Part to host the application. Put the home page in Edit mode. There are a number of ways to do this including selecting Edit Page from the Site Actions menu. Set the focus of where you want to insert the web part by clicking the page—in this case click on the right-side bar below the image and above the Bear video. Use the Ribbon to insert the web part. On the Ribbon click the Insert tab under the Editing Tools context sensitive group. On the Insert tab, click the Web Part button under the Web Parts group. This opens the Web Parts Gallery, which enables you to browse and insert any web part, as shown in Figure 4.17. To insert the Silverlight Web Part select Media and Content from the Categories pane and then select Silverlight Web Part from the Web Parts pane and click the Add button.

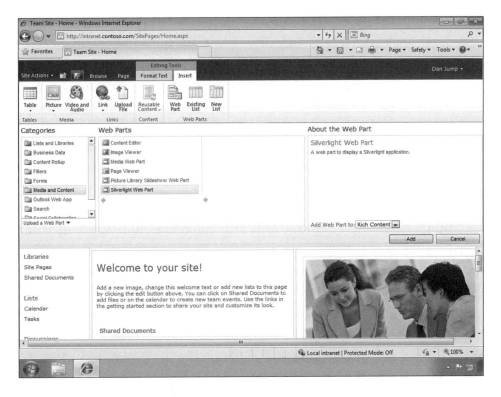

FIGURE 4.17: Insert the Silverlight Web Part

When you click the Add button, SharePoint prompts you for the URL to the Silverlight application. You can paste in the path to the Silverlight .xap file that you copied earlier or just type in the URL, which is http://intranet.contoso.com/Shared%20Documents/SPNetFlix.xap. You now see the Silverlight NetFlix Web Part on the right.

Setting Web Part Properties

The Silverlight Web Part is added using the default properties. If you scroll down the page where you added the Silverlight Web Part you see that the application is cut off and the title of the Web Part is Silverlight Web Part. You can use the standard Web Part Tool pane to edit these properties. To open the Web Part Tool pane, select Edit Web Part from the Web Part context menu. In the Web Part Tool pane, change the title property to SP Net-Flix and change the Height property to 400 pixels.

Passing Initialization Parameters

The Tool pane is also where you can set additional initialization parameters for the Silverlight application. To pass parameters, expand the Other Settings properties at the bottom of the Tool pane and set them in the Custom Initialization Parameters field. The Custom Initialization Parameters field is a comma delimited string of keys and values. If you wanted to pass the parameters for `ReleaseYear` and `Rating` you would do something like "`ReleaseYear=2010,Rating=PG13`". This, of course, assumes that your Silverlight application knows about these parameters and knows how to parse them, as shown in Figure 4.18.

Another thing to be aware of is that the Silverlight Web Part URL encodes the value of this property. Your Silverlight application needs to decode the values back before it uses them. You can use the `System. Windows.Browser.HttpUtility.UrlDecode` method to convert it back to the unencoded string. For example if you had a key and value pair of `K1:K2=V1:V2`, then your Silverlight application would see the key and value as `K1%3AK2=V1%3AV2`. The encoding converts the colon to a `%3A` value. A more common scenario is passing URLs as parameters. Imagine you want to pass a parameter such as `ServerName=http://www.MyServer.com`. This would be encoded as `ServerName=http%3A%2F%2Fwww%2EMyServer%2Ecom`. Calling `System.Windows.Browser.HttpUtility.UrlDecode("http%3A%2F%2 Fwww%2EMyServer%2Ecom")` would convert it back to http://www. MyServer.com. You need to decode both the key and the value.

The Silverlight Web Part also supports two replacement token values in the custom initialization parameters property. The first is the `{webpartid}`, which expands to be the ID of the web part, also known as the *storage key value*. This is the same value returned by the `Microsoft.SharePoint. WebPartPages.GetStorageKey(WebPart)` method, which is a Guid value. For example if you set the custom initialization parameters property of the Silverlight Web Part to `MyWebPartId={webpartid}`, then at runtime this is actually expanded to something similar to `MyWebPartId= %7B5CC5B6C6%2D546C%2D4484%2DB543%2D392B0743EA53%7D`. Decoded in Silverlight, the final key and value pair would be `MyWebPartId={5CC5B6C6- 546C-4484-B543-392B0743EA53}`. The second replacement token is `{pageurl}`, which returns the relative URL of the page that the Silverlight

Web Part is on. For example setting the initialization parameters property to `MyPageUrl={pageurl}` is expanded at runtime to something similar to `MyPageUrl=%2FSitePages%2FSLWP%2Easpx`. Decoding this in Silverlight would result in the final key and value pair of `MyPageUrl=/SitePages/SLWP.aspx`.

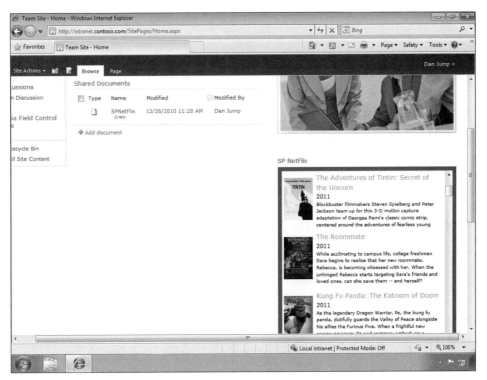

FIGURE 4.18: Silverlight NetFlix Web Part movie browser

Five Seconds to Load

The Silverlight Web Part makes it very easy to add your Silverlight applications to SharePoint without writing any code. The Silverlight Web Part was designed to make this easy and fast without interfering with the functionality of SharePoint. As part of this design, a built-in timeout mechanism throws an exception if the Silverlight application takes longer than five seconds to download and load. The reason for this is to reduce the load time for the entire page by limiting the time to load any individual web part.

This works well for smaller widget-style Silverlight applications but can become an issue for larger applications. One way you hit this timeout is as developers add more functionality to their applications, the size of the Silverlight .xap file grows as resources such as images, videos, and fonts are embedded. Sometimes this is difficult to debug during development because you are calling the local SharePoint instance, so the download is very fast and you do not hit the timeout. The same application on a slower connection might hit the timeout limit, or maybe it occurs only during peak hours when the network is busy. Testing your Silverlight applications under various network conditions is one way to understand if you have this issue. Ultimately you need to use various Silverlight techniques to reduce the load time of your application, such as splitting the application into multiple .xap files or moving resources out of the .xap file. Visit the Silverlight.net site for more ways to reduce the load time of your application.

Other Hosting Options

There are a number of ways to host the Silverlight application without writing custom code. You saw earlier in this chapter how to host Silverlight in the built-in Silverlight Web Part. Next you see two more options for hosting Silverlight in SharePoint. The first way is using the Content Editor Web Part and the second is hosting Silverlight in an IFrame. These are just a couple of examples because hosting Silverlight is ultimately just a simple HTML object tag, so wherever or however you can put this HTML tag in SharePoint, you should be able to host the Silverlight application.

Content Editor Web Part

The Content Editor Web Part (CEWP) is a general purpose web part that allows users to add content directly into the web part without any coding required. The CEWP has three basic ways to enter content. The first is to use the rich text editor. This is a common option for content authors to add formatted text content to a site. The second way, to add content by editing the HTML source directly, is more powerful and used by developers and designers. Linking to an external file is the third way and is my preferred way to add content because it allows for better editing and tool support.

You can add the Content Editor Web Part just like any other web part. The CEWP is located in the Media and Content Categories folder in the Web Part Gallery. When you first add the CEWP it has default text telling you that you need to put the web part in Edit mode to add content. When the CEWP is in Edit mode you can click in the body area of the web part to add content. In this mode you can add content using the Editing Tools tab on the Ribbon. You are not able to add any script using the rich text editing tools. Any script code is automatically stripped out when you save the web part. The Rich Text Editor does not allow you to add a Silverlight application.

HTML Source Code Editor

Editing in the HTML Source view of the CEWP allows you to add script, including the Silverlight object tag. Opening the CEWP for HTML Source editing is hidden under Format Text Ribbon tab in Markup group, where there is a split button called HTML. Expand the HTML split button and select Edit HTML Source. This opens a model dialog for you to enter the HTML source code that you wish to appear in the CEWP. Using this dialog is difficult because there are no tools or other help in editing the text. Let's start by adding some basic tags. Enter the following code in the HTML Source dialog and click OK:

```
?<h1>My First CEWP</h1>
```

The text is then formatted with the h1 tag. This is the same as you could do with the rich text editor, but it is a good way to make sure you have the CEWP working before adding the Silverlight object tag.

Open the Edit HTML Source dialog again and add the code in Listing 4.1. This code comes directly from the TestPage.html file which is automatically generated by the Visual Studio Silverlight project in the bin directory.

LISTING 4.1: Placing Silverlight in the Content Editor Web Part

```
<div id="silverlightControlHost">
    <object data="data:application/x-silverlight-2,"
            type="application/x-silverlight-2"
            width="100%" height="100%">

        <param name="source" value="/Shared%20Documents/SPNetFlix.xap" />
        <param name="onError" value="onSilverlightError" />
```

```
            <param name="background" value="white" />
            <param name="minRuntimeVersion" value="4.0.50826.0" />
            <param name="autoUpgrade" value="true" />

            <a href="http://go.microsoft.com/fwlink/?LinkID=149156&v=4.0.50826.0"
                style="text-decoration: none">
                <img
                    src="http://go.microsoft.com/fwlink/?LinkId=161376"
                    alt="Get Microsoft Silverlight"
                    style="border-style: none" />
            </a>
        </object>
        <iframe id="_sl_historyFrame"
                style="visibility: hidden;
                height: 0px; width: 0px;
                border: 0px">
        </iframe>
    </div>
```

As soon as you click OK to accept the HTML Source dialog, you see the Silverlight application loaded in the CEWP, as shown in Figure 4.19.

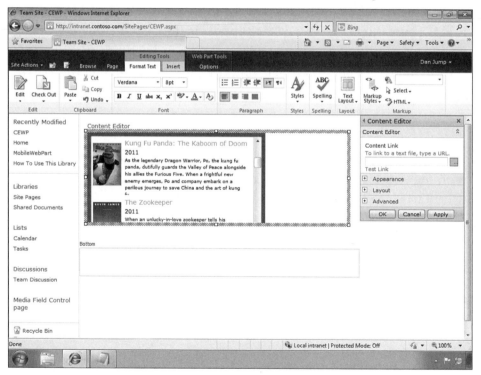

FIGURE 4.19: Silverlight loaded in the Content Editor Web Part

One of the challenges with using the CEWP is that the Web Part modifies your source code. For example, the code that you just entered is changed to the code shown in Listing 4.2 after it is saved. You can see that the code has been modified with additional attributes, and the formatting is not as clean as when it was entered. This makes it difficult to debug and update your source code.

LISTING 4.2: A Silverlight Tag after CEWP Reformatting

```
    <div id="silverlightControlHost">
        <object width="100%" height="100%" data="data:application/x-
oleobject;base64,QfXq3+HzJEysrJnDBxUISgAJAABtOwAA2BMAAAwAAAB3AGgAaQB0AGUAAAAAAA
AAAAAAAAAAAABEAAAALwBTAGgAYQByAGUAZAAlADIAMABEAG8AYwB1AG0AZQBuAHQAcwAvAF-
MAUABOAGUAdABGAGwAaQB4AC4AeABhHAHAAAAA8AAAAAAAACYAAABvAG4AUwBpAGwAdgB1AHIIAbAB-
pAGcAaAB0AEUAcgByAG8AcgAAAAAAAAAAAAAAAAAAAAAAAAAAAAAAAAAAAAAAAAAAAAAAAAAABAAAAAQAAAAAAAA
AAAAAAAAAAABgAAAA0AC4AMAAuADUAMAA4ADIANgAuADAAAAAKAAAAd-
AByAHUAZQAAAAAAAAAAAAAAAAAAAAA=="
            type="application/x-silverlight-2" althtml="
        &lt;a
href=&quot;http://go.microsoft.com/fwlink/?LinkID=149156&amp;v=4.0.50826.0&quot
;
            style=&quot;text-decoration: none&quot;&gt;
            &lt;img

src=&quot;http://go.microsoft.com/fwlink/?LinkId=161376&quot;
            alt=&quot;Get Microsoft Silverlight&quot;
            style=&quot;border-style: none&quot; /&gt;
        &lt;/a&gt;
     " althtml="
        &lt;a
href=&quot;http://go.microsoft.com/fwlink/?LinkID=149156&amp;v=4.0.50826.0&quot
;
            style=&quot;text-decoration: none&quot;&gt;
            &lt;img

src=&quot;http://go.microsoft.com/fwlink/?LinkId=161376&quot;
            alt=&quot;Get Microsoft Silverlight&quot;
            style=&quot;border-style: none&quot; /&gt;
        &lt;/a&gt;
     ">
            <param name="source" value="/Shared%20Documents/SPNetFlix.xap" />
            <param name="onError" value="onSilverlightError" />
            <param name="background" value="white" />
            <param name="minRuntimeVersion" value="4.0.50826.0" />
            <param name="autoUpgrade" value="true" />
            <a
href="http://go.microsoft.com/fwlink/?LinkID=149156&v=4.0.50826.0"
style="text-decoration: none">
```

```
                   <img src="http://go.microsoft.com/fwlink/?LinkId=161376"
alt="Get Microsoft Silverlight"
                     style="border-style: none" />
            </a>
        </object>
        <iframe id="_sl_historyFrame" style="border-bottom: 0px; border-left:
0px; width: 0px;
            height: 0px; visibility: hidden; border-top: 0px; border-right:
0px"></iframe>
           </div>
```

You can also add script code to the CEWP. The script block is added directly to the HTML Source Editor above or below your `div` tag. For example the Silverlight test page creates a script block in the head tag to handle exceptions. Copy the script block from the head tag of the test page and paste it into the top of the HTML Source Editor dialog of the CEWP. This script is shown in Listing 4.3.

LISTING 4.3: Silverlight Error Handling Script

```
<script type="text/javascript">
    function onSilverlightError(sender, args) {
        var appSource = "";
        if (sender != null && sender != 0) {
            appSource = sender.getHost().Source;
        }

        var errorType = args.ErrorType;
        var iErrorCode = args.ErrorCode;

        if (errorType == "ImageError" || errorType == "MediaError") {
            return;
        }

        var errMsg = "Unhandled Error in Silverlight Application " +
            appSource + "\n";

        errMsg += "Code: " + iErrorCode + "     \n";
        errMsg += "Category: " + errorType + "        \n";
        errMsg += "Message: " + args.ErrorMessage + "       \n";

        if (errorType == "ParserError") {
            errMsg += "File: " + args.xamlFile + "       \n";
            errMsg += "Line: " + args.lineNumber + "        \n";
            errMsg += "Position: " + args.charPosition + "        \n";
```

```
            }
        else if (errorType == "RuntimeError") {
            if (args.lineNumber != 0) {
                errMsg += "Line: " + args.lineNumber + "      \n";
                errMsg += "Position: " + args.charPosition + "      \n";
            }
            errMsg += "MethodName: " + args.methodName + "      \n";
        }

        throw new Error(errMsg);
    }
</script>

<div id="silverlightControlHost">
… Omitted for brevity
</div>
```

Linked File

The Content Editor Web Part also allows you to add content by linking to a file that will be displayed in the CEWP, as shown in Figure 4.20. This is the best approach for using the CEWP with Silverlight, as it allows you to create the file separately using tools such as Visual Studio and Expression Web and Expression Blend. Linking to the file makes it easy to create, update, and debug your source code because the file is not changed by the CEWP, unlike using the HTML Source Code Editor dialog.

To see how this works, create a new page and add a CEWP to the page. In this example you use the test HTML page that is generated by Visual Studio in the bin directory when you create a Silverlight application. First you need to modify this file to point to the Silverlight .xap file in SharePoint by changing the following line:

```
<param name="source"value="/Shared%20Documents/SPNetFlix.xap"/>
```

The CEWP also doesn't allow Form tags in the link files, so you need to delete the Form tag from the test page as well.

There is one other small change you can make to the test page. You can change the height and width properties to the actual size of the Silverlight application. These values by default are set to 100%, which causes scroll bars to appear in the CEWP. When these changes have been made, copy this file to the Shared Documents Library and copy the shortcut after it has been uploaded. Next put the CEWP in Edit mode using the Web Part menu and selecting Edit Web Part. On the Web Part Tool pane enter the path to the test page that you uploaded to the Shared Documents Library in the Content Link property. In this example the path is /Shared%20Documents/SPNet-FlixTestPage.html. Click the Test Link hyperlink to verify the link is valid.

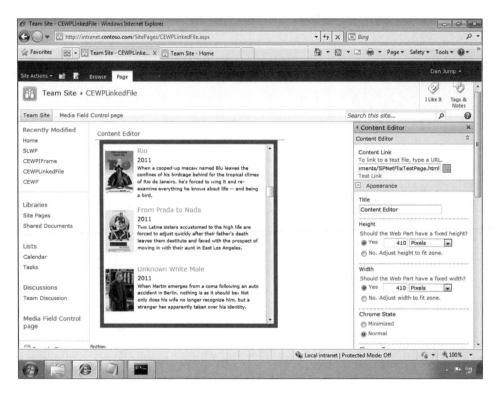

FIGURE 4.20: Content Editor Web Part with a linked content file

IFrame

SharePoint supports loading content as an IFrame. This is also supported in the Content Editor Web Parts. Everything that you learned about the CEWP earlier in this chapter applies to loading content from an IFrame as well.

Instead of loading the Silverlight object tag directly, you can load a page that is running the Silverlight application remotely. Using an IFrame is a good technique for leveraging resources on another server or in the cloud such as running on Windows Azure.

Using SharePoint Designer you can add a simple aspx page to the Site Pages Library that does not have any page layout associated to it. In other words, it appears to be a blank page with no SharePoint page layout or master page. Add the Silverlight test page code to this page, as shown in Figure 4.21.

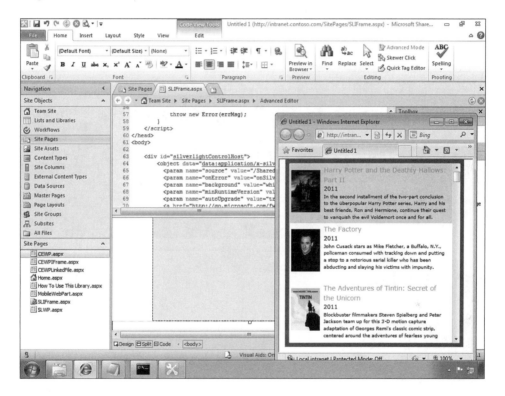

FIGURE 4.21: Building a simple aspx page in SharePoint Designer

You could have used an existing page from Windows Azure or some other location for this example, but when you have a page you want to use you can reference it in the CEWP. To add a Silverlight application running in an IFrame, add a CEWP to a page in SharePoint. Edit the HTML Source of the CEWP, adding the following code. The `src` property of the IFrame is the URL to the page where the Silverlight application is running. Add the following code to the CEWP:

```
<iframe src="http://intranet.contoso.com/SitePages/SLIFrame.aspx "
    scrolling="no" frameborder="0" style="width:410px; height:410px">
</iframe>
```

After you close the HTML Editor Source dialog you see the IFrame loaded with the Silverlight application, as shown in Figure 4.22. In all of these examples you can see that they look the same to the end user, but they all have different implementations.

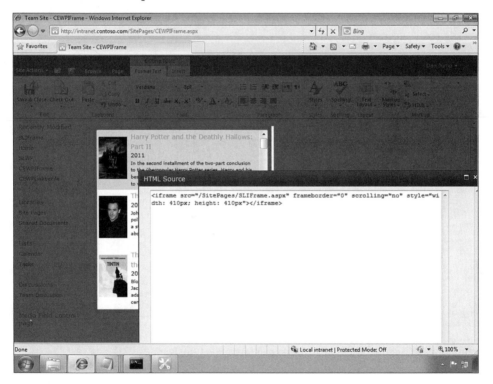

FIGURE 4.22: Using the Content Editor Web Part to load Silverlight in an IFrame

Summary

You have seen that SharePoint offers a number of features that leverage the power of Silverlight to provide a rich user experience. Silverlight enables integration of audio and video to your pages and lists using the Media Player Web Part or the Media Field Control. Silverlight enables you to navigate a large number of items in the Create Content dialog and the Organization Browser. Silverlight also enables you to visualize information in the form of your workflows. But I think the most valuable point of this chapter is to understand how all of these various Silverlight applications that ship with SharePoint work and what design problems they solve. Ultimately you can use this knowledge in the design of your own applications. Let's recap some of the lessons learned:

- **Down-level Support**—You can never guarantee that end users have Silverlight installed, so you should provide a down-level experience that still allows them to accomplish the tasks at hand. Depending on your target audience, this might be more or less of a concern. For example, if you are developing Enterprise solutions, then you have a great deal of control over the desktop environment and can require that Silverlight is installed. If you are targeting Internet or extranet scenarios, then you have much less control over the software installed on the desktop.

- **Install experience**—Building off the down-level experience pattern just described, you should also provide an easy and informative upgrade experience for users who do not have Silverlight installed. You can see this in some of the examples that ship with SharePoint. You should provide a link or warning message that informs the user that a better experience is available. Also users are more likely to install Silverlight if they perceive a benefit, so provide information and Help screens that explain and demonstrate added value.

- **Ribbon Support**—The biggest user interface change in SharePoint 2010 is the inclusion of the Fluent User Interface, which includes the Ribbon. You should integrate the Ribbon into your Silverlight applications.

- **JavaScript API**—Silverlight applications can communicate with JavaScript through the HTML Bridge feature. There is a rich JavaScript client-side object model in SharePoint including the Ribbon. It is important that your Silverlight applications are tightly integrated in the composite application model where web parts are added at runtime to work together. Having a JavaScript API allows other web parts and other SharePoint controls to automate your Silverlight applications.

- **More than Just Web Parts**—SharePoint is more than just web parts. You can leverage all of the user interface elements of SharePoint to host Silverlight in more places. For example, hosting Silverlight directly on the page layout pages or the master pages becomes a powerful way to leverage Silverlight across the entire site in a consist manner. Hosting Silverlight in individual field controls enables you to add rich data entry with mini Silverlight applications providing a small UI surface to enter or view rich field data.

- **Skinning and localization**—Your Silverlight applications should fit naturally into the SharePoint site they are hosted in. This includes skinning the control to match the look and feel of the host site. You can provide minimal functionality such as matching the site's theme, or you can provide a full skinning model that developers can extend at runtime. SharePoint and Silverlight both have deep localization and globalization capabilities that you should take advantage of. These features sync the locales between your Silverlight applications and SharePoint. If the site is in German, your Silverlight application should be as well for the best user experience.

- **Pluggable providers**—Architecting your Silverlight applications to be extensible is a good pattern to follow. This allows you or other developers to add functionality to your application in the future at runtime. A pluggable model also makes it easier for large teams to work together building a large size Silverlight application. Decomposing your application into smaller parts also makes the application easier and faster to download, which greatly enhances the user experience and perception of the application.

- **Diagnostics**—It is important to consider the debugging and operational aspects of building your Silverlight applications. Adding deep diagnostic capabilities into your applications makes it easier for developers and administrators to monitor and troubleshoot your application. SharePoint provides a rich logging environment; you should integrate into this same logging structure with your Silverlight applications as well. If possible avoid creating your own nonstandard logging mechanism.

- **Visio JavaScript API**—Visio provides a JavaScript client object model for automating Visio diagrams hosted in SharePoint. Think about how you can leverage the richness of Visio to provide a drawing surface for overlaying your Silverlight applications. Visio gives you a jump start by providing a drawing and shapes data model to build on.

You also saw that using the Silverlight Web Part was not the only way to host Silverlight applications without writing any code. You saw that you could host Silverlight applications using the Content Editor Web Part either directly in the Web Part or linked to an external file. And finally you learned that it is possible to host Silverlight applications that are running remotely on another server or in the cloud such as on Windows Azure using an IFrame. All of these approaches provide you a number of ways to accomplish the same result of hosting Silverlight in SharePoint but give you the flexibility to choose the method that best fits your scenario.

▊ 5 ▪

Web Part Development

WEB PARTS ARE ONE of the most fundamental user interface components in SharePoint. Web parts enable developers to create visual components that can be configured by end users. This is core to the concepts of SharePoint as a composite application model in that you can compose applications from smaller building blocks, such as web parts. Out-of-the-box, Visual Studio supports creating web parts and Visual Web Parts. The difference between the two Visual Studio projects is that Visual Web Parts can be created using a visual designer, and the web part template is written using code only. In this chapter you learn how to leverage Visual Studio to create Silverlight Web Parts. These are web parts that use Silverlight as the user interface.

Silverlight Web Parts

In Chapter 4, "A First Look at Silverlight in SharePoint," you saw a couple of techniques for hosting Silverlight in SharePoint using the built-in Silverlight Web Part and using the Content Editor Web Part (CEWP). Both of these techniques required you to manually upload the Silverlight application's .xap file to SharePoint and then to manually create a web part to host the .xap file. Using this method to host Silverlight is problematic for a couple of reasons. First, it is a totally manual process and as such is prone to user error. Doing this manually doesn't follow good application lifecycle management (ALM) practices such as using source control, testing, and deployment. To avoid all of these issues you want to also package all of your SharePoint applications into a SharePoint solution package, a .wsp file.

It is important to understand what is going on under the covers. First you will see how to manually build a Visual Studio project to package and deploy the Silverlight application. This process is not obvious and requires a number of steps. Because of this Microsoft has released a Silverlight Web Part extension project for Visual Studio that automates the process of creating a Silverlight Web Part. Later in the chapter you use this extension to build a Silverlight Web Part.

Manually Building a Silverlight Web Part

The first task you need to solve is how to package and deploy your Silverlight application in your SharePoint .wsp package. Start by creating a new Silverlight project in Visual Studio. Next, create an empty SharePoint project in the same Visual Studio solution that the Silverlight project is in. You will have something similar to the project structure in Figure 5.1.

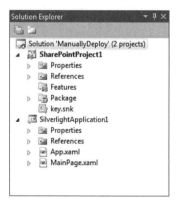

FIGURE 5.1: Default Silverlight and SharePoint projects

At this point you have two projects in the solution, Silverlight and SharePoint, but they are not connected in any way. Normally to reference another project, you add a project reference to the other project in the solution. A Visual Studio project reference will make sure to build the referenced project before including the output of the referenced project into the refering project. In the case of Silverlight this does not work because the output you want to reference is not a .dll but the .xap Silverlight application's package file. So the SharePoint tools had to come up with a different way to do this. This is the technique that is not totally obvious, but it is not too bad after you see it once.

Now that you have two projects, the task is to get the Silverlight .xap file into the SharePoint project. Modules are the ways in which you deploy files to SharePoint. Add a new Module Project Item to the SharePoint project in Visual Studio. The new Module Project Item contains a Sample.txt file and an Elements.xml file. The Elements.xml, shown in Listing 5.1, describes where to deploy the Sample.txt file. In this the URL property specifies a folder called Module1. If this folder does not exist in SharePoint, it is automatically created.

LISTING 5.1: Elements.xml in a New Module

```xml
<?xml version="1.0" encoding="utf-8"?>
<Elements
        xmlns="http://schemas.microsoft.com/sharepoint/">
  <Module Name="Module1">
    <File Path="Module1\Sample.txt"
                 Url="Module1/Sample.txt" />
  </Module>
</Elements>
```

Go ahead and delete the Sample.txt file because it is not needed. You are now ready to add a reference to the Silverlight project. Click the Module1 node in the SharePoint project to view the Properties window. In the Properties window for the Module there is a property named Project Output References. This is a collection property; click the ellipse to open the Project Output References dialog window. Click the Add button to add a new reference. In the reference's properties, set the Deployment Type to Element File. Choose the Silverlight project from the Project Name drop-down property list. In Figure 5.2 you can see that the Project Output References dialog adds a reference to the Silverlight project and adds the path to the Elements.xml file.

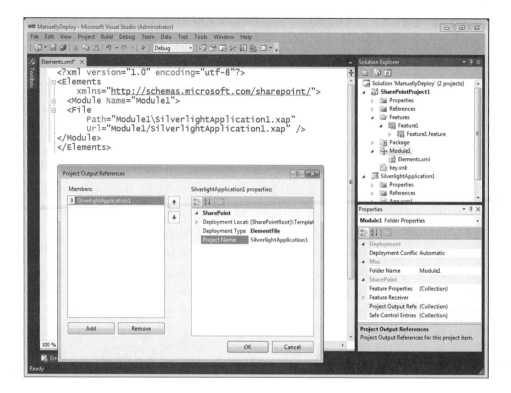

FIGURE 5.2: Project Output References

Also notice that the Module folder only contains the Elements.xml file, which has been updated as shown in Listing 5.2.

LISTING 5.2: Elements.xml to Deploy a Silverlight Application

```xml
<?xml version="1.0" encoding="utf-8"?>
.<Elements
        xmlns="http://schemas.microsoft.com/sharepoint/">
  <Module Name="Module1">
  <File
        Path="Module1\SilverlightApplication1.xap"
        Url="Module1/SilverlightApplication1.xap" />
</Module>
</Elements>
```

This is because there is only a refence to the Silverlight application. The actual .xap is not stored in the SharePoint project. Visual Studio also ensures the Silverlight is built before the SharePoint project if it is dirty, just like it does when adding a project reference.

Build, package, and deploy the SharePoint project to SharePoint by pressing F5. Visual Studio deploys and activates the feature that then deploys the Silverlight application's .xap file; in this case to the Module1 folder. You can verify that the Silverlight application was deployed using SharePoint Designer. Open SharePoint Designer and browse to the All Files folder of the site you deployed the solution to. Under the All Files folder you see the Module1 folder, which contains the SilverlightApplication1.xap file that you just deployed, as shown in Figure 5.3.

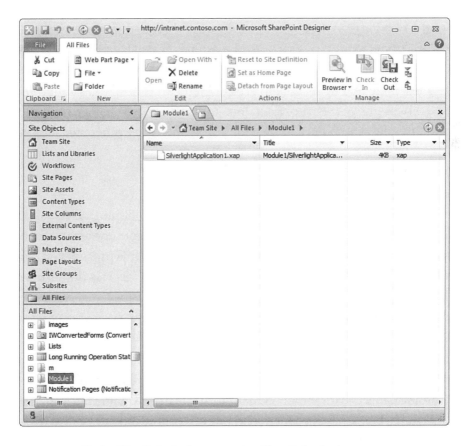

FIGURE 5.3: Verify the Silverlight deployment using SharePoint Designer

After you have deployed the solution, users can add Silverlight Web Parts to pages. All they need is the path to the deployed .xap file, for example http://intranet.contoso.com/Module1/SilverlightApplication1.xap. You could also take the next step and add a web part directly to your project. But Microsoft has already done all of these steps for you in a Visual Studio extension, which you can download for free. Let's take a look at how to do this using the extension.

Visual Studio Silverlight Web Parts Extension

Microsoft has created a Visual Studio extension to automatically build Silverlight Web Parts. With this extension you can avoid doing all of the manual steps from the previous section. The extension also has a couple of other nice features, such as it automatically creates the web part for you and creates a test page that hosts the Silverlight Web Part. This makes it simple to add a Silverlight Web Part project item and press F5 and have a fully functional Silverlight Web Part created for you without any other steps for you to do.

Installing the Extension

The Silverlight Web Part project item templates are not part of Visual Studio out-of-the-box, so you need to download them from the Visual Studio Gallery and install them. But Visual Studio has made this process very easy and quick to not only install but uninstall as well. In fact it is built directly into Visual Studio.

Before you install the Silverlight SharePoint web parts extension, you need to install the Visual Studio 2010 SharePoint Power Tools extension. Click Tools and then Extension Manager from the main menu. In the Extension Manager Gallery click Online Gallery from the menu on the left. When the online gallery loads, enter **Visual Studio 2010 SharePoint Power Tools** in the search box. Click the Download button. Follow the prompts to download and install the extension.

Click Tools and then Extension Manager from the main menu. In the Extension Manager Gallery click Online Gallery from the menu on the left. When the online gallery loads, enter **Silverlight SharePoint Web Parts** in the search box. Click the Download button, as shown in Figure 5.4. Follow the prompts to download and install the extension.

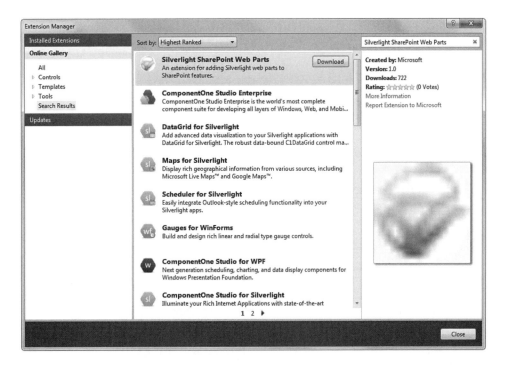

FIGURE 5.4: Visual Studio Extension Manager

The extension does have a dependency on another extension that Microsoft ships called the Visual Studio 2010 SharePoint Power Tools, as shown in Figure 5.5. This extension adds support for sandboxed compatible Visual Web Parts. If you see this warning, click Close and install the Visual Studio 2010 SharePoint Power Tools first. Also be sure to restart Visual Studio after installing the power tools extension.

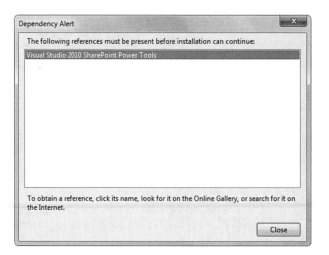

FIGURE 5.5: Dependency Alert

Click Install to accept the EULA and install the extension, as shown in Figure 5.6.

FIGURE 5.6: Install Visual Studio Extension

You can confirm that both extensions are installed from the Extension Manager dialog, as shown in Figure 5.7. In this case you can see that there is a warning to restart Visual Studio, which is required after installing any extension.

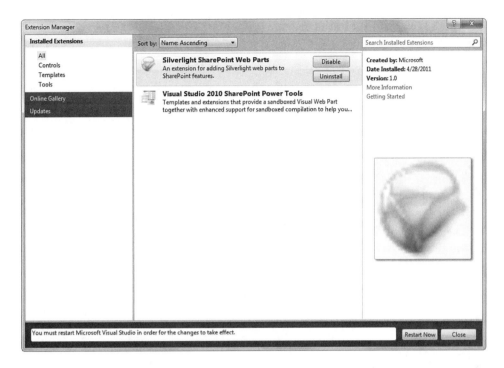

FIGURE 5.7: Restart Visual Studio after installation

With the Silverlight SharePoint Web Part extension successfully installed you are ready to start creating Silverlight Web Parts. Let's look at the two different types of Silverlight Web Parts that you can create with the extension—Silverlight Web Parts and Custom Silverlight Web Parts.

Building a Silverlight Web Part

SharePoint ships with a web part for hosting Silverlight applications. The Silverlight Web Part project template uses this web part to host the Silverlight application. When developers create Silverlight applications for SharePoint, they generally follow one of two patterns. The first is that a Silverlight developer has created a Silverlight application and now wants to deploy it to SharePoint. The second pattern is that a SharePoint developer wants to add an existing Silverlight application to the SharePoint project. But what both of these patterns have in common is that you have one Silverlight and one SharePoint project in a single SharePoint solution and you want to connect them.

Let's take a look at an example of how to do this using the Silverlight Web Part extension project item. Create or open a Silverlight project in Visual Studio. In this example you can open the SLGrid Silverlight application that is located in the sample code, as shown in Figure 5.8.

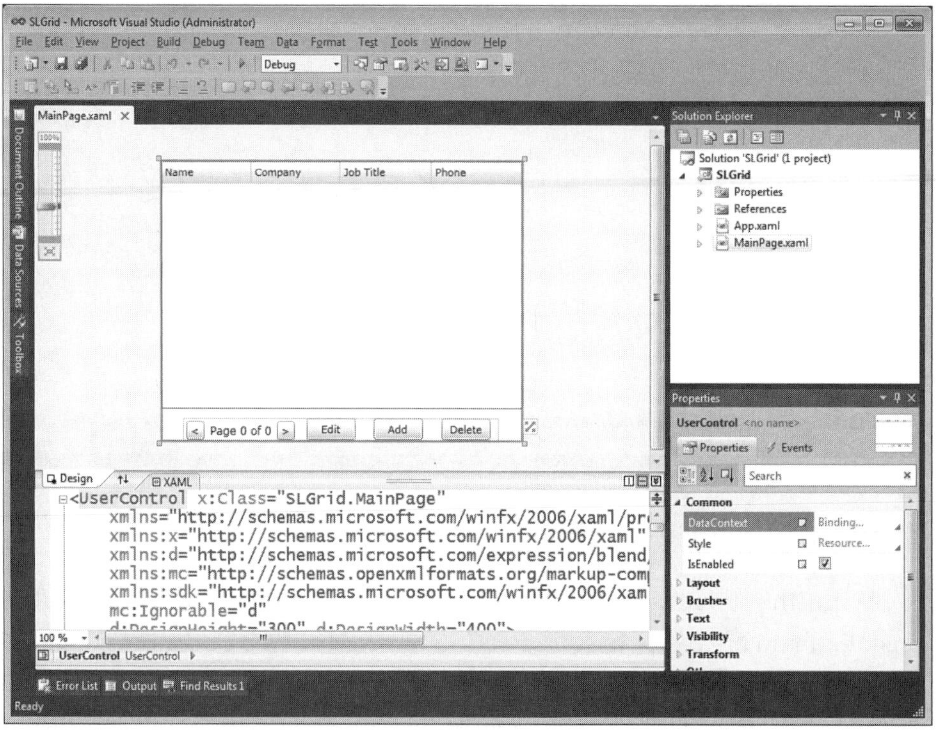

FIGURE 5.8: SLGrid.sln Silverlight application

A developer iterates on the Silverlight application using Expression Blend or Visual Studio until it is ready to be deployed to SharePoint. The SharePoint developer adds a new empty sandboxed SharePoint project to the SharePoint solution. There are a couple of housekeeping tasks you need to do because SharePoint was added after the Silverlight project. First, set the SharePoint project as the startup project. This causes the SharePoint project to deploy to SharePoint when you press F5. You should always enable Silverlight debugging. This setting is somewhat hidden on the SharePoint tab of the Project Properties page; most of the time you need to scroll down to see the setting, as shown in Figure 5.9.

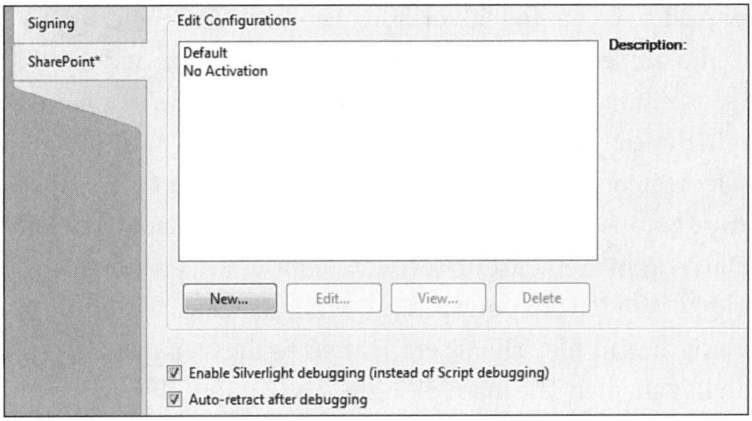

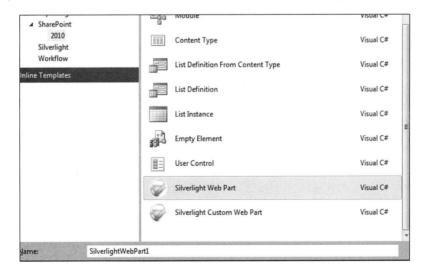

FIGURE 5.9: Enable Silverlight debugging

In your Visual Studio solution you now have one Silverlight and one SharePoint project. Technically it does not matter how you got to this state, whether you started with the SharePoint project or the Silverlight project. After you are in this state you can connect the two projects together by adding a Silverlight Web Part. Right-click the SharePoint project and add a new project item. In the new project item, click the Silverlight Web Part project item in the SharePoint\2010 node, as shown in Figure 5.10.

FIGURE 5.10: Add a Silverlight Web Part

Click Add to create the Silverlight Web Part. The Silverlight Web Part project template sees that you only have one SharePoint and one Silverlight project so it automatically connects them. If you had zero or more than one Silverlight project you would be prompted to create a new Silverlight project or select the one you would like to connect. I don't recommend using this feature because the Silverlight project is created using a default name.

The Silverlight Web Part project item template does more than just add a Silverlight Web Part to your project. First, it creates a module to deploy the Silverlight .xap file. This is equivalent to the steps you did manually earlier in this chapter. The main difference is that the Silverlight application is deployed to the Master Pages gallery. Specifically it is deployed to the ClientBin folder, and a subfolder is created that matches the package name, which is typically the same as the Visual Studio project's name. The Visual Studio replacement token, `$SharePoint.Package.Name$`, is used to dynamically create the folder in the Elements.xml file as shown in Listing 5.3.

LISTING 5.3: Elements.xml with SharePoint Package Name Token

```
<?xml version="1.0" encoding="utf-8"?>
<Elements xmlns="http://schemas.microsoft.com/sharepoint/">
  <Module Name="SLGrid"
Url="_catalogs/masterpage/ClientBin/$SharePoint.Package.Name$">
    <File Path="SLGrid\SLGrid.xap" Url="SLGrid.xap" />
  </Module>
</Elements>
```

The project item template also creates a Silverlight Web Part definition file using the built-in Silverlight Web Part. This is equal to you manually adding a Silverlight Web Part from the Web Parts gallery. Unlike doing this manually, the web part that is created has all of the properties already set, including the URL property, which points to the location of the Silverlight .xap file. You can edit the SLGridWebPart.webpart file's properties to change other values such as description, height, width, and title. The content of SLGridWebPart.webpart is shown in Listing 5.4.

LISTING 5.4: SLGridWebPart.webpart File Sets WebPart Values

```xml
<webParts>
  <webPart xmlns="http://schemas.microsoft.com/WebPart/v3">
    <metaData>
      <type name="Microsoft.SharePoint.WebPartPages.SilverlightWebPart,
Microsoft.SharePoint, Version=14.0.0.0, Culture=neutral,
PublicKeyToken=71e9bce111e9429c" />
      <importErrorMessage>Cannot import this Web
      Part.</importErrorMessage>
    </metaData>
    <data>
      <properties>
        <property name="HelpUrl" type="string" />
        <property name="AllowClose" type="bool">True</property>
        <property name="ExportMode" type="exportmode">All</property>
        <property name="Hidden" type="bool">False</property>
        <property name="AllowEdit" type="bool">True</property>
        <property name="Direction" type="direction">NotSet</property>
        <property name="TitleIconImageUrl" type="string" />
        <property name="AllowConnect" type="bool">True</property>
        <property name="HelpMode" type="helpmode">Modal</property>
        <property name="CustomProperties" type="string" null="true" />
        <property name="AllowHide" type="bool">True</property>
        <property name="Description"
                  type="string">SilverlightSLGrid</property>
        <property name="CatalogIconImageUrl" type="string" />
        <property name="MinRuntimeVersion" type="string" null="true" />
        <property name="ApplicationXml" type="string" />
        <property name="AllowMinimize" type="bool">True</property>
        <property name="AllowZoneChange" type="bool">True</property>
        <property name="CustomInitParameters" type="string" null="true"
                  />
        <property name="Height" type="unit">480px</property>
        <property name="ChromeType" type="chrometype">None</property>
        <property name="Width" type="unit">640px</property>
        <property name="Title" type="string">SilverlightSLGrid</property>
        <property name="ChromeState" type="chromestate">Normal</property>
        <property name="TitleUrl" type="string" />
        <property name="Url"
        type="string">~site/_catalogs/masterpage/ClientBin/$SharePoint.Package.
        Name$/SLGrid.xap</property>
        <property name="WindowlessMode" type="bool">True</property>
      </properties>
    </data>
  </webPart>
</webParts>
```

The final item created by the project item template is a test page called SLGridWebPartPage.aspx that hosts the Silverlight Web Part, SLGridWeb-Part.webpart. This is a nice feature for developing the solution as you immediately have a page that you can run without taking any other steps. This page uses the SharePoint Wiki Page template. The SLGridWebPart-Page.aspx page is a lot of standard wiki page code; the important section is at the very bottom where the Silverlight Web Part is hosted. This is equivalent to you creating a new wiki page in the Site Pages Library and inserting the SLGridWebPart onto the page. Although it is perfectly fine to ship this with the test page, developers generally delete it before going to production. You can see Listing 5.5 for the Silverlight Web Part that is inserted in the wiki field node of the wiki page.

LISTING 5.5: Silverlight Web Part in the Page Wiki Field

```
<!-- Silverlight Web Part -->
<WebPartPages:SilverlightWebPart
    runat="server"
    Height="480px"
    Url="~site/_catalogs/masterpage/ClientBin
/$SharePoint.Package.Name$/SLGrid.xap"
    ExportMode="All"
    ChromeType="None"
    ApplicationXml=""
    HelpMode="Modal"
    Description="SLGrid Web Part"
    ID="g_c24198d9_d504_4132_b56c_585e456d8855"
    Width="640px"
    Title="SLGrid"
    __MarkupType="vsattributemarkup"
    __WebPartId="{90D205F0-8BF4-4138-BCB5-7A947C14BDA9}"
    WebPart="true"
    __designer:IsClosed="false">
</WebPartPages:SilverlightWebPart>
```

Though all of this detail is interesting, there is nothing that you need to change. You simply add the Silverlight Web Part and press F5 to deploy the solution to SharePoint. In this example the SLGrid application uses the client object model to display a grid of contacts, as shown in Figure 5.11.

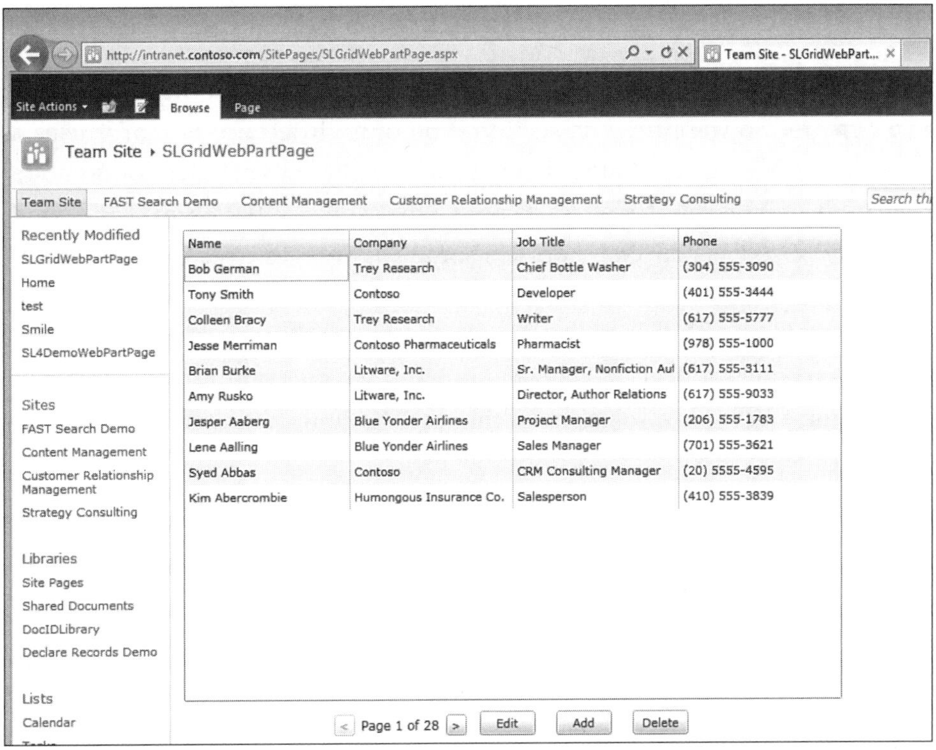

FIGURE 5.11: Silverlight Web Part test page

Adding Silverlight Web Parts using this Project Item template is very simple to use and deploy, but it has some issues. The first is that the built-in Silverlight Web Part has a five-second timeout. This means that your Silverlight application needs to load and start up in five seconds. This is perfect for small applications, but it might be a problem for larger applications or those on slow networks. This is where the Custom Silverlight Web Part comes in. It offers another way to host your Silverlight applications. The second issue is that it is not possible to customize the web part that hosts the Silverlight control. In the next section you learn how to create and extend a custom Silverlight Web Part.

Building a Custom Silverlight Web Part

A custom Silverlight Web Part is very similar to the Silverlight Web Part you created in the previous section. The only difference is that it uses a sandboxed Visual Web Part to host the Silverlight application as opposed to the built-in Silverlight Web Part control that ships with SharePoint. Using the sandboxed Visual Web Part has some advantages over the built in Silverlight Web Part host, such as not having the five-second timeout. A custom Silverlight Web Part enables you to interact with the web part page that the Silverlight application is hosted on. You see an example of this later in the chapter. You can also include other HTML items with your custom web part such as JavaScript, CSS, and images.

Create a Custom Silverlight Web Part just like you did in the previous section. Add a Silverlight project and a SharePoint project to a Visual Studio solution. In this case you can use the SLGrid project that you used in the previous section. After you create the two projects, you need to connect them together. Open the Add New Item dialog for the SharePoint project. Choose the Silverlight Custom Web Part project item, as shown in Figure 5.12.

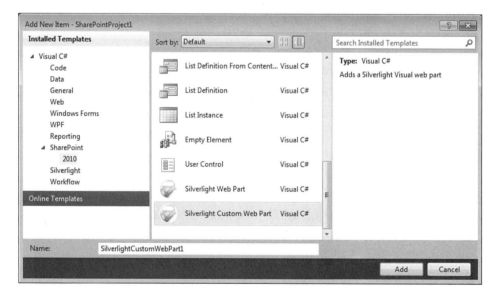

FIGURE 5.12: Add a Custom Silverlight Web Part

The Visual Studio project has the same items as it did when you added a Silverlight Web Part. There is a module that deploys the Silverlight .xap file. There is a wiki test page that hosts the Silverlight Web Part. The difference is now there is a sandboxed Visual Web Part instead of just a .webpart definition file. The sandboxed Visual Web Part Project Item template comes from the Visual Studio 2010 SharePoint Power Tools extension, which you installed as a prerequisite to the Silverlight Web Parts extension. The sandboxed Visual Web Part is implemented as an ASP.NET user control (.ascx). What makes this user control special is that normally you cannot deploy user controls as part of a SharePoint sandboxed solution because the .ascx file must be written to the _layouts directory in SharePoint. But because this is a sandboxed solution, you are not allowed to do this. To work around this problem the Visual Studio team wrote a custom sandboxed Visual Web Part that compiles the .ascx control to code before deploying it to SharePoint. This avoids the file restrictions of the sandbox as there is nothing to write to the file system. The Silverlight Web Part extension takes advantage of this special Visual Web Part to host the Silverlight application, as shown in Figure 5.13. This is important because Silverlight runs on the client, so there should never be a restriction that it cannot run in a sandboxed solution. Also by using the Visual Web Part it makes it easier for developers to extend the web part using the Visual Design tools in Visual Studio.

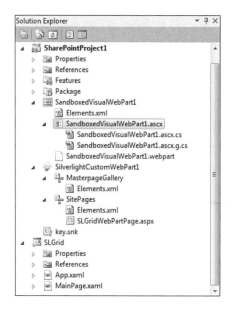

FIGURE 5.13: Custom Silverlight Web Part

The sandboxed Visual Web Part contains the code to host the Silverlight application. Open this page in Visual Studio to see the hosting code. This code is the same code that the Silverlight project generates in the test pages when you build the project. The only change to that generated code is the insertion of SharePoint tokens for the `source` and `initparams`.

First is the Silverlight error handling code in Listing 5.6. This code is unchanged from what is generated by the Silverlight project system.

LISTING 5.6: Error Handling Script in the Custom Silverlight Web Part

```
<!-- Silverlight Error Handler -->
<script type="text/javascript">
function onSilverlightError(sender, args) {
    var appSource = "";
    if (sender != null && sender != 0) {
        appSource = sender.getHost().Source;
    }

    var errorType = args.ErrorType;
    var iErrorCode = args.ErrorCode;

    if (errorType == "ImageError" || errorType == "MediaError") {
        return;
```

```
        }

    var errMsg = "Unhandled Error in Silverlight Application " + appSource +
"\n";

    errMsg += "Code: " + iErrorCode + "    \n";
    errMsg += "Category: " + errorType + "    \n";
    errMsg += "Message: " + args.ErrorMessage + "    \n";

    if (errorType == "ParserError") {
        errMsg += "File: " + args.xamlFile + "    \n";
        errMsg += "Line: " + args.lineNumber + "    \n";
        errMsg += "Position: " + args.charPosition + "    \n";
    }
    else if (errorType == "RuntimeError") {
        if (args.lineNumber != 0) {
            errMsg += "Line: " + args.lineNumber + "    \n";
            errMsg += "Position: " + args.charPosition + "    \n";
        }
        errMsg += "MethodName: " + args.methodName + "    \n";
    }

    throw new Error(errMsg);
}
</script>
```

The next section of code, shown in Listing 5.7, is the code that inserts Silverlight on the page. The two properties to call out are `source` and `init-Params`. The `source` property is the URL to the Silverlight .xap file host in SharePoint. The `initParams` are parameters passed to the Silverlight application when it is started. There is one special parameter called `MS.SP.url`. The `MS.SP.url` parameter is used by the client object model to set the `ClientContext.Current` value. Without the `MS.SP.url` parameter, `Client-Context.Current` returns null. You should always pass this parameter if you want to access the client context, even if you are creating your own Silverlight Web Parts.

LISTING 5.7: Silverlight Object Tag in the Custom Silverlight WebPart

```
<!-- Silverlight Control -->
<div id="silverlightControlHost" style="position:relative; height:480px;
width:640px;">

    <object data="data:application/x-silverlight-2," type="application/x-
silverlight-2"
```

```
            width="100%" height="100%">
            <param name="source" value="<%=  Microsoft.SharePoint.SPContext.
Current.Web.Url
%>/_catalogs/masterpage/ClientBin/SLGridCustomWebPartPackage/SLGrid.xap" />
            <param name="onError" value="onSilverlightError" />
            <param name="background" value="white" />
            <param name="minRuntimeVersion" value="4.0.50401.0" />
            <param name="autoUpgrade" value="true" />
            <param name="initParams" value="MS.SP.url=<%=
Microsoft.SharePoint.Utilities.SPHttpUtility.HtmlEncode(Microsoft.SharePoint.SP
Context.Current.Web.Url) %>" />
            <a href="http://go.microsoft.com/fwlink/?LinkID=149156&v=4.0.50401.0"
style="text-decoration: none">
                <img src="http://go.microsoft.com/fwlink/?LinkId=161376" alt="Get
Microsoft Silverlight"
                    style="border-style: none" />
            </a>
        </object>
        <iframe id="_sl_historyFrame" style="visibility: hidden; height: 0px;
width: 0px;border: 0px"></iframe>
</div>
```

You could run the project at this point. There is nothing more you need to do to deploy this to SharePoint. But let's take a look at one more advantage of using the custom Silverlight Web Part by extending the application to interact with the user control hosting the Silverlight application. Open the Visual Web Part in the Visual Studio Code Editor and add the following div tag below the closing script tag and above the Silverlight object tag:

```
<div id="SLDiv"></div>
```

This div tag could really go anywhere on the page. In this example it appears above the Silverlight application within the web part. Next you need to add some code to the SLGrid application's MainPage.xaml.cs file to populate this div tag with the currently selected user. In the Loaded event of the MainPage, add the code to handle the selection changed event of the data grid as shown in Listing 5.8.

LISTING 5.8: MainPage_Loaded Event

```
void MainPage_Loaded(object sender, RoutedEventArgs e)
{
    clientContext = ClientContext.Current;
    listDataGrid.SelectionChanged +=
```

```
    new listDataGrid_SelectionChanged;
RefreshData();
}
```

The selection changed event handler retrieves the current list item from the data grid. Note that because we are using data binding with the client object model, the list item is an actual SharePoint List Item object. Extract the FullName field from the list item and call the SetSLDiv() function. Set-SlDiv() uses the Silverlight HTML Bridge to get a reference to the SLDiv tag that you added to the user control. When you have a reference to the div tag, you can set the innerhtml property with the FullName of the list item, and you could even set other values such as the style properties. Add the code in Listing 5.9 to the MainPage.xaml.cs file in theSilverlight application SLGrid.

LISTING 5.9: Displaying SharePoint ListItem Properties in a Div Tag

```
void listDataGrid_SelectionChanged(
    object sender, SelectionChangedEventArgs e)
{
    ListItem selectedListItem =
        (ListItem)listDataGrid.SelectedItem;
    string fullName = "No Selected Item";
    if(selectedListItem != null)
        fullName =
            selectedListItem["FullName"].ToString();
    SetSLDiv(string.Format("<h1>{0}</h1>", fullName));
}

private void SetSLDiv(string InnerHTML)
{
    HtmlElement SLDiv =
        HtmlPage.Document.GetElementById("SLDiv");
    if (SLDiv != null)
    {
        SLDiv.SetProperty("innerhtml", InnerHTML);
        SLDiv.SetStyleAttribute("color", "blue");
    }
}
```

Run the project by pressing F5, which compiles both the Silverlight project and the SharePoint project. It packages the SharePoint project, adding a copy of the Silverlight .xap file to the package. F5 also deploys the package to the SharePoint sandboxed Solution Gallery, activates the solution, launches Internet Explorer, and attaches the Visual Studio debugger. You can see in Figure 5.14 that Bob is selected in the Silverlight grid, that `div` tag has been set with his full name, and the color has been set to blue.

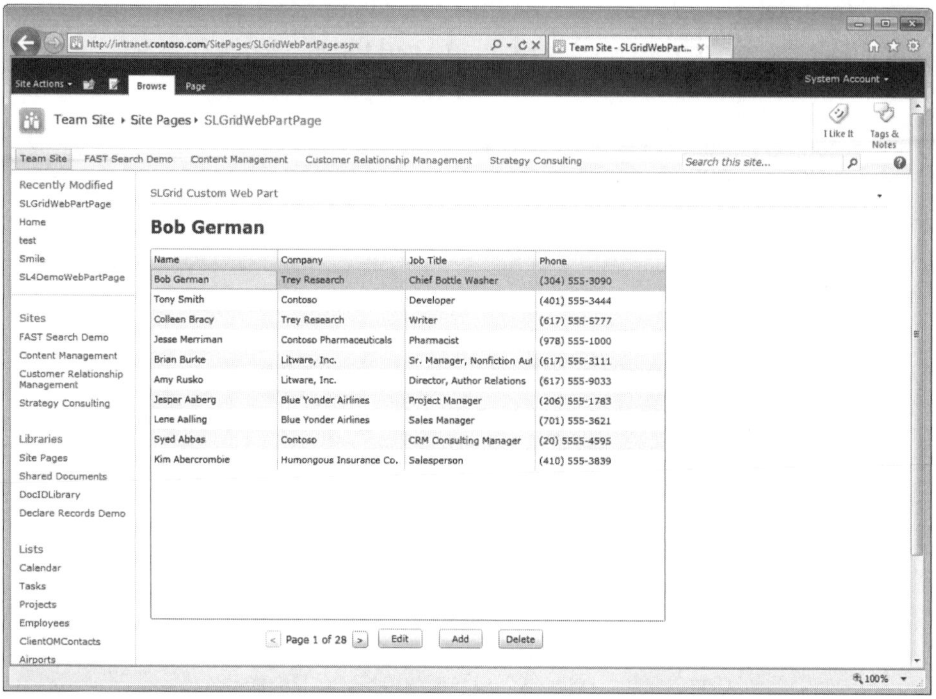

FIGURE 5.14: Silverlight interacting with HTML

The custom Silverlight Web Part is as easy to use as the built-in Silverlight Web Part and opens up a number of new scenarios.

Connecting Web Parts

A cool feature of SharePoint web parts is the ability to connect them together. This allows business users to compose their own mash-ups and dashboards of related information. For example, a master/detail display could allow users to select an item in one web part and then see details and related information in other web parts on the page. The only thing is that SharePoint's web part connections run on the server, so a page refresh is required to update the connected web parts.

In this section, you will learn to build Silverlight web parts that can be connected, but since Silverlight runs on the client, the update will be immediate with no need for a page refresh. The strategy to do this is to use a SharePoint server-side web part connection to broker a direct Silverlight connection on the web page. Figure 5.15 shows the web parts in the ConnectedWebParts sample in the code download. When the web parts are connected, anything that's typed into the source web part also appears in one or more connected target web parts.

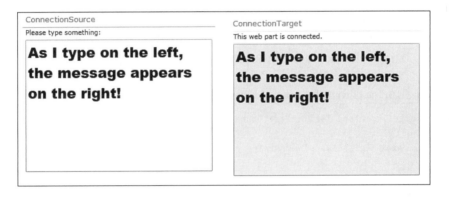

FIGURE 5.15: Connected web parts

You can try this on your development machine if you place the two web parts on the page. Edit either web part; then pull down the same drop-down next to the web part title you used to edit the web part. This time, a Connections choice appears to let you connect the web parts as shown in Figure 5.16.

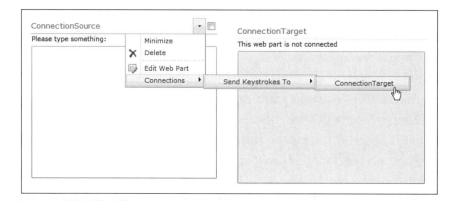

FIGURE 5.16: Connecting SharePoint web parts

Fortunately, SharePoint allows developers to create any kind of connection they like. In this case the connection is called ISilverlightConnection, and it defines a simple registration method for web parts that wish to connect. Listing 5.10 shows the interface.

LISTING 5.10: The ISilverlightConnection Interface

```
public interface ISilverlightConnection
{
    void RegisterReceiver(string receiverName);
}
```

The ConnectionSource Web Part implements the ISilverlight Connection, and ConnectionTarget consumes it. The strategy is for each ConnectionTarget to register a unique receiver name by calling the RegisterReceiver() method in the source. Both web parts then pass the receiver name to their corresponding Silverlight applications, which can then use Silverlight's messaging API to send messages. The ConnectionSource web part is capable of handling several receiver names if multiple target web parts are connected; go ahead and try this if you like. This is shown in Figure 5.17.

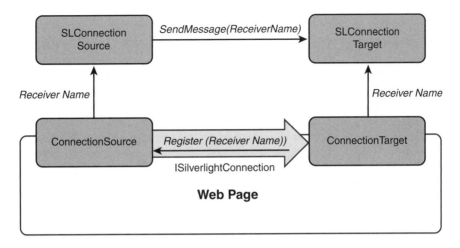

FIGURE 5.17: Brokering Silverlight communication with a server-side connection

Using Silverlight in Composite Controls

The sad truth is that sandboxed solutions don't allow web part connections, and the Silverlight SharePoint Web Parts used earlier in this chapter use a sandboxed solution. To handle this, the web parts are written from scratch. A Visual Web Part would work, but this is a good opportunity to show you how to use Silverlight in composite controls, as explained in Chapter 2, "Introduction to SharePoint Development." These concepts are used in other web parts later in the book as well as in editor parts, where a visual solution is not available. It's also used in a navigation control in Chapter 13, "Creating Silverlight Navigation," and a field control in Chapter 15, "Creating a Silverlight Field Control," where, again, a composite control is the only option.

Beginning with a farm solution, each web part was added as a simple, nonvisual web part. As you recall from Chapter 2, instead of using a design surface containing ASP.NET controls and HTML, child controls are added in code by overriding a method called `CreateChildControls()`.

To facilitate placing Silverlight on the page, a new SilverlightPlugin web control has been provided in the code download. It contains the same Javascript error handler and `<object>` tag as the standard Silverlight test page, which you might have noticed in the Custom Silverlight Visual Web Part. This time they're in string constants that contain tokens such as {0}

and {1} that hold values for the source, InitParams, and other properties.
CreateChildControls() fills in the tokens and adds both the Javascript and
<object> tag to the page, as shown in Listing 5.11.

LISTING 5.11: CreateChildControls() in the SilverlightPlugin Control

```
private const string SILVERLIGHT_EXCEPTION_SCRIPT_BLOCK = @"
    <script type=""text/javascript"">
    function {0}Error (sender, args) {{

    // Boilerplate error handler goes here, same as in any Silverlight
    // web page. The full code is in the code download.

    </script>";

private const string SILVERLIGHT_OBJECT_TAG = @"
  <div style=""overflow-x: hidden; position:relative; width:{0};
      height:{1};"">
    <object data=""data:application/x-silverlight-2,""
      type=""application/x-silverlight-2"" width=""{0}"" height=""{1}"">
      <param name=""source"" value=""{2}""/>
      <param name=""onError"" value=""{3}Error"" />
      <param name=""background"" value=""white"" />
      <param name=""minRuntimeVersion"" value=""4.0.50401.0"" />
      <param name=""initparams"" value=""{4}"" />
      <param name=""autoUpgrade"" value=""true"" />
       <!-- Rendering for browsers without Silverlight follows -->
       <!-- The code download contains the full code for this →
    </object>
    <iframe id=""_sl_historyFrame""
      style=""visibility:hidden;height:0px;width:0px;border:0px"">
    </iframe>
  </div>";

protected override void CreateChildControls()
{
    base.CreateChildControls();

    if (Source != null && Source != "")
    {
        // Ensure we have set the height and width
        string width = (this.Width == Unit.Empty)
                            ? "100%" : this.Width.ToString();
        string height = (this.Height == Unit.Empty)
                            ? "100%" : this.Height.ToString();

        // Render error handling script
        this.Controls.Add(new LiteralControl(
```

```
      String.Format(SILVERLIGHT_EXCEPTION_SCRIPT_BLOCK,
          this.ClientID)));

      this.Controls.Add(new LiteralControl(
      String.Format(SILVERLIGHT_OBJECT_TAG, width, height, this.Source,
          this.ClientID, this.InitParameters)));
  }
}
```

It's important to ensure the `Height` and `Width` properties are set on the Silverlight `<object>` tag, as they both default to zero. Leaving them out will result in a 0x0 pixel Silverlight application that won't show on the page at all.

It would be typical to add Javascript to the page by calling `Page.RegisterClientScriptBlock()`, but this would preclude using the `SilverlightPlugin` control in sandboxed solutions in the future because the sandbox does not allow access to the `Page` object. Instead, the web part's `clientID` property, which is guaranteed to be unique on the page, is used to make the error handler's method name unique, and the script is generated inline, as in the Silverlight Custom Visual Web Part.

The `SilverlightPlugin` control shows up in other solutions later in this book in standard (nonvisual) web parts as well as editor parts and navigation and field controls. It makes writing composite controls with Silverlight easy and encapsulates the details about placing Silverlight on the page.

Making the Connection

Listing 5.10 shows the `ISilverlightConnection` interface used to connect the web parts in this example. The *provider* (ConnectionSource) web part implements the interface, and the *consumer* (ConnectionTarget) web part makes use of the interface. In SharePoint the connection provider always implements the interface; in this case, the consumer calls the provider's `RegisterReceiver()` method, but event handlers are often used to allow information to flow from provider to consumer.

Listing 5.12 shows the ConnectionSource web part. The `[ConnectionProvider]` attribute tells SharePoint that the connection is available, and the `ConnectionInterface()` method hands SharePoint an object that implements the `ISilverlightConnection` interface. Because this web part only supports one kind of connection, the easiest approach is for the web part itself to implement the interface and pass itself back in this method. If you ever want to implement more than one kind of connection provider in a single web part, you'll find yourself having to implement a separate class for each interface and manage them in your web part.

LISTING 5.12: ConnectionSource Web Part Implements a Connection Provider

```
public class ConnectionSource : WebPart, ISilverlightConnection
{
    // Register with SharePoint as a connection provider
    // The provider name will appear in the connection message, as
    // in, "Send Keystrokes To"
    [ConnectionProvider("Keystrokes")]
    public ISilverlightConnection ConnectionInterface()
    {
        return this;
    }

    // ISilverlightConnection members
    void ISilverlightConnection.RegisterReceiver(string receiverName)
    {
        EnsureChildControls();

        if (silverlightPlugin.InitParameters == null ||
            silverlightPlugin.InitParameters == "")
        {
            silverlightPlugin.InitParameters = "SendOn=" + receiverName;
        }
        else
        {
            silverlightPlugin.InitParameters += ";" + receiverName;
        }
    }

    private SilverlightPlugin silverlightPlugin;
    protected override void CreateChildControls()
    {
        base.CreateChildControls();

        silverlightPlugin = new SilverlightPlugin();
        silverlightPlugin.Source = SPContext.Current.Site.Url +
            "/ClientBin/SLConnectionSource.xap";

        this.Controls.Add(silverlightPlugin);
    }
}
```

The RegisterReceiver() method begins by calling EnsureChildControls(), which is a method in all ASP.NET controls that checks to see if CreateChildControls() has been called and calls it if it wasn't. That way, the code that follows can be sure that the SilverlightPlugin control has been created.

The code passes the receiver name to its Silverlight application using its InitParam property. This is standard operating procedure in Silverlight: If you want to pass one or more values to Silverlight, place them in the InitParam property in the format name1=value1, name2=value2 and the Silverlight application is presented with a dictionary object containing the name-value pairs in its application startup event. In later chapters you learn how to pass more complex data in a hidden form field on the web page and to pass a reference to the form field in InitParam; for now the receiver name(s) can go in directly. The code uses the convention of a semicolon to separate receiver names, so as more target web parts register themselves the receiver names are simply appended to the InitParam value.

Listing 5.13 shows the ConnectionTarget web part, which registers as a connection consumer. Instead of implementing a method decorated with the [ConnectionProvider] attribute, this web part includes a [ConnectionConsumer] attributed method. As you can see, it uses its own client ID, which is sure to be unique and HTML-safe, as the receiver name, and it registers with the provider and also passes the same ID to its Silverlight application.

LISTING 5.13: ConnectionTarget Web Part Implements a Connection Consumer

```
public class ConnectionTarget : WebPart
{
    // Register with SharePoint as a connection consumer
    // The consumer name will appear in the connection message, as
    // in, "Get Keystrokes From"
    [ConnectionConsumer("Keystrokes")]
    public void GetConnectionInterface
        (ISilverlightConnection providerPart)
    {
        providerPart.RegisterReceiver(this.ClientID);
        EnsureChildControls();
        silverlightPlugin.InitParameters = "ReceiveOn=" +
            this.ClientID;
    }
```

```
SilverlightPlugin silverlightPlugin;

protected override void CreateChildControls()
{
    base.CreateChildControls();

    silverlightPlugin = new SilverlightPlugin();
    silverlightPlugin.Source = SPContext.Current.Site.Url +
        "/ClientBin/SLConnectionTarget.xap";

    this.Controls.Add(silverlightPlugin);
}
}
```

Now both the source and target Silverlight applications have the receiver name, so they can communicate directly on the client. Listing 5.14 shows the `Application_Startup` event in the SLConnectionTarget application; as you can see it simply retrieves the list of receiver names from `Init-Params` and passes them to the main page by setting a public property.

LISTING 5.14 : The Application_Startup Event Passes InitParams to Main Page

```
private void Application_Startup(object sender, StartupEventArgs e)
    {
        MainPage page = new MainPage();
        this.RootVisual = page;

        if (e.InitParams.ContainsKey("SendOn"))
        {
            page.SendOnConnectionNames = e.InitParams["SendOn"];
        }
    }
```

The main page is extremely simple. It consists of a textbox, whose `KeyUp` event is hooked as shown in Listing 5.15. Each time the event fires, the content of the text box is sent to all receivers.

LISTING 5.15: SLConnectionSource Sends Information on the KeyUp Event

```
internal string SendOnConnectionNames { get; set; }

private void messageTextBox_KeyUp(object sender, KeyEventArgs e)
{
    foreach (string receiverName in SendOnConnectionNames.Split(';'))
    {
```

```
        LocalMessageSender msgSender =
            new LocalMessageSender(receiverName);
        msgSender.SendAsync(messageTextBox.Text);
    }
}
```

The SLConnectionTarget Silverlight application's job is to listen on its receiver and display messages sent to it in a text box. It uses the same Application_Startup code to pass in the receiver name, but instead of sending the main page, it receives as shown in Listing 5.16.

LISTING 5.16: SLConnectionTarget Receives and Displays Text

```
LocalMessageReceiver msgReceiver;

internal void SetupReceiver(string receiverName)
{
    msgReceiver = new LocalMessageReceiver(receiverName);

    msgReceiver.MessageReceived += (s, e) =>
        {
            Dispatcher.BeginInvoke(() =>
                {
                    this.messageTextBox.Text = e.Message;
                });
        };

    msgReceiver.Listen();
    this.StatusTextBlock.Text = "This web part is connected.";
}
```

The MessageReceived event handler is called whenever a new message is received and is implemented as an anonymous function as discussed in Chapter 3. In Silverlight, the user interface always needs to be updated on the UI thread, so a second anonymous function is passed Dispatcher.BeginInvoke(), which runs it on the UI thread. Anonymous functions are a big help with all the asynchronous activity in a Silverlight application.

The last thing to do is to listen on the event, by calling the Listen() method. Now any time a user types into the ConnectionSource web part, all connected ConnectionTargets are updated immediately with every key stroke.

Summary

In this chapter you have seen how to manually create Silverlight Web Parts that can host a Silverlight application in SharePoint. Creating the web parts manually is a little tedious and not very straight forward for beginners. This was the reason the Silverlight Web Part extension was created. The Silverlight Web Part extension automates all of the steps required to create Silverlight Web Parts. The extension also gives you the flexibility to use either the built-in Silverlight Web Part or use a sandboxed Visual Web Part.

You learned about some of the limitations of the built-in web part. You also saw how you could extend the Visual Web Part by interacting with the HTML tags in the web part. All of these options should be used in ways that make the most sense for your particular solution. The Silverlight Web Part extension helps you jump start your Silverlight Web Part projects and reduces the steps to get Silverlight running in SharePoint.

You've also learned how to connect web parts so you can show master-detail relationships, dashboards, and mash-ups. In the process, you also learned how to manually put Silverlight in a web control, which is helpful when writing navigation controls, field controls, and editor parts.

6

Expression Blend, Data Binding, and Sample Data

EXPRESSION BLEND IS AN INTEGRATED development environment for designers who want to create Windows Presentation Foundation (WPF), Silverlight, and Windows Phone applications. In this case think of IDE as Interactive Design Environment. Blend's power comes from the rich declarative designers that allow developers to build entire applications without writing any code. Using just XAML and other components, designers can build visually stunning applications. Then designers can wire up functionality declaratively using Behaviors. Later in this chapter you learn how to use Behaviors and how to create your own custom Behaviors. As amazing as Blend is for designers, the real power of Blend comes from the integration with Visual Studio and developers. Expression Blend and Visual Studio work hand-in-hand to seamlessly integrate designing and developing. You see later in this chapter how designers and developers can work together to create SharePoint applications. You also see that designers can create a great design without any knowledge of SharePoint, and the developers can create great looking SharePoint applications without knowing anything about design or graphic arts. This lets each discipline focus on its core strengths.

SketchFlow is a feature of Blend that you use to rapidly create interactive prototypes. In this chapter you walk through the process of creating a prototype from beginning to end using SketchFlow. You also learn how to publish your prototypes to SharePoint and leverage SharePoint data using the Client Object Model and data binding. Let's get started by understanding Behaviors in Expression Blend, which are the glue that designers use to add interactivity.

Behaviors

Behaviors in Silverlight provide a way to componentize a unit of functionality that can be attached to various user interface objects at design time and runtime. Behaviors also provide for a design-time tool experience in Expression Blend. This further allows the separation of design and code to occur. Developers can create new Behaviors that can be consumed by designers without writing any code. In Blend Behaviors appear in the Asset Gallery just as any other control that you can drag onto the design surface or the Objects and Timeline panel.

Let's get started with a simple example of Behaviors in action. Open a new Silverlight application in Blend and add a button to the design surface. Open the Assets panel and click the Behaviors item on the left to filter by showing only the Behaviors. On the left in Figure 6.1, you can see a count of the number of Behaviors that Blend sees, and in the right pane you see a list of the Behaviors. Hovering over an item displays a Tooltip with the description, class name, namespace, and assembly.

FIGURE 6.1: Behaviors in Asset Gallery

Click and drag the `PlaySoundAction` onto the button on the design surface, or you can drop the Behavior onto the visual tree in the objects and timeline panel. When you have the Behavior attached to the button control, you can set the properties. In this case the only important one is the source property under the common properties group. Set this to the path of a Silverlight audio file (*.mp3, *.mp4, *.asf, *.asx, *.wma, *.wmv). You can find some sample audio files in the Expression Blend Samples directory at C:\Program Files (x86)\Microsoft Expression\Blend 4\Samples\en. Copy the start.mp3 file from the BeeHive.zip sample. Press F5 to run the project. Click the button to hear the start.mp3 sound play. Close the application and return to Blend. You can also specify the trigger that causes the Behavior to start. By default, for a button it is the click event, but you can see a list of all of the events in the Event Name drop-down property under the Triggers group. There are many events aside from the common ones such as Mouse Enter and Mouse Leave or the Left and Right Button down, you have other ones such as drag events and binding events.

Let's take a look at one simple example. This time you add a Behavior to drag the canvas around the screen. A Canvas element is a container that can contain other XAML elements. Start by grouping your button into a new canvas. Right-click your button, choose Group Into from the context menu, and then select Canvas. This creates a new canvas and adds all of the selected objects onto the canvas, in this case your button. By default the canvas is sized to fit the selected objects; resize the canvas a little to make it easier to grab and drag. Next you need to attach a Behavior to the new canvas. Open the Assets Gallery again and from the Behaviors filter drag the MouseDragElementBehavior onto the new canvas that you just created. Select the MouseDragElementBehavior object in the Objects and Timeline panel. Notice how there is no trigger to set. This is because this Behavior is based on the Behavior<T> class, which does not let you change the trigger or target. To make the drag operation stand out a little more, change the background color of the LayoutRoot canvas to Red, as shown in Figure 6.2. Press F5 to build and run your application. You hear that the sound still plays when you click the button, and now you can click and drag the surface of the application.

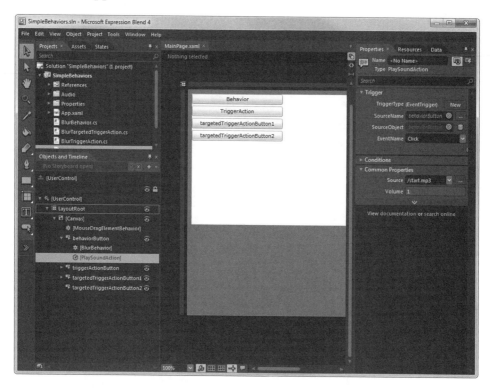

FIGURE 6.2: Expression Blend Behaviors

As a designer you can see how easy it is to add interactivity to your designs without needing to write any code. And as a developer you can create Behaviors for your designers, and you can use existing Behaviors yourself. This reduces your testing and debugging because you can reuse already tested and working code, thus reducing the amount of code you must write.

Building Your Own Behaviors

There are three types of Behaviors—`Behavior<T>`, `TriggerAction<T>`, and `TargetedTriggerAction`. Behaviors are attached to objects in Blend and provide a declarative way to add functionality. If you are familiar with Triggers and Actions in WPF or previous versions of Silverlight, you can think of Behaviors as encapsulating these two concepts.

Behavior‹T›

The first type of Behavior is the `Behavior<T>` class. This type of Behavior acts on the object it is attached to. This Behavior does not have a trigger or target associated with it. The Behavior is responsible for attaching to the events that it is concerned about. As you saw earlier, the `MouseDragBehavior` is a good example. The `MouseDragBehavior` has no triggers; it just attaches to the drag and drop events to work seamlessly in the background as expected.

Let's look at a simple Behavior to blur the attached object when you mouse over the object. To create a blur Behavior, add a new class to your project called `BlurBehavior` using Visual Studio. Your `BlurBehavior` must derive from `System.Windows.Interactivity.Bahavior`. Next you must override the `OnAttached` and `OnDetaching` methods. These methods are where you hook and unhook any events you want to handle in your Behavior. In the case of the `BlurBehavior` example, you want to handle the `MouseEnter` and `MouseLeave` events. When the mouse events fire, you can set the `Effects` property of the `AssociatedObject`. The `AssociatedObject` is a property on the base class that is set to a reference to the object that the Behavior was attached to.

Replace the code from Listing 6.1 in your `BlurBehavior` class to see it in action.

LISTING 6.1: Code for a Custom Blur Behavior

```csharp
using System;
using System.Net;
using System.Windows;
using System.Windows.Controls;
using System.Windows.Documents;
using System.Windows.Ink;
using System.Windows.Input;
using System.Windows.Media;
using System.Windows.Media.Animation;
using System.Windows.Shapes;

using System.Windows.Interactivity;
using System.Windows.Media.Effects;
using System.ComponentModel;

namespace SimpleBehaviors
{

    [Description("This is my Blur Behavior")]
    public class BlurBehavior : Behavior<FrameworkElement>
    {
        BlurEffect blur = new BlurEffect();

        public BlurBehavior()
            : base()
        {
            //set the default blur
            BlurRadius = blur.Radius;
        }

        protected override void OnAttached()
        {
            base.OnAttached();

            AssociatedObject.MouseEnter += AssociatedObject_MouseEnter;
            AssociatedObject.MouseLeave += AssociatedObject_MouseLeave;
        }

        protected override void OnDetaching()
        {
            base.OnDetaching();

            AssociatedObject.MouseEnter -= AssociatedObject_MouseEnter;
            AssociatedObject.MouseLeave -= AssociatedObject_MouseLeave;
        }

        void AssociatedObject_MouseEnter(object sender, MouseEventArgs e)
```

```
    {
        blur.Radius = BlurRadius;
        AssociatedObject.Effect = AssociatedObject.Effect = blur;
    }

    void AssociatedObject_MouseLeave(object sender, MouseEventArgs e)
    {
        AssociatedObject.Effect = null;
    }

    // Property Panel code here

    }
}
```

When you have created your Behavior you should set the `Description` attribute on the class. The `Description` attribute is used by Expression Blend in the tool tip of the Behavior in the Asset Gallery. Compile the project and then open the project in Blend. You see you `BlurBehavior` in the Asset Gallery. To test the Behavior, add a button to the design surface. From the Asset Gallery drag the `BlurBehavior` onto the button you just created. You can press F5 to run the project; however, you will need the code in the next section as well for this to compile. You can see that hovering over the button causes it to blur with a radius of five pixels.

But what if you want to configure the Blur Radius? You can add properties to your Behaviors by using a `DependencyProperty`. Also be sure to add the `Description` attribute and the `Category` attribute. These are used by Blend in the properties panel on the right. If you do not specify a `Category` attribute for your properties, they appear in the category called Common Properties. Add the code from Listing 6.2 to the bottom of the `BlurBehavior` class.

LISTING 6.2: Dependency Property to Control the Blur Radius

```
// Property Panel
public static readonly DependencyProperty BlurRadiusProperty =
DependencyProperty.Register("BlurRadius", typeof(double), typeof(BlurBehavior),
null);

[Category("Blur Properties")]
[Description("Sets the Blur Radius of the Effect")]
public double BlurRadius
```

```
    {
        get
        {
            return (double)base.GetValue(BlurRadiusProperty);
        }
        set
        {
            base.SetValue(BlurRadiusProperty, value);
        }
    }
}
```

Now in Expression Blend when you select the `BlurBehavior` object that is attached to the button in the Objects and Timeline panel, you see a new property category and property on the right in the Property panel. Set the `BlurRadius` to 10 and run the application, as shown in Figure 6.3. You now see that the object is more blurry now that you increased the radius.

FIGURE 6.3: Custom Behavior properties

TriggerAction<T>

The `TriggerAction` Behavior is very similar to the `Behavior<T>` Behavior except that now it has a trigger associated to it. This means that the designer can declaratively set the trigger that fires this Behavior.

Let's create a `TriggerAction` Behavior that blurs the attached object when the trigger is hit. In Visual Studio add a class to your project called `BlurTriggerAction`. Your `BlurTriggerAction` must derive from `System.Windows.Interactivity.TriggerAction`. Next you must override the `OnAttached` and `OnDetaching` methods. Although you could attach to events here just as you did in the `BlurBehavior`, it is generally not a best practice to do so. The key to the `TriggerAction` Behavior is that when the trigger is hit, it calls the `Invoke` method. So you must override the `Invoke` method and put your implementation to blur the attached object here. Replace the code from Listing 6.3 in the `BlurTriggerAction` class.

LISTING 6.3: Custom Trigger Action

```csharp
using System;
using System.Net;
using System.Windows;
using System.Windows.Controls;
using System.Windows.Documents;
using System.Windows.Ink;
using System.Windows.Input;
using System.Windows.Media;
using System.Windows.Media.Animation;
using System.Windows.Shapes;

using System.Windows.Interactivity;
using System.Windows.Media.Effects;
using System.ComponentModel;

namespace SimpleBehaviors
{
    [Description("This is my Blur TriggerAction
Behavior"),Category("MyBehaviors")]
    public class BlurTriggerAction : TriggerAction<FrameworkElement>
    {
        BlurEffect blur = new BlurEffect();

        public BlurTriggerAction()
            : base()
        {
            //set the default blur
            BlurRadius = blur.Radius;
        }

        protected override void Invoke(object parameter)
        {
            AssociatedObject.Effect =
                AssociatedObject.Effect == null ?
                this.AssociatedObject.Effect = blur :
                this.AssociatedObject.Effect = null;
        }

        protected override void OnAttached()
        {
            base.OnAttached();
        }

        protected override void OnDetaching()
        {
            base.OnDetaching();
        }
```

```
// Property Panel
public static readonly DependencyProperty BlurRadiusProperty = Depen-
dencyProperty.Register("BlurRadius", typeof(double), typeof(BlurTriggerAction),
null);


[Category("Blur Properties")]
[Description("Sets the Blur Radius of the Effect")]
public double BlurRadius
{
    get
    {
        return (double)base.GetValue(BlurRadiusProperty);
    }
    set
    {
        base.SetValue(BlurRadiusProperty, value);
    }
}
    }
}
```

To test this Behavior, add a button to the design surface. From the Asset Gallery drag the `BlurTriggerAction` to the button. In the Properties pane, you can now set the Trigger event for the Behavior, as shown in Figure 6.4. In this example the Trigger is set to the click event of the button. When you run the application, clicking the button causes it to blur.

FIGURE 6.4: TriggerAction Behavior

TargetedTriggerAction

The `TargetedTriggerAction` is the same as the `TriggerAction` Behavior except that it adds the ability to specify a target. This target is the object the action occurs on; in this example it is the object that is blurred when the trigger is fired. A common scenario for this type of Behavior is to attach to a button to control an image or video so that when the button is clicked, the video plays.

Let's create a new `TargetedTriggerAction` Behavior to demonstrate this. In Visual Studio create a new class called `BlurTargetedTriggerAction`. This class must derive from the `System.Windows.Interactivity.TargetedTriggerAction`. The code in Listing 6.4 is nearly identical to the `BlurTriggerAction` Behavior that you created in the previous section. The major difference is that you now use the `Target` property to reference the object that you perform the action on.

In the other two Behavior types, you used `AssociatedObject` as the object to perform the action upon, but now the target is declaratively set and dynamic. You can also override the `OnTargetChanged` event that runs when the object being targeted changes.

LISTING 6.4: Targeted Trigger Action

```
using System;
using System.Net;
using System.Windows;
using System.Windows.Controls;
using System.Windows.Documents;
using System.Windows.Ink;
using System.Windows.Input;
using System.Windows.Media;
using System.Windows.Media.Animation;
using System.Windows.Shapes;

using System.Windows.Interactivity;
using System.Windows.Media.Effects;
using System.ComponentModel;

namespace SimpleBehaviors
{
    [Description("This is my Blur TriggerAction Behavior")]
    public class BlurTargetedTriggerAction : TargetedTriggerAction<Frame-
workElement>
    {
```

```csharp
        BlurEffect blur = new BlurEffect();


        public BlurTargetedTriggerAction()
            : base()
        {
            //set the default blur
            BlurRadius = blur.Radius;
        }

        protected override void Invoke(object parameter)
        {
            Target.Effect =
                Target.Effect == null ?
                Target.Effect = blur :
                Target.Effect = null;
        }

        protected override void OnTargetChanged(FrameworkElement oldTarget,
FrameworkElement newTarget)
        {
            base.OnTargetChanged(oldTarget, newTarget);
        }

        protected override void OnAttached()
        {
            base.OnAttached();
        }

        protected override void OnDetaching()
        {
            base.OnDetaching();
        }

        // Property Panel
        public static readonly DependencyProperty BlurRadiusProperty =
            DependencyProperty.Register(
                "BlurRadius", typeof(double),
                typeof(BlurTargetedTriggerAction),
                new PropertyMetadata(OnBlurChanged));


        [Category("Blur Properties")]
        [Description("Sets the Blur Radius of the Effect")]
        public double BlurRadius
        {
            get
            {
```

```
                return (double)base.GetValue(BlurRadiusProperty);
            }
            set
            {
                base.SetValue(BlurRadiusProperty, value);
            }
        }

        static private void OnBlurChanged(DependencyObject obj,
DependencyPropertyChangedEventArgs e)
        {
            System.Diagnostics.Debug.WriteLine(
                "BlurRadius property changed from {0} to {1}",
                    e.OldValue, e.NewValue);
        }

    }
}
```

To test this Behavior, add a button to the design surface. From the Asset Gallery drag the BlurTargetedTriggerAction to the button. In the Properties pane you can now set the TargetObject and TargetName properties for the Behavior, as shown in Figure 6.5. In this example the target is set to another button. When you run the application, clicking the button causes the targeted button to blur.

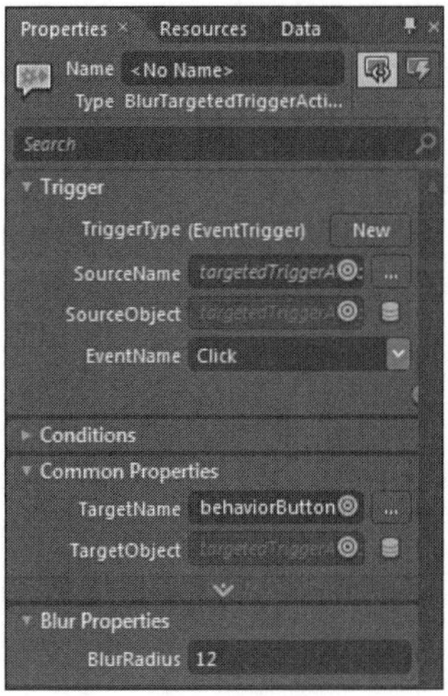

FIGURE 6.5: TargetedTriggerAction Behavior properties

One more interesting note about this example is setting the `typeMeta-Data` parameter of the `DependencyProperty`. This is the last parameter and can be null. But you can also provide a callback method here that is called when the property changes. You can see in the preceding example that an `OnBlurChanged` handler writes the old and new values to the debug window.

Another question that comes up next is how do you debug this? This event fires in design mode as the designer updates the property in Expression Blend. In the next section you see how you debug your Behaviors at both design time and run time.

Debugging Behaviors

Debugging Behaviors in Visual Studio is just like debugging other Silverlight code. Simply set a breakpoint on the line of code you wish to break on and press F5 in Visual Studio to build and attach the debugger. Visual Studio stops at the breakpoint when your Behavior runs.

A more useful tip is how to debug the Behavior as it is running in Expression Blend. When your project is open in Blend, it is actually running your code behind the scenes as you develop it. Sometimes you might wish to debug how the designer interacts with your Behavior during design time. To debug your Behavior in the designer, open the project in Visual Studio as well as Expression Blend. From Visual Studio open the Attach to Process dialog from the Debug menu. In the Attach to Process dialog, select the Blend process that is running your Behavior; normally there will be only one. When you are attached to the Blend process, you can switch back to Blend and exercise the Behavior, and Visual Studio stops on breakpoints just as it did when the project was running in the browser.

Behaviors are a very powerful feature of Silverlight and Expression Blend. They allow developers to create packages of functionality that designers can attach to objects in the designer. In this chapter you have only seen a small slice of what Behaviors can do. You can find more information and sample Behaviors on the Expression Gallery located here: http://gallery.expression.microsoft.com.

SketchFlow

SketchFlow is a part of Expression Blend that uses sketching to let you quickly go from an idea and rough sketches to a fully working prototype. It allows you to explore many different design ideas rapidly.

SketchFlow solves three basic issues that designers face with creating prototypes. The first problem is how to create rapid, dynamic, and interactive prototypes that are cheap to build and iterate. The second problem is how to communicate your design to key stakeholders. The third issue is how to gather feedback from users about the design.

Building a Prototype

Building a prototype allows all of the participants in a project to understand the design and intent of an application. So it is important to be able to create these prototypes as rapidly as possible. In the past you might have prototyped on whiteboards or the back of a napkin at a coffee shop. For many the next level is to capture the whiteboard with a camera and throw the images into a PowerPoint slide deck. This is a fast and easy way to get your design out to people, but with PowerPoint you can't navigate or interact with the design.

SketchFlow enables you to take a design to the next level by making it interactive. At its most basic level, creating a prototype in SketchFlow is as fast as doing it in PowerPoint with all of the benefits of Blend and Sketch-Flow, such as navigation, interaction, documentation, and user feedback.

The best way to understand the process is to start at the beginning and walk through to the completion of a prototype. SketchFlow allows you to pay as you go, so your prototype can evolve in the areas that you need to in order to communicate the design of the application. In this scenario you have an idea for a SharePoint application that allows you to browse and update a list of contacts. You get together with your design team in a conference room and design the application on the whiteboard. At the end of the meeting someone takes photos of screens on the whiteboard. You can find the sample whiteboard images used here in the download code for this chapter. It is also very common to start your prototyping directly in Blend with no prior screenshots or images like the ones in Figure 6.6.

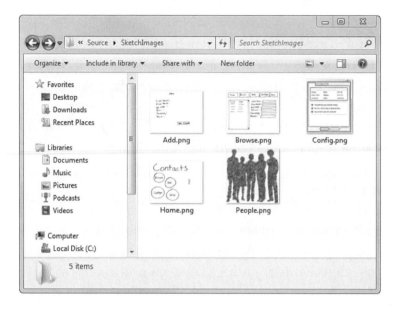

FIGURE 6.6: Whiteboard screens captured during design session

The next step that many do is throw these images into a PowerPoint slide deck and send them out to the team, as shown in Figure 6.7. As the applications grow in size and complexity, PowerPoint becomes less useful for communicating the design. It is also difficult in PowerPoint to understand the navigation of the application and get a feel for the animations and flow.

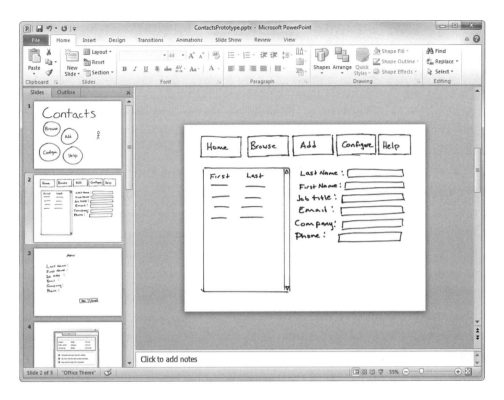

FIGURE 6.7: PowerPoint prototype

You are ready to create your SketchFlow prototype. In Blend create a new Silverlight SketchFlow Application project called ContactsPrototype. Blend creates two projects, ContactsPrototype and ContactsPrototype-Screens. The ContactsPrototypeScreens project is the one you will design the screens for that make up the application. The ContactsPrototype project is just the wrapper that wraps the screens with the SketchFlow player. The SketchFlow player is used to gather feedback from the users. You learn more about this in the next section. The screens project starts with one default screen called Screen 1. Every screen created in SketchFlow is backed by an .xaml file in the project; Screen 1 is backed by the file Screen_1.xaml. The screens project also contains a file called Sketch.Flow. The Sketch.Flow file is an .xml definition file for the SketchFlow designer. You don't need to worry about this file in any way as Blend takes care of updating it. The last file created in the default project is the SketchStyles.xaml file. This is a

Resource Dictionary containing all of the sketch styles that give your prototype the look of a hand-drawn sketch. This is actually a very important aspect to SketchFlow. Nothing is worse than going to a review meeting with a customer and spending the time explaining why the control is in that color or size. People see the sketched styles and can focus on the overall design of the application or its functionality and not on minor fit and finish design elements.

You must now transfer the design from the whiteboard session to SketchFlow. The first step is to lay out the screens and connect them together. Start by renaming Screen 1 to Home by double-clicking the blue square in the SketchFlow Map panel. Each node in the SketchFlow Map Panel represents a screen in your application. Think about these screens as whiteboards where you can sketch your designs. Connecting these nodes together allows you to model the flow and navigation of your application. Next create the Browse screen by dragging the Create a Connected Screen icon to a new location on the map, as shown in Figure 6.8. The screen menu appears when you hover over one of the screens on the map. The other options are to connect to an existing screen or create a component screen. You learn more about component screens in the next section. The last icon on the screen context menu is to change the visual tag. The visual tag simply means the background color of the screen in the map. The visual tags of screens by default are blue, and component screens are green. The other colors you can choose are yellow, orange, red, violet, gray, and white. The visual tags are helpful to group like screens together by color.

FIGURE 6.8: Create a connected screen

Continue creating the Browse, Add, Config, and Help screens using the same process. All of the screens should be connected to the Home screen. One good tip to keep in mind is that after you drag a new screen, you have the chance to name it. If you name the screen before clicking off it, then the backing .xaml file will have the same name. If you click off the screen or rename it later, the label and screen will be file out of sync. This is not really a big problem, but it makes it easier to understand if they match when you look at the project in the Projects panel or in Visual Studio. Your initial screen design should look something like what's shown in Figure 6.9.

FIGURE 6.9: Initial screen design

Now you have the initial screens created, but at this point they are just blank space for you to add the design to. As mentioned before, SketchFlow allows you to pay as you go so you can simply drag the images that you captured from the whiteboard design session onto the corresponding screens. Double-click each screen in the SketchFlow Map panel to open it on the art board. Drag the image file from Windows Explorer onto the screen and resize it to fit. This is easiest if you have a multi-monitor development setup, but if not, simply resize both the Blend and Explorer windows so you can drag and drop between them. The default screen resolution is 640x480, and the images are quite large. It might be faster to set the Width and Height properties in the Property panel to 640x480 and all of the Margin Properties to 0. When you have done this for all of the screens, your prototype is at the same stage as your PowerPoint Prototype. Unlike PowerPoint, the prototype is interactive, and the user can navigate between screens, as shown in Figure 6.10.

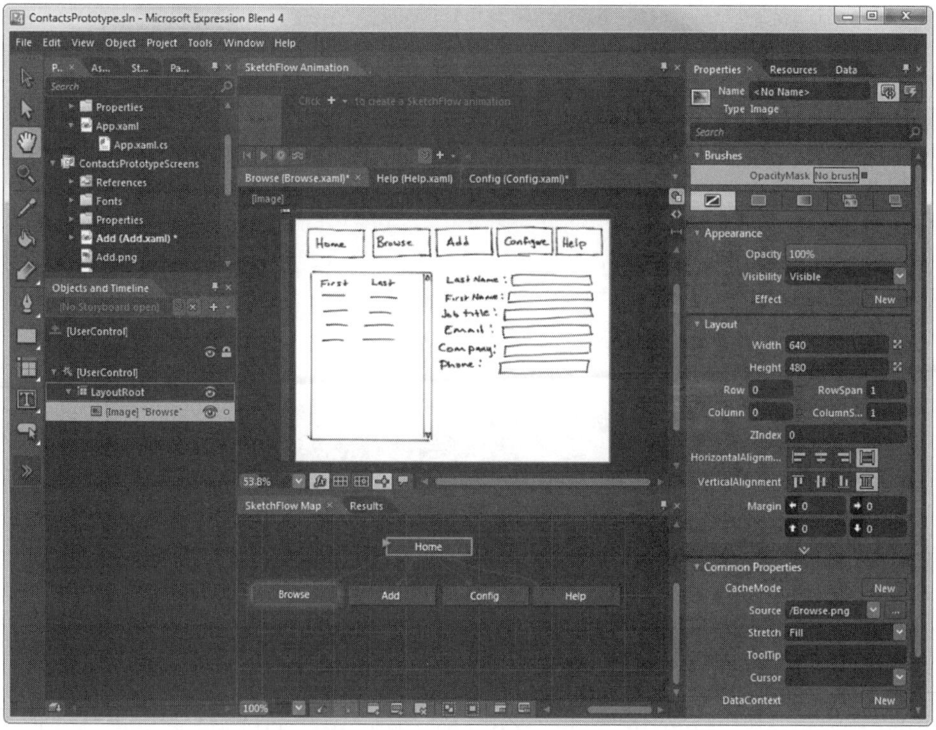

FIGURE 6.10: Completed Sketchflow navigation

SketchFlow Player

At this point you have only created the screens and connected them together. Your screen designs are just images of the whiteboard mock-ups. This might be the ending point for many of your prototypes; remember, the goal is to do just enough to convey the design and Behavior to stakeholders. Let's run the project to see the SketchFlow Player in action. Press F5 to launch your prototype. You can see the SketchFlow Player in Figure 6.11.

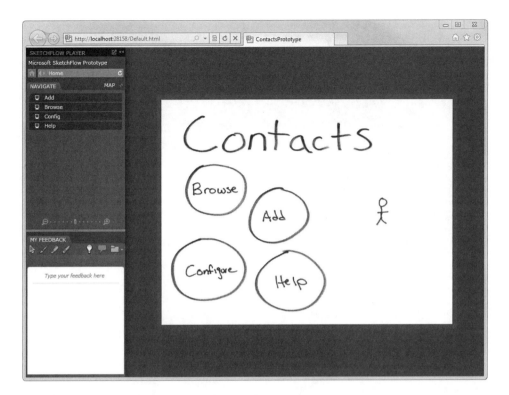

FIGURE 6.11: This the prototype running in the SketchFlow Player

Although you haven't added any interactivity yet, the SketchFlow Player allows you to jump to any screen from the Navigate panel. Above the Navigate panel is a Home button you can click to jump back to the Home screen where there is a navigation control that lets you navigate up and down the screen based on the connections you made on the Sketch-Flow map. The Map button toggles a SketchFlow map overlay view of the screens indicating which screen you are currently on, as shown in Figure 6.12. The Map view also allows you to navigate by clicking a screen in the map.

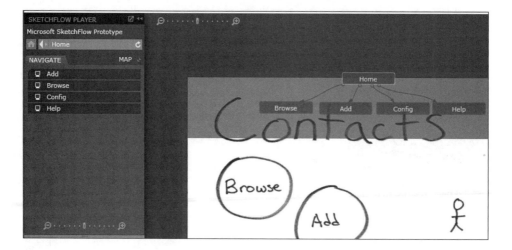

FIGURE 6.12: SketchFlow Player Map view

You learn about gathering feedback from the player in the next section. Let's continue on with the prototyping process to add additional functionality. Close the browser window and return to the Contacts Prototype in Blend.

There are many techniques you can use when building your prototypes in Blend. Though it is not possible to cover all aspects of prototyping in SketchFlow in the space allowed in this book, a few examples are discussed. The first thing you want to do is enable the buttons on the home page so that when you click a button, it navigates to another screen. This is a prototype, so you want to trade fast and good enough for complete. In this case you could create a round button that you would place on the screen, but this would take too long and deliver minimal value to understanding the design. Instead you can cheat a little and place a transparent button over the round button images on the home page. Open the Home screen and drag a button-Sketch control over the circle labeled Browse. You can use any control from Blend, but you want to try and use the sketch controls if possible. They are located in the Assets Gallery under the Styles-Sketch Styles category. Resize the button to cover the circle. It should look something like Figure 6.13.

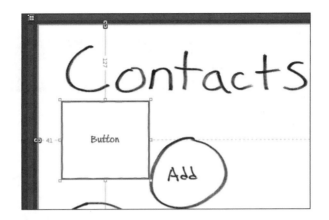

FIGURE 6.13: Create a Browse button

Set the Opacity property to 0% to hide the button. Next, you want to wire up the button's click event to navigate to the Browse screen. Right-click the button you just created and select Browse under the Navigate To context menu. Under the Navigate To context menu you have the option for Forward and Back and a list of the screens in the current map. Continue this process adding buttons to all of the circle buttons on the Home screen.

One last thing to do on the Home screen is to update the people image on the right. The stick man doesn't convey enough about the design intent here, so you want to update the image; not with a final image, but a little more detailed sketch. Drag an image into this space. You can use the People.png from the SketchImages folder in the Source for this chapter. When you are done, your Home screen should look something like what's shown in Figure 6.14. The buttons are at 30% opacity so that you would be able to see them in this screen shot, but you can make them totally invisible if you choose to.

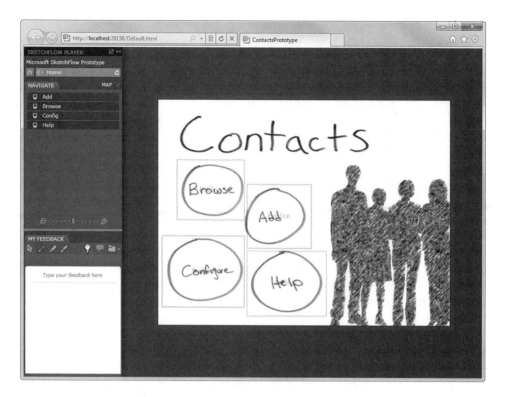

FIGURE 6.14: Completed Contacts Prototype Home screen

The user can now click the round buttons on the Home screen and navigate to the correct screen. This is starting to feel more like a real application already. Let's continue with some of the other screens.

If you still have the SketchFlow Player running, close it and return to Blend. Open the Help screen, which is blank. There were no whiteboard mock-ups made of this screen. This is a common occurrence when doing iterative designs. Maybe you thought of some new screens as you started to lay out the map, or maybe the screens are going to be designed in another phase of the project; whatever the reason, you should probably tell the user what is going on. To do this add a Note-Sketch control to the screen and enter some text in the note such as: "This Help Screen will be added in Phase 2," as shown in Figure 6.15.

FIGURE 6.15: Note to give the user more details about the Help screen

At this point you are done with the prototype. You see in the last section how to hook up the Browse screen with sample data from SharePoint and how to then hand the prototype to a developer to bind live SharePoint data to the prototype. But before that there are two more important features of SketchFlow prototyping—documenting the design and gathering feedback from the users.

Documenting the Design

When designing applications it is important to communicate and document the design. This allows everyone involved with the project to know what the current status is with the design. You also need a way to archive the design process so that you can go back and learn from the decisions that were made or understand what has already been tried. SketchFlow includes a feature to generate a design document using Microsoft Word.

Generate a Word design document by choosing Export to Microsoft Word from the File menu of Blend. In the Export to Word dialog, set the file name and location to save the document to, as shown in Figure 6.16. You can also choose to include feedback. You learn more about feedback in the next section. You can also choose to have the document opened when it is completed. The last option is to use a Word template. This only allows you to set the styles in Word; other regions of placeholders are ignored other than the headers and footers. Click OK to generate the design document.

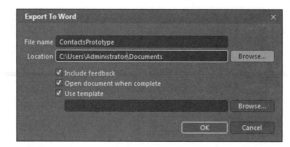

FIGURE 6.16: Create a design document in Word

When the document is generated, you have a nicely formatted Word document that contains an image of the SketchFlow map and all of the screens from your design are captured in the document. You can see an example of the generated Word document in Figure 6.17.

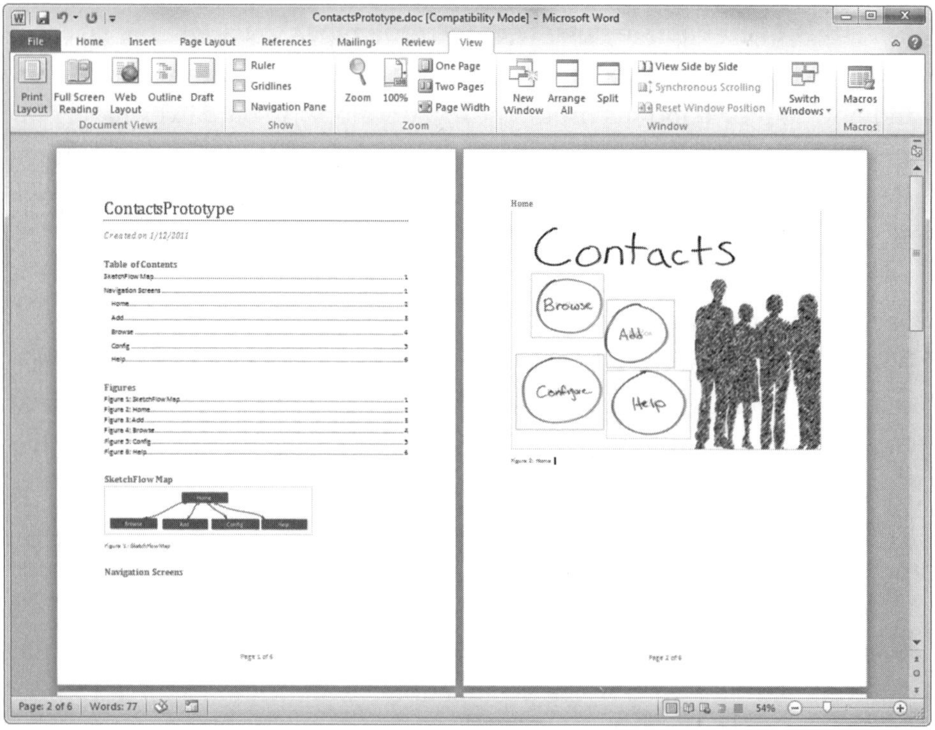

FIGURE 6.17: Generated design document

Feedback

The main goal of prototyping is to gather feedback from users and stake-holders. The SketchFlow Player gives users the ability to comment on each screen. Users can add or remove short notes in the bottom left of the Sketch-Flow Player for each screen. Users can also add ink annotations directly on the surface of each screen, as shown in Figure 6.18. There are eight colors to choose from and four pen sizes. The player also includes a highlighter tool, which is similar to the ink tool. The main difference between the ink and the highlight tools is that the highlighter draws using a semi-transparent ink, which enables you to see what is under the highlighted region.

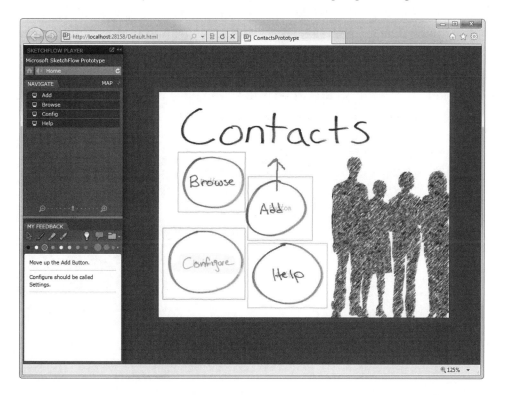

FIGURE 6.18: SketchFlow feedback

Exporting and Importing Feedback

After you have added all of your feedback to the prototype, you need to export it. Click the folder icon in the feedback panel of the Player and choose Export Feedback. You also have the option to clear your feedback if you need to start over or change your mind about the comments you added. If you click the Clear Feedback button, you are asked to confirm before it is actually cleared. Next in the Feedback Author Information dialog, enter your name and initials. This makes it easy to understand who made which comments when all of the feedback is aggregated together. In the Save As dialog, browse to the folder you wish to save the feedback file to and give it a name.

After you have exported your feedback, you can send this file to the designer. The designer can import all of feedback files they receive directly in Blend. To import the SketchFlow feedback you need to make the Sketch-Flow Feedback panel visible in Blend from the Window menu. In the SketchFlow Feedback panel, click on the plus icon to import a .feedback file. After the feedback file is imported, you can select the active feedback item in the panel, which shows you the comments and overlays any ink annotations directly on the art board. As you open other screens, the comments that appear are filtered to the active screen, as shown in Figure 6.19.

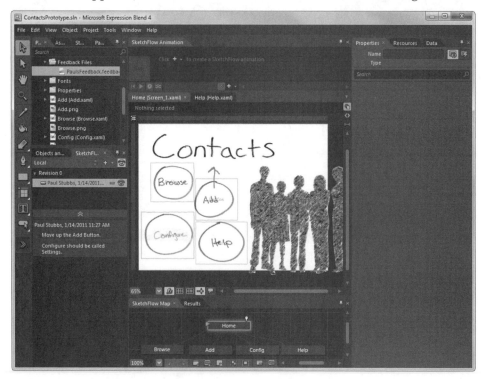

FIGURE 6.19: Feedback imported into Blend

Publishing to SharePoint

You have seen how easy it is to create and view a prototype and to gather feedback from users. But one of the new features of Expression Blend is the ability to publish prototypes directly to a SharePoint document library. Let's take a look at how the process changes when publishing to SharePoint.

There are two ways you can prepare your prototype so that users can view it. The first is from the File menu—choose Package SketchFlow Project. This creates a folder with the Silverlight .xap file and a default.aspx and a default.html test page. You can then send this to the user or put it on a file share for them to access or on an ASP.NET web site. The second and preferred way is to publish the prototype directly to a SharePoint library. Choose Publish to SharePoint from the File menu. In the Publish to SharePoint dialog, enter the URL to the document library and a name for the folder, as shown in Figure 6.20.

FIGURE 6.20: Publish to SharePoint dialog

After publishing is complete, you can run the prototype from the following URL, http://intranet.contoso.com/Shared Documents/ContactsPrototype/ContactsPrototype_v2/Default.aspx.

Notice that under the ContactsPrototype folder, there's a sub folder with the same name appended with a version number. Each time you publish to SharePoint, a new versioned folder is created. This makes it very easy to keep all of your design iterations organized. In the versioned folder you see the same files that you would see if you just packaged the SketchFlow project. Also under the versioned folder in SharePoint is a feedback folder. What is really cool about publishing to SharePoint is that the SketchFlow player is aware that it is running in SharePoint and saves the users' feedback directly on the SharePoint site in the feedback folder for each version.

Users and designers don't need to worry about how to export and import their feedback. In the SketchFlow Player there is a new feedback option to Upload to SharePoint. The user is asked for his name and initials just like before, but after that there are no other prompts. The feedback is saved automatically back in the SharePoint library. Another new feature that appears in the player when you publish to SharePoint is the Shared tab in the feedback section. The Shared tab displays all of the feedback files that have been submitted to SharePoint. This enables all of the users to collaborate on the feedback. In Figure 6.21 you can see that version 3 is published and there are comments from both version 2 and 3. Clicking the Revision 2 link takes you to that version of the prototype.

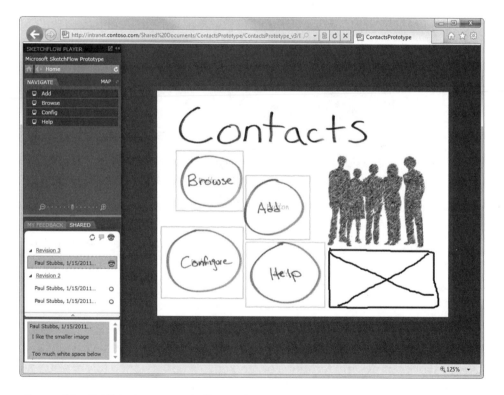

FIGURE 6.21: Published prototype in SharePoint

Design with Data

The prototype so far has progressed from static images to a more interactive model with navigation and controls. The next step of the prototype design is to add data to a few controls so that users can really get a good feel for how the application will behave. Blend includes a sample data feature that allows designers to design the application using a set of mocked up or random data as the data source without being connected to a live data source. This gives the designers the ability to design with data that closely represents what the real data will look like without needing to know anything about the final data source. For SharePoint applications this allows designers who might not know anything about SharePoint to create great interactive applications. And it allows SharePoint developers who might not know anything about cool designs to hook up those applications with very little effort. It allows large teams to divide the work and have the design and developer teams be loosely coupled.

Generating SharePoint Sample Data

Expression Blend has the ability to create its own random sample data. When developing applications for SharePoint, the data list already exists or is already defined. You want to generate a simple sample .xml file of that SharePoint list that you can give to your designers. In the source folder you will find a simple console application that uses the Client Object Model, which you learn more about in Chapter 8, "Accessing SharePoint Data with the Client Object Model," to generate a sample data file. Listing 6.5 contains the code to generate the sample data file. When the contacts list is returned from SharePoint it loops through the row items, generating the .xml file with the XMlTextWriter class. This code is generic and can be used on any SharePoint list. The code generates the correct field nodes for a given list. You only need to change the list name parameter in the GetByTitle method. You can also adjust the number of rows returned or create a completely new CAML query to return a very specific set of items.

LISTING 6.5: Code to Generate Sample Data

```
using System;
using System.Collections.Generic;
using System.Linq;
using System.Text;
using Microsoft.SharePoint.Client;
using System.Xml.Linq;
using System.Xml;


namespace GenerateSampleData
{
    class Program
    {
        static void Main(string[] args)
        {
            ClientContext context = new ClientContext
("http://intranet.contoso.com");
            ListItemCollection sampleListItems = default(ListItemCollection);
            List sampleList = context.Web.Lists.GetByTitle("Contacts");

            //Filter the items returned
            CamlQuery qry = new CamlQuery();
            qry.ViewXml = "<View><RowLimit>5</RowLimit></View>";
            sampleListItems = sampleList.GetItems(qry);

            //Call the SharePoint Server
            context.Load(sampleListItems);
            context.ExecuteQuery();

            XmlTextWriter writer =
                new XmlTextWriter("C:\\ContactsSampleData.xml", null);
            writer.Formatting = Formatting.Indented;

            //Write the root element
            writer.WriteStartElement("SharePointListItems");

            //Iterate through all of the rows
            foreach (ListItem item in sampleListItems)
            {
                //Write the ListItem element
                writer.WriteStartElement("ListItem");

                //iterate through the fields
                foreach (
                    KeyValuePair<string, object> fieldValue in
item.FieldValues)
                {
```

```
            writer.WriteElementString(
                fieldValue.Key,
                (fieldValue.Value ?? string.Empty).ToString());
        }

        // end the ListItem element
        writer.WriteEndElement();
    }

    // end the root element
    writer.WriteEndElement();

    //Write the XML to file and close the writer
    writer.Close();
        }
    }
}
```

Using Sample Data

When you have generated a sample .xml data file from SharePoint, you can add this file to your SketchFlow prototype. Open the Contacts Prototype project again in Blend. The first thing you need to do is import the sample data. From the Data tab, choose Import Sample Data from XML… under the sample data drive icon, as shown in Figure 6.22. The other data icon on the far right has a little line under it, which is meant to represent a network and is used to create a data source.

FIGURE 6.22: Import SharePoint Sample Data

In the Import Sample Data from XML dialog, you must enter a name for the sample data and a path to the sample data .xml file. The path to the sample data file can be a fully qualified path or an http URL, or even a relative path if you have included the .xml file in your project. In this example, name your data source Contacts to match the name of the SharePoint list; although naming them the same is not required, it makes it easier to remember where the data is coming from. You can also define the scope of the sample data. The default is to define in the project, which makes the sample data available to all screens in the prototype. The last option enables you to see the sample data even when the application is running. This is the option you want to start with because you have not connected it to Share-Point list data yet. Click OK to create the sample data source. Figure 6.23 shows the completed Import Sample Data from XML dialog.

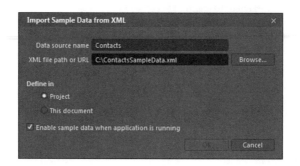

FIGURE 6.23: Import Sample Data from XML Dialog

Now that the sample data has been imported into the prototype, you are ready to add it to the application. In the example you create a master detail view on the Browse screen. Open the Browse screen so that it is visible on the art board. According to the screen image that was mocked up, you want to create a list box with the first and last names of each contact. With the sample data feature you can create a list box by selecting and dragging the fields onto the art board. Rename the list box to `ContactsListBox`. In the data panel on the right, expand the sample data tree to view the list of fields under the `ListItemCollection`. Select the `lastname` and the `title` fields; `title` is actually the first name. At the top of the data panel there are two icons on the left, List Mode and Details Mode. List Mode is the default and creates a list box on the screen. Details Mode creates individual fields for each field selected when you drag it to the art board.

First you want to create the list box, so verify that List Mode is selected and drag the `title` and `lastname` fields onto the art board. A list box is created displaying sample data values; resize the list box to cover the list box image of the mock-up and set the background color to white to hide the image underneath.

Next you want to add the details to the right of the list box you just created. Set the data panel to Details Mode and select the fields you want to see. In the mock-up, the designer wants to see firstname, lastname, jobTitle, email, company, and phone. Select all of those fields together and drag them onto the art board. Resize the detail fields to cover the details image of the mock-up and set the background of the grid they are grouped into to white. At this point reorder and play with the design of the fields so that they match the mock-up and look good to you. When you are done, you should have something that looks like what you see in Figure 6.24.

FIGURE 6.24: SharePoint sample data in the prototype

When you press F5 to run the prototype, you see that you have a fully functional master/detail form, and as you select items in the list box that the details change to match the selected item. You can also publish the new version to SharePoint as well. The sample data enables the designers to complete the prototype, knowing that the design will fit once it is connected to live data.

Databinding SketchFlow to SharePoint Data

The last part of developing the SketchFlow prototype is to actually hook it up to live SharePoint data. You can call SharePoint data in a number of different ways such as using web services, WCF Data services or the Client Object Model. All of these methods are discussed later in the book.

For this example you use the Client Object Model to retrieve a collection of Contact list items. Add the following code to the code behind for the Browse.xaml class. Skip to Chapter 8 to learn more about how to use the Client Object Model. You also need to add a reference to the Microsoft. SharePoint.Client.Silverlight.dll and the Microsoft. SharePoint.Client. Silverlight.Runtime.dll from the SharePoint root folder under \14\ TEMPLATE\LAYOUTS\ClientBin. The key to this code is to set the ItemsSource property of the list box to the contacts list item collection returned by the Client Object Model. The rest of the code in Listing 6.6 is just a standard Client Object Model call to return list items.

LISTING 6.6: Databinding SketchFlow to SharePoint Data

```
using System;
using System.Windows;
using System.Windows.Controls;
using System.Windows.Documents;
using System.Windows.Ink;
using System.Windows.Input;
using System.Windows.Media;
using System.Windows.Media.Animation;
using System.Windows.Shapes;

using Microsoft.SharePoint.Client;

namespace ContactsPrototypeScreens
{
    public partial class Browse : UserControl
    {
        ClientContext ctx;
        ListItemCollection contactsListItems;

        public Browse()
        {
            // Required to initialize variables
            InitializeComponent();
```

```
            //Get SharePoint List after page loads
            this.Loaded += ThisPage_Loaded;
        }

        void ThisPage_Loaded(object sender, RoutedEventArgs e)
        {
            //Get Client Context
            ctx = new ClientContext("http://intranet.contoso.com");

            if (ctx != null) //null if we are not in SharePoint
            {
                //Get Contacts from SharePoint
                List contactsList = ctx.Web.Lists.GetByTitle("Contacts");
                contactsListItems =
                    contactsList.GetItems(CamlQuery.CreateAllItemsQuery());

                ctx.Load(contactsListItems);
                ctx.ExecuteQueryAsync(ContactsLoaded, ContactsLoadedFail);
            }
        }

        //ContactsLoadedFail
        void ContactsLoadedFail(object sender, ClientRequestFailedEventArgs
args)
        {
            //TODO: Handle any Error;
        }

        //ContactsLoaded
        void ContactsLoaded(object sender, ClientRequestSucceededEventArgs
args)
        {
            //call back on the UI thread
            Deployment.Current.Dispatcher.BeginInvoke(
                delegate
                {
                    ContactsListBox.ItemsSource = contactsListItems;
                });
        }
    }
}
```

Databinding to Indexers

In the code behind you returned a list item collection and set the data source of the list box to the contactsListItems. But if you ran this, it would actually not work because the Client Object Model returns list item collections back as a collection of dictionary values. This means you need to change the data binding syntax of the XAML code to bind correctly to the dictionary objects. For example, when you drag the sample data onto the art board, Blend sets the Binding to just the name of the field to bind to:

```
<TextBlock Text="{Binding Title}">
```

A Dictionary collection is a known as an Indexer. This is because you can reference a specific item using an index value or key. Lists in SharePoint are very dynamic; designers can change the fields in a list very easily either in the browser or using SharePoint Designer. For the Client Object Model to handle the dynamic nature it returns the list results as a collection of field values. You need to change the binding syntax to handle this by setting the Path attribute. Change all of the bindings in the Browse.xaml file to use the indexer binding syntax like the following example.

```
<TextBlock Text="{Binding Path=FieldValues[Title]}">
```

When you have all of the bindings changed and have the code behind in place to load the Contacts list, you can publish the SketchFlow prototype to SharePoint. Figure 6.25 shows the sketch running in SharePoint with databinding.

In SharePoint, you can see all of the Contacts list items in the list box. Everything still works as before; as you select an item in the list box the details are displayed on the right.

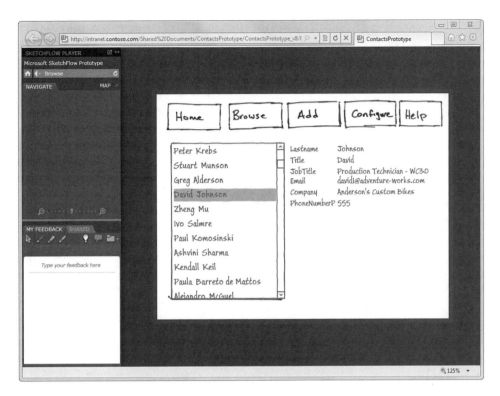

FIGURE 6.25: SketchFlow prototype with live SharePoint data

Summary

Expression Blend is a powerful tool for designers and developers to create rich Silverlight applications. Behaviors are key to allowing designers to create interactivity and animations declaratively without writing any code. Developers can easily create Behaviors in Visual Studio that are integrated into the Blend UI for designers to use. Another key to Blend is SketchFlow prototypes. Building prototypes that can be created rapidly adds interactivity and navigation as needed to communicate the intent of the design. SketchFlow also enables you to publish your prototypes to SharePoint, giving you a central location for versioning, documentation, and feedback.

7

Accessing SharePoint Using the HTML Bridge

S ILVERLIGHT IS DESIGNED to be hosted on web pages, and it's no sur-prise that developers would want a way for their Silverlight applica-tions to interact with the pages that host them. This is provided by the HTML Bridge, which connects a Silverlight application with the browser's HTML Document Object Model and Javascript. This chapter shows you how to optimize your solutions by passing information on the web page and accessing it via the HTML Bridge instead of making extra requests to the server. It also shows you how to call SharePoint's Javascript and JQuery from your Silverlight applications.

Passing Data to Silverlight with the HTML Bridge

Figure 7.1 shows a typical Silverlight application interacting on the net-work. It begins when a user clicks on a web page and the browser issues an HTTP Get request. On a good day, the server (in this case SharePoint) responds with a Get response containing some HTML to be rendered. What the diagram doesn't show is that the web browser will likely issue a flurry of additional Get requests for any number of images, style sheets, Javascript files, and other objects referenced in the HTML, unless they are already in the browser's cache. In this case, let's assume one of these objects is a Silverlight application (.xap) file, referenced in an <object> tag.

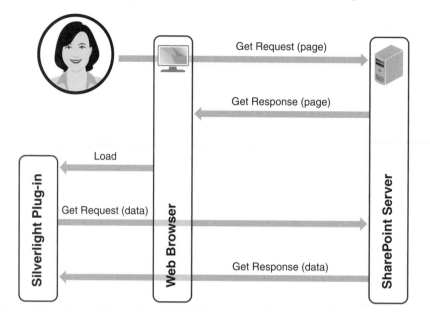

FIGURE 7.1: Typical Network Interaction in a Silverlight application

The browser loads the Silverlight application, and as soon as it starts running, it realizes that it needs some data to display. To get the data, it makes some sort of network request using the Client Object Model, RESTful services, or some other protocol and waits for a response. Assuming the needed data was already on the server when the web page was requested and we already knew what we'd need, this round trip is "wasted" because rather than passing a reference to the data on the web page, we could have just sent the data itself. It's not terrible, but it does add load to the web server and slows down the client experience. There is a better way!

This chapter proposes an alternative, depicted in Figure 7.2. The data needed by Silverlight is embedded in the web page, so the Silverlight application doesn't need to make another round trip to the server. This can noticeably speed up the user interface, especially when a page is loading and the browser is requesting a lot of other resources, and it certainly reduces load on the server. It's easy to pass data to your Silverlight application in a hidden field or even in the `InitParams` property of the Silverlight object tag.

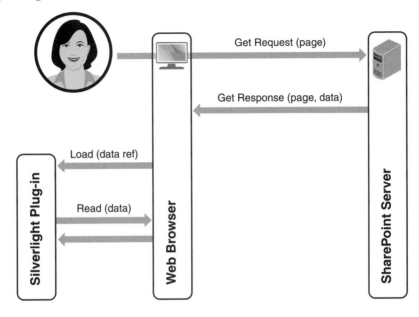

FIGURE 7.2: Piggybacking data on the SharePoint page

This technique isn't only useful for optimizing network traffic; there are situations where you really need to pass data on the web page because users expect the data to be processed when the page is posted back. An example of this is in the *editor part* later in this chapter. An editor part is a control that runs in the web part editing panel to allow users to configure some aspect of the web part. When editing a web part, users expect all their changes to be saved or cancelled when they press the OK, Apply, or Cancel buttons in the SharePoint UI. If a Silverlight application located in the web part editing panel were to use the client object model or a web service to update the settings as the user selects them, it would be too soon. Instead, the Silverlight application pushes its data into a hidden field on the page that is handled along with all the other fields during postback processing so all of the changes are saved or cancelled together.

Passing Data on the Web Page

Early on in this book, you learned a simple way to pass data to Silverlight using the InitParams parameter in the Silverlight <object> tag. This is indeed on the web page, and is a good start, but InitParams is really intended for passing a few values needed for application startup, specified as name/value pairs and accessed as a Dictionary object. For example, if InitParams is specified as

```
<param name="initparams" value="message=hello,urgency=normal" />
```

the application will be passed a Dictionary object containing two keys ("message" and "urgency") and their values ("hello" and "normal"). This can be accessed in the Application_Startup event as shown in Listing 7.1, which passes the information to the Silverlight user control in its (modified) constructor.

LISTING 7.1: Accessing InitParams from the Silverlight Application_Startup Method

```
private void Application_Startup(object sender, StartupEventArgs e)
{
    if (e.InitParams.ContainsKey("message") &&
        e.InitParams.ContainsKey("urgency"))
    {
        string message = e.InitParams["message"];
        string urgency = e.InitParms["urgency"];
        this.RootVisual = new MainPage(message, urgency);
    }
}
```

Although some developers have reported success passing large amounts of serialized data in InitParams, it's generally easier and more flexible to pass it in a hidden field on the page. Visible fields can also be used, and sometimes using a TextBox can be helpful during debugging.

Access to the field from Silverlight is provided by the Silverlight HTML Bridge. The Silverlight HTML Bridge provides dynamic access to the hosting web page, as well as access to and from Javascript functions and objects. You can easily retrieve and change any content on the web page using this technology.

> **▪. TIP**
>
> Silverlight maintains a security setting called `enableHtmlAccess`, which controls whether a web page wants its HTML and Javascript to be available to Silverlight. This security setting could block Silverlight's ability to access data in a page field, as shown in this chapter.
>
> By default, `enableHtmlAccess` is true when the web page and Silverlight applications both come from the same DNS domain and otherwise is set to false. For example, if you host your .xap file on http://server.abc.com and your web page on http://www.xyz.com, by default Silverlight won't be able to access the page.
>
> To manually enable access, include the `enablehtmlaccess` property in the Silverlight object tag, as follows:
>
> ```
> <param name="enablehtmlaccess" value="bool"/>
> ```
>
> Set "bool" to true or false to enable or disable access. There are similar issues when calling web services across DNS domains in Silverlight; this is covered in Chapter 11, "Accessing External Data."

To start, consider a simple example. (The solution is called Chapter07a.sln in the downloadable code.) If you want to create a similar project yourself, begin with a SharePoint sandboxed solution and add a simple web part. Then add a Silverlight application project, but don't bother to allow it to create a test application.

In the SharePoint project, add a new Module item and call it ClientBin. Delete the Sample.txt file that comes with the module. Click the module and view its properties and then open up the Project Output References collection. Add a new Project Output Reference by clicking the Add button. Set the Deployment Type to ElementFile and for Project Name, select the Silverlight project. Figure 7.3 shows the Project Output Reference dialog box. This tells SharePoint to deploy the Silverlight project's .xap file to the /ClientBin directory when the SharePoint solution is deployed.

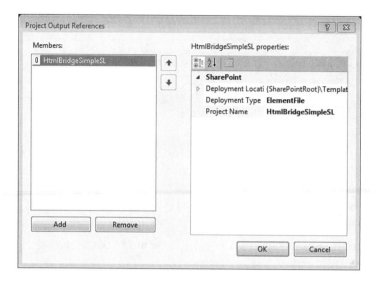

FIGURE 7.3: Setting a Project Output Reference to deploy the Silverlight .xap file

In the web part, a hidden HTML field is created along with the Silverlight plug-in in `CreateChildControls()`; this is shown in Listing 7.2. The code uses the same custom Silverlight plug-in control that was introduced in Chapter 5, "Web Part Development"; your best bet is to copy it from the code download.

LISTING 7.2: Passing Data to Silverlight in a Hidden Field

```
protected override void CreateChildControls()
{
    HiddenField hidden = new HiddenField();
    hidden.Value = "Hello, world.";
    this.Controls.Add(hidden);

    SilverlightPlugin silverlight = new SilverlightPlugin();

    SPSite currentSite = SPContext.Current.Site;
    silverlight.Source =
        ((currentSite.ServerRelativeUrl == "/") ? "/" :
         currentSite.ServerRelativeUrl + "/") +
         "ClientBin/Chapter10SimpleSL.xap";

    silverlight.InitParameters = "controlId=" + hidden.ClientID;
    this.Controls.Add(silverlight);
}
```

The code passes a message, "Hello, world," in a hidden field and passes the client ID of the hidden field to Silverlight in the `initparams` property.

> **■ TIP**
>
> The URL manipulation for the Silverlight source file in Listing 7.2 is to ensure the solution works in a site collection at the root of a web application (such as http://myserver/) or under a managed path (such as http://myserver/sites/something/). Unfortunately the SharePoint Server API returns / for the former case, but only /sites/something (with no trailing /) in the latter, so the code needs to add the extra / when building the .xap file's URL.
>
> To thoroughly test your solutions, ensure they work properly in the root of a web application and under a managed path. For each of these, test the web part in the top-level site and in a child site.

Doing a "view source" in a web browser displaying the web part shows the hidden field (the control IDs are shortened for readability):

```
<input type="hidden" name="ctl00$m$g..." id=" ctl00$m$g..."
 value="Hello, world." />
```

The HTML source also shows that the hidden field's control ID is passed in `initparams`:

```
<object data="data:application/x-silverlight-2,"
        type="application/x-silverlight-2" width="100%" height="100%">
  <param name="source"
   value="/sites/book/ClientBin/Chapter10SimpleSL.xap"/>
   ...
  <param name="initparams" value="controlId= ctl00$m$g..." />
   ...
</object>
```

The next step is when the Silverlight application starts up and fires its `Application_Startup` event in App.xaml.cs. The code retrieves the control ID and passes it to the user control, as shown in Listing 7.3.

LISTING 7.3: Passing the Hidden Field's Control ID into the Silverlight Application

```
private void Application_Startup(object sender, StartupEventArgs e)
{
    if (e.InitParams.ContainsKey("controlId"))
    {
        string controlId = e.InitParams["controlId"];
        this.RootVisual = new MainPage(controlId);
    }
}
```

Finally, the message is passed to the main page in its constructor, which displays the message in a text box. Change the `MainPage` constructor in MainPage.xaml.cs as shown in Listing 7.4.

LISTING 7.4: Displaying Data from the Hidden Field

```
public MainPage(string controlId)
{
    InitializeComponent();

    HtmlDocument doc = HtmlPage.Document;
    HtmlElement hiddenField = doc.GetElementById(controlId);
    string message = hiddenField.GetAttribute("value").ToString();

    MessageTextBlock.Text =
        "The message from the server is: " + message;
}
```

The `HtmlPage`, `HtmlDocument`, and `HtmlElement` classes are part of the HTML Bridge and are in the `System.Windows.Browser` namespace. The `HtmlDocument` object corresponds to the web browser's Document object, and as in Javascript there is a function to get an element by ID. When the hidden field element is in hand, its value attribute can be accessed (or even updated) just as in Javascript.

When the project is deployed and the web part placed on a SharePoint page, the simple message is shown in the Silverlight application, as seen in Figure 7.4.

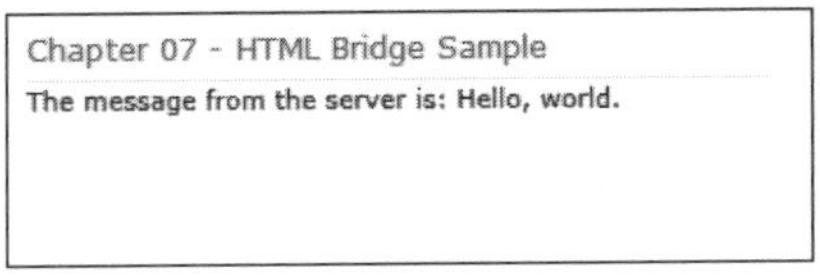

Chapter 07 - HTML Bridge Sample
The message from the server is: Hello, world.

FIGURE 7.4: Simple demonstration of the HTML Bridge

Passing SharePoint Library Content to Silverlight

Passing "Hello world" from server to client isn't all that exciting, and indeed such a message could be passed in InitParams rather than using a hidden field. To demonstrate a more interesting example, consider the PictureView Web Part included as the Chapter07b.sln solution in the code download. As shown in Figure 7.5, this web part displays images from a picture library as a slide show.

FIGURE 7.5: The PictureView Web Part

This is the kind of web part that might find its way onto the home page of a web site, rotating the pictures of the day. If traffic is high, avoiding the extra round-trip is especially appealing. The web part reads the picture library and passes Silverlight the data needed to render pictures in a hidden field.

There's too much code in this solution to include all of it in the chapter listings, so it's best to start right off with the Chapter07b.sln solution from the code download. The chapter, however, endeavors to explain all the concepts required to follow the code. For those who don't want to build the sample, you still learn how to use the HTML Bridge to shuttle data structures between SharePoint and Silverlight.

Open the sample solution in Visual Studio 2010 and deploy it to a test SharePoint site where you have a Picture Library that contains some pictures. Place the PictureView Web Part on the page and edit it. In the editing panel, select the picture library you wish to display, and you should be presented with a slide show of the images in the web part.

> **■ TIP**
>
> Another advantage of retrieving SharePoint data on the server is the possibility of caching. This solution could be made even more scalable by caching the list of pictures on the server. This is easily done using the ASP.NET Cache object.
>
> Just remember that SharePoint implements security trimming on both the server and client APIs; if a user doesn't have permission to read an item, it is hidden from the API. This is a cool feature that comes with no additional code; end users just see what they're supposed to without any developer work. However, caching one user's content and showing it to another could be a problem. If security is a concern, be sure to take this into account before designing server-side caching into your solution.

This project begins much as the previous one. It starts with a SharePoint sandboxed solution called Chapter07b, which contains a standard web part. The solution also contains two Silverlight applications. The Picture-ViewSL project displays the pictures, and PictureViewEditorPartSL is used when editing the web part. In the SharePoint project, a module called ClientBin contains output references to the Silverlight application projects. To complete the setup, the `SilverlightPlugin` class seen in Chapter 5 is back to place the Silverlight application on the page.

Listing 7.5 shows the web part's `CreateChildControls()` method, which places the hidden field and Silverlight objects on the page. Notice that both of the child controls are in fields so they can be accessed later on during web part processing.

LISTING 7.5: CreateChildControls() Creates a Hidden Field and Silverlight Plugin Control

```
HtmlInputHidden inputControl;
SilverlightPlugin silverlightControl;

protected override void CreateChildControls()
{
    inputControl = new HtmlInputHidden();
    this.Controls.Add(inputControl);

    silverlightControl = new SilverlightPlugin();
    this.Controls.Add(silverlightControl);
}
```

You might wonder why `CreateChildControls()` doesn't pass any data to Silverlight as it did in the previous example. The reason is that the picture data won't necessarily be available during `CreateChildControls()`because that comes too early in the page rendering cycle. If a user edits the web part and changes its properties, to select a new picture library for example, the changes won't show up until the postback occurs during page rendering. This is long after `CreateChildControls()` has run. To make the changes show up immediately when the web part is edited, the code to read the picture data is in `OnPreRender()`, which always runs after postback processing. This is shown in Listing 7.6.

The code checks to be sure the user has selected a picture library, and if so it passes the picture information to Silverlight in a collection of `PictureList` objects. The next section describes the `PictureList` class and explains the mysteries of its `Serialize` method, which turns the whole list into an HTML-safe string. For now just observe the use of the SharePoint server API to get the picture data and put it in the hidden field. The hidden field's client-side ID is passed to the Silverlight applications in `InitParams`, just like in the last example.

Listing 7.6: Sending Picture Data to Silverlight

```
protected override void  OnPreRender(EventArgs e)
{
    base.OnPreRender(e);

    try
    {
        // Ensure there is a picture library selected
        if (this.PictureLibraryName == null ||
            this.PictureLibraryName == "")
        {
            throw new Exception("Please select a picture library ");
        }

        // Build the server URL (to be pre-pended to image URL's to
        // make them absolute)
        Uri serverUri = new Uri(this.WebUrl);
        string serverUrl = serverUri.Scheme + "://" +
                              serverUri.DnsSafeHost;
        if (serverUri.Port != 80)
        {
            serverUrl += ":" + serverUri.Port.ToString();
        }

        // Build the picture list
        PictureList pictureList = new PictureList();
        pictureList.ServerUrl = serverUrl;
        pictureList.WebUrl = this.WebUrl;
        pictureList.PictureLibName = this.PictureLibraryName;

        using (SPSite site = new SPSite(this.WebUrl))
        {
            using (SPWeb web = site.OpenWeb())
            {
                SPList picList = web.Lists[this.PictureLibraryName];
                foreach (SPListItem li in picList.Items)
                {
                    pictureList.List.Add(new Picture(li.Title,
                        serverUrl + li.File.ServerRelativeUrl));
                }
            }
        }
        inputControl.Value = pictureList.Serialize();

        // Set up Silverlight plug-in
        SPSite currentSite = SPContext.Current.Site;
        silverlightControl.Source =
            ((currentSite.ServerRelativeUrl == "/") ?
                  "/" : currentSite.ServerRelativeUrl + "/") +
```

```
                    "ClientBin/PictureViewSL.xap";

                silverlightControl.InitParameters = "InputControlID=" +
                    inputControl.ClientID;

                base.CreateChildControls();

            }
            catch (Exception ex)
            {
                this.errorSet = true;
                this.errorMessage = ex.Message;
            }
        }
    }
```

As you can see, the code loops through the picture library and adds a `Picture` object to the `PictureList` for each item it finds. During the process it changes each picture's URL from relative to an absolute by adding the `http://servername` portion in front. The Silverlight `Bitmap` object that eventually reads the images expects an absolute URL. When the `PictureList` completes, it is serialized and stuffed into a hidden input control.

You might notice the exception handling sets a flag called `errorSet` and saves away the error message in a field called `errorMessage`. In case an exception is thrown, the overridden `Render()` method displays the error message instead of the child controls as shown in Listing 7.7.

LISTING 7.7: Exception Handling in the Web Part Render() Method

```
// Exception handling fields
private bool errorSet = false;
private string errorMessage = "";

// Render exception if any, otherwise let the base class render the
// Controls collection
protected override void Render(HtmlTextWriter writer)
{
    if (!this.errorSet)
    {
        base.Render(writer);
    }
    else
    {
        writer.Write("Error: " +
            HttpContext.Current.Server.HtmlEncode(this.errorMessage));
    }
}
```

Serializing Using the Data Contract JSON Serializer

To see how the picture data is serialized, take a look at Listing 7.8. This code defines the `PictureList` and `Picture` classes and can be found in PictureList.cs in both the SharePoint and PictureViewSL projects in the code download. To make it serializable, the classes are decorated with a `DataContract` attribute, and each serializable property is marked as a `DataMember`.

LISTING 7.8: Picture and PictureList Classes

```
using System.IO;
using System.Runtime.Serialization;
using System.Runtime.Serialization.Json;

[DataContract]
public class Picture
{
    public Picture(string title, string url)
    {
        this.Title = title;
        this.Url = url;
    }

    public Picture()
    {
    }

    [DataMember]
    public string Title { get; set; }
    [DataMember]
    public string Url { get; set; }
}

[DataContract]
public class PictureList
{
    [DataMember]
    public string ServerUrl { get; set; }

    [DataMember]
    public string WebUrl { get; set; }

    [DataMember]
    public string PictureLibName { get; set; }

    [DataMember]
```

```
    public List<Picture> List { get; set; }

    public PictureList()
    {
        this.List = new List<Picture>();
    }
}
```

The code defines a `Picture` class to hold the information about each picture and a `PictureList` class, which as the name implies is a list of pictures. Some other random information needed by the Silverlight application is also included in the `PictureList` class; an advantage of this technique is that it's extremely easy to change the data payload by simply editing `DataMember` properties.

This is a good start, but there is still no code to serialize the data so it can be placed in a hidden field on the server side and reconstituted from the field in Silverlight. .NET provides serializers for XML and JSON, the JavaScript Object Notation; of these the latter is more compact and has the advantage that it can be evaluated by Javascript. To use the JSON serializer, you must add references to `System.Runtime.Serialization` and `System.ServiceModel.Web`; these are available both on the server and in Silverlight.

Actually serializing and deserializing the `PictureList` is only a few lines of code, as shown in Listing 7.9. Deserializing is provided in a static `Load()` method to make it easy for callers to obtain a `PictureList` already loaded from some serialized data. Both methods are part of the `PictureList` class.

LISTING 7.9: Serializing and Deserializing the Picture List

```
public string Serialize()
{
    DataContractJsonSerializer js =
        new DataContractJsonSerializer(this.GetType());
    string result = "";

    using (MemoryStream ms = new MemoryStream())
    {
        js.WriteObject(ms, this);
        result = Encoding.UTF8.GetString(ms.ToArray(), 0,
            Convert.ToInt32(ms.Length));
```

```
        }

        return result;
    }

    public static PictureList Load(string serializedObject)
    {
        DataContractJsonSerializer js =
            new DataContractJsonSerializer(typeof(PictureList));
        PictureList result = null;

        using (MemoryStream ms = new
            MemoryStream(Encoding.UTF8.GetBytes(serializedObject)))
        {
            Object o = js.ReadObject(ms);
            if (o is PictureList)
            {
                result = o as PictureList;
            }
            ms.Close();
        }
        return (result);
    }
}
```

Notice that the serialized JSON is in UTF8 format; this encoding is specified in the JSON specification.

It's not too hard, by the way, to put the `Serialize()` and `Load()` methods in a reusable class, so any derived class you might cook up can easily be serialized; this is the `SerializableObject` class found in Chapters 10, 13, and 15. To make this work, the `Load()` method needs to use a generic to allow it to return the derived type at runtime. This is shown in Listing 7.10.

LISTING 7.10: SerializableObject Base Class

```
// Serializable Object - Base class to allow quick serialization and
// deserialization of derived classes. To use, pass the derived
// class as T.

[DataContract]
public class SerializableObject <T> where T : SerializableObject<T>
{
    // Serialize the object and return it as a string
    public string Serialize()
    {
        DataContractJsonSerializer js =
            new DataContractJsonSerializer(this.GetType());
```

```
        string result = "";

        using (MemoryStream ms = new MemoryStream())
        {
            js.WriteObject(ms, this);
            result = Encoding.UTF8.GetString(ms.ToArray(), 0,
                Convert.ToInt32(ms.Length));
        }

        return result;
    }

    // Deserialize the object from the provided string
    public static T Load(string serializedObject)
    {
        DataContractJsonSerializer js =
            new DataContractJsonSerializer(typeof(T));
        T result = null;

        using (MemoryStream ms = new
            MemoryStream(Encoding.UTF8.GetBytes(serializedObject)))
        {
            Object o = js.ReadObject(ms);
            if (o is T)
            {
                result = o as T;
            }
            ms.Close();
        }
        return (result);
    }
}
```

Retrieving the Data in Silverlight

On the Silverlight side, the process of getting the PictureList begins in the Application_Startup event handler in App.xaml.cs, which, as before, passes the control ID of the hidden field that contains the data. This is shown in Listing 7.11.

LISTING 7.11: Retrieving the Hidden Field ID in the Application_Startup Event

```
private void Application_Startup(object sender, StartupEventArgs e)
{
    MainPage p = new MainPage();
    this.RootVisual = p;
```

```
        if (e.InitParams.ContainsKey("InputControlID"))
        {
            p.ReadPictureDataFromPage(e.InitParams["InputControlID"]);
        }
}
```

The event handler calls a method called `ReadPictureDataFromPage()` in the `MainPage` class. Reading the data is just a question of accessing the hidden field and calling the `Load()` method, as shown in Listing 7.12.

LISTING 7.12: Reading the Picture Data from the Hidden Field

```
// Private fields for picture data and selection
private IEnumerable<Picture> currentPictures;
private int currentPictureIndex = 0;

internal void ReadPictureDataFromPage(string inputControlID)
{
    // Use the browser DOM to find the element and parse it
    HtmlDocument doc = HtmlPage.Document;
    HtmlDocument doc = HtmlPage.Document;
    HtmlElement hidden = doc.GetElementById(controlId);
    string jsonString = hidden.GetAttribute("value").ToString();

    // Get picture data from json
    PictureList p = PictureList.Load(jsonString);
    currentPictures = p.List;

    // Display the first image and start the timer to show them all
    DisplayImage(0);
    timer.Start();
    VisualStateManager.GoToState(this, "Playing", true);
}
```

Introducing the Visual State Manager

At the end of Listing 7.12 there are a few lines of code to display the first image, start the timer, and to go to a state in the *Visual State Manager (VSM)*, which is the topic of this section.

```
DisplayImage(0);
timer.Start();
VisualStateManager.GoToState(this, "Playing", true);
```

The first image is displayed using the `DisplayImage()` method, and the timer is started to begin showing the pictures as a slide show. Then the VSM is called to set the application's play/pause controls to the Playing state. `DisplayImage()` uses the VSM to show the fade transition between images, so it makes sense to understand it before digging into `DisplayImage()` itself.

The VSM is a powerful part of Silverlight and Windows Presentation Foundation that greatly simplifies managing the user interface states for an application. VSM manages *states*, such as whether the slide show is playing or paused. These are grouped into *state groups*, which are sets of states that govern independent aspects of the user interface. PictureView has a number of state groups that control its presentation:

- **PlayStates (Paused, Playing)**—These states control whether the application is playing a slide show or is paused.
- **CurrentItemStates (FirstItem, MiddleItem, LastItem)**—These states control the disabling of the Previous and Next buttons for the first and last items in the list, so you can't advance beyond the last image or before the first.
- **MouseStates (MouseOver, MouseOut)**—These states control the fading in of controls when the mouse hovers over the application.
- **DisplayImageStates (MainImageShowing, AltImageShowing)**—These states are used to smoothly fade between images.

The XAML code defines a set of animations or *storyboards* to be played when each state is entered. The storyboards change control properties over a period of time. For example, entering the MouseOver state gradually changes the opacity of the player controls to 100%, and entering the Mouse-Out state fades it to 0%.

Figure 7.6 shows these state groups being edited in Expression Blend. In the figure, the MouseOver state is selected; this brings the MouseOver timeline into the Objects and Timeline panel. A timeline is used to define the

Silverlight animation, and the points on the timeline relate to property settings to be attained when that point in time is reached. Expression Blend makes it easy to create and edit these timelines by "recording" the property settings when an object and point in time are selected. For a video walkthrough of how to configure Visual State Manager states in Expression Blend, see http://bit.ly/SPSL_BlendVSM.

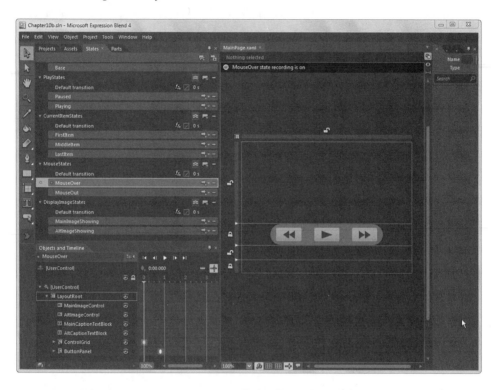

FIGURE 7.6: Working with the Visual State Manager in Expression Blend

When they've been set up in XAML, it's easy to switch between visual states in code, as in this example:

```
private void LayoutRoot_MouseEnter(object sender, MouseEventArgs e)
{
    VisualStateManager.GoToState(this, "MouseOver", true);
}
```

Displaying and Caching Images

Loading the pictures smoothly is the intent of the `DisplayImageStates` state group. Silverlight displays images using its `Image` control, and PictureView has not one but two of them. The `MainImageControl` is shown when the `DisplayImageStates` group is in `MainImageShowing` state, and the `AltImageControl` is shown in `AltImageShowing` state.

`DisplayBitmap()`is called when an image is to be shown; it loads a bitmap into whichever image control isn't showing, and the VSM plays an animation that fades out the old image while fading in the new one. This is shown in Listing 7.13.

LISTING 7.13: Fading Between Bitmaps with the Visual State Manager

```
// Alternate between main and alt image controls, beginning with main
private enum ImageControlStates { MainImageShowing, AltImageShowing }
private ImageControlStates currentImageControlState =
        ImageControlStates.MainImageShowing;

// Display a bitmap on whichever image control isn't being used, then
// change visual and local states
private void DisplayBitmap(BitmapImage bitmap, string caption)
{
    switch (this.currentImageControlState)
    {
        case ImageControlStates.MainImageShowing:
            {
                AltImageControl.Source = bitmap;
                AltCaptionTextBlock.Text = caption;
                VisualStateManager.GoToState(this, "AltImageShowing",
                  true);
                this.currentImageControlState =
                  ImageControlStates.AltImageShowing;
                break;
            }
        case ImageControlStates.AltImageShowing:
            {
                MainImageControl.Source = bitmap;
                MainCaptionTextBlock.Text = caption;
                VisualStateManager.GoToState(this, "MainImageShowing",
                    true);
                this.currentImageControlState =
                    ImageControlStates.MainImageShowing;
                break;
            }
    }
}
```

You might have noticed that back in Listing 7.12 there was a call to `DisplayImage(0)`. `DisplayImage()` calls `DisplayBitmap()` and also adds bitmap caching.

Silverlight does not cache downloaded images, nor does the browser's cache help with this. `DisplayImage()` caches the images in a dictionary object. Though this doesn't persist after the user leaves the web page, it works for as long as the slide show is left cycling. This is shown in Listing 7.14.

LISTING 7.14: Code to Display Images from SharePoint

```
// Bitmaps are cached in this Dictionary
private Dictionary<int, BitmapImage> imageCache =
    new Dictionary<int, BitmapImage>();

// DisplayImage - Displays an image by its index
private void DisplayImage(int pictureIndex)
{
    // Get the selected picture information
    Picture picture = currentPictures.ElementAt<Picture>(pictureIndex);

    // Try to get the bitmap from cache, or load it up
    BitmapImage bitmap;
    if (imageCache.ContainsKey(pictureIndex))
    {
        bitmap = imageCache[pictureIndex];
    }
    else
    {
        bitmap = new BitmapImage(new Uri(picture.Url));
        imageCache[pictureIndex] = bitmap;
    }

    // Display the bitmap and remember the current picture index
    DisplayBitmap(bitmap, picture.Title);
    currentPictureIndex = pictureIndex;

    // Cache the next image if necessary
    if (currentPictureIndex < (currentPictures.Count<Picture>() - 1) &&
        !imageCache.ContainsKey(pictureIndex+1))
    {
        Picture nextPicture =
            currentPictures.ElementAt<Picture>(pictureIndex + 1);
```

```
        imageCache[pictureIndex+1] =
            new BitmapImage(new Uri(nextPicture.Url));
    }

    // Set visual state depending on what item we are now showing
    if (currentPictureIndex <= 0)
    {
        VisualStateManager.GoToState(this, "FirstItem", true);
    }
    else if (currentPictureIndex <
            (currentPictures.Count<Picture>() - 1))
    {
        VisualStateManager.GoToState(this, "MiddleItem", true);
    }
    else
    {
        VisualStateManager.GoToState(this, "LastItem", true);
    }
}
```

DisplayImage() is passed an index for the picture to be displayed, and it starts by looking in the imageCache dictionary for a bitmap with that index. If it's not found, the bitmap is loaded from SharePoint and added to the cache:

```
        bitmap = new BitmapImage(new Uri(picture.Url));
        imageCache[pictureIndex] = bitmap;
```

Then the bitmap is displayed by calling DisplayBitmap(). Display Image() also attempts to cache the next image in advance so it can be displayed quickly when the time comes.

DisplayImage() also manages the CurrentItemStates group, which governs the display of the control buttons. When the first image is displayed, the Previous button must be hidden, just as the Next button is concealed when the last image is shown. The code simply switches to the appropriate visual state to show and hide the buttons as needed.

Much of the rest of the MainPage code is spent in button event handlers and the timer, all of which end up calling DisplayImage(). However, there are a couple more nuggets to explore next, namely the code behind the Full Screen and Print buttons.

Full Screen and Printing in Silverlight

If you press the Full Screen button on the web part, the application runs in full screen. The code only needs to flip the `IsFullScreen` flag, as shown in Listing 7.15.

LISTING 7.15: Running Silverlight Full Screen

```
private void FullScreenButton_Click(object sender, RoutedEventArgs e)
{
    App.Current.Host.Content.IsFullScreen =
        !App.Current.Host.Content.IsFullScreen;
}
```

Be aware, however, that there are some security limitations when running in full screen. This is to prevent an application from simulating another user interface, such as a login screen or web browser, to illicitly obtain information from a user. To that end, it's not possible to start an application in full screen mode; it can only be changed in an event handler that follows some user action. In addition, the user is prompted for consent, and keyboard use is limited while in full screen mode.

If you press the Print button on the web part, you are presented with the operating system's Print dialog box and given an opportunity to print the currently displayed picture. Again the code is pretty simple, as shown in Listing 7.16. `InitializePrinting()` is called from the MainPage constructor, so printing is always ready when a user clicks the button.

LISTING 7.16: Printing in Silverlight

```
private PrintDocument pDoc = new PrintDocument();

private void InitializePrinting()
{
    pDoc.PrintPage +=
        new EventHandler<PrintPageEventArgs>(pDoc_PrintPage);
}

void pDoc_PrintPage(object sender, PrintPageEventArgs e)
{
```

```
    if (this.currentImageControlState ==
        ImageControlStates.AltImageShowing)
    {
        e.PageVisual = this.AltImageControl;
    }
    else
    {
        e.PageVisual = this.MainImageControl;
    }
}

private void PrintButton_Click(object sender, RoutedEventArgs e)
{
    pDoc.Print("Silverlight Photo");
}
```

Web Part Editing and Posting Back with the Web Page

The PictureView Web Part could employ a simple text field to contain the URL of the picture library to be displayed, but that's a pain for users who would have to type the long URL exactly or paste it in from the browser's address bar. To simplify matters, PictureView includes an *Editor Part* to provide a custom, Silverlight-based editing experience. As shown in Figure 7.7, the editor part allows the user to select a picture library in the current or a different site and to preview the first few pictures before completing the selection.

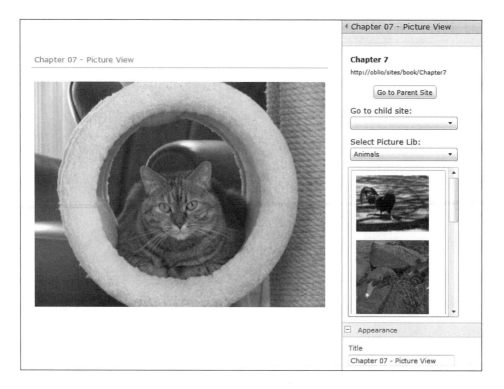

FIGURE 7.7: PictureView Editor Part

This also provides another key example of HTML Bridge use. The editor part runs in the panel that swings out from the right when a user edits a web part. There are many fields on the panel, and the users rightfully expect that all or none of them will be saved when they click OK or Cancel. The same thing happens in a dialog box, on an administrative form, or during web page editing: Updating is an all-or-nothing affair across multiple web form fields. The Silverlight application uses a hidden field to post back the data along with the other fields on the page.

Under the covers, this editor part operates on two strings: the site URL and picture library name. They are exposed as public properties in the PictureView Web Part, as shown in Listing 7.17.

LISTING 7.17: Editable Properties of the PictureView Web Part

```
[Personalizable(PersonalizationScope.Shared),
 WebBrowsable(false),
 WebDescription("URL of Web Site"),
 WebDisplayName("Web URL"),
 System.ComponentModel.Category("Configuration")]
public string WebUrl { get; set; }

[Personalizable(PersonalizationScope.Shared),
 WebBrowsable(false),
 WebDescription("Name of Picture Library"),
 WebDisplayName("Picture Library"),
 System.ComponentModel.Category("Configuration")]
public string PictureLibraryName { get; set; }
```

If the `WebBrowsable` attribute were set to true, SharePoint would generate a pair of text boxes for these properties, but because our Silverlight editor part renders the information, it is set to false. Next you must tell the web part about the editor part so it will be displayed when the web part is edited; this is accomplished by overriding the `CreateEditorParts()` method as shown in Listing 7.18.

LISTING 7.18: CreateEditorParts() Method

```
public override EditorPartCollection CreateEditorParts()
{
    ArrayList editorPartArray = new ArrayList();

    PictureViewEP editorPart = new PictureViewEP();
    editorPart.Height = Unit.Pixel(450);
    editorPart.ID = this.ID + "_editorPart";
    editorPartArray.Add(editorPart);

    // If no site is already selected, use this site
    if (string.IsNullOrEmpty(WebUrl))
    {
        Uri pageUrl = HttpContext.Current.Request.Url;
        string webUrl = SPContext.Current.Web.ServerRelativeUrl;

        if (pageUrl.IsDefaultPort)
        {
            WebUrl = pageUrl.Scheme + "://" + pageUrl.Host + webUrl;
        }
        else
        {
```

```
            WebUrl = pageUrl.Scheme + "://" + pageUrl.Host + ":" +
                pageUrl.Port + webUrl;
        }
    }

    return new EditorPartCollection(editorPartArray);
}
```

The Editor Part itself is a composite control called `PictureViewEP`, which is derived from the `EditorPart` class. Listing 7.19 shows the editor part's `CreateChildControls()` method; as you can see it uses two hidden fields, which just happens to correspond with the two web part properties from Listing 7.17. As before, the hidden field IDs are passed to the Silverlight application using `InitParams`.

LISTING 7.19: CreateChildControls() in the Editor Part

```
private HiddenField webUrlField = new HiddenField();
private HiddenField pictureLibraryField = new HiddenField();

protected override void CreateChildControls()
{
    base.CreateChildControls();

    // Add hidden fields to store the web address and picture library
    this.Controls.Add(webUrlField);
    this.Controls.Add(pictureLibraryField);

    // Add the Silverlight application which will edit these values
    SilverlightPlugin sl = new SilverlightPlugin();
    SPSite site = SPContext.Current.Site;
    sl.Source = ((site.ServerRelativeUrl == "/") ? "/" :
                site.ServerRelativeUrl + "/") +
                "ClientBin/PictureViewEditorPartSL.xap";
    sl.InitParameters =
        "webUrlClientID=" + this.webUrlField.ClientID +
        ",pictureLibraryClientID=" + this.pictureLibraryField.ClientID;
    sl.Width = this.Width;
    sl.Height = this.Height;

    this.Controls.Add(sl);
}
```

All editor parts must implement a pair of methods, `ApplyChanges()` and `SyncChanges()`, to keep the editor part in sync with the web part being edited. `SyncChanges()` is called to tell the editor part to load the values from the web part prior to editing, and `ApplyChanges()` tells the editor part to save the updated values back to the web part.

Listing 7.20 shows the PictureView editor part's implementation of these methods. All they really need to do is copy the web part properties into the hidden fields (in `SyncChanges()`) and back again (in `Apply-Changes()`). Notice that both methods call `EnsureChildControls()`; this method calls `CreateChildControls()` if it hasn't already run and ensures that the hidden fields have been created before attempting to move data in and out of them.

LISTING 7.20: SyncChanges() and ApplyChanges() in the Editor Part

```
// SyncChanges - Override to update the EditorPart controls
// with the latest web part properties
public override void SyncChanges()
{
    this.EnsureChildControls();

    if (this.WebPartToEdit is PictureView)
    {
        PictureView webPart = this.WebPartToEdit as PictureView;
        webUrlField.Value = webPart.WebUrl;
        pictureLibraryField.Value = webPart.PictureLibraryName;
    }
}


// ApplyChanges - Override to update the web part with the
// latest EditorPart control values
public override bool ApplyChanges()
{
    if (this.WebPartToEdit is PictureView)
    {
        PictureView webPart = this.WebPartToEdit as PictureView;
        webPart.WebUrl = webUrlField.Value;
        webPart.PictureLibraryName = pictureLibraryField.Value;
    }
    return true;
}
```

The Silverlight application can now read and write its settings to the hidden fields, and the editor part take cares of updating the web part settings in its `ApplyChanges()` method. When the Silverlight application starts up, it saves away both fields and initializes the user interface based on their initial values. Listing 7.21 shows the PictureViewEditorPartSL application's `MainPage` constructor. Just as in the earlier examples in this chapter, the `Application_Startup()` event handler takes the IDs of the two hidden fields from `InitParams` and passes them in.

Listing 7.21: Silverlight Editor Part MainPage Constructor

```
// Fields on the hosting web page, used to pass data between
// server and client
private HtmlElement webUrlField;
private HtmlElement pictureLibraryField;
private string originalPictureLibraryName;

public MainPage(string webUrlClientID, string pictureLibraryClientID)
{
    InitializeComponent();

    // Get the fields on the hosting page
    HtmlDocument doc = HtmlPage.Document;
    webUrlField = doc.GetElementById(webUrlClientID);
    pictureLibraryField = doc.GetElementById(pictureLibraryClientID);

    // If we have a picture library name, remember it
    if (pictureLibraryField != null &&
        pictureLibraryField.GetAttribute("value") != null)
    {
        this.originalPictureLibraryName =
            pictureLibraryField.GetAttribute("value").ToString();
    }

    // If we have a web URL, then start the UI
    if (webUrlField != null &&
        webUrlField.GetAttribute("value") != null)
    {
        LoadSiteData(webUrlField.GetAttribute("value").ToString());
    }
}
```

`LoadSiteData()` uses the Client Object Model to populate the child site and picture library combo boxes and to show the picture library preview.

The Client Object Model is covered in detail in Chapter 8, "Accessing Share-Point Data with the Client Object Model."

As the user browses within the editor part to various sites and picture libraries, the Silverlight application continually saves the selected site and picture library in the hidden fields. For example, when the user selects a picture library, the combo box's event handler stuffs the library name into the hidden field and shows a preview of the images in the library. This is shown in Listing 7.22.

LISTING 7.22: Updating the Picture Library Field

```
// Library_SelectionChanged - When the user selects a picture library,
// save it to the web page for post-back
private void Library_SelectionChanged(object sender,
                                      SelectionChangedEventArgs e)
{
    if (this.LibraryComboBox.SelectedValue != null)
    {
        pictureLibraryField.SetAttribute("value",
            this.LibraryComboBox.SelectedValue.ToString());
        ShowPreview(this.SiteUrlTextBlock.Text,
            this.LibraryComboBox.SelectedValue.ToString());
    }
}
```

Using this technique, a Silverlight application can be the user interface for nearly any ASP.NET control; in this case it was an editor part, but it could just as easily be a field control (like the one in Chapter 15) or a control on a web form. Silverlight stuffs updated data into the hidden field(s) just as a user would type into a textbox or click a radio button, so the user gets a richer experience without disrupting the page postback logic.

Calling SharePoint Javascript and JQuery from Silverlight

SharePoint's user interface includes a number of user interface elements like status bars and dialog boxes that developers can use in their solutions. Simple Javascript APIs are provided; using them can save you work and also help your solution fit visually into SharePoint. Table 7.1 shows some of the most useful of these functions.

TABLE 7.1: Commonly Used SharePoint UI Functions

Element	Javascript Function	Description
Dialog Box	`SP.UI.ModalDialog.showModalDialog()`	Dims the screen and shows a web page in a modal dialog box
Notification	`SP.UI.Notify.addNotification()`	Shows a notification message
Status Bar	`SP.UI.Status.addStatus()`	Shows a message in the status bar

The sample solution Chapter07c.sln shows a simple Silverlight Web Part that shows a JQuery progress bar in the SharePoint status bar. JQuery is a popular Javascript library that includes client-side widgets such as this progress bar.

When the button is pushed, the Silverlight application simulates a long-running process and advances the progress bar over a period of about 10 seconds. When the progress bar reaches 100%, the status bar is hidden. Figure 7.8 shows two of these web parts, each with its own progress bar.

> ■ **TIP**
>
> There are two web parts and progress bars in Figure 7.8 because it was tricky to get two of them to work together on the page. This will be evident in the code.
>
> When testing your solutions, decide if you want to support multiple instances on a page and if so, test it. It's easy to hard-code an object ID or to add some Javascript, and it might work fine until a second instance is added to the page.

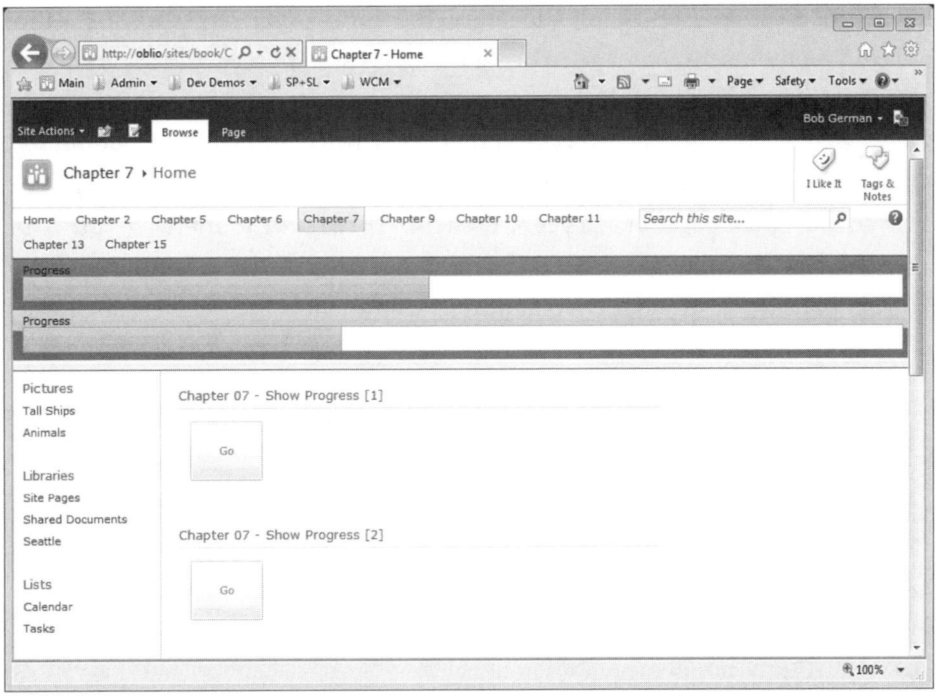

FIGURE 7.8: JQuery progress bars in the SharePoint Status Bar

This solution begins with a Custom Silverlight Web Part from the Silverlight SharePoint Web Parts extension described in Chapter 5. This automatically creates a sandboxed Visual Web Part to host the Silverlight application and deploys the Silverlight .xap file to the Master Page Gallery in SharePoint.

From this starting point, the first challenge is to deploy JQuery and its progress bar widget to SharePoint so we can use it in the solution. They come as a set of scripts (.js files), style sheets (.css files) and images (.png) files, which are used to render the progress bar. This is an easy one: Simply add a module to your SharePoint project called jQuery and add all the files. Visual Studio packages them up and deploys them to a folder called jQuery in SharePoint. Because the module is part of a site collection feature, the jQuery folder shows up in the top-level site of the site collection. For documentation on the JQuery and the progress bar, see http:// bit.ly/SPSL_JQueryProgressBar.

With the files deployed, the next step is to place the `<script>` and `<link>` elements on the page to bring in the Javascript files and style sheets. The tricky part is that if there is more than one instance of the web part on the page, you only want one set of `<script>` and `<link>` elements. In a SharePoint farm solution this could be handled by using the `ClientScriptManager.RegisterClientScriptBlock()` method on the server side, but alas this isn't accessible in a sandboxed solution. Instead this is handled with client script added to the ShowProgressWP.ascx file, shown in Listing 7.23.

LISTING 7.23: Javascript to include JQuery Library Only Once on a Page

```
<script type="text/javascript">
// Ensure jQuery and extensions are loaded
if (window.ch7jquery == undefined)
{
    ch7jquery = new Object();

    ch7jquery.load = function (url)
    {
        var head= document.getElementsByTagName('head')[0];
        var element;
        if (url.indexOf('.js') > 0)
        {
            element= document.createElement('script');
            element.type= 'text/javascript';
            element.src= url;
        }
        else
        {
            element = document.createElement('link');
            element.type = 'text/css';
            element.rel = 'stylesheet';
            element.href = url;
        }
        head.appendChild(element);
    }
    ch7jquery.load ('<%=SPContext.Current.Site.Url%>/jQuery/jquery-
1.4.4.min.js');
    ch7jquery.load ('<%=SPContext.Current.Site.Url%>/jQuery/jquery-ui-
1.8.11.custom.min.js');
    ch7jquery.load ('<%=SPContext.Current.Site.Url%>/jQuery/jquery-ui-
1.8.11.custom.css');
}
</script>
```

The other change to the .ascx file is to pass the client control ID to the Silverlight application in `InitParams` so it can be used to uniquely name its scroll bar. This is easily added to the `InitParams` parameter:

```
<param name="initParams" value="MS.SP.url=<%=
Microsoft.SharePoint.Utilities.SPHttpUtility.HtmlEncode(Microsoft.SharePoint.SP
Context.Current.Web.Url) %>,clientID=<%= this.ClientID %>" />
```

Being able to edit the .ascx file to add script and change the object tag is a big convenience of the Custom Silverlight Web Part.

On the Silverlight side, the `Application_Startup` event handler passes the client control ID to the `MainPage` constructor, which saves it away to use in uniquely naming the HTML objects it creates when someone pushes the button. It also starts a `DispatcherTimer`, which ticks at regular intervals to update the progress bar. By now you're probably used to seeing `Dispatcher.BeginInvoke()` used to queue up work for the UI thread; the `DispatcherTimer` takes care of this for you. (If it's not familiar, see the Tip on this topic in Chapter 3, "Introduction to Silverlight Development.") The constructor code is shown in Listing 7.24.

LISTING 7.24: MainPage Constructor for JQuery Sample

```
DispatcherTimer timer = new DispatcherTimer();
private int progressValue = 0;
private string clientID;


public MainPage(string clientID)
{
    InitializeComponent();

    timer.Tick += new EventHandler(timer_Tick);
    timer.Interval = TimeSpan.FromMilliseconds(100);

    this.clientID = clientID;
}
```

When the button is clicked, its event handler cooks up a script block, embedding the unique client control ID in the script to make the status bar ID and progress bar ID unique across multiple instances of the web part.

Running Javascript is as easy as calling the `HtmlPage.Window.Eval()` method. This and the rest of the `MainPage` code are in Listing 7.25.

LISTING 7.25: Code to Animate a JQuery Progress Bar in a SharePoint Status Bar

```
private void GoButton_Click(object sender, RoutedEventArgs e)
{
    string scriptBlock =
        "var statusId_" + clientID + "=SP.UI.Status.addStatus" +
        " ('','Progress <div id=\"progressbar_" + clientID +
        "\"></div>');" +
        "SP.UI.Status.setStatusPriColor(statusId_" + clientID +
        ", 'red');" +
        "$(\"#progressbar_" + clientID + "\").progressbar({value: 0, height:
10});";

    ShowProgress(this.progressValue = 0);
    HtmlPage.Window.Eval(scriptBlock);
    timer.Start();
    GoButton.IsEnabled = false;
}

private void ShowProgress(int i)
{
    HtmlPage.Window.Eval("$(\"#progressbar_" + clientID +
        "\").progressbar(\"option\", \"value\", " + i.ToString() + ");");
}

void timer_Tick(object sender, EventArgs e)
{
    if (this.progressValue < 100)
    {
        this.progressValue += 1;
        ShowProgress(this.progressValue);
    }
    else
    {
        timer.Stop();

        HtmlPage.Window.Eval("SP.UI.Status.removeStatus(statusId_"+
            clientID + ");");
        GoButton.IsEnabled = true;
    }
}
```

Summary

The HTML Bridge is an elegant and efficient way to optimize network utilization and provide expected postback behavior in Silverlight. It also can be used to access Javascript and JQuery elements on the page to provide seamless integration between Silverlight and the rest of the SharePoint UI.

In the next few chapters you explore several other ways for Silverlight to interact with SharePoint: through the Client Object Model, RESTful services, and traditional web services. Powerful as these tools are, it's worth remembering that the HTML Bridge is available, too, and if you were just delivering or posting back a whole page anyway, it might be your best choice!

◤8◾

Accessing SharePoint Data with the Client Object Model

THE SHAREPOINT CLIENT OBJECT MODEL (CLIENT OM) for Silverlight offers a new client API for accessing SharePoint data. Share-Point actually has three separate Client Object Models—JavaScript, .NET CLR, and Silverlight. In this book we only cover the Silverlight Client OM, but when you learn one, the others are easy because they are similar. The Client OM will be very familiar to SharePoint developers who have used the server API. This makes learning to program SharePoint with Silverlight as easy as creating a traditional SharePoint application that runs on the server.

Client Object Model Goals

In the past, developers had limited options to access SharePoint data from client applications. If your application were not on the server, you really only had .asmx Web Services as a programming option. Although this is still a viable and powerful option for many SharePoint solutions, the Client OM makes developing core SharePoint scenarios much easier. As more developers looked to expand the way they communicated with SharePoint and the types of devices and languages increased, it was clear that a new API was needed.

To handle all of the requests, the SharePoint team designed the Client OM as a proxy on the Server API. A proxy is generated for each platform and language that the SharePoint team wants to support. For SharePoint 2010 they shipped with support for the .NET Common Language Runtime, JavaScript, and Silverlight.

Understanding that the Client OM is just a wrapper on the server API also helps you understand how to use and learn programming on the client. Many times if you know the method or object name on the server, you can find the same method or object on the client. The only real exception to this is that some classes that are prefixed with SP on the server have dropped the prefix on the client. For example SPWeb on the server is just Web on the client. Generating the client API as a proxy to the server solves the first goal of being consistent. It is important that there should be a common or very similar way to program on the client no matter which client platform you are targeting.

Another goal of the Client OM is to be efficient. The Client OM is going to be calling across the network or the Internet to send and retrieve data. It is very important to have an efficient calling pattern that minimizes the number of calls to the server and reduces the number of roundtrips and the amount of data sent back and forth for each call.

The Client OM is efficient in two ways. The first is that you explicitly call the server—no behind-the-scenes calls are made. Developers decide when to call the server based on their needs. The second way is that developers need to be explicit about the amount of data that is returned. By default the Client OM does not return all properties or all fields in a list. Being explicit about the data returned reduces the amount of data across the wire and increases the perceived responsiveness of the Silverlight applications.

Hello World

The best way to understand the Client OM is starting with a simple example. This code snippet updates the title property of the SharePoint web site. You learn all of the details on how this snippet works throughout the chapter, but this should give you a sense of the coding style and pattern of the Client OM. The code has been stripped down to just the items that relate to the Client Object Model. The full sample is included with the source for the chapter.

All of the Client Object Model classes are contained in two assemblies that are located in the layouts\clientbin folder in C:\Program Files\ Common Files\Microsoft Shared\Web Server Extensions\14\ TEMPLATE\LAYOUTS\ClientBin. Add a reference to these two files, Microsoft.SharePoint.Client.Silverlight.dll and Microsoft.SharePoint. Client.Silverlight.Runtime.dll. Add the using statement.

```
using Microsoft.SharePoint.Client;
```

Define two class variables for the ClientContext and the Web objects. This makes it easy to use these objects across the asynchronous callbacks.

```
ClientContext clientContext;
Web site;
```

This sample uses the Silverlight navigation pages, as shown in Listing 8.1. When the user navigates to this page, he needs to call SharePoint to get the site title. Set a reference to ClientContext using the static property called Current. Set a reference to the Web property of the clientContext and then add this to the query stack by calling the Load() method.

At this point, everything has happened on the client. Call the Execute-QueryAsync() method to send the query to SharePoint. The query is sent to SharePoint asynchronously, and the results are returned to the succeed-edCallback() or the failedCallback() methods, depending on success or failure.

LISTING 8.1: Hello World ClientOM Sample

```
// Executes when the user navigates to this page.
protected override void OnNavigatedTo(
    NavigationEventArgs e)
{
    // Get the client context for the site
    clientContext = ClientContext.Current;

    // Get the Web Site Title
    site = clientContext.Web;

    // Add the site to the query
    clientContext.Load(site);
```

```
    // Call the SharePoint Server with the query
    clientContext.ExecuteQueryAsync(
        succeededCallback, failedCallback);
}
```

The succeededCallback() method is called when the query was success-fully executed on the SharePoint server. The method is called on a back-ground thread, which is different from the UI thread. To communicate with the UI thread, you need to call the BeginInvoke() method of the Dispatcher object, as shown in Listing 8.2.

LISTING 8.2: Handling a Successful Callback from the Client OM

```
private void succeededCallback(
    object sender, ClientRequestSucceededEventArgs args)
{
    // Update the UI with the site's title
    this.Dispatcher.BeginInvoke(() =>
    {
        siteTitle.Text = site.Title;
    });
}
```

Failed results are returned to the failedCallback() method. The args parameter contains information about the exception. In Listing 8.3, the ValidationSummary control is used to display exception information to the user.

LISTING 8.3: Handling a Failed Callback from the Client OM

```
private void failedCallback(
    object sender, ClientRequestFailedEventArgs args)
{
    // Display the error message in the UI
    this.Dispatcher.BeginInvoke(() =>
    {
        ValidationSummaryItem error =
            new ValidationSummaryItem(
                "Request failed. " + args.Message);
        validationSummary.Errors.Add(error);
    });
}
```

The successful path shown in Listing 8.2 shows how the Client OM can read SharePoint content when it returns the `site` object and the `title` property. Updating data using the Client OM is straightforward as well. To update the `title` property, set the new value of the property and call `Update()`. The `Update()` method flags the object to be updated on the query. There is no need to call `Load()` in this case.

Just like when reading data from the server, no calls to the server occur until the `ExecuteQueryAsync()` method is called. Consider the code in Listing 8.4, which updates the title of the site and turns the border of the text box green if it is successfully set.

LISTING 8.4: Setting SharePoint Content with the Client OM

```
private void UpdateButton_Click(
    object sender, RoutedEventArgs e)
{
    // Set the new site title
    site.Title = siteTitle.Text;

    // flag the site to be updated
    site.Update();

    // Call the SharePoint Server with the query
    clientContext.ExecuteQueryAsync(
        updateSucceededCallback, updateFailedCallback);
}

private void updateSucceededCallback(
    object sender, ClientRequestSucceededEventArgs args)
{
    // Set the border green
    this.Dispatcher.BeginInvoke(() =>
    {
        siteTitle.BorderBrush =
            new SolidColorBrush(Colors.Green);
    });
}

private void updateFailedCallback(
    object sender, ClientRequestFailedEventArgs args)
{
    // Display the error message in the UI
    this.Dispatcher.BeginInvoke(() =>
    {
        ValidationSummaryItem error =
```

```
            new ValidationSummaryItem(
                "Request failed. " + args.Message);
        validationSummary.Errors.Add(error);
    });
}
```

This is one of the simplest examples you see with the Silverlight Client Object Model, but it is a good way to learn the pattern used by all Client OM calls. The first step is to get a reference to the `ClientContext`. In the next section you learn about the various ways to do this. The second step is to build the query by referencing objects and setting them on the `Load()` and `LoadQuery()` methods. After you have loaded all of the queries on the `ClientContext`, you send and execute them on the server using the `ExecuteQueryAsync()` method. The last step is to handle the succeeded or failed results. All programming using the Client OM follows this pattern.

Now that you have a basic understanding of how to program with the Client OM, you get to learn a few of the details around how it works and then finish the chapter with some coding examples of common tasks you will perform.

Client Context

The `ClientContext` is the central object used to program the Client Object Model. This should be a familiar concept if you have programmed using the `Context` object of the SharePoint server API. `ClientContext` maintains the object identities for objects returned using the `Load()` method. `ClientContext` makes calls to the server and parses the results back into objects on the client.

One of the first programming tasks is to set the context for `ClientContext`; that is the site that the context refers to. The most basic way to set the `ClientContext` is to hard code the URL.

```
ClientContext clientContext =
    new ClientContext("http://intranet.contoso.com");
```

Generally this is not the best approach. Because the Silverlight application is deployed to multiple sites, you need to pass the parameter in as an `initParam`. One scenario where this might be used is if you are targeting a site other than the one that the application is deployed to. A better approach is to use the static property of the `ClientContext` class called `Current` to return an instance of the `ClientContext` object.

```
ClientContext clientContext = ClientContext.Current;
```

The `Current` property is available when using the Silverlight Web Part. If you are creating your own Web Part or using the Object tag directly on the page, you might encounter the error "Unhandled Error in Silverlight Application Object reference not set to an instance of an object." This error occurs because the Current property returns a null value. Behind the scenes the Client Object Model looks for an `initParam` called MS.SP.url. The Silverlight Web Part automatically sets the MS.SP.url parameter to the URL of the current site. If you are not using the Silverlight Web Part, you need to set this property yourself. For example, if you are using a Visual Web Part, then you could set it in the following way:

```
<param
   name="initParams"
   value="MS.SP.url=<%=
   Microsoft.SharePoint.Utilities.SPHttpUtility.HtmlEncode(
   Microsoft.SharePoint.SPContext.Current.Web.Url) %>" />
```

There are scenarios in which the Silverlight application is not running in the context of a web part but is in fact running in the Out of Browser host. The Out of Browser feature allows the Silverlight application to run in a special mode on the desktop outside of any web browser host. This gives the Silverlight application additional features such as access to the file system and COM automation. One of the limitations of the Out of Browser mode is that there are no `initParams`. The technique to work around this limitation is to cache the parameters in isolated storage when the application is opened in the browser. This works because generally the application opens when in the browser, even if for only a moment before it is installed in Out of Browser mode.

Load and LoadQuery

You might have noticed that the Client Object Model has two load methods, `Load()` and `LoadQuery()`. The `Load()` method does an in-place loading of the data returned from the server. All of the data returned from the server is stored and tracked inside of the `ClientContext` object. The `Client Context` tracks the object IDs of the items and properties returned from the server. For example if you call the server for the web object but do not return the title on the first call, you could subsequently call the server again for the title. The `Title` property is now filled in and ready to be used. This convenience does come with some trade-offs. For example, because the objects returned from the server are stored in the `ClientContext` object, it means that all of the data will only be garbage collected in the Silverlight application when the `ClientContext` object is cleaned out.

The `LoadQuery()` method returns the results as new objects. These objects are not part of the `ClientContext` and a result can be easily managed and discarded when not needed any more. Another difference between `Load()` and `LoadQuery()` is the type of queries you can write. The Client OM supports two types of queries: LINQ query syntax and method syntax. LINQ query syntax is a more natural declarative query language. This format is one that you are probably more familiar with and what people think of when they write LINQ queries. Listing 8.5 shows an example of a LINQ query to return visible Lists.

LISTING 8.5: Using LINQ Query Syntax with the Client OM

```
private void loadQueryButton_Click(object sender, RoutedEventArgs e)
{

    ClientContext clientContext = ClientContext.Current;
    ListCollection lists = clientContext.Web.Lists;

    var query = from list
                in lists
                where list.Hidden != false
                select list;

    IEnumerable<List> listsCollection = clientContext.LoadQuery(query);

    clientContext.ExecuteQueryAsync(
```

```
    // Succeeded Callback
    (ss, se) =>
    {
        // Execute on the UI thread
        Deployment.Current.Dispatcher.BeginInvoke(() =>
        {
            //Databind the List of Lists to the listbox
            listBox1.ItemsSource = listsCollection;
            listBox1.DisplayMemberPath = "Title";
        });
    },
    // Failed Callback
    (fs, fe) =>
    {
        // Not Implemented
    });
}
```

Listing 8.6 is the equivalent code that uses the method syntax query and the Load() method. The results are exactly the same as the LoadQuery() example just described. Both examples return a list of List objects that are not hidden and bind them to the list box control.

LISTING 8.6: Using Method Syntax with the Client OM

```
private void loadButton_Click(object sender, RoutedEventArgs e)
{

    ClientContext clientContext = ClientContext.Current;

    ListCollection lists = clientContext.Web.Lists;

    clientContext.Load(lists,
            lc => lc.Where(
                list => list.Hidden != false)
            .Include(
                list => list.Title));

    clientContext.ExecuteQueryAsync(
        // Succeeded Callback
        (ss, se) =>
        {
            // Execute on the UI thread
            Deployment.Current.Dispatcher.BeginInvoke(() =>
            {
                //Data bind the List of Lists to the listbox
                listBox1.ItemsSource = lists;
```

```
                listBox1.DisplayMemberPath = "Title";
            });
        },
        // Failed Callback
        (fs, fe) =>
        {
            // Not Implemented
        });
}
```

Object Model

The Silverlight Client OM supports a wide range of programming tasks against the server. Most of the examples you commonly see are against lists, list items, and document libraries. Although these are the cornerstone of the types of applications you write with the Client OM, there are many other interesting areas supported. For example you can work with site collections and sites. You can program against files and folders within a document library. You can create content types, pages, and web parts. You can work with users' roles and security. Unlike working with OData services (as explained in Chapter 9), the Client OM allows you to program against more features of a SharePoint site other than list and library data.

In this chapter you see how to do many of these tasks, but you won't see examples of everything you can do with the Client OM. You can visit the Microsoft SharePoint Client Object Model Resource Center at http://bit.ly/SPSL_ClientOMResourceCenter for links to more examples and documentation.

Let's start with a basic look at some of the ways to interact with list data. In the sample project included with this chapter you find a data grid that uses data binding to display the list data from SharePoint, as shown in Figure 8.1.

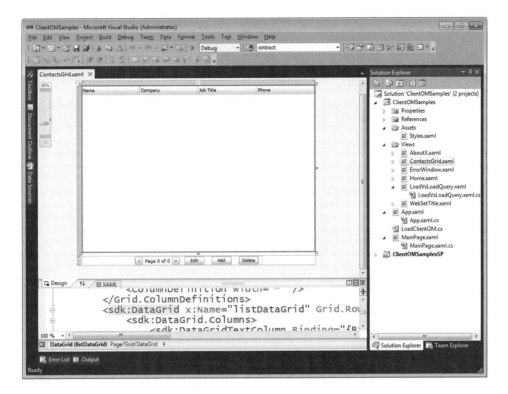

FIGURE 8.1: Data grid for data binding

Retrieving List Data

Retrieving list data from SharePoint is the most common use of the Client OM. The first thing you need to do is to call the GetByTitle() method of the list collection to return the specific list. Remember at this point you haven't called the server yet. You are just building up the query that will be sent to the server.

You must pass a CAML query to the GetItems method. You might remember CAML queries and the Collaboration Application Markup Language from Chapter 2, "Introduction to SharePoint Development." In this case you want to return all of the items so you can use the static method CreateAllItemsQuery() on the CamlQuery class to create a query that returns all of the items. In a real-world scenario you would pass a more complex query to filter and sort the items returned to reduce the network traffic. You see how to do paging later in this chapter without writing any CAML queries. Next you call the `Load()` method of the `ClientContext` object to add the query to the call back to the server. Finally, to actually execute the call on the server, call the `ExecuteQueryAsync()` method as shown in Listing 8.7.

LISTING 8.7: Reading a SharePoint List with the Client OM

```
//Get Contacts from SharePoint
ListCollection lists = clientContext.Web.Lists;
contactsList =
    lists.GetByTitle("ClientOMContacts");

contactsListItems =
    contactsList.GetItems(
        CamlQuery.CreateAllItemsQuery());

//load the list so we can get the item count for paging
clientContext.Load(contactsListItems);

clientContext.ExecuteQueryAsync(
    // Succeeded Callback
    (ss, se) =>
    {
        // Execute on the UI thread
        Deployment.Current.Dispatcher.BeginInvoke(() =>
        {
                // Databind the List Items Collection to the Datagrid
            listDataGrid.ItemsSource = contactsListItems;
        });
    },
    // Failed Callback
    (fs, fe) =>
    {
        // Not Implemented
    });
```

The `ExecuteQueryAsync()` method is an asynchronous call to the server with two callbacks for succeeded and failed. As in this example, one way to handle the callbacks is to use an anonymous delegate to handle them inline;

this was explained in Chapter 3, "Introduction to Silverlight Development." In this case there are two parameters, `Sender` and `ClientRequest-SucceededEventArgs`. When the results return from the server, you need to display them in the data grid. Data binding is the easiest way to do this. Set the `ItemsSource` property of the `datagrid` to the list collection.

Next you use a special data binding syntax for each field in the XAML of the data grid. This is required because the Client OM returns a loosely typed collection of items in a dictionary object. This means you need to bind to the items using an indexer reference as opposed to directly to the object. The indexer binding syntax is the name of the field in the dictionary, in this case `FieldValues`, then the fieldname in square brackets, as shown in Listing 8.8.

LISTING 8.8: Data Binding to a List Item Collection

```
<sdk:DataGrid x:Name="listDataGrid"
              Grid.Row="0" Margin="0,0,0,10"
              AutoGenerateColumns="False"
              CanUserSortColumns="False">
    <sdk:DataGrid.Columns>
        <sdk:DataGridTextColumn
            Binding="{Binding Path=FieldValues[FullName]}"
            Header="Name" Width="*" />
        <sdk:DataGridTextColumn
            Binding="{Binding Path=FieldValues[Company]}"
            Header="Company" Width="*" />
        <sdk:DataGridTextColumn
            Binding="{Binding Path=FieldValues[JobTitle]}"
            Header="Job Title" Width="*" />
        <sdk:DataGridTextColumn
            Binding="{Binding Path=FieldValues[WorkPhone]}"
            Header="Phone" Width="*" />
    </sdk:DataGrid.Columns>
</sdk:DataGrid>
```

When you run the application, you see the Contacts list data displayed in the data grid, as shown in Figure 8.2.

Client Object Model Samples			Contacts Datagrid ▼
Name	Company	Job Title	Phone
Bob German	Trey Research	Chief Bottle Washer	(304) 555-3090
Tony Smith	Contoso	Developer	(401) 555-3444
Colleen Bracy	Trey Research	Writer	(617) 555-5777
Jesse Merriman	Contoso Pharmaceutic	Pharmacist	(978) 555-1000
Brian Burke	Litware, Inc.	Sr. Manager, Nonfictic	(617) 555-3111
Amy Rusko	Litware, Inc.	Director, Author Relat	(617) 555-9033
Jesper Aaberg	Blue Yonder Airlines	Project Manager	(206) 555-1783
Lene Aalling	Blue Yonder Airlines	Sales Manager	(701) 555-3621
Syed Abbas	Contoso	CRM Consulting Mana	(20) 5555-4595
Kim Abercrombie	Humongous Insuranc	Salesperson	(410) 555-3839

FIGURE 8.2: SharePoint Contact List

Updating List Data

Updating an item using the Client OM, as shown in Listing 8.9, is as simple as setting the new values for an item. The work comes from getting a reference to the item you want to update. In this example, with the data grid you already have a reference to the item. Cast the `SelectedItem` of the data grid to a `ListItem` object. Set the values of the properties you want to change. In this case you only need to call the `Update()` method of the item. Calling the `Update()` method is enough to flag that record for update when you call the `ExecuteQueryAsync()` call.

LISTING 8.9: Updating List Data with the Client OM

```
ListItem item = (ListItem)listDataGrid.SelectedItem;

// prepend the value with an X as a test
item["Title"] = "X " + item["Title"];
item["FullName"] = "X " + item["FullName"];
item["Company"] = "X " + item["Company"];
item["JobTitle"] = "X " + item["JobTitle"];

item.Update();
```

```
clientContext.ExecuteQueryAsync(
    // Succeeded Callback
    (ss, se) =>
    {
        // Execute on the UI thread
        Deployment.Current.Dispatcher.BeginInvoke(() =>
        {
            // Remember the selected index before refresh
            int index = listDataGrid.SelectedIndex == 0
                ? 1 : listDataGrid.SelectedIndex - 1;

            // refresh the databinding to the List Items Collection
            listDataGrid.ItemsSource = null;
            listDataGrid.ItemsSource = contactsListItems;

            // Set the selected item and show it
            listDataGrid.SelectedIndex = index;
            listDataGrid.UpdateLayout();
            listDataGrid.ScrollIntoView(
                listDataGrid.SelectedItem,
                listDataGrid.Columns[0]);
        });

    },
    // Failed Callback
    (fs, fe) =>
    {
        // Not Implemented
    });
```

When the record is updated on the server, you need to do a little work on the data grid to refresh the bindings and scroll back to the record that was updated. This is not strictly required but provides a good user experience.

Deleting List Data

One of the easiest operations to do with the Client OM is to delete a List item. When you have a reference to the item you want to delete, call the DeleteObject() method of the ListItem, using the code from Listing 8.10.

LISTING 8.10: Deleting List Data with the Client OM

```
ListItem item = (ListItem)listDataGrid.SelectedItem;
item.DeleteObject();

clientContext.ExecuteQueryAsync(
    // Succeeded Callback
    (ss, se) =>
    {
        // Execute on the UI thread
        Deployment.Current.Dispatcher.BeginInvoke(() =>
        {
            // Remember the selected index before refresh
            int index = listDataGrid.SelectedIndex == 0
                ? 1 : listDataGrid.SelectedIndex - 1;

            // refresh the databinding to the List Items Collection
            listDataGrid.ItemsSource = null;
            listDataGrid.ItemsSource = contactsListItems;

            // Set the selected item and show it
            listDataGrid.SelectedIndex = index;
            listDataGrid.UpdateLayout();
            listDataGrid.ScrollIntoView(
                listDataGrid.SelectedItem,
                listDataGrid.Columns[0]);
        });

    },
    // Failed Callback
    (fs, fe) =>
    {
        // Not Implemented
    });
```

Just as you did with the Update()method, you can do a little work to refresh the data grid view. Again this is a just a function of the data grid and not part of the Client OM.

Creating List Data

Creating a new List item is almost the same as updating a List item. The only difference is you create a new record using the ListItemCreation Information() object in the AddItem() method of the List. When you have a reference to the new instance of a List item, you can set the field values just as you did when you updated a record. Call the Update() method of the new item after you have set all of the field values. Finally, calling ExecuteQueryAsync()creates the new List item on the server. Use the code in Listing 8.11 to create a new List item.

LISTING 8.11: Creating List Data with the Client OM

```
ListItem newItem =
    contactsList.AddItem(
        new ListItemCreationInformation());

newItem["Title"] = "TestName";
newItem["FullName"] = "TestName";
newItem["Company"] = "TestCompany";
newItem["JobTitle"] = "TestJob";
newItem["WorkPhone"] = "555-123-1234";

newItem.Update();
clientContext.Load(newItem);
clientContext.ExecuteQueryAsync(
    // Succeeded Callback
    (ss, se) =>
    {
        // Not Implemented
    },
    // Failed Callback
    (fs, fe) =>
    {
        // Not Implemented
    });
```

Paging

One of the best ways to handle large lists of data is to use paging. Paging returns items in small increments. For example if you set the page size to ten, then only ten items will be returned at a time. This allows the user to flip through all of the data if needed without overwhelming the server or the network connection.

Let's take a look at the data grid example you saw earlier and see what it takes to add paging support. In this case you want to be able to page forward and backward through the List items, know what page you are on, and know how many total pages of data there are. First add a couple of buttons to handle the navigation forward and backward through the List items. Then add some text to indicate what page you are on. These controls are shown in Listing 8.12.

LISTING 8.12: Adding Paging Buttons and Text

```
<Button x:Name="PreviousPageButton"
        Click="PreviousPageButton_Click"
        Content="&lt;"
        Width="20"
        Height="20"
        Margin="3,0"/>
<TextBlock x:Name="PageNumberTextBlock"
        Text="Page 0 of 0"
        TextWrapping="Wrap"
        Margin="3,0"
        FontSize="12"
        Padding="0,5,0,0"/>
<Button x:Name="NextPageButton"
        Click="NextPageButton_Click"
        Content="&gt;"
        Width="20"
        Height="20"
        Margin="3,0"/>
```

Next you need a few class level variables to hold information about the page size, the current page, and the Client OM page query object called `ListItemCollectionPosition()`. In this case the page size is set to ten, as shown in Listing 8.13.

LISTING 8.13: Variables to Hold Paging Information

```
// Hold paging info
ListItemCollectionPosition itemPosition = null;
// Start with 10 so you can see paging in action
int pageSize = 10;
int currentPage = 1;
```

Next when you get the data from the server, you pass the paging information as well. Start by resetting the navigation buttons to disabled. This is because you do not want the user to navigate until you have retrieved the list data from the server. Otherwise the user could click the button faster than you can retrieve the data, causing multiple calls to the server at the same time.

The next change is to pass the page size to the `CreateAllItemsQuery()` method, as shown in Listing 8.14. This still creates a CAML query that returns all items, but now it only returns the number of items specified in the page size. You also initialize the `ListItemCollectionPosition` property by passing in the next data page to use. In the first run when you are on the first page, this is null.

LISTING 8.14: Retrieving Paged Data with the Client OM

```
// Disable paging buttons until the data returns
PreviousPageButton.IsEnabled = false;
NextPageButton.IsEnabled = false;

//Get Contacts from SharePoint
ListCollection lists = clientContext.Web.Lists;
contactsList =
    lists.GetByTitle("ClientOMContacts");

// Get items with paging support
CamlQuery query =
    CamlQuery.CreateAllItemsQuery(pageSize);
query.ListItemCollectionPosition = itemPosition;

contactsListItems =
    contactsList.GetItems(query);

//load the list so we can get the item count for paging
clientContext.Load(contactsList);
clientContext.Load(contactsListItems);

clientContext.ExecuteQueryAsync(
    // Succeeded Callback
    (ss, se) =>
    {
        UpdatePaging();

        // Execute on the UI thread
        Deployment.Current.Dispatcher.BeginInvoke(() =>
        {
            // Databind the List Items Collection to the Datagrid
            listDataGrid.ItemsSource = contactsListItems;
        });
    },
    // Failed Callback
```

```
(fs, fe) =>
{
    // Not Implemented
});
```

After the call returns from the server, you need to call the Update
Paging() method, which is discussed next. Finally data bind the list collection to the data grid. The only difference here is that there are only a few
items being bound to the data grid. The way you data bind doesn't change
because you are paging.

The UpdatePaging() method is a helper method you can create to
encapsulate all of the paging functionality in one place. The first thing to
do is calculate the text for the current page. You can return the total list
size from the ItemCount property of the list. Next save a reference to the
ListItemCollectionPosition object. The ListItemCollectionPosition
object is the key to paging; in particular, the PageInfo property contains the
paging query string used to determine which data page to return. Finally,
enable the correct navigation buttons based on what page you are on. The
UpdatePaging() method is shown in Listing 8.15.

LISTING 8.15: Updating Paging Controls

```
private void UpdatePaging()
{
    // Calculate the data pages
    int pageCount = (int)Math.Ceiling(
                            (double)contactsList.ItemCount /
                            (double)pageSize);
    string pageText = string.Format("Page {0} of {1}",
                            currentPage,
                            pageCount);

    // Get the current data page query
    itemPosition =
        contactsListItems.ListItemCollectionPosition;

    // Execute on the UI thread
    Deployment.Current.Dispatcher.BeginInvoke(() =>
    {
        PageNumberTextBlock.Text = pageText;

        // Enable paging buttons
        PreviousPageButton.IsEnabled = (currentPage > 1);
```

```
        NextPageButton.IsEnabled = (currentPage < pageCount);

    });
}
```

Let's first look at the Forward navigation button event handler. This is the easiest one to understand because there is really nothing to do. When you call for a `ListCollection` that uses paging, SharePoint sets the `ListItemCollectionPosition` object to the next data page. Each time you call the server, you automatically get the next page of data. This might be useful if want to return all of the data from the server at once, one page at a time. Listing 8.16 shows the click event handler of the Forward button; you only need to increment the page count and refresh the data. The next data page query is already set.

LISTING 8.16: Next Page Button Click Event Handler

```
private void NextPageButton_Click(object sender, RoutedEventArgs e)
{
    currentPage++;

    RefreshData();
}
```

Navigating backward is a little more difficult because you need to build the `ListItemCollectionPosition` object yourself. All you really need to do is set the `PagingInfo` property to the correct data page, as shown in Listing 8.17. The format of the `PagingInfo` property is a string of key and value pairs separated by an ampersand.

The first parameter is the `Paged=TRUE`, which tells the server you are paging. The next parameter is the `PagedPrev=TRUE`. If this property is true, it tells the server that you are paging backward. If this property is false or omitted, then you are paging forward. The last parameter is `p_ID`. This is the SharePoint record ID for a record in the data page. If you are paging forward, this is the record ID of the last record. If you are paging backward, this is the record ID of the first record of the current data page. In this case you can retrieve the first record ID from the list collection as record zero.

LISTING 8.17: Previous Page Button Click Event Handler

```
private void PreviousPageButton_Click(
    object sender, RoutedEventArgs e)
{
    currentPage--;

    // Build the paging query string
    string pageInfo =
        String.Format(
        "Paged=TRUE&PagedPrev=TRUE&p_ID={0}",
            contactsListItems[0].Id);

    itemPosition = new ListItemCollectionPosition();
    itemPosition.PagingInfo = pageInfo;

    RefreshData();
}
```

Paging in SharePoint is a little obscure and not well documented. Walking through the sample included with this chapter can help you gain a better understanding of how it works.

Document Upload

The Client OM supports uploading documents to a document library. The sample code included in this chapter demonstrates how to capture an image from a webcam and upload the image file to a SharePoint document library.

Silverlight doesn't have any built in way to convert a raw image from the webcam into an image file such as a .png or .jpg. For this you need to leverage some other code. The code used in the sample code can be found on codeplex at http://imagetools.codeplex.com/. This code adds an extension to the `System.Windows.Media.Imaging.WriteableBitmap` class to convert the webcam image to a .png, by default. The conversion is also pluggable so that you can add additional file converters.

The first part of the code in Listing 8.18 converts the `WriteableBitmap` object into a `MemoryStream` that contains the .png image from the webcam. You need to obtain a reference to the `Library` that you will copy the file to.

From the List object, create a new file definition using the FileCreationInformation class. Set the Contents property of the file definition to Byte array from the MemoryStream representation of the .png file. The Url property is the name the image file will be in SharePoint. With the FileCreationInformation object populated with the details of the file, you just add it to the Files collection of the Library object.

LISTING 8.18: Converting a WriteableBitmap to a PNG Stream and Uploading to SharePoint

```
ImageTools.Image image = (ImageTools.Image)bitmap.ToImage();
PngEncoder encoder = new PngEncoder();
MemoryStream PNGstream = new MemoryStream();
encoder.Encode(image, PNGstream);

clientContext = ClientContext.Current;

// Get the Library
List library =
    clientContext.Web.Lists.GetByTitle("Shared Documents");

// Prepare the File to Upload
FileCreationInformation fileCreationInformation =
                    new FileCreationInformation();
fileCreationInformation.Content = PNGstream.ToArray();
fileCreationInformation.Overwrite = true;
fileCreationInformation.Url = "TestWebCamImage.png";
library.RootFolder.Files.Add(fileCreationInformation);

clientContext.ExecuteQueryAsync(succeededCallback, failedCallback);
```

Creating Ribbon Custom Actions

The Client OM also supports creating Ribbon Custom Action Commands. In this example you create a custom action on the Site Actions menu, as shown in Listing 8.19. The first thing to do is to set a couple of variables to hold the collection of custom actions and the ClientContext. You can return a collection of the custom actions from the Web object using the UserCustomActions property. Then call the server to fill the collection with the custom actions.

LISTING 8.19: Adding a Ribbon Custom Action with the Client OM, Part 1

```
UserCustomActionCollection userCustomActions;
ClientContext clientContext;

// Add Ribbon Custom Action
private void AddRibbonCustomAction()
{
    clientContext = ClientContext.Current;

    userCustomActions = clientContext.Web.UserCustomActions;

    clientContext.Load(userCustomActions);
    clientContext.ExecuteQueryAsync(succeededCallback, failedCallback);
}
```

When the collection of custom actions is returned from the server, you can add a new custom action to the collection. Before you add a new custom action, you should be sure that the action doesn't already exist. In this example in Listing 8.20, you can iterate through all of the custom actions deleting any that already exist. To add a new custom action, call the Add() method of the UserCustomActions collection. When you have a new custom action, you can set all of the required properties such as the location for the item. In this case Microsoft.SharePoint.StandardMenu refers to the Site Actions menu. You must also set the Url to navigate to when the custom action menu item is clicked. You should also set the Title, Description, and ImageUrl. Just like when adding a new List item, you call the Update() method of the userCustomAction object.

LISTING 8.20: Adding a Ribbon Custom Action with the Client OM, Part 2

```
private void succeededCallback
    (object sender, ClientRequestSucceededEventArgs e)
{
    // Loop backward through the collection to clean out old actions
    for (int x = userCustomActions.Count - 1; x >= 0; x--)
    {
        if (userCustomActions[x].Url.Contains("Smile"))
        {
            userCustomActions[x].DeleteObject();
        }
    }

    // Add the Custom Action
```

```
    UserCustomAction userCustomAction = userCustomActions.Add();

    userCustomAction.Location = "Microsoft.SharePoint.StandardMenu";
    userCustomAction.Group = "SiteActions";
    userCustomAction.Sequence = 101;
    userCustomAction.Title = "This is my Custom Action";
    userCustomAction.Description = "My Custom Action.";
    userCustomAction.Url = @"~site/SitePages/default.aspx";
    userCustomAction.ImageUrl = "_layouts/1033/images/RTEIMG.GIF";

    userCustomAction.Update();

    clientContext.ExecuteQueryAsync(succeededCallback2, failedCallback);
}

private void succeededCallback2
    (object sender, ClientRequestSucceededEventArgs e)
{
    // Not Implemented
}

private void failedCallback
    (object sender, ClientRequestFailedEventArgs e)
{
    // Not Implemented
}
```

Server Side Exception Handling

In regular programming you can wrap your code in a try/catch block to handle exceptions. This allows you to execute an alternate code path if an exception occurs. For example, you might use the code shown in Listing 8.21.

LISTING 8.21: Typical Exception Handling Code

```
    public void RunCode()
    {
        try
        {
            MessageBox.Show("Executing try block");
            throw new NullReferenceException();
        }
        catch
        {
```

```
            MessageBox.Show("Caught the exception");
        }
        finally
        {
            MessageBox.Show("Running the finally block.");
        }
    }
```

The Client Object Model has a similar concept that allows you to create server-side try/catch blocks. This is important in that there are many times where you expect an exception to occur. The server-side exception handling allows you to handle the exception and run an alternate code path without returning to the client.

The Client Object Model contains a class called Exception HandlingScope. The ExceptionHandlingScope class provides a wrapper for the try/catch and finally statements. The exception handling pattern is the same as you do on the client.

Begin by creating an instance of the ExceptionHandlingScope class. In the following example, which is part of the webcam sample project, you need to delete a wiki page from the Site Pages list. This page might or might not exist. If it doesn't exist then the code throws an exception, but in this case it doesn't matter, and you want the code to continue executing without returning to the client. Listing 8.22 shows how to use this.

LISTING 8.22: Server Side Exception Handling with the Client OM

```
ExceptionHandlingScope ex =
    new ExceptionHandlingScope(clientContext);

using (ex.StartScope())
{
    using (ex.StartTry())
    {
        // Delete the existing Wiki Page if it exists
        SP.File existingPage =
                clientContext.Web.GetFileByServerRelativeUrl(
                "/SitePages/Smile.aspx");
        existingPage.DeleteObject();
        clientContext.Load(existingPage);
    }
    // Do this if there is an exception on the server
    using (ex.StartCatch())
```

```
    {
        // Do nothing
    }

    // Always do this
    using (ex.StartFinally())
    {
        // Do nothing
    }
}
```

Server-side exception handling is a good way to optimize your code to reduce the number of calls to the server. There are also a number of properties of the `ExceptionHandlingScope` class that tell you information about the server side exceptions. These are `ErrorMessage`, `HasException`, `ServerErrorCode`, `ServerErrorValue`, and `ServerStackTrace`. When the call returns from the server, you can query these properties to see if there was an exception handled on the server and find more details about what that exception was.

Deployment and Redistribution

The last thing that you need to think about with the Client Object Model is how to redistribute the Client OM assemblies. Microsoft does ship a redistributable package of the Client OM assemblies for Silverlight and the .NET CLR. You can download the package at http://on-msn.com/SPSL_ClientOMRedist. This package also allows you to develop SharePoint solutions without the need to install SharePoint Foundation.

Redistributing the two Client OM assemblies in your Silverlight .xap package is not a best practice. A better approach is to dynamically load the assemblies at runtime. This allows you to avoid the issues of servicing the assemblies. For example, what do you do if Microsoft updates them in a future Service Pack? If you embed them in every Silverlight Web Part you create, then you would need to recompile and redeploy each one of these web parts. Including the assemblies inside of your .xap file also increases the size by 407KB. That is not a huge amount, but over a large deployment it adds up. Another benefit of loading the Client OM at runtime is that the assemblies are cached by the browser. This caching benefits the user because for every Silverlight application that uses the Client OM, the assemblies are only downloaded once and are pulled from the browser cache. The caching benefits the server by reducing the load of downloading the assemblies for every user for every Silverlight Web Part. The code to download the Silverlight Client OM at runtime is very generic, and you can write it once and it can be reused again in every application.

Dynamically loading the Client OM has two basic steps. The first step is to download the Client OM assemblies, which are packaged as a Silverlight .xap package file located in /_layouts/clientbin/Microsoft.SharePoint.Client.xap file. You can also pass an Action delegate so you can tell your application that you have finished downloading and loading the Client OM assemblies. Download the .xap package using the WebClient class. Even though your code downloads the .xap file every time the app runs, it is not a problem because Internet Explorer actually returns the .xap from the browser cache. Listing 8.23 shows how to load the assemblies at runtime.

LISTING 8.23: Dynamically Loading the Client OM, Part 1

```
private Action action;

public LoadClientOM(Action action)
{
    this.action = action;
    WebClient client = new WebClient();
    client.OpenReadCompleted += ReadCompleted;
    client.OpenReadAsync
        (new Uri("/_layouts/clientbin/Microsoft.SharePoint.Client.xap",
         UriKind.Relative));
}
```

The second step is to extract the Client OM assemblies from the Microsoft.SharePoint.Client.xap package you downloaded and load the assemblies. Loading the assemblies makes them available to the rest of your application. For each assembly you want to load from the downloaded .xap package, you extract the assembly as a stream using the GetResourceStream method. When you have the stream, you can pass the stream to the `Load()` method of an `AssemblyPart` class. And then finally you can callback on the `Action` delegate to tell the calling application that the assemblies have been loaded and are ready to be used. This is shown in Listing 8.24.

LISTING 8.24: Dynamically Loading the Client OM, Part 2

```
void ReadCompleted(object sender, OpenReadCompletedEventArgs e)
{
    Stream assemblyStream;
    AssemblyPart assemblyPart;

    // Load Client Runtime
    assemblyStream = Application.GetResourceStream(
        new StreamResourceInfo(e.Result, "application/binary"),
        new Uri("Microsoft.SharePoint.Client.Silverlight.Runtime.dll",
            UriKind.Relative)).Stream;

    assemblyPart = new AssemblyPart();
    assemblyPart.Load(assemblyStream);

    // Load Client OM
    assemblyStream = Application.GetResourceStream(
        new StreamResourceInfo(e.Result, "application/binary"),
        new Uri("Microsoft.SharePoint.Client.Silverlight.dll",
            UriKind.Relative)).Stream;

    assemblyPart = new AssemblyPart();
    assemblyPart.Load(assemblyStream);

    // Callback on the passed Delegate
    if (action != null) action();
}
```

Summary

The Client Object Model is the key to building SharePoint solutions using Silverlight. Although some of the data functionality is covered by the WCF Data Services, you have seen that the Client OM covers much more of the functionality of SharePoint. This enables you to not only consume data from SharePoint, but to create fully functional client-side applications that can do much of what you can do on the server. The power of the Client OM not only comes from how much you can do against SharePoint but in how easy it is to create those applications. The Client OM makes client-side asynchronous programming easy to do across a number of clients such as Silverlight and JavaScript. The Client OM also makes it easy for you to create very efficient applications that are fast across the network and reduce the load on the server.

9

Accessing SharePoint Data with WCF Data Services

I N THE LAST CHAPTER you learned about SharePoint's Client Object Model. This chapter introduces another option for accessing SharePoint list data in Silverlight. WCF Data Services, also known as ADO.NET Data Services, provides easy access to SharePoint list data using REST and the Open Data Protocol.

A major advantage of using WCF Data Services rather than the Client Object Model or Web Services interfaces to SharePoint is that Visual Studio can generate client-side proxy classes that provide strongly-typed access to list data. This can reduce coding errors and makes list fields available in Visual Studio IntelliSense. For example, where in the Client Object Model you might retrieve an `IEnumerable<ListItem>`, in WCF Data Services you can retrieve an `IEnumerable<Task>` and be able to reference the task columns as properties of the Task object.

Another advantage is that WCF Data Services uses a standard, the Open Data Protocol (OData), to access SharePoint. This can give you the flexibility to use the same code to access other OData services as well as SharePoint.

REST and the Open Data Protocol

REST and RESTful interfaces have become increasingly popular over the last several years. REST means Representational State Transfer and is actually an architectural pattern rather than a specific technology. For example, although nearly all RESTful interfaces are based on the HTTP protocol, a carrier-pigeon–based system could implement REST as long as it had a uniform way to address resources, used stateless servers, and conformed to a handful of other design principles.

The World Wide Web works on the same design principles, but REST is more general and allows for any kind of data and client states, instead of being limited to page rendering in a web browser. Because the Web itself follows REST, conventional web servers, gateways, proxies, and firewalls are already designed to handle RESTful traffic.

When a RESTful web service is implemented using the HTTP protocol, the resource being acted upon is specified in the URI, the MIME type specifies the data format, and the HTTP verb (GET, PUT, POST or DELETE) specifies the action to be taken. Depending on whether the URI specifies a collection (that is, ends with a /) or a specific entity, the verbs might have different meanings; for example a GET of a collection typically lists the collection, whereas a GET of a specific entity is expected to return the entity's associated data.

Beyond this, there is no single REST protocol, just as there is no single type of blue jeans: It's an easily recognized style but not an exact standard. Although many of the advantages of REST can be realized by just following the pattern, interoperability requires standards. That's where OData comes in.

OData is a protocol that allows for database-style Create, Read, Update and Delete (CRUD) operations over the Web. OData is an abbreviation for Open Data Protocol; for details see http://www.odata.org. OData access is mostly RESTful and is based on HTTP and familiar technologies such as the Atom Publishing Protocol and JavaScript Object Notation (JSON).

OData's mission is to bridge silos of data and to promote an ecosystem of compatible data consumers and providers. A single client, such as Excel 2010, can access any number of OData services without any programming, and an OData service such as the eBay catalog can be accessed by a wide variety of client applications.

Since its introduction in November 2009, quite a number of OData implementations have become available. At this writing, client libraries were available for Javascript, PHP, Java, iPhone, Silverlight and .NET, as well as being built into client applications such as Excel 2010.

On the server side, Microsoft SQL Server 2008 R2 exposes its reporting services data as OData, as does Microsoft Dynamics CRM 2011, the cloud-based SQL Azure and, of course, SharePoint Server 2010. IBM Websphere also supports the standard, and SAP has announced that its products will as well. In addition, eBay and Netflix have published their catalogs as OData; Windows Live provides OData access to photos, contacts and status messages; and many smaller web sites allow their content to be queried using the standard.

Getting Started with WCF Data Services

WCF Data Services provides both a client library and data services framework to make it easy to consume and produce OData interfaces in .NET and Silverlight. This technology was originally called *ADO.NET Data Services*, and the name change doesn't seem to have fully taken effect because the terms are used interchangeably on the Microsoft web site. At this writing, the download is still for "ADO.NET Data Services Update," even though much of the documentation is labeled "WCF Data Services."

The good news is that SharePoint 2010 supports OData through this same services framework; the bad news is that the framework code is not installed as a prerequisite, so before using OData, it's important to ensure that WCF Data Services has been installed on the SharePoint servers to be accessed. Download http://bit.ly/SPSL_DataServicesUpdate and make it a part of your standard SharePoint installation. Ensure that this is installed on your development machine before attempting any of the OData examples in this chapter.

The examples in this chapter make use of a Contacts list in SharePoint. If your test site doesn't already contain a Contacts list, create one by selecting More Options on the Site Actions menu in SharePoint. Because WCF Data Services is strongly typed, your list name is important because that will be the class name used in your solution; the sample in this chapter uses a contact list called, simply, Contacts.

For the paging and caching examples later in this chapter, it will be helpful to have quite a few contacts in there, so if you have some in Microsoft Outlook you might want to move them into your SharePoint list as test data. To do this, navigate into the list from the computer where you run Outlook; you might need to log in using basic authentication prompts if this machine isn't in your SharePoint development domain. Click the List tab and then the Connect to Outlook button. (Of course this assumes you have Microsoft Outlook 2007 or 2010 installed.) You are presented with a security prompt; if you allow the connection, Outlook connects to the contacts list in SharePoint. From here you can drag any contacts you have in Outlook into the SharePoint list. On the Send/Receive tab in Outlook, press Send/Receive All Folders to sync your changes into SharePoint. Now you should be able to see your contacts in the SharePoint list.

When WCF Data Services is installed and working on the SharePoint farm, you can use any web browser to query data directly from SharePoint. For example, if your site is at http://intranet.contoso.com/sites/Chapter09/, browse to http://intranet.contoso.com/sites/Chapter09/_vti_bin/listdata.svc. The service responds by enumerating the lists on the site, as shown in Figure 9.1.

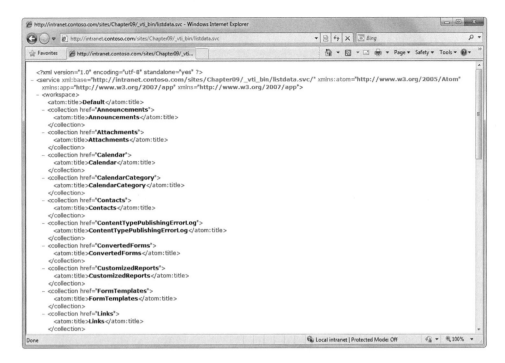

FIGURE 9.1: Enumerating a site's list with OData

The URI can be extended to query specific list data; for example, appending /Contacts to the URL enumerates the items in the Contacts list as an ATOM feed. If you're using Internet Explorer, it recognizes the Atom Pub format and offers to subscribe to it as a feed. If you wish to see the XML directly, you can turn this off. On the Tools menu, select Internet Options; then on the Content Tab click the Settings button for Feeds and Web Sites. If you uncheck the Turn on Feed Reading View checkbox, the browser displays simple XML thereafter.

Many other sorts of queries are possible, as shown in Table 9.1.

TABLE 9.1: OData Query URLs

Use This Format	To Perform This Query
`Listdata.svc/Contacts`	Retrieve all items in the Contacts list
`Listdata.svc/Contacts(1)`	Retrieve the first item in the Contacts list
`Listdata.svc/Contacts(1)/FullName`	Retrieve the single column FullName from the first item in Contacts
`Listdata.svc/Contacts?$select=FullName,JobTitle`	Retrieve selected columns from the Contacts list
`Listdata.svc/Contacts?$orderby=LastName`	Retrieve all items in the Contacts list, sorted by LastName
`Listdata.svc/Contacts?$skip=20&$top=10`	Skip the first 20 items in Contacts and retrieve the next 10 items (for paging)
`Listdata.svc/Contacts?$filter=JobTitle eq 'Developer'`	Retrieve all items in the Contacts list which have "Developer" in the JobTitle field

Binding to a SharePoint List Using WCF Data Services

WCF Data Services generates object wrappers for the OData service, allowing you to code to a strongly typed object model in your Silverlight application. To do this in your own Silverlight project, right-click Service References in Solution Explorer and enter the URL for the site that contains your contacts list, ensuring you append the service address /_vti_bin/ listdata.svc after the site URL. Give the service a namespace such as Share-PointContent. The Add Service Reference dialog box is shown in Figure 9.2; note that under Services: you need to double-click the data context if you want to see the lists expanded as in the screen shot.

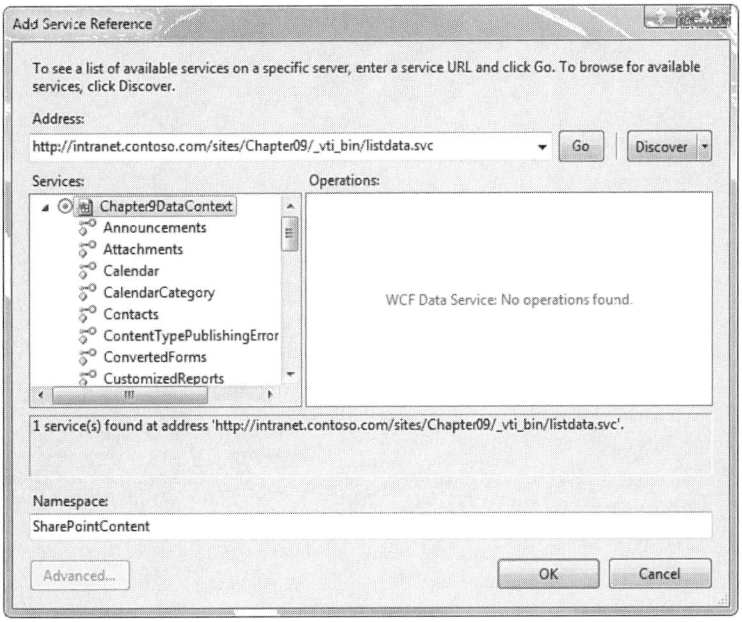

FIGURE 9.2: Adding a service reference to ListData.svc

This queries the web service description and generates an entity data model to allow you to access the service. Note that in the code download this step has already been done for you. The namespace and object class of the entity data model are determined when the service reference is added; in Figure 9.2 the class is `SharePointContent.Chapter9DataContext`.

Three web parts with accompanying Silverlight applications are provided to accompany this chapter: Contact Grid Simple, Contact Grid, and Contact Grid (Silverlight 5). The first two of these are shown in Figure 9.3. The simple version is a minimal implementation to bind the contacts list to a Silverlight DataGrid and perform full Create, Read, Update, and Delete (CRUD) operations on it, and the full version adds sorting, filtering, paging, and caching to the solution to show how to manage large data sets.

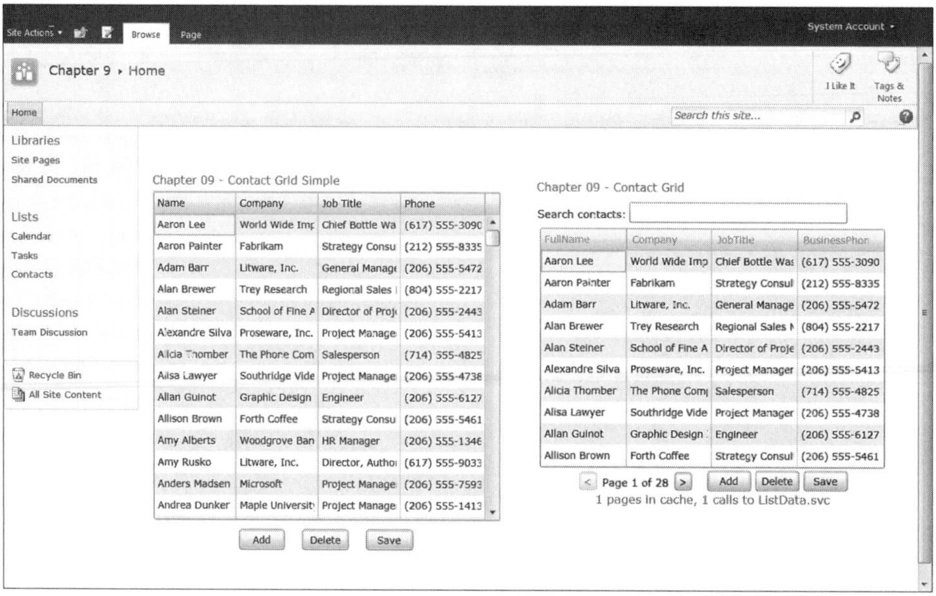

FIGURE 9.3: Simple and full contact grid web parts

There is a Silverlight project for each of the web parts, and a SharePoint project is set up to deploy them along with simple web parts to place them on the page. To set this up from scratch, you begin with an empty Share-Point project and add the Silverlight applications to the same solution. A module called ClientBin is added to deploy the .xap files, as described in Chapter 7; see Figure 7.3 for a screen shot.

The web parts are quite simple and use the `SilverlightPlugin` object to place the Silverlight application on the page and pass in the site URL; `SilverlightPlugin` was introduced in Chapter 5, "Web Part Development"; see Listing 5.2 for details. Listing 9.1 shows the ContactGridSimpleWP Web Part in its entirety except for the `using` statements and class declaration.

LISTING 9.1: ContactGridSimpleWP Web Part

```
protected override void CreateChildControls()
{
    SilverlightPlugin sl = new SilverlightPlugin();

    sl.Source = SPContext.Current.Site.RootWeb.Url.ToString() +
        "/ClientBin/ContactsGridSimpleSL.xap";
    sl.InitParameters = "siteUrl=" +
```

```
                    SPContext.Current.Web.Url.ToString();

            this.Controls.Add(sl);
        }
```

As you can see, not much work is done in the server side of the web part; it simply passes the site URL. Next, let's look at the simplified web part's Silverlight application in detail. It uses the standard DataGrid control with three buttons below it, laid out using a StackPanel. The XAML for this is shown in Listing 9.2.

LISTING 9.2: XAML for Simple Contact Grid Web Part

```xml
<Grid x:Name="LayoutRoot" Background="White">
  <Grid.RowDefinitions>
    <RowDefinition Height="*" />
    <RowDefinition Height="25" />
  </Grid.RowDefinitions>
  <Grid.ColumnDefinitions>
    <ColumnDefinition Width="*" />
  </Grid.ColumnDefinitions>
  <sdk:DataGrid x:Name="listDataGrid" Grid.Row="0"
                      Margin="0,0,0,10" AutoGenerateColumns="False"
                      CanUserSortColumns="False">
    <sdk:DataGrid.Columns>
      <sdk:DataGridTextColumn Binding="{Binding FullName}"
                      Header="Name" Width="*" />
      <sdk:DataGridTextColumn Binding="{Binding Company}"
                      Header="Company" Width="*" />
      <sdk:DataGridTextColumn Binding="{Binding JobTitle}"
                      Header="Job Title" Width="*" />
      <sdk:DataGridTextColumn Binding="{Binding Path=BusinessPhone}"
                      Header="Phone" Width="*" />
    </sdk:DataGrid.Columns>
  </sdk:DataGrid>
  <StackPanel Grid.Row="1" Orientation="Horizontal"
                      HorizontalAlignment="Center">
    <Button Content="Add" Height="23" Margin="10,0,10,0"
                      Name="AddButton" VerticalAlignment="Top"
                      Width="54" Click="AddButton_Click"
                      Grid.RowSpan="2" />
      <Button Content="Delete" Height="23" Margin="10,0,10,0"
                      Name="DeleteButton" VerticalAlignment="Top"
                      Width="54" Click="DeleteButton_Click"
                      Grid.RowSpan="2" />
      <Button Content="Save" Height="23" Margin="10,0,10,0"
                      Name="SaveButton" VerticalAlignment="Top"
```

```
                    Width="54" Click="SaveButton_Click"
                    Grid.RowSpan="2" />
    </StackPanel>
</Grid>
```

As you can see, the DataGrid contains binding expressions relating the field names from the SharePoint list to the data columns in the grid. Later on, the code creates a two-way data binding to this grid.

The Silverlight coding begins in App.xaml.cs, where the `Application_Startup` method is modified to take the site URL out of `InitParams` and pass it into the main page, whose constructor has been modified to accept the site URL as an argument. This is shown in Listing 9.3.

LISTING 9.3: Application_Startup Event Handler

```
private void Application_Startup(object sender, StartupEventArgs e)
{
    string siteUrl;
    if (e.InitParams.TryGetValue("siteUrl", out siteUrl))
    {
        MainPage p = new MainPage(siteUrl);
        this.RootVisual = p;
    }
}
```

Things get more interesting in the MainPage's constructor, which begins the process of connecting the `DataGrid` to the SharePoint Contacts list as shown in Listing 9.4. First, the code creates a new instance of `SharePoint-Content.Chapter09DataContext`; this object represents the runtime context of the WCF Data Services connection. This class was generated by Visual Studio when the service reference was made to ListData.svc. If you refer back to Figure 9.2, you can see the namespace and context name were chosen at that point. `SharePointContent.Chapter09DataContext` provides Entity Framework Object Services, which allow strongly-typed queries, inserts, updates, and deletes of the SharePoint Contacts list.

LISTING 9.4: MainPage Creates DataContext

```
SharePointContent.Chapter9DataContext dataContext;

public MainPage(string siteUrl)
```

```
{
    InitializeComponent();

    // Set up the data context and display the data
    dataContext = new SharePointContent.Chapter9DataContext(
        new Uri(siteUrl + "/_vti_bin/listdata.svc", UriKind.Absolute));

    RefreshData();
}
```

Chapter9DataContext is derived from the DataServiceContext class in the System.Data.Services.Client namespace provided by WCF Data Services. The DataServiceContext constructor takes a Uri as an argument; this allows the code to act on the site where the web part is installed rather than the one used when adding the service reference. Note that in order for this to work, the Contacts list in the target site must be identical to the one in the site where the service reference was made!

The final data binding, shown in Listing 9.5, is done in a separate method called RefreshData(), which is called from the MainPage constructor as well as later on when rows are added or deleted in the DataGrid.

LISTING 9.5: Binding the DataGrid to the SharePoint Contacts List

```
bool needsRefresh = false;

// Retrieve and display data
private void RefreshData()
{
    DataServiceQuery<SharePointContent.ContactsItem> q =
        (DataServiceQuery<SharePointContent.ContactsItem>)
        (
            from contact in dataContext.Contacts
                orderby contact.FullName
                select contact
        );

    q.BeginExecute((IAsyncResult result) =>
    {
        Dispatcher.BeginInvoke(() =>
        {
            q = result.AsyncState as
                DataServiceQuery<SharePointContent.ContactsItem>;
```

```
        IEnumerable<SharePointContent.ContactsItem> items =
            q.EndExecute(result);
        dataServiceCollection = new
            DataServiceCollection<SharePointContent.ContactsItem>
            (items);
        listDataGrid.ItemsSource = dataServiceCollection;

        needsRefresh = false;
    });
}, q);
}
```

RefreshData() begins with a LINQ query against the Entity Framework objects that selects the entire list, sorted by FullName. The query is strongly typed, and IntelliSense makes coding quick and less error-prone than with the traditional SharePoint Object Model.

The LINQ code constructs the query but doesn't actually issue it to SharePoint; to do that you need to call the BeginExecute() method. BeginExecute() expects to be passed a delegate, which it calls when a response has been received, in typical Silverlight asynchronous style. In this case, the delegate is defined as an anonymous function, taking a single IAsyncResult as its argument.

When this callback function is invoked, another anonymous function is used to switch over to the Silverlight UI thread using Dispatcher. BeginInvoke(). When this second anonymous function runs, it has the results in hand and is on the UI thread so it can bind the results to the Data-Grid.

The IAsyncResult passed in contains a Result property, which contains the now-populated Object Services representation of the Contacts list. Invoking the EndExecute method returns an IEnumerable collection of results, which in this case are ContactsItem objects generated to represent items in the SharePoint Contacts list.

Debugging Data Binding with Silverlight 5

Even though this is a Silverlight 4 project, if you have loaded Silverlight 5 (or the Silverlight 5 Beta), you can debug your data binding by simply setting a breakpoint in your XAML. This is shown in Figure 9.4.

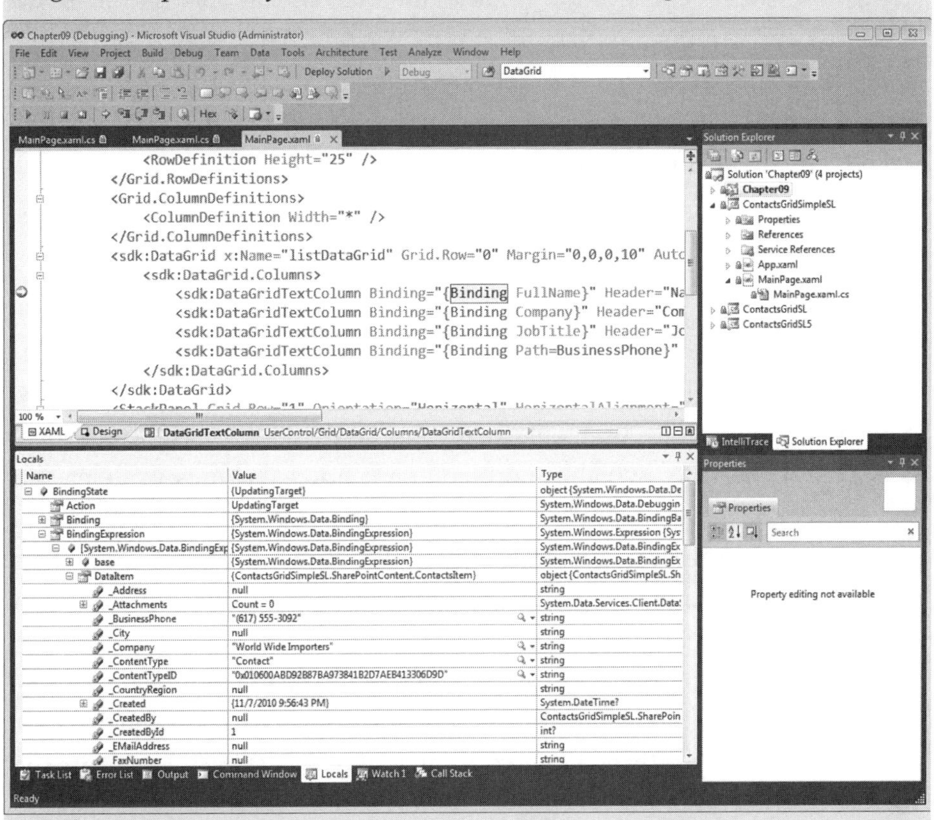

FIGURE 9.4: Data binding debugging with Silverlight 5

When you run your project in the debugger, the breakpoint is hit as the data binding expression is about to be evaluated. In the Locals debugger pane you see a BindingState object that contains all the details about the data binding. If you need to inspect the data item, it's right inside the BindingExpression within the BindingState object. This can save a lot of time when troubleshooting data binding expressions.

Updating SharePoint Data

At this point you could simply bind the IEnumerable collection to the Data-Grid and be done with it; indeed it would faithfully render the contact list. However, that would only give you a one-way binding, and two-way binding is necessary if you want to update the data back in SharePoint. To do this you need to enlist another class in the System.Data.Services.Client namespace: the DataServiceCollection class. Its constructor can be passed an IEnumerable collection, so it's easy enough to pass in the contacts list. Recall these lines from Listing 9.5:

```
IEnumerable<SharePointContent.ContactsItem> items =
    q.EndExecute(result);
dataServiceCollection = new
DataServiceCollection<SharePointContent.ContactsItem>(items);
```

DataServiceCollection is an ObservableCollection, which as the name implies, is a collection that can be observed. In this case, the observer is WCF Data Services, which is notified of any adds, changes, or deletes in the collection. DataServiceCollection can then update the data source with these changes on demand. When the DataServiceCollection is bound to the DataGrid, the binding is two-way, and changes in the grid can be written back to SharePoint.

This write-back is not implicit; indeed if every change to the object collection were immediately written back, it would result in a very chatty user interface. In this case, the user needs to press the "Save" button to write the data back to SharePoint. Listing 9.6 shows the Save button's click event handler, which saves any changes back to SharePoint.

LISTING 9.6: Save Button Saves Changes to SharePoint

```
private void SaveButton_Click(object sender, RoutedEventArgs e)
{
    dataContext.BeginSaveChanges(SaveChangesOptions.Batch,
    delegate(IAsyncResult asyncResult)
    {
        Dispatcher.BeginInvoke(() =>
        {
            try
            {
```

```
        dataContext.EndSaveChanges(asyncResult);
        MessageBox.Show("Changes saved");

        if (needsRefresh) RefreshData();
    }
    catch (Exception ex)
    {
        MessageBox.Show("Error: " + ex.InnerException.Message);
    }
        });
    }, dataContext);
}
```

Saving data is done in the same asynchronous pattern as querying data and begins with invoking the data context's `BeginSaveChanges()` method. Again, an anonymous delegate is used, along with a call to `Dispatcher.BeginInvoke()` to ensure that a second anonymous function runs in the Silverlight UI thread. If `EndSaveChanges()` is successful, it reports the results back to the user; if not it shows an error message.

You might notice a Boolean field `needsRefresh` was declared just before the `RefreshData()` method and was set to false in `RefreshData()`. This flag is used when rows are added to the grid to refresh and re-sort the data. If the flag is set, `RefreshData()` is called.

At this point, users can click the DataGrid and update the cells, and the changes are written back to SharePoint when they click Save. The only thing that remains is to implement the Add and Delete button click events so users can add and delete rows in the DataGrid.

Clicking the Add button creates a new `ContactsItem` object and adds it to the `DataServiceCollection`. The new item will be at the end of the collection and therefore appears at the bottom of the `DataGrid`, so the last row is selected and scrolled into view to make it visible to the user. The Delete button is even simpler: It simply deletes the selected row. The add and delete code is shown in Listing 9.7.

LISTING 9.7: Adding a Contact to the Collection

```
// Add a new item to the grid and position there
private void AddButton_Click(object sender, RoutedEventArgs e)
{
    SharePointContent.ContactsItem c =
```

```
                new SharePointContent.ContactsItem();

    dataServiceCollection.Add(c);
    listDataGrid.SelectedIndex = dataServiceCollection.Count - 1;
    listDataGrid.ScrollIntoView(listDataGrid.SelectedItem,
                                listDataGrid.Columns[0]);
    needsRefresh = true;
}


// Delete an item from the grid
private void DeleteButton_Click(object sender, RoutedEventArgs e)
{
    int i = listDataGrid.SelectedIndex;
    dataServiceCollection.RemoveAt(i);
}
```

The DataGrid now implements all of the "CRUD" (Create, Read, Update and Delete) operations on a SharePoint list, and all the heavy lifting is done by WCF Data Services.

Paging through Large Data Sets

This example is fine as long as you don't mind downloading the entire SharePoint list every time you want to display the data. And that's okay if the list is short, but if the list becomes too large it would waste a lot of time and bandwidth retrieving rows of data the user might never choose to view. The solution is to provide a way to page through the data and to find contacts through a user query function. These features are included in the full ContactsGridWP Web Part.

As a first step to implement paging, additional controls are added below the DataGrid to page through the data. The out-of-the-box paging control would allow paging through objects in memory, but this solution implements its own so it can fetch the pages from SharePoint as they're needed. The extra controls are shown in Listing 9.8.

LISTING 9.8: Paging Controls for the Contacts Grid

```xml
<StackPanel x:Name="PagingControlsStackPanel" Orientation="Horizontal"
 HorizontalAlignment="Center">
  <Button x:Name="PreviousPageButton" Click="PreviousPageButton_Click"
        Width="20" Content="&lt;" Height="20" Margin="3,0"/>
```

```
    <TextBlock x:Name="PageNumberTextBlock" Text="Page 1 of x"
            TextWrapping="Wrap" Margin="3,0" FontSize="12"
            Padding="0,5,0,0"/>
    <Button x:Name="NextPageButton" Click="NextPageButton_Click" Width="20"
            Content="&gt;" Height="20" Margin="3,0"/>
    <Button x:Name="AddButton" Width="50" Content="Add" Margin="15,0,0,0"
            Click="AddButton_Click" />
    <Button x:Name="DeleteButton" Width="50" Content="Delete"
            Margin="5,0,0,0" Click="DeleteButton_Click" />
    <Button x:Name="SaveButton" Width="50" Content="Save" Margin="5,0,0,0"
            Click="SaveButton_Click" />
</StackPanel>
```

Instead of retrieving all the rows of the Contacts list, the code retrieves the rows in "pages" of pageSize rows and stores each "page" in its own DataServiceCollection object in a local cache. The UI state is maintained in a set of local fields shown in Listing 9.9. At any given time, the currentPage field contains the page number being displayed.

LISTING 9.9: Fields to Maintain State of Contact Grid

```
// Current page number
private int currentPage = 0;

// Page size and Row Count
private const int pageSize = 10;        // # of rows to display in grid
private long totalRowCount = 0;         // total rows in result set

private long totalPageCount
{
    get { return ((totalRowCount - 1) / pageSize) + 1; }
}
```

To display the number of pages and avoid allowing the user to page past the end of the data, the code needs to know how many rows are on the server. This can be retrieved along with each page of data and is stored in totalRowCount so the totalPageCount property will be accurate and can be displayed in the paging user interface.

Listing 9.10 shows the code to retrieve and display a page of data. Note that the code samples that can be downloaded with this book also include caching, filtering, and sorting logic, which are discussed later in this chapter; therefore this Listing is simpler than the download.

LISTING 9.10: Code to Retrieve a Page of Data

```
private void DisplayPage(int pageNum)
{
    // Remember new state
    currentPage = pageNum;

    DataServiceQuery<SharePointContent.ContactsItem> q =
        (DataServiceQuery<SharePointContent.ContactsItem>)
            (from contact in dataContext.Contacts.IncludeTotalCount()
            select contact).Skip<SharePointContent.ContactsItem>
            (pageNum * pageSize).Take<SharePointContent.ContactsItem>
            (pageSize);

    try
    {
        // Kick off the query as an asynchronous request
        q.BeginExecute((IAsyncResult result) =>
        {
            // Ensure we're running on the UI thread
            Dispatcher.BeginInvoke(() =>
            {
                // Process the result
                q = result.AsyncState as
                        DataServiceQuery<SharePointContent.ContactsItem>;
                QueryOperationResponse<SharePointContent.ContactsItem>
                  queryResponse = q.EndExecute(result) as
                  QueryOperationResponse<SharePointContent.ContactsItem>;

                if (queryResponse != null)
                {
                    this.totalRowCount = queryResponse.TotalCount;

                    this.dataServiceCollection = new
                      DataServiceCollection<SharePointContent.ContactsItem>
                      (queryResponse);

                    // Bind to the DataGrid and save away in cache
                    listDataGrid.ItemsSource = this.dataServiceCollection;

                    // Update the other controls on the page
                    UpdatePageControls(1);
                }
            });
        }, q);
    }
    catch (Exception ex)
    {
        // If here, something bad happened, so tell the user
```

```
        Dispatcher.BeginInvoke(() =>
        {
            MessageBox.Show("Error retrieving data: " + ex.Message);
        });
    }
}
```

Notice that the LINQ query is more elaborate than in the previous example. First, the `.Skip<T>()` and `.Take<T>()` methods have been added to the query to fetch just the page we want. One more piece of information is needed, however, and that's the total number of rows matching the query so we know how many pages there are. Fortunately, OData and WCF Data Services can accommodate that without requiring an extra round-trip to the server. To request the total row count, the method `IncludeTotalCount()` is called while referencing the Contacts object.

Following the LINQ query, the code is pretty similar to the simplified Contacts grid example from earlier in this chapter. The result is passed into an anonymous delegate function, and the `Dispatcher` is used to ensure you're on the UI thread.

The result processing is a bit different, however, because it needs to extract the total count from the result set. The `EndExecute()` method returns an `IEnumerable<ContactsItem>` suitable for data binding or access via a `DataServiceCollection`, but if you count the items in the collection, you'll only get the count for one page of data. To get at the total row count, you need to cast the `IEnumerable` interface to its underlying object, which is a `QueryOperationResponse<ContactsItem>`; this is the object that allows access to the total row count.

After binding the `DataServiceCollection` to the DataGrid control, the code calls a private method called `UpdatePageControls()`. As shown in Listing 9.11, it simply displays the page number and disables the Previous or Next button when the user is at the first or last page, respectively. It also maintains some simple statistics for demonstration purposes.

LISTING 9.11: Updating Controls after a Paging Operation

```
// Update paging buttons and status messages
private void UpdatePageControls(int callsToService)
{
```

```
// Enable and disable paging buttons to prevent moving back
// from the first page or forward from the last
this.PreviousPageButton.IsEnabled = (currentPage > 0);
this.NextPageButton.IsEnabled = (currentPage < totalPageCount - 1);

this.PageNumberTextBlock.Text = "Page " + (currentPage + 1) +
                        " of " + totalPageCount.ToString();

// Show a sneak peek at the cache for demonstration purposes
this.callsToListDataSvc += callsToService;
this.StatusTextBlock.Text = this.cache.Keys.Count() +
                    " pages in cache, " +
                    this.callsToListDataSvc +
                    " calls to ListData.svc";
}
```

Allowing the user to page through the data is simple: When the Previous and Next buttons are clicked, the new page is displayed using the DisplayPage() method as shown in Listing 9.12.

LISTING 9.12: Paging Button Click Event Handlers

```
// Handle paging buttons
void PreviousPageButton_Click(object sender, RoutedEventArgs e)
{
    DisplayPage(--currentPage);
}

void NextPageButton_Click(object sender, RoutedEventArgs e)
{
    DisplayPage(++currentPage);
}
```

Caching Paged Data

An easy way to cache pages of data is to keep the DataServiceCollection objects as they are retrieved, and to reuse them as the user pages back and forth. The cache is just a generic Dictionary collection with the page number as its key and a DataServiceCollection as its value. Adding a page to cache is simple; AddToCache() is called after retrieving a new page in DisplayPage(). This is shown in Listing 9.13.

LISTING 9.13: Caching Code in Contacts Grid Web Part

```
// Here is the cache:
private Dictionary<int, DataServiceCollection
    <SharePointContent.ContactsItem>> cache = new Dictionary
    <int, DataServiceCollection<SharePointContent.ContactsItem>>();

// Add a page of data to the cache
private void AddToCache(int pageNumber,
    DataServiceCollection<SharePointContent.ContactsItem> page)
{
    cache[pageNumber] = page;
}


// Attempt to display a cached page of data, or return false if it
// isn't available
private bool DisplayFromCache(int pageNumber)
{
    if (cache.ContainsKey(pageNumber))
    {
        // If here, we found the cached page; go ahead and display it
        DataServiceCollection<SharePointContent.ContactsItem>
            bindingCollection = cache[pageNumber];
        listDataGrid.ItemsSource = bindingCollection;
        UpdatePageControls(0);
        return true;
    }
    else
    {
        // If here, no luck; tell caller to get the page from SharePoint
        return false;
    }
}

private void ClearCache()
{
    cache.Clear();
}
```

The strategy is to try to display a page from cache before requesting it from SharePoint. This function returns true if it's able to display the page from cache or false to indicate that we need to use WCF Data Services to get the data. In addition, a simple method is provided to clear the cache.

A minor update to the DisplayPage() method checks the cache before requesting data, and if a new page is retrieved, adds it to the cache. This is shown in Listing 9.14.

LISTING 9.14: DisplayPage() Tries to Use Cache Before Retrieving a Page

```
private void DisplayPage(int pageNum)
{
    // Remember new state
    currentPage = pageNum;

    // Try to display from cache if available
    if (!DisplayFromCache(pageNum))
    {
        // Retrieve and display from SharePoint as before
        // (code is not repeated from the earlier listing...)

        // After binding the page to the DataGrid,
        //    add this line to save it in cache:
        AddToCache(pageNum, this.dataServiceCollection);
    }
}
```

Filtering and Sorting the Data

The whole idea of paging is to handle large data sets, yet if there were thousands of contacts in the Contacts list, users would quickly tire of paging through hundreds of grids full of data. A filtering feature allows the user to type a few characters of the contact's information to quickly narrow down the list of choices. In addition, users often like to click the grid headings to sort the data to their liking. Both of these features have been included in the full ContactsGrid Silverlight application.

An AutoCompleteBox from the Silverlight Toolkit (http://silverlight. codeplex.com/) has been added above the `DataGrid` so users can type a filter string to narrow down the data set. The `Populated` event fires if the user pauses more than 250 milliseconds while typing, as specified in the `MinimumPopulateDelay` property. When this happens, the code updates the grid with a new filter for a very interactive user experience. The added controls are shown in Listing 9.15.

LISTING 9.15: AutoCompleteBox for Filtering the Results Set

```
<StackPanel Orientation="Horizontal">
    <TextBlock Text="Search contacts:" FontSize="12" Padding="0,8,0,0" />
    <sdk:AutoCompleteBox HorizontalAlignment="Left"
```

```
               x:Name="filterAutoCompleteBox"
               Margin="3" VerticalAlignment="Top" Text=""
               Height="23" Width="249"
               MinimumPopulateDelay="250"
               MinimumPrefixLength="0"
               Populated="filterAutoCompleteBox_Populated"/>
</StackPanel>
```

An `AutoCompleteBox` is similar to a `TextBox` and is intended to offer possible completions for what the user is typing, similar to the search suggestions SharePoint shows. In this case there won't be any suggestions, but the `AutoCompleteBox`'s `Populate` event is useful for refreshing the data when the user pauses in typing rather than triggering a new query for each keystroke.

When the `AutoCompleteBox` fires its `Populate` event, the event handler sets the filter field to whatever the user has typed, clears the cache, and displays the first page of data as shown in Listing 9.16.

LISTING 9.16: AutoCompleteBox Event Handler to Filter Results

```
// Field to hold current filter string
private string filter = "";

// Handle filtering
private void filterAutoCompleteBox_Populated(object sender,
                                          PopulatedEventArgs e)
{
    this.filter = this.filterAutoCompleteBox.Text;
    this.ClearCache();
    this.DisplayPage(0);
}
```

Another difference between this and the simplified contacts grid is that this one implements sorting. The DataGrid control would gladly handle this by simply setting its `CanUserSortColumns` property to true, but this would just sort the data that was in the grid. To sort the whole data set, the sorting needs to happen on the server so the code needs to flush the cache and do a new query with the required sort order.

The user initiates a sort by clicking a column heading. If the data was already sorted in ascending order by the column the user has clicked, then it is sorted in descending order instead. Listing 9.17 shows the column heading Click event handler.

LISTING 9.17: Column Heading Click Event Handler

```
// Field to hold current sort order
private string orderby = "FullName asc";

private void SortHeading_Click(object sender, RoutedEventArgs e)
{
    HyperlinkButton btn = sender as HyperlinkButton;
    if (btn != null)
    {
        if (this.orderby == btn.Content.ToString() + " asc")
        {
            this.orderby = btn.Content.ToString() + " desc";
        }
        else
        {
            this.orderby = btn.Content.ToString() + " asc";
        }

        this.ClearCache();
        this.DisplayPage(0);
    }
}
```

The only thing left to do to enhance the DisplayPage() method to include the filter and orderby terms in the LINQ query. Listing 9.18 shows the whole query, including what was shown in the earlier listing of DisplayPage() with the addition of dynamic query terms for sorting and filtering.

LISTING 9.18: LINQ Query with Sorting, Filtering, and Paging

```
// Begin with the basic list query...
DataServiceQuery<SharePointContent.ContactsItem> q =
    (DataServiceQuery<SharePointContent.ContactsItem>)
        (from contact in dataContext.Contacts.IncludeTotalCount()
         select contact).Skip<SharePointContent.ContactsItem>
         (pageNum * pageSize).Take<SharePointContent.ContactsItem>
         (pageSize);

// ... then add the dynamic query terms
q = q.AddQueryOption("$orderby", orderby);
```

```
if (filter != "")
{
    q = q.AddQueryOption("$filter", "substringof('" +
        this.filter + "', FullName) or substringof('" +
        this.filter + "', Company) or substringof('" +
        this.filter + "', JobTitle) or substringof('" +
        this.filter + "', BusinessPhone)");
}
```

The `AddQueryOption()` method allows any query string option to be added to the query. This allows the `$orderby` and `$filter` query string parameters to be added at runtime rather than baking them into a LINQ query that is evaluated at compile time. The filter term is applied to all four of the displayed data fields by specifying a logical "or" of four substring expressions. Consult the OData standard for details on how to construct query options on your own.

Using Silverlight 5 to Bind Style Setters

Silverlight 5 introduces the ability to bind data to *style setters*, a feature that was already available in Windows Presentation Foundation. Style setters are XAML elements that declare visual styles to be displayed by setting specific properties. For example, a bold style might use a style setter that sets the `Bold` property to true. In this next example, you learn how to bind style setters in the Contacts Grid to highlight rows based on the data.

After using the Contacts Grid Web Part, users reported they would like the grid to highlight managers and directors so they can be identified at a glance. This information is already in each contact's JobTitle field; the key is to convert it to a form that is useful for data binding and then bind it to a style that sets the grid cells' background.

A grid cell's background property is set to a Silverlight `Brush` object, so a *value converter* is needed to convert the `JobTitle` string into a `Brush` for data binding. The binding expression references the value converter, and the class's `Convert()` method is called during data binding. The value converter is shown in Listing 9.19.

LISTING 9.19: Data Binding Value Converter from Contact to Brush

```
public class JobTitleToBrushConverter : IValueConverter
{
    public object Convert(object value, Type targetType,
            object parameter, System.Globalization.CultureInfo culture)
    {
        Color resultColor = Colors.Transparent;
        if (value is string)
        {
            string jobTitle = value as string;
            if (jobTitle.IndexOf("Director") >= 0)
            {
                // Pale green background
                resultColor = Color.FromArgb(225, 144, 227, 100);
            }
            else if (jobTitle.IndexOf("Manager") >= 0)
            {
                // Pale yellow background
                resultColor = Color.FromArgb(255, 255, 255, 165);
            }
        }
        Brush result = new SolidColorBrush(resultColor);
        return result;
    }

    public object ConvertBack(object value, Type targetType,
            object parameter, System.Globalization.CultureInfo culture)
    {
        // Should never be called in this application
        throw new NotImplementedException();
    }
}
```

The style is declared immediately after opening the `UserControl` tag in MainPage.xaml, as shown in Listing 9.20. The style affects all `DataGridCell` elements; these are the cells in the `DataGrid`.

LISTING 9.20: Style to Change Cell Background Based on Job Title

```
<UserControl.Resources>
    <local:JobTitleToBrushConverter x:Key="JobTitleToBrushConverter" />
    <Style TargetType="sdk:DataGridCell">
        <Setter Property="Background" Value="{Binding JobTitle,
                Converter={StaticResource JobTitleToBrushConverter}}" />
    </Style>
</UserControl.Resources>
```

Figure 9.5 shows the finished project; any contact with Manager or Director in the JobTitle field is highlighted. Notice you can edit the job title of one of the contacts and the style changes immediately based on the data binding.

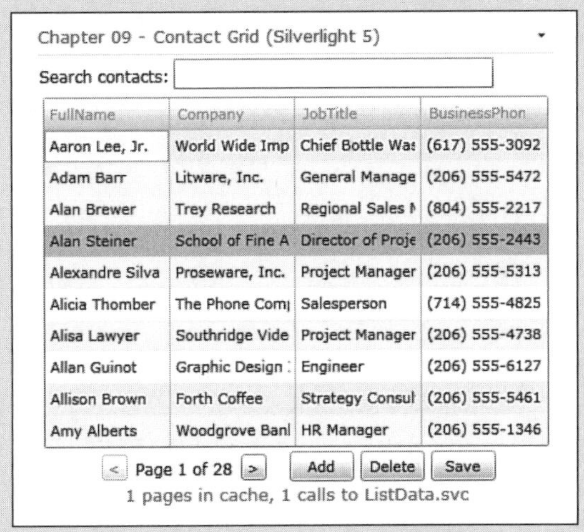

FIGURE 9.5: Finished Contact Grid with data-bound style setters

Summary

OData and WCF Data Services are extremely useful for accessing Share-Point list data and other data sources from Silverlight. Two-way data binding makes it easy to display and update SharePoint data from any Silverlight control that supports it. Large data sets can be accessed efficiently by using the paging features of WCF Data Services. The type-safe approach can be a blessing or a curse, depending on the application; the Client Object Model might be a better choice if your solution needs the flexibility to access lists and fields that are determined at runtime.

10.

Accessing SharePoint with Web Services

PRIOR TO SHAREPOINT 2010, the primary way to access SharePoint data from client-side technologies such as Silverlight was to use its web services interface. Introduced in SharePoint 2003, web services provide access to SharePoint content and shared services. The primary user of these services has been the Microsoft Office client, which provides deep integration with SharePoint for document management, meeting coordination, and a variety of other collaborative tasks. They are well documented on the MSDN web site, and though some have been deprecated over the years, most are still available for use.

Web services open up the world of SharePoint shared services that span many site collections and web applications to provide core features such as enterprise search and social networking. Much of this chapter revolves around the sample SearchView Web Part that shows how to use these services from Silverlight. The sample also follows the Model View ViewModel (MVVM) pattern and has a section that explains how to use it. The SearchView web part project will show you how to access SharePoint shared services, which are only accessible using web services. You'll learn how to use these services to search for content and people, and to provide the new Search Suggestions available in SharePoint 2010. You'll also learn how to access SharePoint's social networking API to read user profiles and post comments, and to read a user's "Activity Feed", which is an ATOM feed. At the end of the chapter, you'll learn to develop your own WCF service to SharePoint in case you can't find a web service that does what you need.

Web Services in SharePoint

SharePoint supports dozens of web services that offer access to nearly every part of the product. Table 10.1 shows a small subset of what's available; for a complete list see http://bit.ly/SPSL_SPWebServices.

TABLE 10.1: Selected SharePoint Web Services

Service	Used for	Minimum Product
Alerts	Manage subscriptions to alerts sent when content changes	SharePoint Foundation
Copy	Copy files between locations in SharePoint	SharePoint Foundation
Lists	Work with lists, libraries and content types	SharePoint Foundation
Published Links	Manage published links shown in Office dialog boxes	SharePoint Server
Search	Enterprise search across SharePoint site collections, people, and external sources	SharePoint Server
Social Data	Access and update ratings, tags, comments, and other social data	SharePoint Server
User Profile	Access and update user profiles	SharePoint Server

The most popular web service in Windows SharePoint Services (renamed SharePoint Foundation in 2010) was surely the Lists.asmx web service, which allows queries and updates on SharePoint lists. This functionality and much more is now available with the Client Object Model and

WCF Web Services. Using traditional web services for manipulating Share-Point list content is no longer de rigueur unless access to older versions of SharePoint is necessary or if the Client Object Model and OData Services are not available from the SharePoint hosting provider.

However, with each version of SharePoint, shared services—those services that can span all content across site collections—become richer and richer. Web services are the best (and only) way to access these services. That's why access to shared services, in particular Search and SharePoint's social networking services, is the focus of this chapter.

> **◾ TIP**
>
> The search and social networking web services used in this chapter are all part of Microsoft SharePoint Server 2010 and are not included in the "free" Microsoft SharePoint Foundation 2010 product. To run the SearchView sample solution, you also need to set up and configure both the search and user profile services.
>
> If you downloaded the *2010 Information Worker Demonstration and Evaluation Virtual Machine* mentioned in Chapter 1, these services should be up and running. If you set up your own server, ensure they are working before attempting to run the SearchView sample. Details on search configuration are available at http://bit.ly/SPSL_SearchConfig, and user profile setup is described at http://bit.ly/SPSL_ProfileConfig.
>
> If you are developing for SharePoint Foundation, you might want to skip to the last section on building your own WCF services; however, you'd miss a lot of information on building solutions with the Model View ViewModel pattern, which is used in the SearchView Web Part sample.
>
> The search web service is available in the "free" Search Server 2010 Express product; however, the profile service is not. If you want to develop on Search Server 2010 Express, you could adapt the solution by removing the social aspects, which are isolated to the Person Detail child window.

The SearchView Web Part Sample Solution

Most of this chapter (except for the custom WCF section) is built on a single solution called the SearchView Web Part. SearchView is able to search content or people, as shown in Figure 10.1.

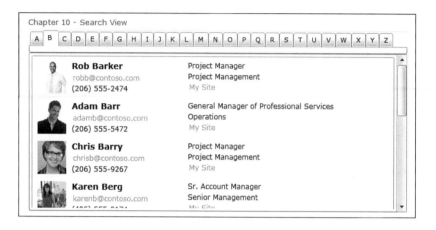

FIGURE 10.1: SearchView Web Part with People Search results and Alpha Tabs Query

There are three ways to issue a search query with SearchView:

- A fixed query can be entered when editing the web part. This allows the web part to serve as a search-driven content rollup.

- The user can enter a search (and is shown Search Suggestions as they type). Optionally a fixed portion of the query can be specified when editing the web part. For example, to provide a search within a particular SharePoint site, a fixed query of "site:http://myserver/sites/mysite/" could be entered, and this term would be added to whatever the user types.

- Alphabetic tabs can be provided for selecting content beginning with a particular letter of the alphabet, again with optional fixed query terms. For example, to make a directory of the Sales department, a People search with alphabetic tabs could be augmented with a fixed query of "department:sales".

When SearchView is configured for People search, the user can click a person in the results display for a summary of his or her user profile, activity feed, and a small text box to leave a comment for the user. This is shown in Figure 10.2.

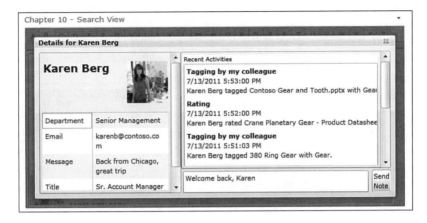

FIGURE 10.2: SearchView People Detail child window

These social features are provided by the User Profile and Social Data web services, and the Activity Feed provides an opportunity to see how easy it is to consume an ATOM feed from SharePoint.

When the web part is edited, the editing experience is directly in the web part. Although this doesn't really have much to do with web services, it is described in the section, "In-Place Web Part Editing Experience," later in this chapter.

The MVVM Pattern

The Silverlight application that provides the SearchView user interface was developed using the MVVM (Model View ViewModel) pattern, which adds a bit of code but also cleans up the design quite a bit. This is a good pattern to follow if web parts start to become complex, such as in this case. The design is shown in Figure 10.3.

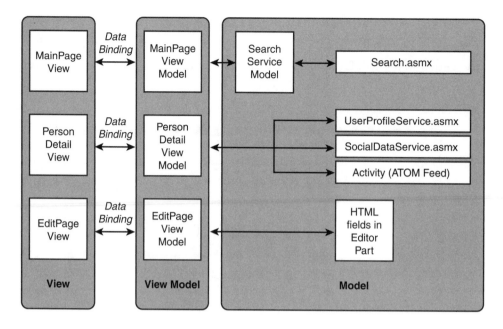

FIGURE 10.3: MVVM Pattern in the SearchView Web Part

The SearchViewSL project has four main .xaml files, each of which defines a View of the application:

- MainPage.xaml provides the primary user interface for SearchView.
- EditPage.xaml provides the editing view.
- PersonDetail.xaml is a child window, which is more or less a dialog box in Silverlight; it shows the social networking user interface when a user clicks on a person in the MainPage view.
- ErrorPage.xaml displays an error message.

Each .xaml file is a view in the MVVM pattern. In classic MVVM style, the views have no code logic, except a couple of lines to create the View-Model, which might annoy MVVM purists! Each view defines a part of the user interface and uses data binding to connect to application data and behaviors in the ViewModel.

A *ViewModel* is a class written specifically for a View to bind to. It includes any number of bindable properties and collections that the View can bind to, and it animates the user interface by manipulating those properties and collections. This design has a number of advantages, including providing a better separation of code and design and facilitating automated testing of the ViewModel. Both of these are possible because the ViewModel contains no code that references the View; it can only update the View indirectly through its exposed properties.

The project includes a ViewModel for each of the major views: MainPageVM.cs is for the MainPage.xaml view, EditPageVM.cs is for the EditPage.xaml view, and PersonDetailChildWindow.cs is for the PersonDetailChildWindow.xaml view.

The Model provides the business logic and data and is called by the ViewModel. In some cases, the ViewModel calls web services or client APIs directly, considering them the Model; in others the Model might include complete business and data layers.

Both approaches are used in the sample solution. SharePoint's web services are complex enough to warrant a `SearchService` class, which acts as the main page's Model; however, the user profile and social networking web services are so simple, they're accessed directly from the `Person DetailVM` class. The Edit Page's ViewModel reads and updates the web part's settings by accessing a hidden field in the SharePoint Editor Part, so that is the Model when editing the web part.

Each ViewModel implements a number of public properties, which the controls in the corresponding View are bound to. Each `ViewModel` implements the `INotifyPropertyChanged` interface, which is used to notify the bound controls that something has changed. The `INotifyPropertyChanged` interface requires you to implement a single event handler, `Property-Changed`, which you need to fire when anything changes that would be visible in the user interface. During data binding, Silverlight notices that `INotifyPropertyChanged` is available, subscribes to the `PropertyChanged` event, and refreshes the UI when it fires.

For readability, each `ViewModel` includes its own implementation of a helper function, `SetWithNotify<T>()`, which reduces the amount of code in the property declarations. It's used in the setter of each property, and its job is to fire the `PropertyChanged` event whenever the property changes. The code is shown in Listing 10.1 along with a sample property; this is at the top of each `ViewModel` class.

LISTING 10.1: Implementing INotifyPropertyChanged

```csharp
public class MainPageVM : INotifyPropertyChanged
{
    // INotifyPropertyChanged Implementation
    public event PropertyChangedEventHandler PropertyChanged;

    // Helper function to update a property and, if it actually changed,
    // fire the event
    private void SetWithNotify<T>(ref T assignTo, T value,
                                  string propertyName)
    {
        bool valueChanged =
            (assignTo == null || !assignTo.Equals(value));
        assignTo = value;
        if (valueChanged && this.PropertyChanged != null)
        {
            this.PropertyChanged(this,
                new PropertyChangedEventArgs(propertyName));
        }
    }

    // Now a bindable property declaration looks like this:
    private string _userQueryString;
    public string UserQueryString
    {
        get { return _userQueryString; }
        set { SetWithNotify<string>(ref _userQueryString, value,
                                    "UserQueryString"); }
    }
}
```

The strategy is to store the property values in private fields, such as _userQueryString. When the corresponding property is set, SetWith Notify<T>() first checks to see if the value is actually changing, which is true if the referenced assignTo field was null or unequal to the new value. Then the field is updated with the new value, and if the value had changed, the event is fired.

There are quite a number of properties set up in this way, generally one or more for binding to each control that needs to show or capture information on the corresponding view.

The Search button is only shown when the application is set up to allow users to enter a free-text query, as shown in Figure 10.4. The button is bound to a command with the XAML as shown in this excerpt from MainPage.xaml:

```
<Button Content="Search"
 Command="{Binding Path=RunSearchQueryCommand}" />
```

RunSearchQueryCommand is a class that implements the ICommand interface at the bottom of the MainPageVM.cs file. When the button is pressed, RunSearchQueryCommand calls a method in the ViewModel to run the search.

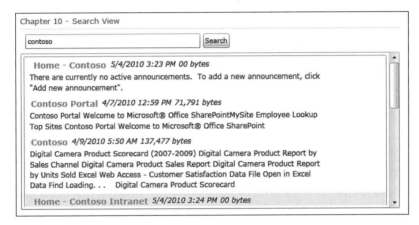

FIGURE 10.4: SearchView Web Part with all content search and user-entered query

Another technique you see is use of the Expression Blend Behavior called CallMethodAction; this is a declarative way to "bind" an arbitrary event to a method in the ViewModel. If Blend is installed, you probably already have the files, which are in C:\Program Files (x86)\Microsoft SDKs\Expression\Blend\Silverlight\v4.0\Libraries; if not, download the SDK at http://bit.ly/SPSL_BlendSDK. If you have Blend 4, reference Microsoft.Expression.Interactions.dll; for Blend 3, reference Expression.samples.interactivity.dll. You need to reference System.Windows.Interactivity and add a couple XML namespaces to your .xaml file:

```
xmlns:i="http://schemas.microsoft.com/expression/2010/interactivity"
xmlns:ei="http://schemas.microsoft.com/expression/2010/interactions"
```

When this is done, it's easy to "bind" an event in the view to a method in the ViewModel. Listing 10.2 shows an example from MainPage.xaml, which calls the ShowPersonDetail() method in response to a click on the person results ListBox.

LISTING 10.2: Using Behaviors to "Bind" a View Event to a ViewModel Method

```
<ListBox ItemsSource="{Binding Path=SearchResults}"
         Visibility="{Binding Path=PeopleSearchVisible}"
         SelectedItem="{Binding Path=SelectedResult, Mode=TwoWay}">
    <i:Interaction.Triggers>
        <i:EventTrigger EventName="MouseLeftButtonUp">
            <ei:CallMethodAction MethodName="ShowPersonDetail"
                                 TargetObject="{Binding}" />
        </i:EventTrigger>
    </i:Interaction.Triggers>
    <ListBox.ItemTemplate>
        <DataTemplate>
            ...
```

Armed with what you already know about data binding and by using Blend behaviors, you can begin to construct cleanly designed MVVM solutions.

In-Place Web Part Editing Experience

SearchView has a lot of configuration information—it allows three kinds of queries (fixed, user-specified, and alphabetic tabs), two kinds of searches (people and all content), and other choices such as the number of results, sort order, and so on. To accommodate this, the web part is edited "in place"—that is, the web part itself is configured right along with all the other settings in the SharePoint Editing panel. Figure 10.5 shows the editing experience. The Editor Part, where settings would normally be edited, appears as just a little text at the top of the editing panel, and the web part itself becomes the main editing surface.

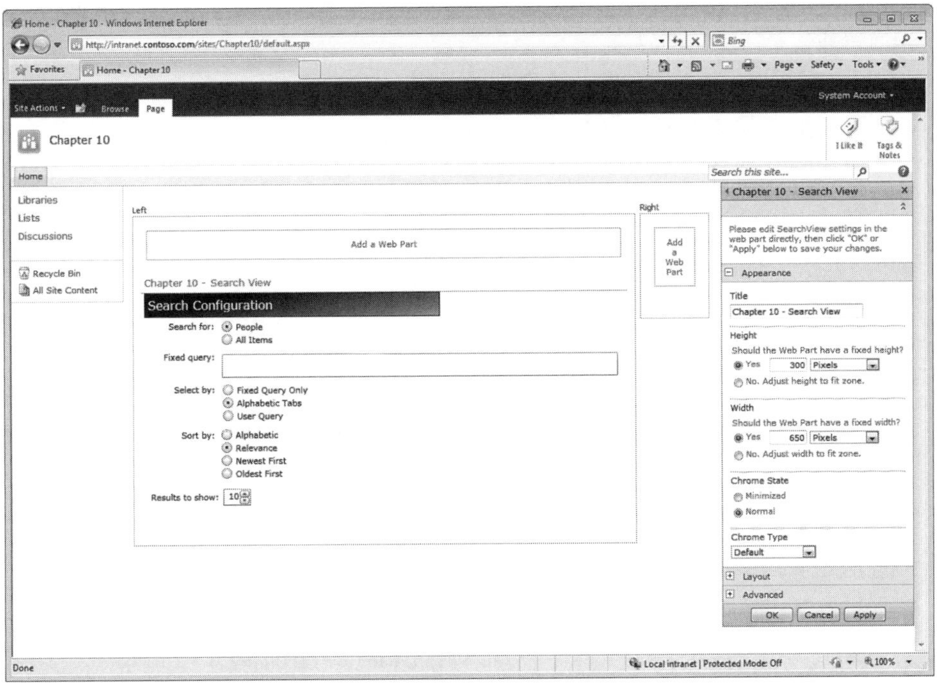

FIGURE 10.5: Editing the SearchView Web Part

All the configuration information is conveniently encapsulated in a class called `QueryInfo`, which has a base class, `SerializableObject`, that allows it to be easily transformed in and out of JSON notation. This is used to store the query info as a simple string in SharePoint's web part store. Chapter 7, "Accessing SharePoint Using the HTML Bridge," goes into detail on this JSON serialization technique, where it was used to pass data to the PictureView Web Part; in this case it's only used by the SearchViewSL Silverlight application to store the user's preferences. Suffice it to say that it's easy to turn the whole `QueryInfo` into an HTML-safe string and back again. Listing 10.3 shows the `QueryInfo` class so you can see what properties can be configured on the web part.

LISTING 10.3: The QueryInfo Class holds Web Part Configuration Settings

```
[DataContract]
public class QueryInfo : SerializableObject
{
    // The constructor fills each property with default values
```

```
public QueryInfo()
{
    SearchFor = SearchOptions.People;
    FixedQuery = "";
    SelectBy = SelectByOptions.Fixed;
    SortBy = SortByOptions.Alphabetic;
    ResultCount = 10;
}

// Search options - what kind of search should we do?
public enum SearchOptions { People, AllItems };
[DataMember]
public SearchOptions SearchFor { get; set; }

// Fixed query - what fixed query terms should be included
// in the search?
[DataMember]
public string FixedQuery { get; set; }

// Select by options - should we just use the fixed query terms,
// or should we include terms from alphabetic tabs or a user-entered
// query?
public enum SelectByOptions { Fixed, AlphaTabs, UserQuery }
[DataMember]
public SelectByOptions SelectBy { get; set; }

// Sort by options - how should we sort the results?
public enum SortByOptions { Alphabetic, Relevance, DateDesc,
                            DateAsc }
[DataMember]
public SortByOptions SortBy { get; set; }

// Result count - how many results should we display?
[DataMember]
public int ResultCount { get; set; }
}
```

The SearchView Web Part (on the server) provides a single string property to store all this information when the web part is edited. The property includes the attributes needed to tell SharePoint to save it along with other web part settings. A second public property, the EditorPartControlID, allows the EditorPart to pass the client-side control ID of a second hidden field over to the web part (more on this in a moment). Listing 10.4 shows both properties. You can view the code in the download in the Chapter10a.sln solution under SearchView in the SearchView.cs file.

LISTING 10.4: EditorPartControlID Property

```
// Web Part Properties
[WebBrowsable(false)]
[Personalizable(PersonalizationScope.Shared)]
public string Query { get; set; } // Serialized QueryInfo

public string EditorPartControlId { get; set; }
```

Notice that the Query property is marked with the attribute [Web Browsable(false)], so SharePoint won't render a text box for the property when the web part is edited. Instead, the SearchView Web Part overrides the CreateEditorPart() method and creates its own Editor Part to handle the editing. This is shown in Listing 10.5.

LISTING 10.5: Overriding the CreateEditorParts() Method

```
public override EditorPartCollection CreateEditorParts()
{
    ArrayList editorPartArray = new ArrayList();

    SearchViewEP editorPart = new SearchViewEP();
    editorPart.ID = this.ID + "_editorPart";
    editorPartArray.Add(editorPart);

    return new EditorPartCollection(editorPartArray);
}
```

The Editor Part is about as simple as they come, nearly as simple as if it had a single text box for editing the web part property. However, it uses a hidden field and pushes the hidden field's client ID back into the web part so it can be handed to Silverlight, which actually does the editing. The EditorPart class, found in SearchViewEP.cs in the code download, is shown in Listing 10.6.

LISTING 10.6: EditorPart for SearchView

```
class SearchViewEP : EditorPart
{
    private HiddenField queryInfoFormField = new HiddenField();

    protected override void CreateChildControls()
    {
        base.CreateChildControls();
```

```
        // Add the hidden field, and instructions to edit the web
        // part on its surface
        this.Controls.Add(queryInfoFormField);
        this.Controls.Add(new LiteralControl(
            "Please edit SearchView settings in the web part " +
            "directly, then click \"OK\" or \"Apply\" below to " +
            "save your changes.<br /><br />"));

        // Pass the hidden field's client ID back to the web part, so
        // it can pass it to Silverlight
        if (this.WebPartToEdit is SearchView)
        {
            SearchView webPart = this.WebPartToEdit as SearchView;
            webPart.EditorPartControlId = queryInfoFormField.ClientID;
        }
    }


    // ApplyChanges - Override to update the web part with the
    // latest EditorPart control values
    public override bool ApplyChanges()
    {
        this.EnsureChildControls();

        if (this.WebPartToEdit is SearchView)
        {
            SearchView webPart = this.WebPartToEdit as SearchView;
            webPart.Query = queryInfoFormField.Value;
        }
        return true;
    }


    // SyncChanges - Override to update the EditorPart controls
    // with the latest web part properties
    public override void SyncChanges()
    {
        this.EnsureChildControls();

        if (this.WebPartToEdit is SearchView)
        {
            SearchView webPart = this.WebPartToEdit as SearchView;
            queryInfoFormField.Value = webPart.Query;
        }
    }
}
```

The SearchView Web Part passes its `QueryInfo` property value to Silverlight in a hidden field, and Silverlight configures the web part accordingly. If the web part is in Edit mode, the web part also passes the Editor

Part's hidden field ID so Silverlight can save changes back to SharePoint when the Editor Part is posted back. This is the same as the Editor Part example in Chapter 7 except that a single Silverlight application is handling both the view and edit functions.

Listing 10.7 shows the web part code to pass the `QueryInfo` via a hidden field and optionally pass the Editor Part's hidden field as well. Notice that this all needs to be done late in the page rendering cycle, during `OnPreRender`, to ensure the property is set and the Editor Part has had a chance to create its hidden field and pass its ID in to the web part.

LISTING 10.7: Web Part Code to Pass QueryInfo in a Hidden Field

```
// Fields for child controls
private HiddenField hidden =
    new HiddenField(); // Hidden field to pass QueryInfo to Silverlight
private SilverlightPlugin sl =
    new SilverlightPlugin();


// Create Child Controls
protected override void CreateChildControls()
{
    // Add the hidden field to pass QueryInfo to Silverlight
    this.Controls.Add(hidden);

    // Set up Silverlight plug-in
    SPSite site = SPContext.Current.Site;
    sl.Source = ((site.ServerRelativeUrl == "/") ?
                "/" : site.ServerRelativeUrl + "/") +
                "ClientBin/SearchViewSL.xap";
    this.Controls.Add(sl);
}

// OnPreRender event handler - By this time in the page rendering
// process, the EditorPart, if present, will have begun rendering and
// will have assigned its control ID. With that and other information,
// we can pass initial parameters to Silverlight
protected override void OnPreRender(EventArgs e)
{
    base.OnPreRender(e);

    string initParams = "";

    // Pass the query information to the Silverlight application in a
    // hidden field
    hidden.Value = (this.Query == null) ? "" : this.Query;
    initParams += ",queryFieldId=" + hidden.ClientID;
```

```
    // If the editor part is open, pass its control Id
    if (this.EditorPartControlId != null &&
        this.EditorPartControlId != "")
    {
        initParams += ",editorPartFieldId=" + this.EditorPartControlId;
    }

    // Finally, pass the web service endpoint addresses
    SPWeb web = SPContext.Current.Web;
    initParams += ",searchEndpointAddress=" + web.Url +
                                    "/_vti_bin/search.asmx";
    initParams += ",profileEndpointAddress=" + web.Url +
                            "/_vti_bin/userprofileservice.asmx";
    initParams += ",socialEndpointAddress=" + web.Url +
                            "/_vti_bin/socialdataservice.asmx";
    sl.InitParameters = initParams;
}
```

As you can see, the web part passes in three endpoint addresses, one for each of the three web services to be used. SharePoint web services are in the /_vti_bin/ folder of each and every SharePoint site; SharePoint makes it appear there as a copy of the service in every site even though in reality, a single copy is installed. It's always best to access web services from within the current site to ensure the client has permission to access the web service (based on their having at least minimal access to the site), as well as to provide the correct context to the web service. That's why the current site URL is used as a base for each of the endpoint addresses.

> ■ **TIP**
>
> Many people wonder about the choice of folder name, _vti_bin, in SharePoint URLs. The curious acronym "vti" stands for Vermeer Technologies, Inc., the inventors of FrontPage web site editing technology, based in Cambridge, Massachusetts. Microsoft acquired Vermeer in 1996, and portions of the "FrontPage Server Extensions" were used in early versions of SharePoint. The URL remains to this day.
>
> Files that appear in the _vti_bin directory in every SharePoint site are actually installed in the ISAPI folder under the SharePoint root, which by default is C:\Program Files\Common Files\Microsoft Shared\Web Server Extensions\14 for SharePoint 2010.
>
> The tip is: Don't delete or mess with those _vti folders, or things will break!

When the Silverlight application starts up, it looks to see if it's in Edit mode or view mode and displays the `EditPage` or `MainPage` view accordingly. Listing 10.8 shows the application startup code from App.xaml.cs in the SearchViewSL project. It captures the `QueryInfo` object and endpoint addresses from `InitParams`.

LISTING 10.8: InitParams Processing in the Application Startup Event

```
// Global properties
public QueryInfo CurrentQueryInfo { get; set; }
public string SearchEndpointAddress { get; set; }
public string ProfileEndpointAddress { get; set; }
public string SocialEndpointAddress { get; set; }

private void Application_Startup(object sender, StartupEventArgs e)
{
    try
    {
        // Determine edit mode from client state
        bool editMode = false;
        HtmlDocument doc = HtmlPage.Document;
        HtmlElement element =
            doc.GetElementById("MSOSPWebPartManager_DisplayModeName");

        if (element != null && element.GetAttribute("value") != null)
        {
            string s = element.GetAttribute("value").ToString();
            if (s.ToLower() == "edit") editMode = true;
        }

        // Get the query settings from the hidden field referenced in
        // InitParams
        string serializedQuery =
            GetInitParamValue(e, "queryFieldId", true);
        this.CurrentQueryInfo = GetQuery(serializedQuery);

        // Get editor part field id, if present
        string editorPartFieldId =
            GetInitParamValue(e, "editorPartFieldId", false);

        // Get endpoint addresses for web service calls
        this.SearchEndpointAddress =
            GetInitParamValue(e, "searchEndpointAddress", true);
        this.ProfileEndpointAddress =
            GetInitParamValue(e, "profileEndpointAddress", true);
        this.SocialEndpointAddress =
            GetInitParamValue(e, "socialEndpointAddress", true);
```

```
    // Now that we have all the necessary information, bring up
    // the UI
    if (editMode)
    {
        // We are editing; ensure we have a queryInfo and run
        // the Edit page
        if (this.CurrentQueryInfo == null)
        {
            this.CurrentQueryInfo = new QueryInfo();
        }
        this.RootVisual =
            new EditPage(this.CurrentQueryInfo, editorPartFieldId);
    }
    else
    {
        // We are viewing; if we don't have a QueryInfo, throw an
        // exception. If we do, then run the Main page.
        if (this.CurrentQueryInfo == null)
        {
            throw new Exception("Please edit the web part to set " +
                                "up a Search View");
        }
        this.RootVisual = new MainPage();
    }
}
catch (Exception ex)
{
    this.RootVisual = new ErrorPage(ex.Message);
}
}
```

You might notice there is a trick for determining if the page is being edited. SharePoint maintains an HTML element called `MSOSPWebPart` `Manager_DisplayModeName` that contains the edit state and can be easily read by Silverlight using the HTML Bridge. Most of the rest of the code is involved with retrieving data out of `InitParams`; in the end the application decides if it should show the main, edit, or error page depending on what it finds there.

Listing 10.9 shows the helper functions used the in the previous listing. The first extracts values from `InitParams`, and the second deserializes the `QueryInfo` structure for passing to the ViewModel.

LISTING 10.9: Helper Functions for InitParams and QueryInfo Processing

```
// GetInitParamValue - extracts a value from InitParms, optionally
// throwing an exception if it is missing
private string GetInitParamValue(StartupEventArgs e, string key,
                                 bool throwExceptionIfMissing)
{
    string value = null;
    if (e.InitParams.ContainsKey(key))
    {
        value = e.InitParams[key];
    }
    else if (throwExceptionIfMissing)
    {
        throw new Exception("The web part did not pass the correct " +
            "initial parameters to the Silverlight application");
    }
    return value;
}

// GetQuery - De-serializes the QueryInfo class passed in from the host
private QueryInfo GetQuery(string queryFieldId)
{
    QueryInfo result = null;

    if (queryFieldId != "")
    {
        // Use the browser DOM to find the element, then parse it
        HtmlDocument doc = HtmlPage.Document;
        HtmlElement element = doc.GetElementById(queryFieldId);
        if (element != null && element.GetAttribute("value") != null)
        {
            string serializedQueryInfo =
                element.GetAttribute("value").ToString();
            if (serializedQueryInfo != "")
            {
                result = QueryInfo.Load<QueryInfo>(serializedQueryInfo);
            }
        }
    }
    return result;
}
```

In Edit mode, the EditPageVM ViewModel interacts with the hidden field in the server-side editor part. The ViewModel writes the whole serialized QueryInfo back into the editor part every time anything on the form changes. If the user saves the changes, the editor part saves it for future display. Now there are two things to do when a property changes: As before, the `PropertyChanged` event must be fired, and also the editor part field must be updated.

As an example, Listing 10.10 shows the declaration of the `SelectBy` property in EditPageVM.cs and the method it calls to update the editor part's hidden field. When the user changes the Search By radio buttons in the Edit Page view, the two-way binding writes to the property. The property setter immediately calls `UpdateEditorPart()` to update the hidden field, so if the next user click is the OK button, the change is saved back to SharePoint.

LISTING 10.10: Updating the EditorPart Hidden Field in a ViewModel Property Setter

```
// Example of a bindable property in the EditPage ViewModel
private QueryInfo.SelectByOptions _selectBy;
public QueryInfo.SelectByOptions SelectBy
{
    get { return _selectBy; }
    set
    {
        SetWithNotify<QueryInfo.SelectByOptions>(ref _selectBy, value,
            "SelectBy");
        UpdateEditorPart();
    }
}

// . . .

// Method to update the field in the editor part for saving back to
// the server; this should be called whenever a UI choice is changed
private void UpdateEditorPart()
{
    QueryInfo queryInfo = new QueryInfo();

    queryInfo.SearchFor = this.SearchFor;
    queryInfo.SelectBy = this.SelectBy;
    queryInfo.FixedQuery = this.FixedQuery;
    queryInfo.ResultCount = this.ResultCount;
    queryInfo.SortBy = this.SortBy;

    string jsonQueryInfoString = queryInfo.Serialize();

    // Use the browser DOM to find the element and parse its contents
    HtmlDocument doc = HtmlPage.Document;
```

```
    HtmlElement element = doc.GetElementById(this.editorPartFieldId);
    if (element != null)
    {
        element.SetAttribute("value", jsonQueryInfoString);
    }
}
```

Accessing Enterprise Search

Enterprise Search has been a major part of SharePoint from the very beginning, and over the years it's become more and more powerful. The SharePoint search engine pre-dates SharePoint itself and was originally released as part of Microsoft Site Server 3.0 back in the late 1990s. It's improved with each version and is now a scalable search engine capable of finding documents, web pages, and people in a wide range of repositories. In addition to SharePoint itself, the SharePoint search engine can index content in file shares, crawlable web sites, Microsoft Exchange public folders, Lotus Notes databases, and business data in the form of Business Connectivity Services entities.

In January 2008, Microsoft acquired a high-end enterprise search vendor, a Norwegian firm called FAST Search and Transfer. FAST offers greater scalability than the SharePoint search engine and includes a number of high-end features such as entity extraction (extracting metadata from document text), deep refiners (ability to refine the search based on metadata about the whole result set, with hit counts) and more advanced linguistics support. The FAST search engine is available for SharePoint Server in a product called FAST Search Server 2010 for SharePoint, greatly simplifying setup and configuration compared to earlier versions.

The good news is that both search engines have a common API, so the examples in this chapter work with either one.

Please don't confuse these enterprise search solutions with the free site-by-site search that's included with SharePoint Foundation! The search code in this chapter requires either the SharePoint or FAST for SharePoint search engines, as found in any of the following products:

- **Microsoft Search Server 2010 Express**—This is a free download and allows a single server to run the standard SharePoint search engine along with SharePoint Foundation 2010.

- **Microsoft SharePoint Server 2010**—This comes in standard and enterprise editions, both of which include the SharePoint search engine and the ability to build multiserver search environments with high availability and scalability.

- **Microsoft FAST Search Server 2010 for SharePoint**—This is an addition to the enterprise edition of Microsoft SharePoint Server 2010.

Keyword Query Language

SharePoint has three query languages: a SQL variant (supported only by the SharePoint standard search engine), Fast Query Language (supported only by FAST) and Keyword Query Language (which works with both). For most applications, Keyword Query Language (KQL) is the syntax of choice, and it's also easy to enter into a search box.

A KQL query consists of free-text keywords, property-restriction keywords, and operators for Boolean, proximity, wildcards and so on. To search for the word dog, the KQL query is simply "dog". To search for dog in the Title property, add a property restriction and search for "title:dog". To search for documents with cat in the body of the document and dog in the Title, search for "cat and title:dog".

Part of the idea of the SearchView Web Part is that it allows part of the KQL query to be set when the site administrator configures the web part and another part by the end user at runtime. For example, if the web part is configured to allow the user to enter a search query, one or more property-restriction keywords can be added when the web part is edited to make a specialized search. The term "site:url" limits results to documents beneath the URL, "fileextension:ext" limits results to the "ext" file extension, "department:sales" limits a people search to people in the sales department.

When the web part is configured for fixed search only, just the search terms entered during web part editing are used and the user can't add anything. When it's configured for user search, the user has an auto-complete box to enter a query, and the fixed terms are added as well. When it's configured for alphabetic tabs, a wildcard search term is added to the fixed search terms, with the `lastname` property restriction for people searches. For example, clicking the S tab does a KQL query for "lastname:s*".

For a full reference on KQL, see the Keyword Query Syntax Reference at http://msdn.microsoft.com/en-us/library/ee558911.aspx.

Accessing the Search Web Service

The first step to accessing the search web service from a Silverlight application is to add a web reference. To do this, right-click the References folder in Visual Studio's Solution Explorer and select Add Service Reference. Enter the URL for your search service, which should be your debugging site (for now) with the path _vti_bin/search.asmx under the site as shown in Figure 10.6. Call your service `SearchQueryService`.

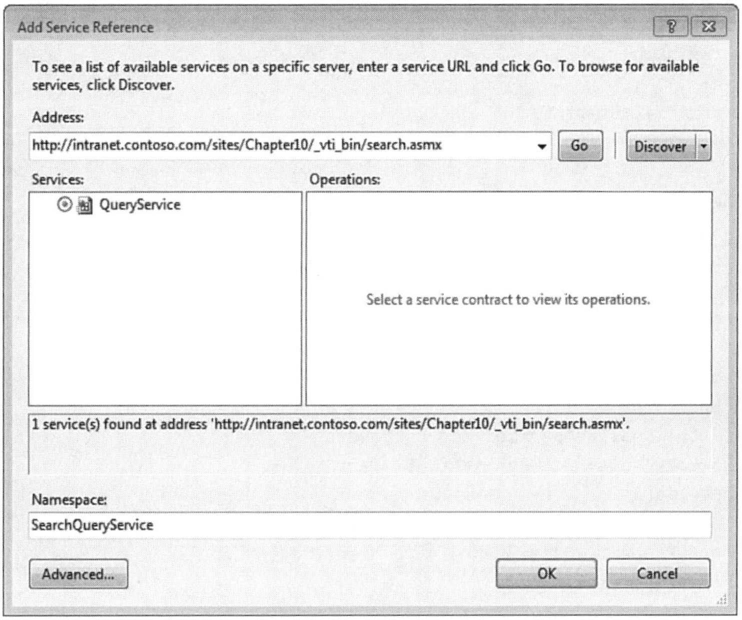

FIGURE 10.6: Adding a reference to the Search.asmx service

With the service reference in place, you're ready to set up and invoke search queries using the service.

Invoking a Search Query

Before invoking the `QueryAsync()` method on the search web service, there's some preparation to do. `QueryAsync()` expects a search query packet, which is an XML structure containing all the details about the search to be performed. The KQL query is just one of many elements in the packet. Listing 10.11 shows an example that does a general search for "dog" and returns the first ten results.

LISTING 10.11: Sample Search Query Packet XML

```xml
<QueryPacket xmlns="urn:Microsoft.Search.Query">
  <Query>
    <QueryId />
    <SupportedFormats>
      <Format revision='1'>
urn:Microsoft.Search.Response.Document:Document</Format>
    </SupportedFormats>
    <Context>
      <QueryText language='en-US' type='STRING'>dog</QueryText>
    </Context>
    <Range>
      <StartAt>1</StartAt>
      <Count>10</Count>
    </Range>
    <Properties>
      <!-- Mandatory Properties -->
      <Property name="Title" />
      <Property name="Path" />
      <Property name="Description" />
      <Property name="Write" />
      <Property name="Rank" />
      <Property name="Size" />
      <!-- Optional Properties for Documents -->
      <Property name="HitHighlightedSummary" />
    </Properties>
    <SortByProperties>
      <SortByProperty name="rank" direction="Descending" />
    </SortByProperties>
  </Query>
</QueryPacket>
```

The SearchViewSL Silverlight application contains pre-built query packets to be used as a starting point. They can be found as XML files in the QueryServiceXml folder, and they're deployed as part of the .xap package for use in the `SearchService` code. There are separate templates for People vs. All Sites or general content searches, and they differ mainly in the properties they return. Only the properties with elements under the `<Properties>` tag are returned, and the search fails if the mandatory properties aren't there at a minimum. Note that the search engine is only capable of returning *managed properties*, which can be set up in the search service administration pages in SharePoint Centeral Administration.

The SearchService class, in SearchService.cs, implements the search data model. It sets up one of these query packets during initialization and stuffs information from the web part setup into the XML from a `QueryInfo` object. Loading the query packet template is simple in Silverlight with LINQ to XML, as shown in Listing 10.12.

LISTING 10.12: Code to Load a Query Packet XML Template in SearchService.cs

```
// Given queryInfo from the server, load the QueryPacket template
// from this project
if (queryInfo.SearchFor == QueryInfo.SearchOptions.People)
{
    this.currentQueryPacket =
        XDocument.Load("QueryServiceXml/QueryPacket-People.xml");
}
else
{
    this.currentQueryPacket =
        XDocument.Load("QueryServiceXml/QueryPacket-AllSites.xml");
}
```

Following this, in a method called `InitializeQueryPacket()`, the various query settings are added to the generic query XML. First, the code checks for a People search and adds a KQL term, "scope:People" to the query packet. It also sets up the fixed portion of the query; the user portion isn't known yet because this is still initialization. Listing 10.13 shows `InitializeQueryPacket()`.

LISTING 10.13: Initializing the Query Packet XML

```
private void InitializeQueryPacket
        (QueryInfo queryInfo, XDocument queryPacket)
{

    // Handle SearchFor People vs. All Sites
    if (queryInfo.SearchFor == QueryInfo.SearchOptions.People)
    {
        XElement queryTextElement =
            queryPacket.Descendants(sq + "QueryText").First<XElement>();
        queryTextElement.Value =
            (queryTextElement.Value + " scope:People").Trim();
    }

    // Handle fixed portion of query
    if (queryInfo.FixedQuery != "")
    {
        XElement queryTextElement =
            queryPacket.Descendants(sq + "QueryText").First<XElement>();
        queryTextElement.Value =
            (queryTextElement.Value + " " + queryInfo.FixedQuery).Trim();
    }

    // Handle SortBy options
    XElement sortByElement =
        queryPacket.Descendants(sq + "SortByProperty").First<XElement>();
    switch (queryInfo.SortBy)
    {
        case QueryInfo.SortByOptions.Alphabetic:
            {
                sortByElement.Attribute("name").Value = "LastName";
                sortByElement.Attribute("direction").Value =
                    "Ascending";
                break;
            }
        case QueryInfo.SortByOptions.DateAsc:
            {
                sortByElement.Attribute("name").Value = "write";
                sortByElement.Attribute("direction").Value =
                    "Ascending";
                break;
            }
        case QueryInfo.SortByOptions.DateDesc:
            {
                sortByElement.Attribute("name").Value = "write";
                sortByElement.Attribute("direction").Value =
                    "Descending";
                break;
```

```
            }
        case QueryInfo.SortByOptions.Relevance:
            {
                sortByElement.Attribute("name").Value = "rank";
                sortByElement.Attribute("direction").Value =
                    "Descending";
                break;
            }
    }

    // Handle ResultCount
    int resultCount = queryInfo.ResultCount;
    XElement resultCountElement = queryPacket.Descendants(sq +
        "Count").First<XElement>();
    resultCountElement.Value = resultCount.ToString();
}
```

At some point the user will click a tab or the Search button, or the Main Page's ViewModel will decide to automatically issue a "fixed-only" query at the end of its initialization. The `SearchService` class has methods for each of these, all using different signatures of `RunQuery()`: One inserts the user query string, and another inserts the alphabetic wildcard query into the query packet before making the request. Listing 10.14 shows the `RunQuery()` method for a user query and the final invocation of the web service.

LISTING 10.14: Running a User Query in SearchService.cs

```
public void RunQuery(string userQueryString)
{
    // Copy the current query packet and inject the user's text
    XDocument q = new XDocument(currentQueryPacket);
    XElement queryTextElement = q.Descendants(sq +
        "QueryText").First<XElement>();
    queryTextElement.Value = queryTextElement.Value + " " +
        userQueryString;

    RunQuery(q);
}

private void RunQuery(XDocument queryPacket)
{
    BasicHttpBinding httpBinding = new BasicHttpBinding();
    httpBinding.MaxReceivedMessageSize = 500000;
    httpBinding.MaxBufferSize = 500000;
```

```
EndpointAddress endpoint =
    new EndpointAddress(this.searchEndpointAddress);

QueryServiceSoapClient queryClient =
    new QueryServiceSoapClient(httpBinding, endpoint);
queryClient.QueryCompleted +=
    new EventHandler<QueryCompletedEventArgs>
    (queryClient_QueryCompleted);

queryClient.QueryAsync(queryPacket.ToString());
}
```

Notice that the local endpoint address (URL of the .asmx file) is passed to the `QueryServiceSoapClient` and replaces the one set in Visual Studio. Also notice that somewhat large results are expected, with the maximum received message and buffer sizes set to 500K bytes.

As with all Silverlight networking, the request is asynchronous. Therefore, an event handler is set up to receive the completion at `queryClient_QueryCompleted`. The next section explains what happens when the query completes and the event is fired.

Handling Query Completion

Search.asmx returns its results in an XML structure; a subset set is shown in Listing 10.15.

LISTING 10.15: Sample Search Results XML

```
<ResponsePacket xmlns="urn:Microsoft.Search.Response">
  <Response>
    <Range>
      <StartAt>1</StartAt>
      <Count>4</Count>
      <TotalAvailable>4</TotalAvailable>
      <Results>
        <Document xmlns="urn:Microsoft.Search.Response.Document">
          <Action>
            <LinkUrl
fileExt="aspx">http://oblio/my/Person.aspx?accountname=virtual\brian</LinkUrl>
          </Action>
          <Properties xmlns="urn:Microsoft.Search.Response.Document.Document">
            <Property>
              <Name>Title</Name>
              <Type>String</Type>
```

```
          <Value>Brian Burke</Value>
        </Property>
        <Property>
          <Name>Path</Name>
          <Type>String</Type>
<Value>http://oblio/my/Person.aspx?accountname=virtual\brian</Value>
        </Property>
        <Property>
          <Name>Write</Name>
          <Type>DateTime</Type>
          <Value>2010-06-29T20:42:20</Value>
        </Property>
        <Property>
          <Name>Rank</Name>
          <Type>Int64</Type>
          <Value>62174552</Value>
        </Property>
        <Property>
          <Name>Size</Name>
          <Type>Int64</Type>
          <Value>0</Value>
        </Property>
       </Properties>
      </Document>
      <!-- More documents were removed for brevity -->
     </Results>
    </Range>
    <Status>SUCCESS</Status>
  </Response>
</ResponsePacket>
```

As you can see, it's a somewhat verbose format with property names and values in subelements. Although this contains the data you need, the format isn't suitable for binding to a Silverlight control. Instead, the Main Page ViewModel expects to bind its search results to a class called ResultsItem, defined in ResultsItem.cs and shown in Listing 10.16.

LISTING 10.16: ResultsItem Class for View Binding

```csharp
// Results Item used to bind search results to the View
public class ResultsItem
{
    public string Title { get; set; }
    public string UserName { get; set; }
    public string Url { get; set; }
    public string Summary { get; set; }
```

```
        public string Date { get; set; }
        public string Size { get; set; }
        public string JobTitle { get; set; }
        public string Department { get; set; }
        public string WorkPhone { get; set; }
        public string Email { get; set; }
        public string EmailUrl { get; set; }
        public string PictureUrl { get; set; }
    }
```

When the search query completes, the XML results need to be converted into a collection of ResultsItem for binding, and then SearchService fires its SearchComplete event to tell the ViewModel that the results are ready. Listing 10.17 shows the queryClient_QueryCompleted event handler, which does this transformation.

LISTING 10.17: Query Completed Event Handler

```
// This event fires when the web service request is completed
void queryClient_QueryCompleted(object sender,
                                QueryCompletedEventArgs e)
{
    // Parse the results and check for errors
    XDocument resultsXml = XDocument.Parse(e.Result.ToString());

    string status = resultsXml.Descendants(sr +
        "Status").First<XElement>().Value;
    var x = resultsXml.Descendants(sr+ "DebugErrorMessage");
    if (x.Count<XElement>() > 0 && x.First<XElement>().Value != "")
    {
        status += "\n" + x.First<XElement>().Value;
    }

    // If the results are successful, display them
    if (status.ToLower() == "success")
    {
        // Project the results into a collection of result items
        IEnumerable<ResultsItem> resultItems =
                from r in resultsXml.Descendants(srd + "Document")
                select new ResultsItem
        {
            Title = getPropertyValue(r, "Title"),
            UserName = getPropertyValue(r, "AccountName"),
            Url = getPropertyValue(r, "Path"),
            Summary = getSummary(r),
            Date = convertDate(getPropertyValue(r, "Write")),
```

```
                Size = convertSize(getPropertyValue(r, "Size")),
                JobTitle = getPropertyValue(r, "JobTitle"),
                Department = getPropertyValue(r, "Department"),
                WorkPhone = getPropertyValue(r,"WorkPhone"),
                Email = getPropertyValue(r,"WorkEmail"),
                EmailUrl = "Mailto:" + getPropertyValue(r, "WorkEmail"),
                PictureUrl = convertPictureUrl(
                                        getPropertyValue(r, "PictureURL"))
            };
            // Fire the event that the search is complete
            this.SearchComplete(this,
                    new SearchCompleteEventArgs (true, resultItems, ""));
    }
    else
    {
        // If here, we had an error. If it's just results not found,
        // report success with no results. If something else
        // happened, report an error status.
        if (status == "ERROR_NO_RESULTS_FOUND")
        {
            this.SearchComplete (this,
                new SearchCompleteEventArgs(true, null, ""));
        }
        else
        {
            this.SearchComplete (this,
                 new SearchCompleteEventArgs (false, null, status));
        }
    }
}
```

You might have noticed in Listing 10.15 that there's a Status XML element at the end of the search results XML that indicates if the request worked or not. A status of "SUCCESS" means that results were found; a status of "EROR_NO_RESULTS_FOUND" is the normal case of an empty result set, and other values indicate various error conditions. Part of parsing the results XML is to determine and handle the request status.

A helper function, getPropertyValue(), is used to extract property values from the search results XML. It uses an XPath query to locate a requested property and return its value as a string and is shown in Listing 10.18.

LISTING 10.18: Helper Function to Extract Property Values from Search Results XML

```
// Namespaces for the search results
private XNamespace sr = "urn:Microsoft.Search.Response";
private XNamespace srd = "urn:Microsoft.Search.Response.Document";
private XNamespace srdd =
                    "urn:Microsoft.Search.Response.Document.Document";

// Utility function to extract a property value from the results set.
// The results are provided in this format:
//
//  <Property>
//      <Name>Write</Name>
//      <Type>DateTime</Type>
//      <Value>2010-06-29T20:42:20</Value>
//  </Property>
//
private string getPropertyValue(XElement element, string propertyName)
{
    // Set up namespace manager for all the various namespaces used in
    // the results
    XmlNamespaceManager namespaceManager =
        new XmlNamespaceManager(new NameTable());
    namespaceManager.AddNamespace("sr", sr.NamespaceName);
    namespaceManager.AddNamespace("srd", srd.NamespaceName);
    namespaceManager.AddNamespace("srdd", srdd.NamespaceName);

    // Copy the element to work around issue where (XPath)
    // extensions don't iterate correctly when called from the LINQ
    // query
    XElement x = new XElement(element);

    // Use XPath to find the <Property> element that contains a <Name>
    // matching our property name
    string xpath = "//srdd:Property[srdd:Name = \"" + propertyName +
                "\"]";
    XElement matchingElement = x.XPathSelectElement(xpath,
                            namespaceManager);

    // If such an element was found, return its value.
    string result = "";
    if (matchingElement != null)
    {
        result = matchingElement.Element(srdd + "Value").Value;
    }

    return result;
}
```

If the query was successful or just returned a "no results" error, the queryClient_QueryCompleted event handler fires its SearchComplete event handler to tell the caller (the ViewModel) the request is completed. Because the SearchService class has already provided the results as a collection of ResultsItems, and the view is bound to such a collection, the ViewModel only needs to copy its collection to its SearchResults property to display the results. Listing 10.19 shows the SearchComplete event handler in the MainPageVM.cs.

LISTING 10.19: Search Complete Event Handler in MainPage ViewModel

```
void searchService_SearchComplete(object sender,
                               SearchCompleteEventArgs e)
{
    if (e.Succeeded)
    {
        this.SearchResults = e.SearchResults;
    }
    else
    {
        MessageBox.Show(e.ErrorMessage);
    }
}
```

Search Suggestions

SharePoint 2010 includes a cool new feature called Search Suggestions, which provides suggested search queries as the user types. It's possible to utilize this feature via the same Search.asmx web service. If you modify the web part to allow selecting by User Query, a text box is shown for the user query, but it's not really a text box. It's actually a user control, Search SuggestionsBox.xaml. This small component does not follow the MVVM pattern but simply calls the Search web service from code-behind.

SearchSuggestionsBox's user interface is a single control, an AutoCompleteBox, which thankfully already implements the UI logic to offer suggestions when a user pauses in typing and allows him to select a suggestion. This is the same AutoCompleteBox used in Chapter 9, "Accessing SharePoint Data with WCF Data Services," from the Silverlight Toolkit on Codeplex.

```
<my:AutoCompleteBox x:Name="UserQueryAutoCompleteBox"
        Text="{Binding Path=UserQueryString, Mode=TwoWay}"
        MinimumPopulateDelay="250" MinimumPrefixLength="1"
        Populating="UserQueryAutoCompleteBox_Populating" />
```

When the user is typing and enters at least `MinimumPrefixLength` characters (1 in this case) and delays for the `MinumPopulateDelay` interval (250
milliseconds in the sample), the `Populating` event fires and the search suggestions are shown. Figure 10.7 shows the Search Suggestions in action.

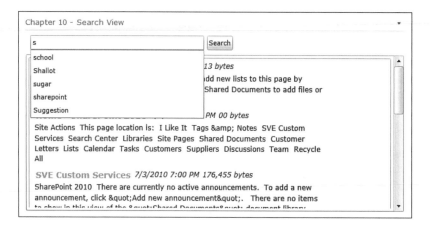

FIGURE 10.7: Search Suggestions in the SearchView Web Part

Before this will work on your server, you need to ensure you have some
search suggestions in the system. Suggestions are based on user queries in
which the user actually clicks one of the results in a SharePoint Search Center site; the idea is if the query is useful, the user clicks at least one of the
results. If a particular query's result is clicked at least six times within a
year, it becomes a search suggestion. Be sure to run the Prepare Query Suggestions timer job (or wait for it to run) after all the clicking in order to see
your search suggestions.

A quicker approach is to use Windows PowerShell to create search suggestions manually. To do this, open the SharePoint 2010 Management Shell
on the Start menu under All Programs/Microsoft SharePoint 2010 Products
and enter the following commands:

```
$ssa=Get-SPEnterpriseSearchServiceApplication
New-SPEnterpriseSearchLanguageResourcePhrase -SearchApplication $ssa
    -Language en-US -Type QuerySuggestionAlwaysSuggest -Name "SharePoint"
$timer=Get-SPTimerJob|? {$_.Name -eq "Prepare Query Suggestions"}
$timer.RunNow()
```

To list the currently available search suggestions, use these commands. (You only need to run the first one once, so if you just added a search suggestion you can skip it.)

```
$ssa=Get-SPEnterpriseSearchServiceApplication
Get-SPEnterpriseSearchQuerySuggestionCandidates -SearchApp $ssa
```

When the user pauses typing in the search box, the `AutoCompleteBox` fires its Populating event, and the code-behind in SearchSuggestionBox.xaml.cs calls the Search web service for suggestions. The web service call is very similar to the general Search query: An XML request packet is created, and the `GetQuerySuggestionsAsync()` method is called. See the sample code for the details.

When the response comes back, it is bound to the `AutoCompleteBox` to show the suggestions as shown in Listing 10.20. Thankfully, the results are simply a collection of strings that don't require any elaborate transformation in order to bind them. If there are no suggestions, an empty collection is returned, and nothing is shown. Notice that after binding, the event handler must call the `PopulateComplete()` method of the `AutoCompleteBox` to notify it that new suggestions have been bound to its `ItemsSource`.

LISTING 10.20: Handling the Search Suggestions Results in SearchSuggestionsBox.xaml.cs

```
// Event handler called when search suggestions have been obtained
// from the server
private void queryClient_GetQuerySuggestionsCompleted
            (object sender, GetQuerySuggestionsCompletedEventArgs e)
{
    Dispatcher.BeginInvoke(() =>
    {
        if (e.Error == null)
        {
            // We have an array of strings, easily bound to the text box
            UserQueryAutoCompleteBox.ItemsSource = e.Result;
            UserQueryAutoCompleteBox.PopulateComplete();
        }
    });
}
```

Accessing Social Data

A major area of advancement in SharePoint 2010 is in its social networking capabilities. The SearchView Web Part can display some of this information when a person is clicked in the People search results ListBox, as shown in Figure 10.2. All this work is done in PersonDetailChildWindowVM.cs, which is the ViewModel for the Person Detail child window.

This section is a great example of why asynchronous networking is a good thing, even if the need to put completion logic in event handlers is annoying at times. The Person Detail ViewModel issues two requests asynchronously: one for the user profile (displayed on the left) and one for the user's activity feed (displayed on the right). Because they are asynchronous, there is no extra work to run them in parallel, and the user interface is updated dynamically with the information as it is returned.

Accessing the User Profile Service

All the user data in the left portion of the Person Detail child window comes from the User Profile Service. The User Profile Service provides access to SharePoint's data about end-users, which is normally imported from Active Directory (or some other directory source) and augmented with information entered by users in their Profile page. To see your profile, click your name in the upper-right corner of most any SharePoint screen and select My Profile. To see just the profile properties, click Edit My Profile under your picture.

Begin by adding a service reference to the user profile service in your development site under /_vti_bin/userprofileservice.asmx. Call the service reference `UserProfileService`.

In an ideal world this would be enough, but in Silverlight 4 the world was not yet ideal, so there's a problem you might need to work around. It turns out that .asmx web services have a different notion of certain data types (namely `guid` and `char`) than Silverlight 4 does, and thus Silverlight chokes on any .asmx web service that uses them. Note that this problem is fixed in Silverlight 5, *even when Silverlight 5 is running a Silverlight 4 application*. Therefore if you're running Silverlight 5 but developing for Silverlight 4, be sure to include the work-around. The work-around is benign and has no known problems with Silverlight 5.

The UserProfileService.asmx has this issue. The solution is to add a behavior to the service reference manually, as described in the Silverlight Team Blog on May 26, 2010, in a posting called, "Workaround for accessing some ASMX services from Silverlight 4." The code download has this solution already in place in the form of the AsmxBehavior.cs and AsmxMessageInspector.cs files. The behavior is added to the web service request in a single line of code, which is highlighted later on in this section. The blog posting can be found at http://bit.ly/SPSL_AsmxWorkaround.

At the end of its initialization, the Person Detail ViewModel (Person DetailChildWindowVM.cs) calls RequestProfileInfo(userName) to issue a request for the user's profile. This is shown in Listing 10.21.

LISTING 10.21: Calling the User Profile Web Service from Silverlight 4

```
// RequestProfileInfo - Requests a user's profile information
public void RequestProfileInfo(string userName)
{
    // Initiate populating the Profile Information
    BasicHttpBinding httpBinding = new BasicHttpBinding();
    EndpointAddress endpoint =
        new EndpointAddress(this.profileEndpointAddress);

    UserProfileServiceSoapClient profileClient =
        new UserProfileServiceSoapClient(httpBinding, endpoint);
    profileClient.GetUserProfileByNameCompleted +=
        new EventHandler<GetUserProfileByNameCompletedEventArgs>
            (GetProfilebyName_Completed);
    profileClient.Endpoint.Behaviors.Add(new AsmxBehavior());
    profileClient.GetUserProfileByNameAsync(userName);
}
```

Notice the second to last line adds the AsmxBehavior to the request endpoint; this institutes the work-around mentioned earlier. Otherwise the request is similar to the Search example and much simpler without the need to set up a complex XML request packet!

The request returns an ObservableCollection<PropertyData>, which is basically a collection of properties. The GetProfilebyName_Completed event handler extracts the user's name and the URL of his picture and stuffs them into ViewModel properties, which are bound to the user interface. Other properties are displayed in a DataGrid, which is bound to a collection of property name-value pairs in the View.

A simple `Dictionary` is used to call out the interesting properties and give them user-friendly names; this is used in a LINQ query to transform the results into the property name-value pairs needed to bind to the `DataGrid`. The `Dictionary` is shown in Listing 10.22 and is defined in PersonDetailChildWindow.xaml.cs.

LISTING 10.22: PropertyMap Dictionary Manages Properties to Be Displayed

```
// This dictionary will be used to map internal property names to
// display names. Properties not found here will not be rendered.
private Dictionary<string, string> PropertyMap =
                            new Dictionary<string, string>
{
    {"WorkPhone", "Work Phone"},
    {"Department", "Department"},
    {"Title", "Title"},
    {"WorkEmail", "Email"},
    {"SPS-Location", "Location"},
    {"SPS-StatusNotes", "Message"}
};
```

Listing 10.23 shows the event handler that is called with the user profile results. Basically all it does is copy user profile properties from the result into the ViewModel's `Properties` collection, which is bound to the View. Because the `Properties` collection is bound to the View in Person-DetailChildWindow.xaml, the results are displayed without any further action.

LISTING 10.23: Copying User Profile Properties to the ViewModel's Properties Collection

```
public void GetProfilebyName_Completed(Object sender,
                        GetUserProfileByNameCompletedEventArgs e)
{
    // Get the properties
    ObservableCollection<PropertyData> result = e.Result;

    // Extract the Preferred Name
    IEnumerable<PropertyData> pdata = from property in result
                            where property.Name == "PreferredName"
                            select property;
    this.PreferredName =
        pdata.First<PropertyData>().Values[0].Value.ToString();
    this.WindowTitle = "Details for " + this.PreferredName;
```

```
    // Extract the Picture URL (or substitute dummy if it's not
    // provided)
     pdata = from property in result
             where property.Name == "PictureURL"
             select property;
     if (pdata.First<PropertyData>().Values.Count > 0)
    {
        this.PictureUrl =
            pdata.First<PropertyData>().Values[0].Value.ToString();
    }
    else
    {
        this.PictureUrl =
            "/_layouts/images/O14_person_placeHolder_192.png";
    }

    // Extract other properties into the ViewModel's Properties
    // collection, based on the PropertyMap dictionary
    this.Properties = from property in result
                      where (property.Values.Count > 0)
                          && PropertyMap.ContainsKey(property.Name)
                      orderby PropertyMap[property.Name]
                      select new PersonProperty
                      {
                          DisplayName = PropertyMap[property.Name],
                          Value = property.Values[0].Value.ToString()
                      };

    // Let the rest of the world know that profile data has been
    // received!
    this.ProfileInfoReceived = true;
}
```

Accessing the Activity Feed

SharePoint 2010 includes an Activity Feed feature that lets users know what other users have been doing. Rating a file, commenting on another user's note board, posting to a blog, or adding a colleague all generate activities in the user's Activity Feed. You can see the Activity Feed in the right of Figure 10.2.

SharePoint displays the activity feed on each user's My Site. To see the activities, find a user in SearchView and click his or her My Site link. The activities are shown under the Recent Activites heading. The activities won't show up until the Activity Feed timer job runs; to run this, issue the following power shell commands (with the first two lines all on one line as you type):

```
$timer=Get-SPTimerJob|?
        {$_.Name -eq "User Profile Service Application_ActivityFeedJob "}
$timer.RunNow
```

You can also run the Activity Feed timer job in SharePoint Central Administration. Under Central Administration click Monitoring; then under the Timer Jobs heading, click Review Job Definitions. Find the job called User Profile Service Application—Activity Feed Job; click it and then at the bottom of the job details page, click the Run Now button.

The activity feed is available as a simple ATOM feed at the My Site root, with the username included. For example, http://intranet.contoso.com/my/_layouts/activityfeed.aspx?consolidated=false&publisher=contoso%5Crong is the activity feed for user contoso\rong.

At the end of initialization, the Person Detail child window calls `RequestActivityFeed(userName)` to request the data to display the user's activity feed. As you can see in Listing 10.24, only a few lines of code are needed to make a web request for the feed. The URL to request is based on the person's My Site URL and the user name, both of which were passed in from the search results.

LISTING 10.24: Requesting the User's Activity Feed

```
// RequestActivityFeed - Kick off the request for an activity (ATOM)
// feed
private void RequestActivityFeed(string userName)
{
    string feedUrl = this.userUrl.Substring(0,
            this.userUrl.IndexOf("Person.aspx")) +
            "_layouts/activityfeed.aspx?consolidated=false&publisher=" +
            System.Windows.Browser.HttpUtility.UrlEncode(userName);

    WebClient wc = new WebClient();
    wc.OpenReadCompleted +=
        new OpenReadCompletedEventHandler(RequestActivityFeedCompleted);
    wc.OpenReadAsync(new Uri(feedUrl));
}
```

When the response comes back, the `OpenReadCompleted` event handler is called. Silverlight provides a `SyndicationFeed` object to make parsing a breeze. From there, the items can be transformed into `ActivityItems`, which are bound to a `ListBox` in the view. When the `Activities` property in the ViewModel is set, it fires the `PropertyChanged` event to tell the view to display the data, as shown in Listing 10.25.

LISTING 10.25: Handling the Activity Feed Completion

```
// Handle the activity feed when it comes back
void RequestActivityFeedCompleted(object sender,
                                    OpenReadCompletedEventArgs e)
{
    // Transform the result stream into a SyndicationFeed for easy
    // ATOM parsing
    XmlReader feedReader = XmlReader.Create(e.Result);
    SyndicationFeed feed = SyndicationFeed.Load(feedReader);

    // Project a collection of ActivityItems for binding to the View
    this.Activities = from item in feed.Items
                    select new ActivityItem
                    {
                        Title = item.Title.Text,
                        Description = FixHtml (item.Summary.Text),
                        PubDate = item.PublishDate.LocalDateTime
                    };
}
```

Adding Social Comments

One of SharePoint 2010's new social networking features is the ability to comment on most anything in SharePoint. It's easy to comment on documents, wiki pages, and the like. Under the covers, the comments are stored in the User Profile database. Each comment is associated with the user who made it and the URL of the item he is commenting on.

If the URL associated with a comment happens to point to a user profile, this becomes a comment on the user and is displayed on the user's note board. Through the Person Detail child window, you can enter a short note and click a button to send it to the user you're viewing; you can see this in the lower right corner of Figure 10.2.

Social comments are managed via the Social Data web service. As before, add a service reference from your Silverlight project, this time for _vti_bin/SocialDataService.asmx. The same .asmx Behavior work-around for using Silverlight 4 with the User Profile service is required for the Social Data service as well.

When the button is pressed, a `Command` object fires and ultimately calls the `PostNote()` method in PersonDetailChildWindow.xaml.cs. As you can see in Listing 10.26, the code creates a simple anonymous event handler to clear the note text when the service returns. Otherwise it's about as simple as calling the `AddCommentsAsync()` method when the binding and endpoint are set up.

LISTING 10.26: Posting a Note for a User with the Social Data Service

```
// PostNote - Posts a note for the user
internal void PostNote()
{
    BasicHttpBinding httpBinding = new BasicHttpBinding();
    EndpointAddress endpoint =
        new EndpointAddress(this.socialEndpointAddress);

    SocialDataServiceSoapClient socialClient =
        new SocialDataServiceSoapClient(httpBinding, endpoint);
    socialClient.AddCommentCompleted += new
        EventHandler<AddCommentCompletedEventArgs>((s, e) =>
        {
            this.NoteToPost = "";
        });
    socialClient.Endpoint.Behaviors.Add(new AsmxBehavior());
    socialClient.AddCommentAsync(this.userUrl, this.NoteToPost, false,
        this.PreferredName);
}
```

Figure 10.8 shows the note, posted back in Figure 10.2, which shows up in the user's note board on her My Site. The posting also shows up in the originating user's activity feed.

FIGURE 10.8: The note sent in Figure 10.2 is delivered.

Updating SearchView for Silverlight 5

Silverlight 5 adds a great feature that enhances the SearchView solution while simplifying its code.

The Silverlight 4 version of the solution contains two `ListBox` controls on its main page, one for people and one for "all items" (generic documents). Silverlight 5 includes *implicit data templates*, previously found only in WPF. Implicit data templates allow you to bind a control to a collection that contains multiple types of objects. During data binding, the data template is selected based on the type of each object. This not only removes the need for two `ListBox` controls, but it also allows for a mix of person and document results in the same display, as shown in Figure 10.9.

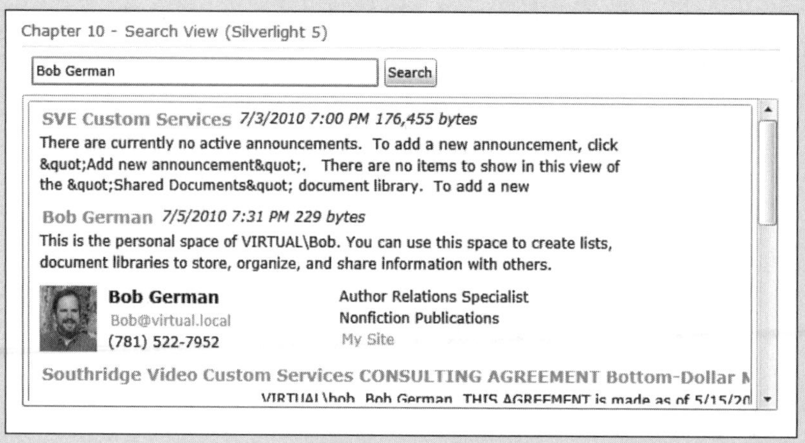

Chapter 10 - Search View (Silverlight 5)

| Bob German | Search |

SVE Custom Services *7/3/2010 7:00 PM 176,455 bytes*

There are currently no active announcements. To add a new announcement, click "Add new announcement". There are no items to show in this view of the "Shared Documents" document library. To add a new

Bob German *7/5/2010 7:31 PM 229 bytes*

This is the personal space of VIRTUAL\Bob. You can use this space to create lists, document libraries to store, organize, and share information with others.

Bob German
Bob@virtual.local
(781) 522-7952

Author Relations Specialist
Nonfiction Publications
My Site

Southridge Video Custom Services CONSULTING AGREEMENT Bottom-Dollar M
VIRTUAL\bob, Bob German. THIS AGREEMENT is made as of 5/15/20

FIGURE 10.9: A Mixture of people and document results with Silverlight 5

The first step to making this work is to introduce different kinds of ResultsItem objects so implicit data binding knows which template to use. In the SearchViewSL5 project, ResultsItem.cs has been updated as shown in Listing 10.27 to include subclasses for general or people results.

LISTING 10.27: Creating Subclasses of ResultsItem

```
// Base class for managing collections of results
public class ResultsItem
{
}

// ResultsItem with all possible fields - for retrieval from XML
public class ResultsItemAll : ResultsItem
{
    public string Title { get; set; }
    public string Url { get; set; }
    public string UserName { get; set; }
    public string Summary { get; set; }
    public string Date { get; set; }
    public string Size { get; set; }
    public string JobTitle { get; set; }
    public string Department { get; set; }
    public string WorkPhone { get; set; }
    public string Email { get; set; }
    public string EmailUrl { get; set; }
```

```
        public string PictureUrl { get; set; }
    }

    // Results Item with general fields - for binding to a general result
    public class ResultsItemGeneral : ResultsItem
    {
        public string Title { get; set; }
        public string Url { get; set; }
        public string UserName { get; set; }
        public string Summary { get; set; }
        public string Date { get; set; }
        public string Size { get; set; }
    }

    // Results Item with Person fields - for binding to a Person result
    public class ResultsItemPerson : ResultsItem
    {
        public string Title { get; set; }
        public string Url { get; set; }
        public string UserName { get; set; }
        public string Summary { get; set; }
        public string Date { get; set; }
        public string Size { get; set; }
        public string JobTitle { get; set; }
        public string Department { get; set; }
        public string WorkPhone { get; set; }
        public string Email { get; set; }
        public string EmailUrl { get; set; }
        public string PictureUrl { get; set; }
    }
```

In addition to `ResultsItemGeneral` and `ResultsItemPerson`, a third subclass called `ResultsItemAll` is defined with all possible properties present; this is used when parsing the XML when it's too early to tell if an item will be a `ResultsItemGeneral` or a `ResultsItemPerson`.

Next, SearchService.cs needs to be smart enough to separate the people and general results into the two subclasses. This is accomplished by introducing a function, `getResultsItem()`, which is used in the select clause of the LINQ query. The function is shown in Listing 10.28, and the updated LINQ query from the `queryClient_QueryCompleted` event handler is shown in Listing 10.29.

LISTING 10.28: Function to Sort Search Result Items into Two Subclasses

```
        private ResultsItem getResultsItem(ResultsItemAll originalResult)
        {
            ResultsItem finalResult = null;
            if (originalResult.UserName == "")
            {
                ResultsItemGeneral r = new ResultsItemGeneral();
                r.Title = originalResult.Title;
                r.Date = originalResult.Date;
                r.Size = originalResult.Size;
                r.Summary = originalResult.Summary;
                r.Url = originalResult.Url;
                r.UserName = originalResult.UserName;

                finalResult = r;
            }
            else
            {
                ResultsItemPerson r = new ResultsItemPerson();
                r.Title = originalResult.Title;
                r.Date = originalResult.Date;
                r.Size = originalResult.Size;
                r.Summary = originalResult.Summary;
                r.Url = originalResult.Url;
                r.UserName = originalResult.UserName;
                // Person-specific properties:
                r.Department = originalResult.Department;
                r.Email = originalResult.Email;
                r.EmailUrl = originalResult.EmailUrl;
                r.JobTitle = originalResult.JobTitle;
                r.PictureUrl = originalResult.PictureUrl;
                r.WorkPhone = originalResult.WorkPhone;

                finalResult = r;
            }

            return finalResult;
        }
```

LISTING 10.29: Updated LINQ Query to Call getResultsItem()

```
// Project the results into a collection of result items
IEnumerable<ResultsItem> resultsItems =
        from r in resultsXml.Descendants(srd + "Document")
        select getResultsItem (new ResultsItemAll
```

```
        {
            Title = getPropertyValue(r, "Title"),
            UserName = getPropertyValue(r, "AccountName"),
            Url = getPropertyValue(r, "Path"),
            Summary = getSummary(r),
            Date = convertDate(getPropertyValue(r, "Write")),
            Size = convertSize(getPropertyValue(r, "Size")),
            JobTitle = getPropertyValue(r, "JobTitle"),
            Department = getPropertyValue(r, "Department"),
            WorkPhone = getPropertyValue(r,"WorkPhone"),
            Email = getPropertyValue(r,"WorkEmail"),
            EmailUrl = "Mailto:" + getPropertyValue(r, "WorkEmail"),
            PictureUrl =
                convertPictureUrl(getPropertyValue(r, "PictureURL"))
        });
```

The result of all this is that the SearchResults property in Main-
PageVM.cs will be a collection with a mix of PeopleResultsItem objects
and GeneralResultsItem objects. The two ListBox controls in Main-
Page.xaml can then be replaced with the single ListBox control shown in
Listing 10.30. The ListBox.Resources element contains two DataTemplate
elements—one for people and one for general results.

LISTING 10.30: Updated Results ListBox

```
<!-- Results List Box shows People and General Results -->
<!--  using Silverlight 5 Implicit Data Binding        -->
<ListBox ItemsSource="{Binding Path=SearchResults}"
        SelectedItem="{Binding Path=SelectedResult, Mode=TwoWay}">
  <i:Interaction.Triggers>
    <i:EventTrigger EventName="MouseLeftButtonUp">
      <ei:CallMethodAction MethodName="ShowPersonDetail"
                        TargetObject="{Binding}" />
    </i:EventTrigger>
  </i:Interaction.Triggers>
  <ListBox.Resources>
    <DataTemplate DataType="local:ResultsItemPerson">
      <Grid>
        <Grid.ColumnDefinitions>
          <ColumnDefinition Width="60" />
          <ColumnDefinition Width="200" />
          <ColumnDefinition Width="*" />
        </Grid.ColumnDefinitions>
        <Image Grid.Column="0" Height="55" Width="55"
```

```
                        Source="{Binding PictureUrl}" Margin="5,2"/>
            <StackPanel Grid.Column="1" Margin="5,2">
                <TextBlock Text="{Binding Title}" FontSize="14"
                        FontWeight="Bold" />
                <HyperlinkButton NavigateUri="{Binding EmailUrl}" FontSize="12"
                        TargetName="_blank" Content="{Binding Email}" />
                <TextBlock Text="{Binding WorkPhone}" FontSize="12" />
            </StackPanel>
            <StackPanel Grid.Column="2" Margin="5,2">
                <TextBlock Text="{Binding JobTitle}" FontSize="12" />
                <TextBlock Text="{Binding Department}" FontSize="12" />
                <HyperlinkButton NavigateUri="{Binding Url}" FontSize="12"
                        TargetName="_blank" Content="My Site" />
            </StackPanel>
        </Grid>
    </DataTemplate>
    <DataTemplate DataType="local:ResultsItemGeneral">
        <StackPanel Orientation="Vertical">
            <StackPanel Margin="5,0,0,0" Orientation="Horizontal">
                <HyperlinkButton NavigateUri="{Binding Url}"
                        Content="{Binding Title}" FontSize="14"
                        FontWeight="Bold" />
                <TextBlock Text="{Binding Date}" FontSize="12"
                        FontStyle="Italic" Margin="5,0,0,0" />
                <TextBlock Text="{Binding Size}" FontSize="12"
                        FontStyle="Italic" Margin="5,0,0,0" />
            </StackPanel>
            <TextBlock Margin="5,0,0,2" Text="{Binding Summary}"
                    FontSize="12" TextWrapping="Wrap" Width="500" />
        </StackPanel>
    </DataTemplate>

</ListBox.Resources>
</ListBox>
```

Building Custom WCF Services for SharePoint

As great as all the SharePoint client-side APIs and web services might be, there inevitably comes a time when you want to do something on the SharePoint server that isn't available in any of them. At that point, the only option might be to write your own web service and deploy it to SharePoint. Fortunately, Visual Studio 2010 and SharePoint 2010 make it pretty easy to do this using Windows Communications Foundation (WCF).

There are a few reasons to write a custom WCF service for SharePoint:

- To access APIs and resources on the server that are not available via client APIs or web services
- To elevate privileges or run under a server-based security context
- To cache information on the server
- To consolidate a series of operations into a single round-trip

The Chapter10b solution in this chapter's code download illustrates the first three of these points. It renders a simple storage meter showing the amount of storage for the current site collection relative to its quota, as shown in Figure 10.10. The quota information is not present in the client-side Site object. Further, accessing this information requires site collection administrative privileges. Finally, the information changes infrequently and is a good candidate for caching on the server rather than looking it up each time.

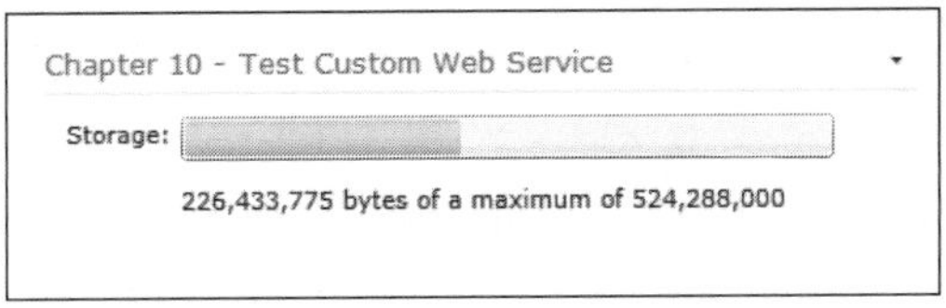

FIGURE 10.10: Web part to display the site collection storage and quota

Creating a Custom Web Service

To begin, create SharePoint and Silverlight projects as usual. This time you need to make it a Farm solution because you need to deploy some files on the web servers and this is not permitted in a sandboxed solution.

Next, add a WCF Service Library project. This project won't actually be used, but it provides an easy way to generate the framework for our WCF service. Copy the Service1.cs and IService1.cs files into your SharePoint project and then delete the WCF Service Library project.

Next, add references to the SharePoint project for System.Runtime. Serialization and System.ServiceModel. These are needed to run the

WCF service. You also need to add a reference to the SharePoint Client Server Runtime, which requires you to browse into the Global Assembly Cache. On the Add Reference dialog box, click the Browse tab and navigate to your Windows directory, and then \assembly\GAC_MSIL\Microsoft. SharePoint.Client.ServerRuntime. There is another directory inside and within that, the DLL to reference—Microsoft.SharePoint.Client.ServerRuntime.dll.

The code that runs in your web service is referenced in a .svc file, which must be deployed to the ISAPI directory; remember, this ends up appearing in the _vti_bin folder under every site in the SharePoint farm. The easiest way to get it there is to use a mapped folder, which maps a Visual Studio folder to a folder in the SharePoint installation directory. To create a mapped folder, right-click the SharePoint project and click Add, and in the fly-out menu select SharePoint Mapped Folder.... A dialog box appears showing you the SharePoint installation directory (or SharePoint Root) structure. Click the ISAPI folder and click OK, and you see an ISAPI folder in your Visual Studio project. Anything placed in that folder will be installed into the corresponding folder on all SharePoint servers when the solution is installed.

Create a text file in the ISAPI mapped folder and name it for your service, ending in .svc. Enter the following markup into the file, substituting your web service object and assembly name (these are for the sample project):

```
<%@ServiceHost Language="C#" Debug="true"
   Service="Chapter10b.TestService, Chapter10b, Version=1.0.0.0,
Culture=neutral, PublicKeyToken=6795e15e830bf8f4"
   Factory="Microsoft.SharePoint.Client.Services.MultipleBaseAddressBa-
sicHttpBindingServiceHostFactory, Microsoft.SharePoint.Client.ServerRuntime,
Version=14.0.0.0, Culture=neutral, PublicKeyToken=71e9bce111e9429c" %>
```

The `Service` attribute tells SharePoint where to find your web service code, which is installed along with the solution. The `Factory` attribute should be copied as-is, all on one line, and tells WCF to use SharePoint's service host factory to host the service.

> **TIP**
>
> Entering an application's full name is a cumbersome process and can be error-prone when application versions and signatures change. SharePoint's configuration files (and WCF's configuration file in this case) frequently need this information, so Visual Studio 2010 has added a feature to make it easier. Instead of the full application name, the token `$SharePoint.Project.AssemblyFullName$` can be used, and Visual Studio substitutes the application name, such as `Chapter10b.TestService`, `Chapter10b`, `Version=1.0.0.0`, `Culture=neutral`, `PublicKeyToken=6795e15e830bf8f4` at compile time.
>
> The tricky part is that by default, Visual Studio only does this for known SharePoint configuration files, so if you want to do it in your .svc file, you need to tell Visual Studio. To do this, right-click the SharePoint project and select Unload Project. All the project items disappear. Right-click the project again, which is now marked unavailable, and select Edit. This enables you to edit the .csproj file directly.
>
> Add this line to the first `<PropertyGroup>` element to enable token substitution in .svc files:
>
> ```
> <TokenReplacementFileExtensions>svc</TokenReplacementFile
> Extensions>
> ```
>
> Save your changes and right-click the project again, this time selecting the Reload Project option. Your project now provides SharePoint token replacement in .svc files.

At this point, you can rename and add your own code to Service1.cs and IService1.cs. The code sample provides a web service called TestService.svc, which has a service contract defined in ITestService.cs and is implemented in TestService.cs. The service is simple and defines a single method, `GetUsageData()`, which returns a small class containing the current site collection storage and quota. Listing 10.31 shows the ITestService.cs service contract.

LISTING 10.31: ITestService Service Contract

```
[ServiceContract]
public interface ITestService
{
    [OperationContract]
    UsageData GetUsageData();
}


[DataContract]
public class UsageData
{
    [DataMember]
    public long Storage { get; set; }
    [DataMember]
    public long StorageWarningLevel { get; set; }
    [DataMember]
    public long StorageMaximumLevel { get; set; }
}
```

The `TestService` implementation is in TestService.cs and derives from the service contract interface `ITestService`. The code is shown in Listing 10.32.

LISTING 10.32: TestService Implementation

```
[BasicHttpBindingServiceMetadataExchangeEndpoint]
[AspNetCompatibilityRequirements
 (RequirementsMode=AspNetCompatibilityRequirementsMode.Required)]
public class TestService : ITestService
{
    public UsageData GetUsageData()
    {
        SPSite site = SPContext.Current.Site;
        // UsageData is defined in ITestService.cs
        UsageData result = HttpRuntime.Cache["USAGE_DATA_" +
            site.ServerRelativeUrl] as UsageData;

        if (result == null)
        {
            result = new UsageData();

            SPSecurity.RunWithElevatedPrivileges(() =>
            {
                using (SPSite elevatedSite = new SPSite(site.ID))
                {
                    result.Storage = elevatedSite.Usage.Storage;
```

```
                    result.StorageWarningLevel =
                        elevatedSite.Quota.StorageWarningLevel;
                    result.StorageMaximumLevel =
                        elevatedSite.Quota.StorageMaximumLevel;
                }
            });

            HttpRuntime.Cache.Add
                ("USAGE_DATA_" + site.ServerRelativeUrl,
                 result, null, DateTime.Now.AddMinutes(10),
                 TimeSpan.Zero, CacheItemPriority.Default, null);
        }
        return result;
    }
}
```

The GetUsageData() method begins by accessing the current SharePoint site collection from SPContext.Current.Site; this is really just to get the site collection URL. The next step is to check the ASP.NET cache to see if the usage data is already in cache. The ASP.NET cache can be accessed as System.Web.HttpRuntime.Cache and is capable of caching any .NET object, in this case a UsageData object for the site. The cache key contains the site URL, as in USAGE_DATA_/sites/chapter10, to ensure it is unique to each site collection. If the cache returns a valid UsageData object, it is returned; if it is null, the new UsageData object must be created.

The usage and quota data are readily available as properties of the SPSite object, so it would seem simple enough to just load them into the new UsageData object and get on with it. However, accessing these properties requires administrative privileges, so if you want the web part to work for everyone, you need to run under elevated privileges. SharePoint's SPSecurity class provides a static method, RunWithElevatedPrivileges, which runs any delegate with the equivalent privileges of a Farm administrator. Needless to say, this API should be used with care.

In this case, the delegate that RunWithElevatedPrivileges will run is an anonymous function declared inline in the code. Notice that the first thing it does is to create a new SPSite object! If the site variable had been used, where SPSite was obtained from the (unelevated) SharePoint context, it would still run under the permissions of the calling user. By creating a new

SPSite object and using the URL of the old one, you get a fully elevated instance of the object and can access all its members.

Finally, the result is added to the ASP.NET cache with a lifetime of ten minutes, so if another request is made within that time, the server processing will be minimal.

Consuming the Custom Web Service

Consuming a custom WCF service is very similar to the .asmx examples earlier in the chapter. Ensure the WCF service is configured correctly before attempting to add a service reference and then add a reference to the .svc file's URL, adding "/MEX" to the end, as in http://myserver/sites/testsite/_vti_bin/TestService.svc/MEX. The /MEX specifies WCF's Metadata Exchange Format.

The sample solution includes a simple Silverlight web part that consumes the test service and displays the site's storage and quota on a Silverlight progress bar. If no quota is set, an arbitrary amount is chosen to control the size of the progress bar. Listing 10.33 shows the Silverlight code, which calls the service and updates the progress bar; in the download, this code is in MainPage.xaml.cs in the TestServiceSL project.

LISTING 10.33: Calling the Custom Web Service

```
BasicHttpBinding binding = new BasicHttpBinding();
EndpointAddress endpoint = new EndpointAddress(endpointAddress);

TestServiceClient tsClient = new TestServiceClient(binding, endpoint);
tsClient.GetUsageDataCompleted += ((s1, e1) =>
{
    UsageData usage = e1.Result as UsageData;
    if (usage != null)
    {
        if (usage.StorageMaximumLevel > 0)
        {
            // Calculate percentage use (progress bar is set for 0-100)
            storageProgressBar.Value =
                100 * usage.Storage / usage.StorageMaximumLevel;
            storageTextBox.Text =
                usage.Storage.ToString("N0") +
                " bytes of a maximum of " +
                 usage.StorageMaximumLevel.ToString("N0");
        }
```

```
        else
        {
            // If no quota is set, use 250MB and simulate a percentage
            storageProgressBar.Value = 100 * usage.Storage / 250000000;
            storageTextBox.Text = usage.Storage.ToString("N0") +
                " bytes";
        }
    }
});

// Call the service
tsClient.GetUsageDataAsync();
```

The sky's the limit with the ability to create your own web services having full access to the SharePoint servers. It is extra work, however, and requires a Farm solution, so it's still better to use SharePoint's out-of-the-box Client Object Model and web services when possible.

Summary

SharePoint 2010's Client Object Model and RESTful list services provide the easiest way to get at SharePoint site content, but there's a lot more to SharePoint than just the site content. SharePoint provides a variety of web services to access its many services, and these can be used in your Silverlight solutions. When all else fails, it's also possible to write and deploy your own web services to SharePoint as a Farm solution.

Given all these possibilities, there's no corner of SharePoint so dark that your Silverlight application can't make use of it!

11

Accessing External Data

THERE ARE SOME CHALLENGES inherent in accessing external data from a SharePoint web part or other user interface extension. Share-Point's Business Connectivity Services (BCS) addresses these challenges, so it should be no surprise that this chapter includes a section on how to set up BCS and use it from Silverlight. However you also learn how to access external data from Silverlight without BCS so you can directly access web services, newsfeeds, and other network resources in your solutions.

One challenge is that for security reasons, sandboxed solution code isn't allowed to make network calls. For example, if you wanted to write an RSS reader that runs in a sandboxed solution, it wouldn't be possible to read the RSS feed in the server code.

Another challenge is the dreaded "multi-hop" authentication problem. The issue here is that even if you can authenticate to a web server (Share-Point in this case), that doesn't mean that SharePoint can authenticate on your behalf to a third tier such as a remote web service or database server. It's possible to do this using SAML claims or Kerberos authentication, but developers rarely have the ability to influence how authentication is set up; those decisions are typically made by the SharePoint deployment team or IT security specialists.

A natural solution to both of these challenges is to access the network from Silverlight on the client. A Silverlight application that is deployed in a sandboxed solution isn't subject to the sandbox limitations; it runs in the Silverlight sandbox on the client, which has no such restriction on network access. Moreover, the multi-hop scenario is avoided because the client computer authenticates directly to the external server in a single hop.

Alas, no solution is perfect, and this one is no exception. A new challenge is introduced by this approach, the challenge of cross-domain access.

Silverlight (as well as other browser plug-ins and all major web browsers) has restrictions on making network calls across DNS domains. Consider, for example, the scenario shown in Figure 11.1. A user browses to a page on a SharePoint server hosted in the intranet.com DNS domain. The page contains a Silverlight application, which attempts to access another domain, external.com, over the network. By default, Silverlight prohibits this as a cross-domain access. If you're wondering why this is so, consider what might happen if external.com were your bank's web site. If you were already logged into the bank web site, or if the login were automatic (as it would be for many servers within an enterprise), the application would have unfettered access to act on your behalf and could empty your bank account or do other malice.

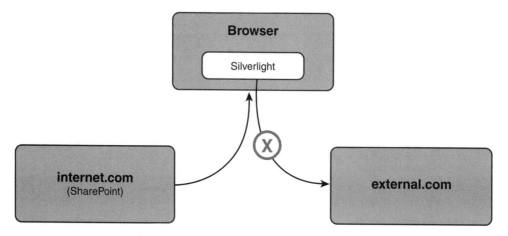

FIGURE 11.1: Cross-domain access from Silverlight

There are a couple ways to address this issue. One is to provide a policy file on the external.com server that explicitly allows access from an external domain. Silverlight looks for a file called clientaccesspolicy.xml, and if it doesn't find it, it looks for the Adobe Flash equivalent of this file, crossdomain.xml. If either of these files is present and includes a policy that allows access, Silverlight permits the access.

> ■ **TIP**
>
> Silverlight looks for the clientaccesspolicy.xml and crossdomain.xml files under the root of the target web server. For example, when attempting to access http://server.external.com/child/grandchild/myservice.svc, Silverlight tries to read http://server.external.com/clientaccesspolicy.xml, ignoring the child and grandchild directories and reading directly under the root of the web server.
>
> Here are some other points to keep in mind:
>
> - Silverlight considers all network access from an "out of browser" application to be cross-domain because the .xap file is installed on the client computer.
> - The SharePoint Client Object Model is not subject to cross-domain policy, but access to SharePoint using OData or web services is.
> - Even with REST and web services access, none of this is an issue when the Silverlight application tries to access data on the same SharePoint server that served up the .xap file because that's not "cross-domain" access.

Listing 11.1 shows a sample clientaccesspolicy.xml file. In this example, it's set to allow any domain to access any path within the server. It's possible to be quite specific as to what domains can access what resources on the server using this file. For example, by setting the `grant-to` element it is possible to limit access to a specific SharePoint site or even an individual .xap file.

LISTING 11.1: Clientaccesspolicy.xml

```xml
<?xml version="1.0" encoding="utf-8"?>
<access-policy>
  <cross-domain-access>
    <policy>
      <allow-from http-request-headers="SOAPAction">
```

```
      <domain uri="*"/>
    </allow-from>
    <grant-to>
      <resource path="/" include-subpaths="true"/>
    </grant-to>
  </policy>
 </cross-domain-access>
</access-policy>
```

Listing 11.2 shows the Adobe Flash policy file, called crossdomain.xml. Although it doesn't allow the server to specify what resource paths are allowed, it still controls the domains that can have access. The advantage of supporting the Flash version of the file is that it's already present on many web servers on the Internet; generally Silverlight developers use the clientaccesspolicy.xml file.

LISTING 11.2: crossdomain.xml

```
<?xml version="1.0"?>
<!DOCTYPE cross-domain-policy SYSTEM
"http://www.macromedia.com/xml/dtds/cross-domain-policy.dtd">
<cross-domain-policy>
  <allow-http-request-headers-from domain="*"
   headers="SOAPAction,Content-Type"/>
</cross-domain-policy>
```

Consider a Silverlight newsfeed reader, which is explained in the next section. If the web part is set to read news headlines from CNN, it works perfectly because CNN provides a policy file that allows any domain to access its services. Other news services, such as BBC and MSNBC, provide policy files that only allow a list of their own domains to have access, so the web part can't access those feeds as long as it's not hosted on one of those domains. Figure 11.2 shows a browser tracing program, Nikhil's Web Development Helper, as the web part attempts to display a feed from a test web site that has no policy file. You can see that it attempts to read both the Silverlight and Flash versions of the file and, when it gets 404 "not found" errors, the access fails.

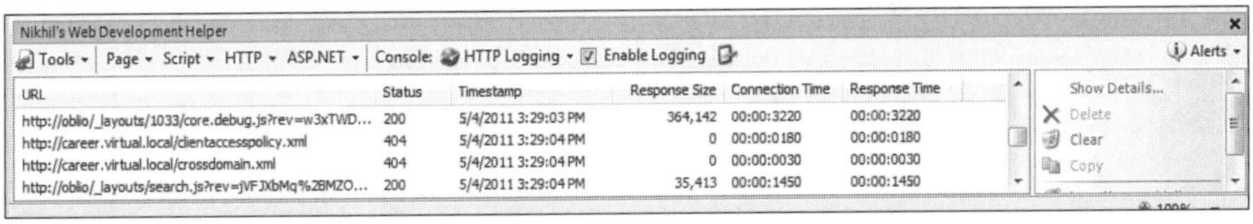

FIGURE 11.2: Attempting to read the cross-domain policy files

In the sections that follow, you learn how to build a newsfeed reader in Silverlight that works subject to cross-domain policy. Then you learn how to avoid the cross-domain issue by setting up a newsfeed proxy on Share-Point (as a Farm solution, so it can retrieve the newsfeed). After that, you learn how to add a cross-domain policy to SharePoint in case you want to allow incoming requests from other domains. Finally, the chapter concludes with a BCS solution that shows how to access a SQL Server database from a Silverlight web part using a SharePoint external list and the Client Object Model.

Building a Feed Reader Web Part

The External Feed Web Part is provided in the code download in a solution called Chapter11a.sln. The Visual Studio solution includes four projects: the SharePoint web solution package, Silverlight 4 and 5 applications, and a test web project that generates an RSS feed. Figure 11.3 shows the External Feed web part pointing to the test web project, which is running at http://localhost:1589/feed.aspx (the port is selected randomly on your workstation).

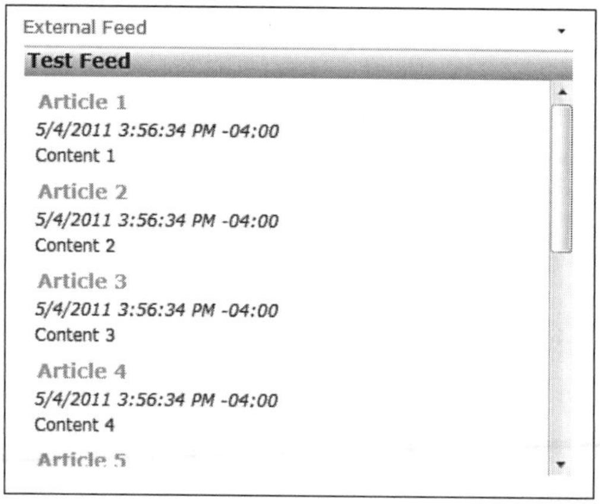

FIGURE 11.3: External Feed Web Part

> **⊾ TIP**
>
> Visual Studio 2010 allows you to set more than one "startup project" that runs when you start the debugger. This can be useful for this example to start both the SharePoint project and the test web site that hosts the RSS feed. To do this, right-click the solution at the top of the Solution Explorer tree and select Set Startup Projects. This brings up a dialog box that allows you to choose a single startup project or to select more than one.

When the web part accesses the feed on the test web site, it's considered a cross-domain access. The web project includes cross-domain policy files, so the web part works fine. This is an ideal environment for testing the policy files. Try removing them entirely or using only the Adobe Flash version of the file.

The web part includes two editable properties, `FeedType` and `Location`. `FeedType` is an enumeration of `Direct`, `Proxy`, and `ExtList`. This same web part is used for all the examples in this chapter, and the `FeedType` property tells the web part if it should access a newsfeed directly, via a SharePoint proxy, or if it should access data via a BCS external list. This section focuses on the first of these choices, direct access.

Listing 11.3 shows the web part server code. There's not much to it: it simply places the Silverlight object tag on the page and passes it the feed type, location, and the current site's URL.

LISTING 11.3: ExternalFeed Web Part

```
public class ExternalFeed : WebPart
{
    public enum FeedOptions {Direct, Proxy, ExtList}

    [WebBrowsable(true)]
    [Personalizable(PersonalizationScope.Shared)]
    public FeedOptions FeedType { get; set; }

    [WebBrowsable(true)]
    [Personalizable(PersonalizationScope.Shared)]
    [Description("URL of feed or external list be displayed")]
    public string Location { get; set; }

    // Silverlight plug-in control
    private SilverlightPlugin sl = new SilverlightPlugin();

    protected override void CreateChildControls()
    {
        // Set up Silverlight plug-in
        SPSite site = SPContext.Current.Site;
        sl.Source = ((site.ServerRelativeUrl == "/")
                        ? "/" : site.ServerRelativeUrl + "/") +
                        "ClientBin/ExternalFeedSL.xap";
        sl.InitParameters = "FeedType=" + this.FeedType.ToString() +
                        ",Location=" + this.Location +
                        ",SiteUrl=" + site.Url;

        this.Controls.Add(sl);
    }
}
```

The Silverlight application follows the MVVM design pattern, as explained in Chapter 10, "Accessing SharePoint with Web Services." Two ViewModels are provided, one for the two newsfeed scenarios (direct and proxy), and one for the BCS external list example. Listing 11.4 shows the Silverlight `Application_Startup` event handler, which creates the Model and connects the appropriate ViewModel.

LISTING 11.4: Silverlight Application_Startup Event Handler

```
private void Application_Startup(object sender, StartupEventArgs e)
{
    // We expect feed type, location and site URL
    // Any less and we display an error
    if (e.InitParams.ContainsKey("FeedType") &&
        e.InitParams.ContainsKey("Location") &&
        e.InitParams.ContainsKey("SiteUrl"))
    {
        if (e.InitParams["Location"] != "")
        {
            // If we have a valid location, create the view
            // and bind the correct ViewModel

            MainPage page = new MainPage();

            switch (e.InitParams["FeedType"].ToLower())
            {
                case "direct":
                    {
                        page.LayoutRoot.DataContext =
                            new SimpleFeedVM(e.InitParams["Location"],
                            "direct",
                            e.InitParams["SiteUrl"]);
                        break;
                    }
                case "proxy":
                    {
                        page.LayoutRoot.DataContext =
                            new SimpleFeedVM(e.InitParams["Location"],
                            "proxy",
                             e.InitParams["SiteUrl"]);
                        break;
                    }
                case "extlist":
                    {
                        page.LayoutRoot.DataContext =
                            new ExternalListVM(page,
                            e.InitParams["Location"]);
                        break;
                    }
            }
            this.RootVisual = page;
        }
        else
        {
            this.RootVisual = new ErrorPage();
        }
    }
}
```

In the case of "direct" access, the code creates a ViewModel called Simple-FeedVM and binds it to the view using its layout root's `DataContext` property. Both the SimpleFeedVM and ExternalListVM ViewModels are based on a common base class called `BaseVM`. The views are bound to the base class (and yes, there are two views: MainPage.xaml to display a list of items and EditDetailChildWindow.xaml, which is used in the BCS example).

As in the MVVM example in Chapter 10, the ViewModels implement the `INotifyPropertyChanged` interface to allow two-way data binding to its properties. The `BaseVM` class implements the required `PropertyChanged` event handler, and its properties raise this event when they are set to tell any bound controls to update themselves. The `BaseVM` properties are

- `string FeedName`: The name of the feed or list to be displayed
- `string FeedUrl`: The URL of a user-clickable link to the information source
- `IEnumerable<FeedItem> Items`: A collection of `FeedItem` objects
- `FeedItem SelectedFeedItem`: The currently selected `FeedItem`

Keep in mind that these properties are different from what we passed from the server to Silverlight; they're binding points for the Silverlight view and its controls. For example, the FeedUrl need not be the location of the information feed—it's a user-clickable link that will be displayed in the Silverlight UI.

The BaseVM.cs file includes a second class, `FeedItem`, which also implements `INotifyPropertyChanged`. The `Items` and `SelectedFeedItem` properties of the `BaseVM` refer to this class, which represents an individual item in a newsfeed or external list. Again, the code is similar to the example in the last chapter, with each property firing the `PropertyChanged` event when it is set. The `FeedItem` properties are

- `int ContactID`: A unique numeric identifier for the feed item
- `string Title`: The title or full name of the item
- `string TitleUrl`: A hyperlink to the item
- `string SubText1`: Descriptive text about the item

- `string SubText2`: Descriptive text about the item
- `string Summary`: Descriptive text about the item

Notice that the properties are all pretty generic, which is an indication that the view will be general in nature so it can display different kinds of information such as a newsfeed item and a contact in an external list.

The `FeedItem` class also implements a `CopyTo()` method, which allows the code to make a copy of a `FeedItem`. This is used in the BCS example when editing the details of an item.

Things start to get more interesting in the `SimpleFeedVM` class, which inherits its properties from `BaseVM` and populates them with a newsfeed. Listing 11.5 shows the constructor, which kicks off the process of requesting the newsfeed, and its completion handler, which uses LINQ to project the results into an `IEnumerable<FeedItem>` for binding to the user interface.

LISTING 11.5: SimpleFeedVM Code to Retrieve a Newsfeed

```
public SimpleFeedVM(string url, string feedType, string siteUrl)
{
    // Read the specified feed using the WebClient
    WebClient wc = new WebClient();
    string feedUrl = url;
    if (feedType == "proxy")
    {
        feedUrl = siteUrl +
            "/_layouts/FeedProxy/GetFeed.aspx?url=" + url;
    }

    wc.DownloadStringCompleted +=
        new DownloadStringCompletedEventHandler
            (wc_DownloadStringCompleted);
    wc.DownloadStringAsync(new Uri(feedUrl));
}

// Completion handler
void wc_DownloadStringCompleted(object sender,
                        DownloadStringCompletedEventArgs e)
{
    if (e.Error == null)
    {
        // If here, we successfully got the newsfeed.
        // Run the result through the StringReader to iron out encoding
        // issues from the source feed
        StringReader reader = new StringReader(e.Result);
```

```
        // Now read into a SyndicationFeed
        XmlReader feedReader = XmlReader.Create(reader);
        SyndicationFeed feed = SyndicationFeed.Load(feedReader);

        // Copy scalar values from the SyndicationFeed to our
        // bindable properties
        this.FeedName = feed.Title.Text;
        this.FeedUrl = feed.Links.Count > 0 ?
                        feed.Links[0].Uri.AbsoluteUri : "";

        // Project the SyndicationFeedItems into a collection of our
        // own FeedItems for binding to the View
        var i = from item in feed.Items
                select new FeedItem
                {
                    Title = item.Title.Text.Trim(),
                    TitleUrl = item.Links.Count>0
                                    ? item.Links[0].Uri.ToString() : "",
                    SubText1 = item.PublishDate.ToString(),
                    SubText2 = item.Authors.Count>0
                                    ? item.Authors[0].Name : "",
                    Summary = FixHtml(item.Summary.Text)
                };
        this.Items = i;
    }
    else
    {
        // If there was a problem, show the error
        this.Items = null;
        System.Windows.MessageBox.Show(e.Error.InnerException.Message);
    }
}
```

Notice that Silverlight conveniently provides a `SyndicationFeed` object to parse the newsfeed, regardless if it's in RSS or ATOM format. The LINQ query enumerates the feed and because newsfeeds can have multiple authors and links, flattens these by selecting the first of each for binding to the user interface.

The only missing piece in Listing 11.5 is a utility method called `StripHtml`, which removes extraneous HTML tags from the newsfeed content. Unfortunately, displaying HTML is a bit of a challenge. Silverlight 4 introduced a `WebBrowser` control, but this is only available for use in out-of-browser applications. Silverlight 5 allows this in trusted browser applications, and this is shown later in this chapter, but still the `WebBrowser` control is too heavy-weight to use in every item in a feed. Therefore the solution just strips out the HTML. Listing 11.6 shows the `StripHtml` method; it's not perfect but removes most of the tags found in RSS feed entries.

LISTING 11.6: StripHtml Strips Out HTML Tags

```
private string StripHtml(string html)
{
    const string BR_REGEX = "<[Bb][Rr].*?>";
    const string HTML_REGEX = "<.*?>";

    string stripped = HttpUtility.HtmlDecode(html);

    // Make all <br /> tags into newlines
    stripped = Regex.Replace(stripped, BR_REGEX, "\n");

    // Now strip away all other tags
    stripped = Regex.Replace(stripped, HTML_REGEX, string.Empty).Trim();

    return stripped;
}
```

To test the web part, add it to a page and point it at the feed.aspx test feed. To do this, expand the TestWeb project, right-click feed.aspx, and click View in Browser. You should see a test feed with ten numbered articles. Copy the URL and paste it into the web part's location property, and because the cross-domain policy is set up, you should see the display just shown in Figure 11.3.

Building a Custom Feed Reader Proxy

Cross-domain policies sometimes get in the way, so it's good to have a few more tricks up your sleeve. The cross-domain policy file is only checked if you're accessing data across domains, so why not employ the SharePoint server as an intermediary? This is shown in Figure 11.4 and is a helpful work-around when a cross-domain policy is not available.

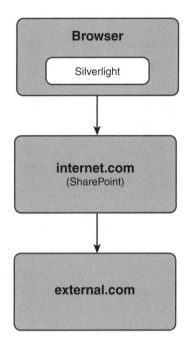

FIGURE 11.4: Using SharePoint to proxy requests

This can have the added advantage that you can cache content in Share-Point, improving performance and reducing thread use on the SharePoint server. However, be sure to respect security; caching can be tricky if different users have different access rights to the cached content.

You can also run afoul of the multihop authentication issue, so the proxy approach is more straightforward when the external site is accessed anonymously or under a single account. BCS handles complex security settings more easily and is preferable for a number of other reasons, but that's a discussion for later in the chapter.

This section examines a proxy solution for newsfeeds. The BCS entity model doesn't map too well to a newsfeed, and many great newsfeeds work with no authentication, so it makes sense to build a feed proxy.

The Chapter11c.sln solution included with the code download contains a Farm solution that adds a newsfeed proxy to SharePoint. The proxy is implemented as a layouts page, which means that it can be accessed under the _layouts directory in any SharePoint site. A custom web service, like the one explained at the end of Chapter 10, could have worked as well. This example using a page shows a simpler alternative and shows how to develop layouts pages in general. It's also accessible from other feed readers because it relays the feed in its original format.

The Visual Studio project consists of a single mapped folder, which is a project folder that is mapped to a physical folder in the SharePoint root directory. In this case, that folder is the Layouts directory that underlies the _layouts folder in SharePoint URLs. Mapped folders are not controlled using the Features infrastructure, so there is no Feature in the project; when the Farm solution is deployed, the proxy page is available in the _layouts directory in every site on the farm.

Within the Layouts folder the solution deploys a folder called Feed-Proxy, and within that a single web page, GetFeed.aspx, which does all the work. Listing 11.7 shows the feed proxy as implemented in the code behind this page. It accepts a newsfeed URL as a query string parameter, and responds with the contents of that newsfeed just as if it came from the source.

LISTING 11.7: Feed Proxy Implemented in GetFeed.aspx.cs

```
protected void Page_Load(object sender, EventArgs e)
{
    string feedString = "";
    Cache currentCache = HttpContext.Current.Cache;

    try
    {
        // Ensure we have a URL
        string feedUrl = Request.QueryString["url"];
        if (string.IsNullOrEmpty(feedUrl))
        {
            throw new Exception("You must specify a URL for the feed");
        }

        // Try to get the feed from cache
        if (currentCache["Feed" + feedUrl] != null)
        {
            feedString = currentCache["Feed" + feedUrl].ToString();
        }
        else
        {
            // If here, the feed was not in cache, fetch it
            WebClient wc = new WebClient();
            feedString = wc.DownloadString(feedUrl);
```

```
            currentCache["Feed" + feedUrl] = feedString;
        }
    }
    catch (Exception ex)
    {
        // Report the exception as an RSS feed
        Response.Clear();
        ReportError(ex);
    }

    // We have the feed, return it with the correct MIME type
    Response.Write(feedString);
    Response.ContentType = "text/xml";
}
```

The code uses the ASP.NET cache to save the feed, so it need not be retrieved each time it is displayed. The cache key contains the feed URL to make it unique. If the feed isn't found in cache, the WebClient object is used to retrieve the feed. This is the same WebClient object used in the last section in Silverlight code, except here it's called synchronously in the style of ASP.NET. The response is sent to the cache and written to the client using a Response.Write statement. All that's left to do is flip the MIME type to "text/xml", and the feed has been sent to our client just as we received it.

You might have noticed in the last section, in Listing 11.5, there is a check for a feed proxy. The snippet of code is repeated in Listing 11.8.

LISTING 11.8: The Silverlight Client Adds the Feed Proxy to a Newsfeed URL

```
    if (feedType == "proxy")
    {
        feedUrl = siteUrl +
            "/_layouts/FeedProxy/GetFeed.aspx?url=" + url;
    }
```

As you can see, the proxy feed type simply puts the feed proxy URL in front of the newsfeed URL. Try it out by editing the External Feed web part and selecting the Proxy connection type. Of course you'll need to ensure that your web server can make outgoing Internet calls; if it can, you should see the feed in Silverlight.

Adding Cross-Domain Policy to SharePoint

What if the tables are turned and you want to allow external users into your SharePoint site? What if you want to use the feed reader to access a cross-domain SharePoint server within your enterprise? Then you need to deploy a cross-domain file on SharePoint.

The simple and most popular approach is to simply copy the policy file in the virtual directory for your web application. This directory is found inside of c:\inetpub\wss\VirtualDirectories on a SharePoint Server; there is a subdirectory for each SharePoint web application.

If you want to control the policy as a SharePoint package, so it is reliably deployed on all web servers in the farm or want to add some logic in defining its contents, this is certainly possible. Such a package is included as the Chapter11b.sln solution in the code download. The solution deploys an HTTP handler, which serves up the policy file anonymously, as shown in Listing 11.9. It is called PolicyHandler in the code download.

Technically, adding any HTTP handler to SharePoint is "unsupported," but this is a nondestructive change that could be removed if you ever had to troubleshoot a problem with Microsoft support.

LISTING 11.9: HttpHandler to Provide the Cross-Domain Access Policy File

```
class ClientAccessPolicyHttpHandler : IHttpHandler
{

    public bool IsReusable
    {
        get { return true; }
    }

    private const string POLICY_XML =
        @"<?xml version='1.0' encoding='utf-8' ?>
          <access-policy>
            <cross-domain-access>
              <policy>
                <allow-from http-request-headers='*'>
                  <domain uri='*' />
                </allow-from>
                <grant-to>
                  <resource path='/' include-subpaths='true' />
                </grant-to> </policy>
              </cross-domain-access>
```

```
        </access-policy>";

    public void ProcessRequest(HttpContext context)
    {
        if (context.Request.Path.ToLowerInvariant() ==
            "/clientaccesspolicy.xml")
        {
            context.Response.ContentType = "text/xml";
            context.Response.Write(POLICY_XML);
        }
    }
}
```

The HTTP handler needs to be declared in web.config. Listing 11.10 shows how to add the HTTP handler to web.config automatically in the feature receiver. The key is to use SharePoint's SPWebConfigModification object. This is explained in more detail in Chapter 13, "Creating Silverlight Navigation."

LISTING 11.10: Adding the HTTP Handler to web.config

```
public override void
                FeatureActivated(SPFeatureReceiverProperties properties)
{
    SPWebConfigModification modification = new SPWebConfigModification();
    modification.Path = "configuration/system.webServer/handlers";
    modification.Name = "add[@name='ClientAccessPolicy']";
    modification.Sequence = 0;
    modification.Owner = "ClientAccessPolicy";
    modification.Type =
     SPWebConfigModification.SPWebConfigModificationType.EnsureChildNode;
    modification.Value =
        "<add name=\"ClientAccessPolicy\" path=\"clientaccesspolicy.xml\""+
        " verb=\"*\" type=\"" +
        typeof(ClientAccessPolicyHttpHandler).AssemblyQualifiedName +
        "\" />";

    SPWebService contentService = SPWebService.ContentService;
    contentService.WebConfigModifications.Add(modification);
    contentService.Update();
    contentService.ApplyWebConfigModifications();
}

public override void
        FeatureDeactivating(SPFeatureReceiverProperties properties)
{
```

```
SPWebConfigModification configModFound = null;

SPWebService contentService = SPWebService.ContentService;
Collection<SPWebConfigModification> modsCollection =
    contentService.WebConfigModifications;

// Find the most recent modification of a specified owner
int modsCount1 = modsCollection.Count;
for (int i = modsCount1 - 1; i > -1; i–)
{
    if (modsCollection[i].Owner == "ClientAccessPolicy")
    {
        configModFound = modsCollection[i];
    }
}

// Remove it and save the change to the configuration database
modsCollection.Remove(configModFound);
contentService.Update();
contentService.ApplyWebConfigModifications();
}
```

Using Business Connectivity Services from Silverlight

Business Connectivity Services (BCS) in SharePoint 2010 has evolved from
SharePoint 2007's Business Data Catalog (BDC). Microsoft loves to keep
us all guessing with new acronyms, so why not a new one for the line-of-
business access component in SharePoint?

BCS allows access to

- Databases, including Microsoft SQL Server and other databases
  compatible with the ODBC standard
- Web and WCF services
- Microsoft .NET Framework assemblies
- Custom data sources

Simple connections to databases and web services can be set up using
SharePoint Designer 2010; .NET and custom data sources require Visual
Studio 2010. The entity model is defined in an XML file that, in the case of

.NET and custom data sources, is backed by code. The model defines entities, such as customers, products and orders, their properties, and relationships among them. Methods can be implemented on entities to allow them to be read, created, updated, and deleted.

When the entity model is complete, there are a number of ways SharePoint and Microsoft Office can consume the data. This is part of the power of BCS: one entity model satisfies a number of use cases, all within the familiar SharePoint user interface. Table 11.1 shows the use cases and the editions of SharePoint that support them.

TABLE 11.1: BCS Features and SharePoint Editions

Feature	SharePoint Edition
External Lists allow business data to be used as if it were a list in SharePoint. This works at both the user interface and API level; however, some features such as versioning don't work on an external list.	SharePoint Foundation 2010
External Data Columns are metadata columns that are based on business data. For example, a user might select a customer from a CRM system rather than entering the data manually. Multiple columns can correspond to asingle business entity; for example several customer fields such as name, address, and phone number can be brought into the list when the customer is selected.	SharePoint Foundation 2010
The **Secure Store** stores identity mappings for users or groups.	SharePoint Server 2010 Standard Edition
External Data Search and **Profile Page** allow users to search for business entities in the Enterprise or FAST search pages. When a user clicks a search result, they are brought to a profile page that contains information about the business entity. A SharePoint administrator can maintain a profile page for each type of business entity and populate it with connected web parts that will pick up the entity's ID and display related information.	SharePoint Server 2010 Standard Edition
User Profile Properties can contain line-of-business data. This is often used to bring in user information that is stored in an HR system.	SharePoint Server 2010 Standard Edition

TABLE 11.1: BCS Features and SharePoint Editions

Feature	SharePoint Edition
External Data Web Parts display business information and can be used by business users to create dashboards and master/detail displays.	SharePoint Server 2010 Enterprise Edition
Office Client Integration allows Microsoft Office programs to use BCS external data columns from the client and allow SharePoint Workspace to take external lists offline.	SharePoint Server 2010 Enterprise Edition

BCS provides flexible authentication options that are configured as part of its entity model. There are three authentication modes available:

- **Pass Through**—The end user's identity is used to access the data source; this requires the ability to do double-hop authentication using technology such as Kerberos or claims.

- **Secure Store Service**—The end user's identity is mapped to an identity stored in the secure store, which is used to access the data source. For example, all users in the Accounting group in Active Directory might connect to a web service using a generic AccountingUser identity. This eliminates the multi-hop authentication issue and also allows for more effective connection pooling, which is of limited value when individual users connect to a data source.

- **Revert to Self**—The SharePoint service account's identity is used to access the data source. This is the simplest option and works well when all SharePoint users have the same permissions when viewing the line-of-business system.

Whole books and tons of other documentation are available on BCS, so this section won't attempt to cover it completely. Instead, you learn to create a simple BCS entity using SharePoint Designer 2010 and to access the data in Silverlight.

The example uses the AdventureWorksLT sample database, which is available at http://bit.ly/SPSL_AdventureWorksLT. Begin by downloading and installing the database according to the accompanying instructions.

When the database is ready, the first step is to open your development web site in SharePoint Designer 2010. Under Site Objects in the left navigation, select External Content Types. The content types display appears, as shown in Figure 11.5, and lists any content types you've previously created.

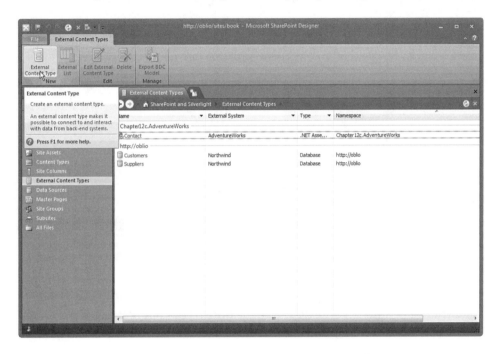

FIGURE 11.5: Creating an External Content Type in SharePoint Designer 2010

Click the new External Content Type button in the Ribbon bar. This opens the new External Content Type form shown in Figure 11.6. Click the New External Content Type link next to the Name: field and set the name to Customers. Also set the Office Item Type to Contact; this allows Microsoft Outlook 2010 and Microsoft SharePoint Workspace 2010 to render the data in a Contact form. This isn't really necessary for the Silverlight exercise but is interesting to try as another way to use the data.

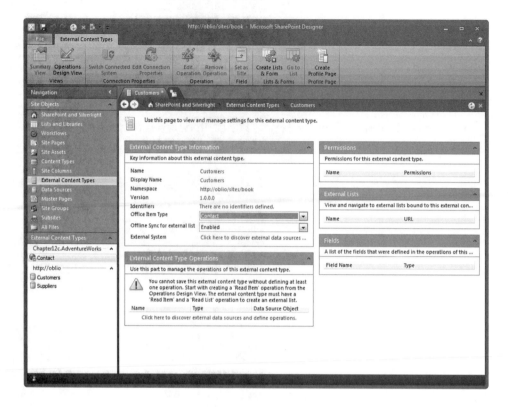

FIGURE 11.6: Filling in the New External Content Type form

Next, click the link under External Content Type Operations to discover external data sources and define operations. This opens the Data Source Explorer, as shown in Figure 11.7.

A data source for the Northwind database was previously registered in the screen shot, but there is no connection to the AdventureWorksLT database. To add one, click the Add Connection button, which prompts you to select a data source type. Select SQL Server, and the SQL Connection dialog box opens up as shown in Figure 11.8.

Notice that there are three connection options that correspond to the three authentication types allowed in BCS. For now, select Connect with User's Identity, which accesses the AdventureWorksLT database with the SharePoint user's identity. If you installed the database on your SharePoint server, multihop authentication won't be an issue because it's literally cross-server hops that are at issue, not connections within a server.

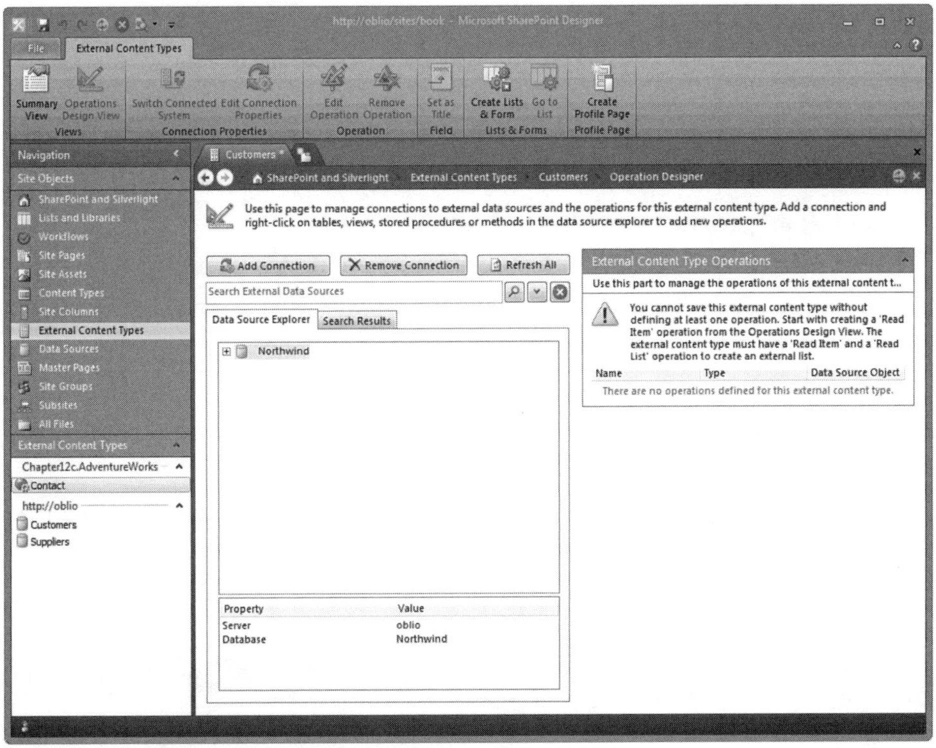

FIGURE 11.7: Data Source Explorer

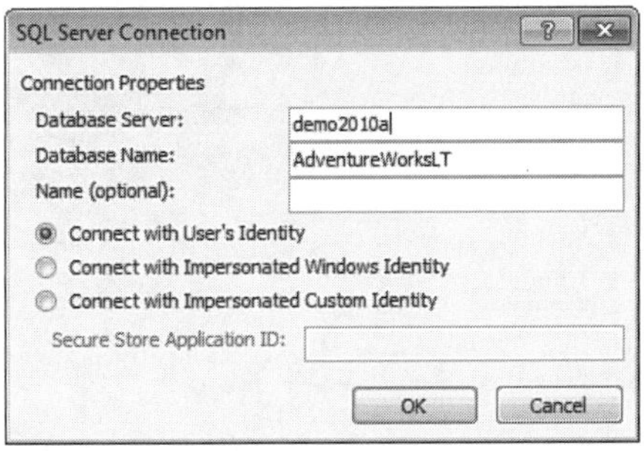

FIGURE 11.8: Create SQL database connection

If you'd prefer to connect as the SharePoint service account, then select Connect with Impersonated Windows Identity. If you'd like to try using the Secure Store, select the third option and enter the Secure Store Application ID to select the identity mapping to use.

Clicking OK closes the dialog box and returns you to the Data Source Explorer, except that now the AdventureWorksLT is available as a data source. Open it up and right-click the Customer table as shown in Figure 11.9. Select Create All Operations from the pop-up menu, and SharePoint Designer faithfully generates all the necessary operations for you. Shouldn't all programming be that easy?

You might notice that it's also possible to create the operations one at a time. There are five possible operations; Create, Read Item, Update and Delete are easily recognizable as the classic CRUD operations. The Read List operation is used to enumerate the entities. It's easy to create a read-only External Content Type by simply omitting the Create, Update, and Delete operations.

If you were to develop an External Content Type in Visual Studio 2010, you would code these operations yourself and could do whatever you wished in your .NET code to access the data.

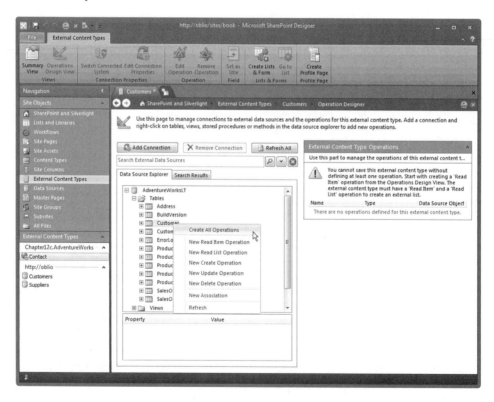

FIGURE 11.9: Create all operations

Because the External Content Type is mapped to one of the Office content types, to create the operations it's necessary to map fields from the data source to Office fields. For example, this allows Outlook to display the FirstName field correctly. This parameter configuration is shown in Figure 11.10. Notice there are a number of errors and warnings at the bottom of the screen, which go away as you map the fields. One by one, select data source fields and set the Office Property drop-down to select the matching Office field.

Because Office doesn't understand globally unique identifiers (GUIDs), there's no way to map the rowguid field, and a warning about that remains at the end of this process.

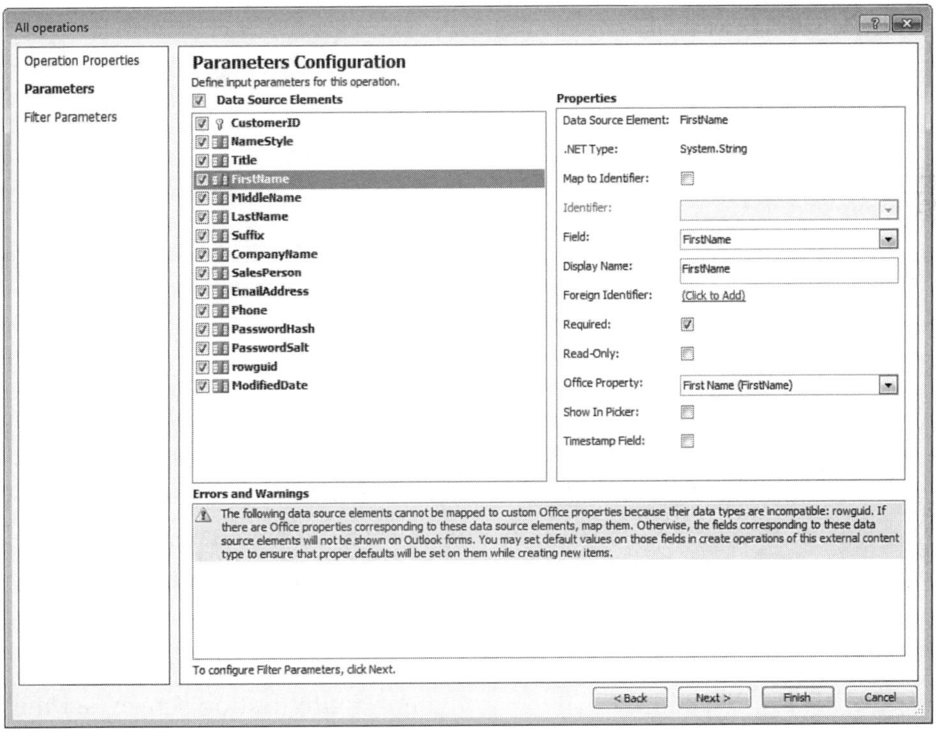

FIGURE 11.10: Mapping fields to Office properties

Next, you can add filter parameters as shown in Figure 11.11.

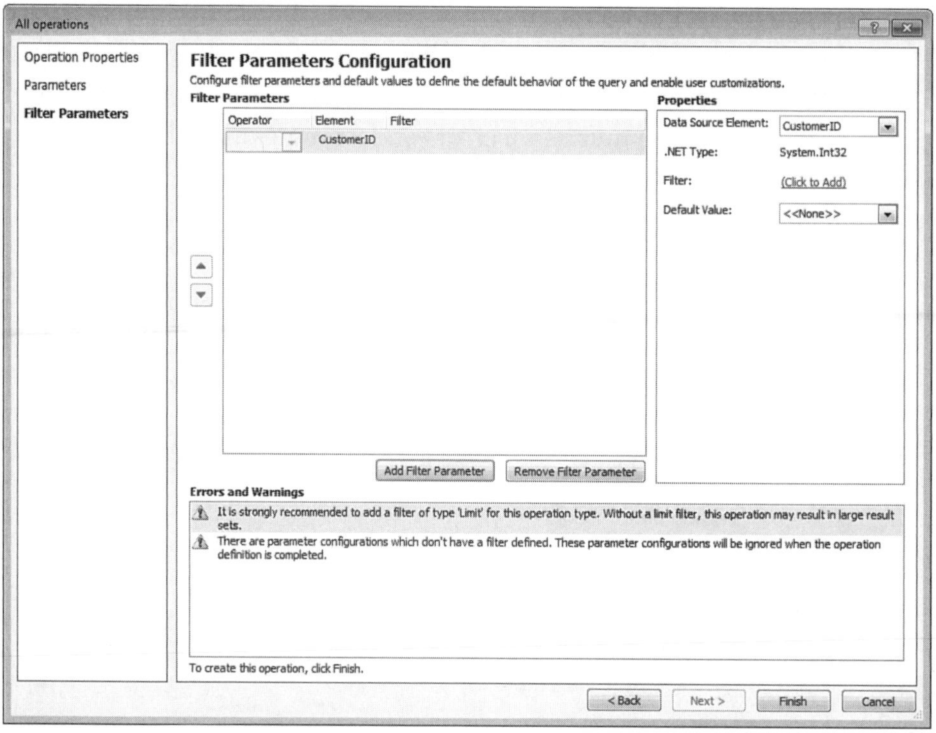

FIGURE 11.11: Adding a filter parameter

Filter parameters can be used to speed up querying the data source and in some instances to show filter options in the SharePoint user interface. At the very least, a Limit filter should be defined to tell SharePoint not to retrieve more than a certain number of rows at one time when reading the list. To do this, click the Add Filter Parameter button to launch the Filter Configuration dialog box as shown in Figure 11.12.

Change the filter type to Limit, leave the Filter field set to CustomerID, and click OK. Back in the Filter Paramaters Configuration screen, set the Default Value (under Properties on the right) to 1000. At this point you can click Finish in the Filter Parameters Configuration screen to complete the new External Content Type.

Before using the new External Content Type, however, you need to give users permission to use it. In this case permission must be granted in two places: in BCS and in the underlying SQL Server database.

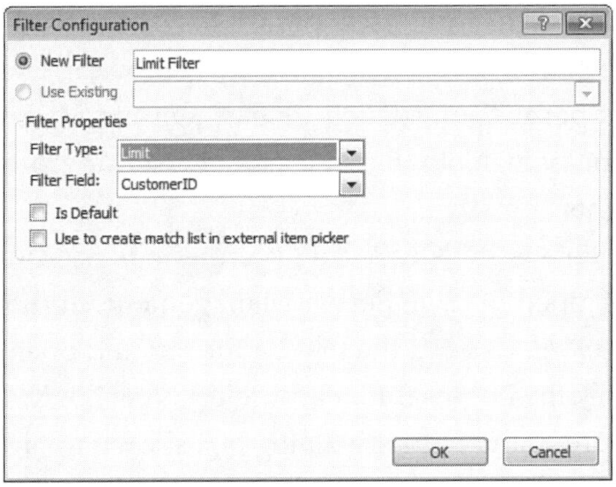

FIGURE 11.12: Configuring a limit filter

To set the BCS permissions, go to Central Administration and under Application Management, click the Manage Service Applications link. Click the Business Data Connectivity Service link, and you see a list of all the BCS services you have created. Select the check box next to the New External Content Type you just created and then click Set Object Permissions in the ribbon bar. You are then presented with the Set Object Permissions dialog box as shown in Figure 11.13.

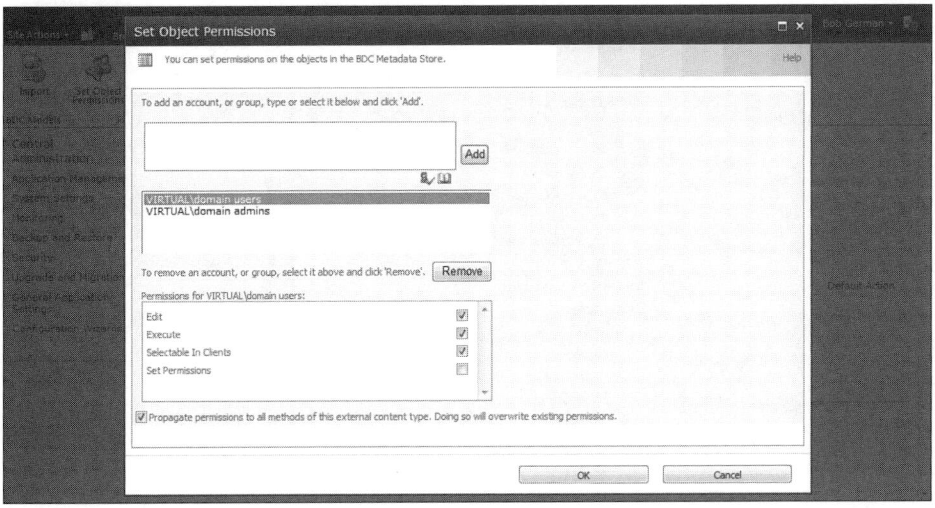

FIGURE 11.13: Setting BCS permissions

Use the dialog box to grant users permission to use the External Content Type. In the screen shot, all domain users are given Edit, Execute, and Selectable in Clients permission, which gives them read/write access to the External Content Type. Note that at least one user or group must have Set Permissions rights.

Because the data is in SQL Server, permissions need to be set there as well. To do this, open up SQL Server Management Studio and connect to your database server. Expand the tree on the left and open up the Security folder. Right-click the Logins folder and select New Login from the pop-up menu. You are presented with the dialog box shown in Figure 11.14.

In the screen shot, all Domain Users are given db_datareader and db_datawriter permissions; this is important because the External Content Type was set to Connect with User's Identity as shown back in Figure 11.8. If you chose to Connect with Windows Impersonated Identity, then grant permissions to the SharePoint service account instead.

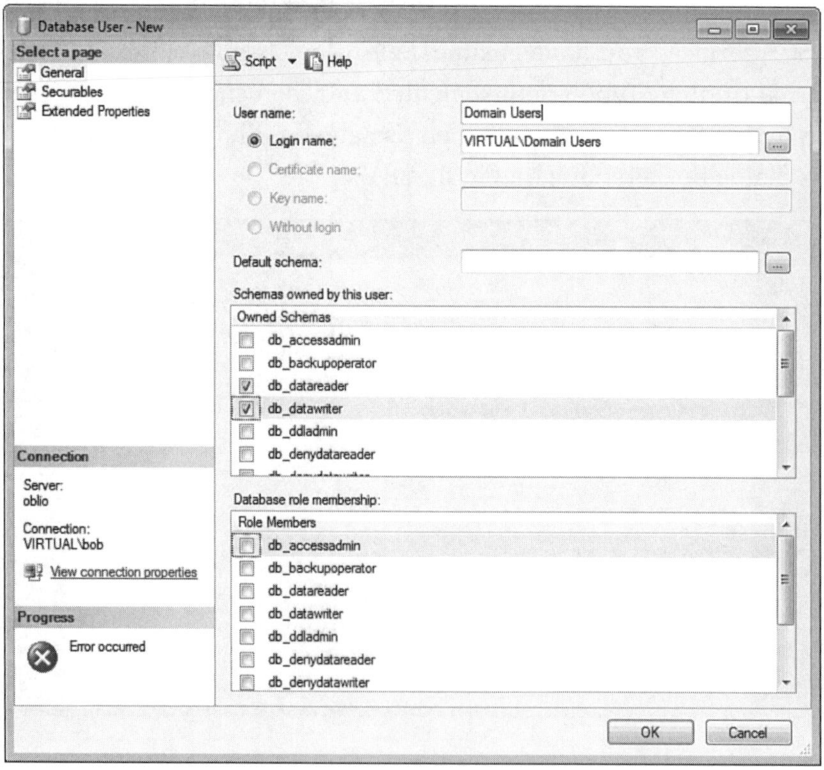

FIGURE 11.14: Adding SQL server permissions

Finally it's time to create a new external list to display the External Content Type. Go back to your browser and open up your development SharePoint site. On the Site Actions menu, select More Options… to create a SharePoint list from many options. Select External List from the Silverlight dialog box that appears; this brings you to the screen shown in Figure 11.15.

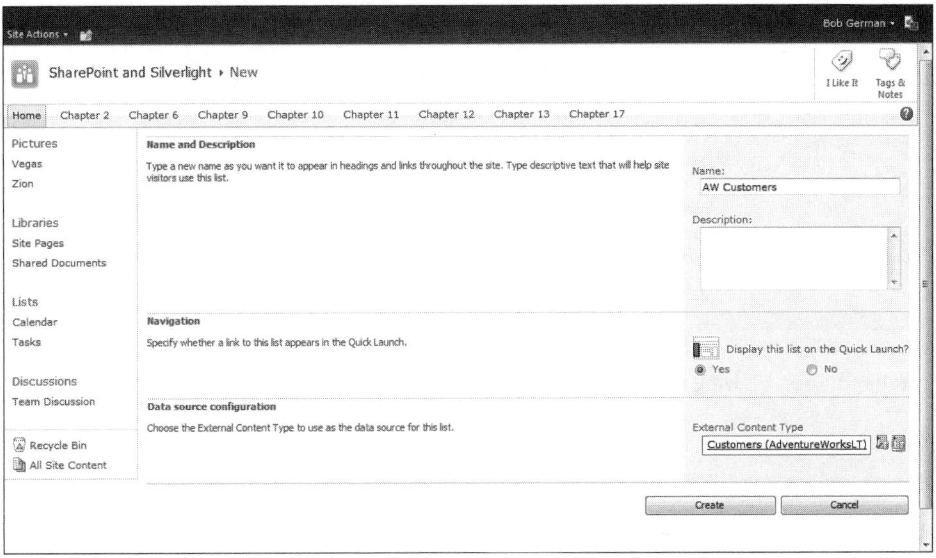

FIGURE 11.15: Adding a new external list

Give the external list a name and select your new External Content Type as the data source. When you click Create, at last your work is rewarded by what should be a working external list of AdventureWorks customers. This is shown in Figure 11.16.

SharePoint's Client Object Model makes it easy to access the external list from Silverlight. (Unfortunately, OData is not supported with external lists.) The External Feed Web Part that showed newsfeeds earlier in the chapter also contains logic to display and edit the AdventureWorks contact list. To do this, edit the web part and select the Ext List feed type. Paste the list URL into the Location property; the web part is smart enough to trim off the web page that displays the list so you can paste in a URL such as http://intranet.contoso.com/Lists/AW%20Customers/Read%20List.aspx. Figure 11.17 shows the web part display.

FIGURE 11.16: Viewing the external list

FIGURE 11.17: Viewing external data in Silverlight

You'll immediately notice that the AdventureWorksLT database has duplicate customer names in it. This isn't a problem with the web part and becomes obvious only when you sort the names.

If you click a name, the web part launches your email program to send them mail given that the names are `mailto:` hyperlinks. If you click elsewhere on one of the entries, an editing form opens up, as shown in Figure

11.18. This form allows the user to edit the customer record, which is written all the way back to the database if the user clicks OK.

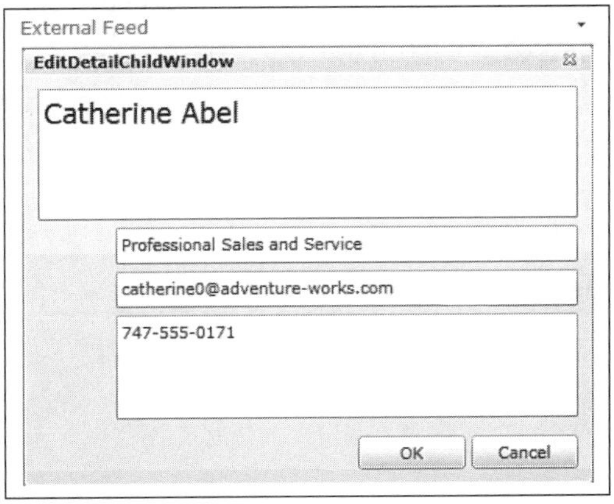

FIGURE 11.18: Editing an external list item

The main Silverlight View shown in Figure 11.17 is the same one that rendered newsfeeds in an earlier example, but now it has a new ViewModel that provides the external list data to the View.

The ViewModel class begins with a CAML query that will sort the customers. The Client Object Model is less forgiving about queries involving external lists, so to make this work it's necessary to use a CAML query that explicitly references the fields in use. The query is shown in Listing 11.11.

LISTING 11.11: CAML Query to Access the External List

```
private const string camlQuery =
        @"<View>
            <Query>
              <OrderBy>
                <FieldRef Name=""LastName""/>
                <FieldRef Name=""FirstName""/>
              </OrderBy>
            </Query>
          <ViewFields>
            <FieldRef Name=""Title""/>
            <FieldRef Name=""FirstName""/>
            <FieldRef Name=""LastName""/>
            <FieldRef Name=""CompanyName""/>
            <FieldRef Name=""EmailAddress""/>
            <FieldRef Name=""Phone""/>
          </ViewFields>
        </View>";
```

The ViewModel, ExternalListVM.cs initiates the query in its constructor. The code to do this is shown in Listing 11.12. Notice that again the fields are explicitly requested in the LoadQuery() method call; this is always a good idea, but in the case of an external list, it's not optional. Any mismatch between the CAML query and LoadQuery() methods are rewarded with a failure message saying that "The given key was not present in the dictionary."

LISTING 11.12: Querying the External List

```
public ExternalListVM(UserControl view, string listUrl)
{
    this.view = view;

    string webUrl;
    string listName;
    ParseUrl(listUrl, out webUrl, out listName);

    // Now use the Client OM to retrieve the external list
    ctx = new ClientContext(webUrl);
    Web web = ctx.Web;
    List list = web.Lists.GetByTitle(listName);

    // Set up a CAML query and issue it against the list
    CamlQuery cq = new CamlQuery();
    cq.ViewXml = camlQuery;
    var listItemQuery = list.GetItems(cq);

    // Load the query, explicitly including the needed fields
    listItems = ctx.LoadQuery<ListItem>
                    (listItemQuery.Include(
                        l => l["Title"],
                        l => l["FirstName"],
                        l => l["LastName"],
                        l => l["CompanyName"],
                        l => l["EmailAddress"],
                        l => l["Phone"]));

    ctx.ExecuteQueryAsync(RequestSucceeded, RequestFailed);
}
```

If the request succeeds, the resulting list items are projected onto FeedItem objects in the ViewModel's Items collection, which is bound to the ListBox in the View. This and the failure processing are shown in Listing 11.13.

LISTING 11.13: Handling Query Completion

```
private void RequestSucceeded
                (Object sender, ClientRequestSucceededEventArgs e)
{
    // If here, the query completed successfully
    view.Dispatcher.BeginInvoke(() =>
        {
            // Project the results into FeedItems that are bound
            // to the Silverlight view
            int i = 0;
            this.Items = from li in listItems
                    select new FeedItem
                    {
                        ContactID = i++,
                        Title = li["FirstName"] + " " +
                                li["LastName"],
                        TitleUrl = "mailto:" + li["EmailAddress"],
                        SubText1 = li["CompanyName"].ToString(),
                        SubText2 = li["EmailAddress"].ToString(),
                        Summary = li["Phone"].ToString()
                    };
        });
}

private void RequestFailed(Object sender, ClientRequestFailedEventArgs e)
{
    // If here, the query failed. For the demo, just report the error
    view.Dispatcher.BeginInvoke(() =>
    {
        MessageBox.Show(e.Message);
    });
}
```

The ShowDetail() method is bound to the MouseLeftButtonUp event in the MainPage View, and when it's pressed, it launches a child window for editing the clicked item. As shown in Listing 11.14, ShowDetail() copies the selected item and binds it to the child window rather than binding directly to the selected item itself. This is to avoid changing the item prematurely in case the user cancels out of the child window.

LISTING 11.14: Method to Display the Detail ChildWindow

```
public override void ShowDetail()
{
    if (this.SelectedItem != null)
```

```
    {
        // First, make a copy of the selected item for editing
        detailItem = new FeedItem();
        this.SelectedItem.CopyTo(detailItem);

        // Create a child window and bind it to the copy
        EditDetailChildWindow child = new EditDetailChildWindow();
        child.Show();
        child.DataContext = detailItem;

        // When the child window closes, if the user wants to save the
        // data then do so
        child.Closed += new EventHandler(UpdateContact);
    }
}
```

Notice that the last thing this code does is to wire up an event handler on the child window, which updates the external list item, but only if the user clicked OK to close the child window. The code for this is shown in Listing 11.15.

LISTING 11.15: Updating the External List item

```
private void UpdateContact(Object sender, EventArgs e)
{
    ChildWindow child = sender as ChildWindow;
    if (child.DialogResult == true)
    {
        // The user clicked "OK" so save their changes.
        // First, copy the values to the corresponding SharePoint
        // list item
        ListItem li =
            this.listItems.ElementAt<ListItem>(detailItem.ContactID);

        li["FirstName"] =
            detailItem.Title.Substring(
                0, detailItem.Title.IndexOf(" ")).Trim();
        li["LastName"] =
            detailItem.Title.Substring(
                detailItem.Title.IndexOf(" ")).Trim();
        li["CompanyName"] = detailItem.SubText1;
        li["EmailAddress"] = detailItem.SubText2;
        li["Phone"] = detailItem.Summary;
        li.Update();
```

```
        // Execute the list update and display an error if any
        ctx.ExecuteQueryAsync(((s0, e0) =>
            {
                // The update succeeded, so show the change
                // in the main view
                view.Dispatcher.BeginInvoke(() =>
                {
                    detailItem.CopyTo(this.SelectedItem);
                });
            }),
            ((s1, e1) =>
            {
                // The update failed, so show a message
                view.Dispatcher.BeginInvoke(() =>
                {
                    MessageBox.Show(e1.Message);
                });
            }));
    }
}
```

If the Child Window returns a true result, the user clicked OK, and the code saves the changes. The code goes back to the ListItem objects that were returned by the Client Object Model and updates the one the user changed. If the query succeeds, the edited item is copied back to the item displayed in the main view, so the user can see the change. If the query fails, a message is shown instead of copying back the item, and the user can see the item was not changed.

Adding a Web Browser Preview with Silverlight 5

Silverlight 4 added a <WebBrowser> element that displays a full web browser within a Silverlight application, but it was only available within trusted out-of-browser applications. In Silverlight 5 <WebBrowser> works even in browser-hosted applications, although they still need to be trusted.

In this section, you learn how to add the web browser control to the Feed Reader Web Part to display a feed preview, as shown in Figure 11.19. This is part of the Chapter11a solution, in a separate web part with a separate Silverlight application called ExternalFeedSL5.

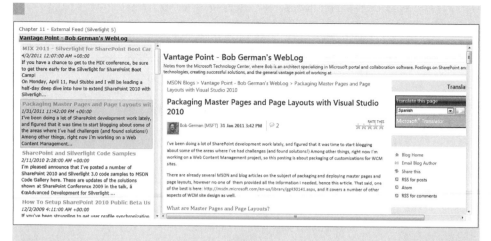

FIGURE 11.19: FeedReader Web Part with Preview Panel

Unfortunately, binding to the Source property is not supported by the WebBrowser control, and such a binding is needed to allow the control to bind with the ExternalFeedVM ViewModel. Fortunately, you can add your own control binding class. Listing 11.16 shows the code to do this, found in the solution in WebBrowserControlBindings.cs.

LISTING 11.16: Adding Control Bindings to the WebBrowser Control

```
public class BindableProperties
{
    public static readonly DependencyProperty SourceProperty =
        DependencyProperty.RegisterAttached(
        "Source",
        typeof(string),
        typeof(System.Windows.Controls.WebBrowser),
        new PropertyMetadata(null, SourcePropertyChanged));

    public static string GetSource(DependencyObject sourceProperty)
    {
        return (string)sourceProperty.GetValue(SourceProperty);
    }

    public static void SetSource(DependencyObject sourceProperty,
                                 string value)
    {
        sourceProperty.SetValue(SourceProperty, value);
```

```
    }

    public static void SourcePropertyChanged
        (DependencyObject sourceProperty,
         DependencyPropertyChangedEventArgs e)
    {
        if (sourceProperty is WebBrowser && e.NewValue != null)
        {
            WebBrowser browser = sourceProperty as WebBrowser;
            browser.Source = new Uri(e.NewValue.ToString());
        }
    }
}
```

This makes it easy to add the WebBrowser control to MainPage.xaml and to bind it to the PreviewUrl property, which has been added to in the ViewModel.

```
<WebBrowser Grid.Row="1"  Grid.Column="1"
    local:BindableProperties.Source="{Binding PreviewUrl}" />
```

The MainPage.xaml view was already set up with a behavior to show details when a user clicks on a feed item; this was used in the External-ListVM in the Silverlight 4 version. When a user clicks a feed item, the behavior calls ShowDetail(), which only needs to set the PreviewUrl property to display the corresponding web page. This is shown in Listing 11.17.

LISTING 11.17: Showing a Preview Web Page

```
        // ShowDetail: Display a preview
        public override void ShowDetail()
        {
            if (this.SelectedItem != null)
            {
                this.PreviewUrl = this.SelectedItem.TitleUrl;
            }
        }
```

At this point the solution would work, except for one thing: The Silverlight application is not trusted, so it only shows an error message. A detailed MSDN article at http://bit.ly/SPSL_TrustedApps explains the process; it is summarized here for your reference. This all happens on the client computer, which runs the Silverlight application.

First, you need to enable in-browser trusted applications by adding a key to the registry. On a 64-bit client, the key goes in HKEY_LOCAL_MACHINE\Software\Wow6432Node\Microsoft\Silverlight\; for 32-bit clients, the location is HKEY_LOCAL_MACHINE\Software\Microsoft\Silverlight\. Use regedit.exe to add a DWORD value called AllowElevatedTrustAppsInBrowser with a value of 1, as shown in Figure 11.20.

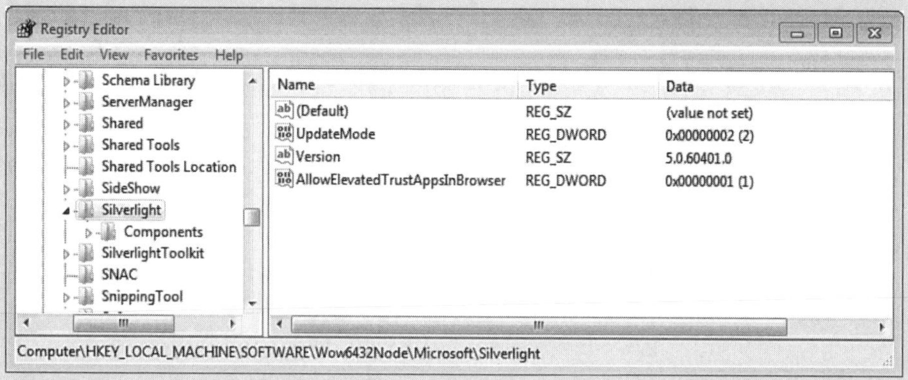

FIGURE 11.20: Setting the Client Registry to Allow Elevated Trust Applications in Browser

Next, you need to sign the .xap file; this option is available in the Signing tab of the Silverlight project properties in Visual Studio 2010 as shown in Figure 11.21. The easiest approach is to simply click Create Test Certificate; however, you might want to use a particular certificate that your clients already trust.

To install the test certificate on your development machine, simply click the More Details button to view the certificate. This is shown in Figure 11.22. Click Install Certificate and follow the wizard to complete the installation.

Now your solution should work, and you can preview any feed item easily within the web part.

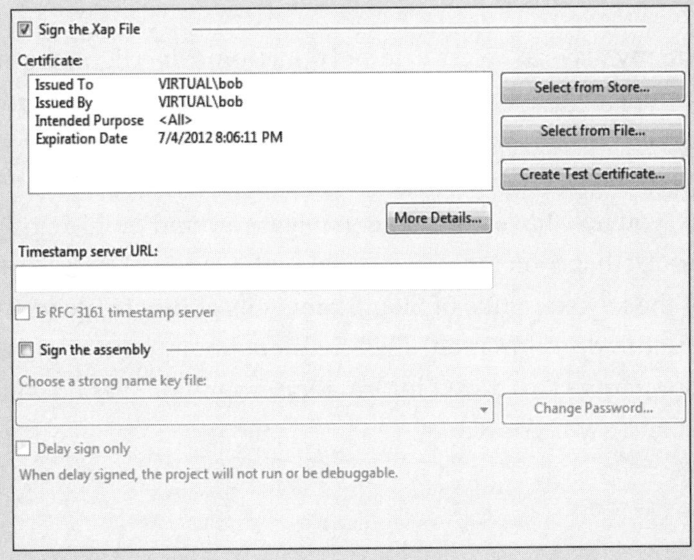

FIGURE 11.21: Signing the .xap file

FIGURE 11.22: Installing the Test Certificate

Summary

There are many ways to access external data from Silverlight; the important thing is to think about security before determining the right approach. BCS is the most flexible and provides for a lot of other use cases, so if your data lends itself to the BCS metadata model, that's probably the best way to go. Otherwise, you now have the tools to navigate around multi-hop and cross-domain issues that come up when you go after external data yourself.

One of the key strengths of SharePoint is its ability to blend structured and unstructured information. This chapter should give you the tools to start bringing more structured information from more varied sources into your solutions.

PART III

Building Solutions

▉ 12.

Windows Phone 7 SharePoint Applications

D EVELOPING WINDOWS PHONE 7 APPLICATIONS for SharePoint is
another area where you can leverage your existing SharePoint skills.
The mobile application space is a white hot and wide open area for developers. You can also have the opportunity to sell your apps in the marketplace and make some money. When you combine the enormous install base
of SharePoint and the number of mobile devices either in the market or
coming in the next year, the numbers are staggering. But building phone
applications that target SharePoint has a number of challenges. Some of the
issues have been worked out, and Microsoft is still working to improve the
experience in other areas. This chapter is not intended to be an all-inclusive
guide for developing Windows Phone applications, but instead you learn
how to get started and see techniques to get around some of the most common issues.

Office Hub

Windows Phone includes a mobile version of Office. This is commonly
referred to as the *Office hub*. Office on the phone includes Word, Excel, PowerPoint, and OneNote. Although the mobile versions are not as fully featured as the full desktop version, you are still able to edit any documents,

and those documents are fully compatible with the desktop version. It is not likely you will want to do a lot of writing on the phone due to its form factor, but it is great to do some reading, commenting, and light editing.

The Office hub includes the SharePoint Workspace Mobile application, shown in Figure 12.1. The SharePoint Workspace syncs your SharePoint Libraries with the phone. When the libraries are synced, you can read or edit the documents using the mobile versions of the Office applications. Any changes you make are efficiently synced back to the SharePoint Server.

SharePoint Workspace Mobile can connect to the SharePoint 2010 site and Online SharePoint 2010 in Office 365, on premise. To connect to an on-premise SharePoint site behind your firewall, you need to use a virtual private network (VPN). The only VPN supported is the Microsoft Forefront Unified Access Gateway (UAG). Microsoft has published a detailed whitepaper for configuring and setting up UAG to connect to your Share-Point sites. The whitepaper is titled, "Building Windows Phone 7 Applications with SharePoint 2010 and Unified Access Gateway" and is located at http://bit.ly/SPSL_UAG.

FIGURE 12.1: Office hub

With all of that said about the Office hub, you should explore and use it to collaborate on your SharePoint documents, but this chapter is about building your own SharePoint applications that can leverage SharePoint data and services. You learn how to build Silverlight phone applications that can read and write SharePoint list data and call other SharePoint services. Let's start by looking at Windows Phone 7 application development framework.

Development Framework

Developing applications for the phone can be done using either Silverlight or XNA, which is targeted at game developers building 3D applications. In this chapter you use Silverlight to develop business applications for the phone that leverage the SharePoint platform. The phone contains a version of Silverlight 3 with a few additions specific to the phone platform. You use Visual Studio and Expression Blend to develop the applications. Silverlight is not supported in the browser on the phone, so you can only use it to build native Silverlight applications. For example, there are APIs to access multitouch, the accelerometer, the camera and microphone, location awareness, and notifications. You can only deploy and install your application from the Windows Phone Marketplace. The marketplace is also how you make money from selling your applications.

Getting Started

The place to start developing Windows Phone applications is App Hub, located at http://create.msdn.com. The App Hub, shown in Figure 12.2, has everything you need to develop phone applications. There are links to download the latest tools and SDK. You can find learning resources such as documentation, hands-on labs, and other quick start samples. There is a rich community forum site for asking questions from others in the community. But the one thing that is missing is information about how to build Windows Phone applications for SharePoint. This is where this chapter comes in to fill the gap in community knowledge around building SharePoint solutions on the phone.

FIGURE 12.2: Developers App Hub site

The App Hub contains a wealth of knowledge. Look around the site, and then come back to the chapter to look at the tools used to build phone applications and begin learning how to configure your development machine.

Development Tools

Developing Windows Phone applications begins like most other Microsoft applications, in Visual Studio or Expression Blend. Building phone applications doesn't actually require a physical phone device; the Visual Studio tools include a Windows Phone Emulator. There are a number of caveats you need to consider when building your developer machine, which you explore later in this chapter.

Visual Studio

Visual Studio 2010 Phone 7 tools contain a number of project templates in both C# and VB, as shown in Figure 12.3. You can find detailed information about all of the project templates on MSDN at http://msdn.microsoft.com/en-us/library/ff402571. For your SharePoint projects you use the first template, Windows Phone Application. This is a simple template containing a single page.

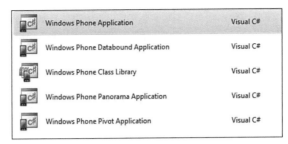

FIGURE 12.3: Visual Studio project templates

The Windows Phone tools in Visual Studio contain a rich XAML editor and a graphical designer. Unlike developing regular Silverlight applications, Visual Studio by default displays the designer and the code side-by-side, as shown in Figure 12.4. This is better optimized for wide-screen monitors and phone developers, as the phone applications tend to be vertically aligned.

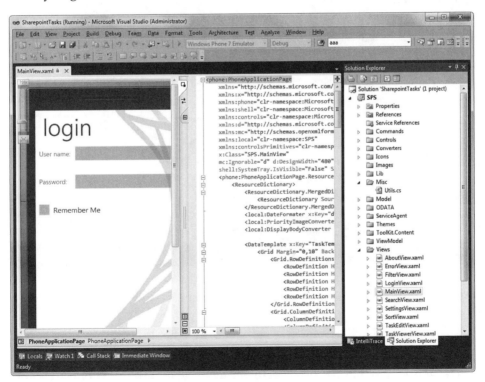

FIGURE 12.4: Windows Phone Designer in Visual Studio

The development model for the phone is identical to regular Silverlight applications. When you have written the code, you can set breakpoints and press F5 to build, deploy, and debug the Windows Phone application. The main difference is that you can choose where to deploy your solution. By default the solution deploys using the Windows Phone emulator as the deployment target, as shown in Figure 12.5. This makes it easy to get started even if you don't actually have a real Windows Phone device. If you do have a device, then select Windows Phone 7 Device as the deployment target. Deploying directly to the device requires that you have the Zune software running on an unlocked device.

FIGURE 12.5: Deploying to the Windows Phone 7 emulator

Although Visual Studio is your main tool for building applications, Expression Blend is a close second. Blend enables your designers to create rich experiences that would be difficult using Visual Studio alone. You get a look at Expression Blend in the next section.

Expression Blend

Designers who are familiar with using Expression Blend for WPF and Silverlight applications will find designing phone applications to be similar if not exactly the same. All of the same features that designers love are there; animations, layout, styles, and more. Many times when you are building complex screens, Blend is better able to display them than the Visual Studio designer, as shown in Figure 12.6. Normally you use them together, switching back and forth as you go from design to code to debugging. Blend and Visual Studio make this a seamless process.

FIGURE 12.6: Expression Blend Windows Phone designer

Although both Blend and Visual Studio are great tools for building Windows Phone applications, Blend, as expected, has more of a focus on the design of your application. Blend helps you make your phone application look like a Windows phone application by setting the default styles that match the Windows Phone style guide. You can read the complete

Windows Phone style guide on MSDN at http://msdn.microsoft.com/en-us/library/aa511258.aspx.

Windows Phone Emulator

Developing applications for the Windows Phone has a low barrier to entry with the help of a full Windows Phone 7 emulator included with the tools, as shown in Figure 12.7. This enables you to build, debug, and test your applications without a physical device. Ultimately you need to deploy to a real phone device and test your application, but the emulator puts that off until you are ready.

The emulator supports networking, storage, keyboard, debugging, and touch. Keyboard support is helpful when you are developing applications, making it easy to enter text information. To enable the keyboard, press the Pause key. You can even tab by quickly pressing the Tab key twice. Keep in mind, though, as you're designing and testing your applications that phone users might not have a keyboard, and requiring them to type long or complex strings can be a problem on a physical device. Also, the emulator supports touch. If you are developing on a laptop or monitor that supports touch, you will be able to interact with the emulator using touch, which more closely simulates how your users will use the application.

> ■ **TIP**
>
> The Windows Phone emulator uses the same underlying hypervisor technology that Hyper-V uses, so they collide if running on the same machine. If you start the emulator on the host machine running Hyper-V, your machine will crash. You see later in the chapter how you can run the emulator in a Windows 7 VHD running in Hyper-V to work around this issue.

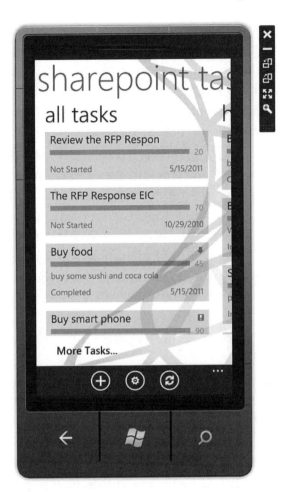

FIGURE 12.7: Windows Phone 7 emulator

Connecting to SharePoint

The most difficult part of building a Windows Phone 7 application against SharePoint is how to authenticate. Authentication with SharePoint from the phone can be difficult because Silverlight on the Windows phone does not support Windows Authentication (NTLM). This means that your Share-Point site must support Forms Based Authentication (FBA) or a proxy technology such as the ForeFront Unified Access Gateway (UAG).

Forms Based Authentication

FBA enables users to log in to a SharePoint site using a simple user name and password. The credential store used by FBA can be anywhere; typically this is SQL Server or Active Directory. You can find more information on how to configure FBA on your SharePoint site from MSDN at http://msdn.microsoft.com/en-us/library/bb975136.aspx.

The login process for FBA requires that you as a developer pass the user name and password to SharePoint authentication.asmx web service. The authentication service returns a secure cookie back that contains the SAML token. This is called the FedAuth cookie and is passed to every subsequent call to SharePoint. In essence the FedAuth cookie becomes the user's credentials. The problem is that the FedAuth cookie is a protected cookie, which means that you as a developer cannot see this cookie. So how do you use a cookie you cannot see? The way you are able to use this protected cookie is through the `System.Net.CookieContainer` class built into the .NET Framework. This provides the programmatic equivalent of the cookie cache in your browser.

Authenticate to SharePoint using the code shown in Listing 12.1 in the `MainPage` class. The first thing is to create an event handler to handle an event when the authentication process is complete. Next create a `Cookie Container` to store the authentication tokens. In this simple example the user name and password are hardcoded, but you would create an actual login screen for the user to enter the credentials. Finally, create a method to handle the `OnAuthenticated` event and call the `Authentication()` method.

LISTING 12.1: Authenticating with SharePoint from Windows Phone 7

```
public partial class MainPage : PhoneApplicationPage
{
    public event EventHandler OnAuthenticated;

    CookieContainer cookieJar = new CookieContainer();

    //Hard coded for Demo
    private string userName = "danj";
    private string userPassword = "pass@word1";


    // Constructor
```

```
public MainPage()
{
    InitializeComponent();

    this.OnAuthenticated += MainPage_OnAuthenticated;
    Authenticate();
}
}
```

You can start the authentication process by calling the authentication.asmx web service. In the example in Listing 12.2, the SharePoint server is called Phone.Contoso.com. You must craft the SOAP web service call by hand using the `HttpWebRequest` class. Add the following code to your `MainPage` class:

LISTING 12.2: Calling the Authentication.asmx Service

```
private void Authenticate()
{
    System.Uri authServiceUri = new
      Uri("http://phone.contoso.com/_vti_bin/authentication.asmx");

    HttpWebRequest spAuthReq = HttpWebRequest.Create(authServiceUri) as
        HttpWebRequest;
    spAuthReq.CookieContainer = cookieJar;
    spAuthReq.Headers["SOAPAction"] =
        "http://schemas.microsoft.com/sharepoint/soap/Login";
    spAuthReq.ContentType = "text/xml; charset=utf-8";
    spAuthReq.Method = "POST";

    //add the soap message to the request
    spAuthReq.BeginGetRequestStream(new AsyncCallback(spAuthReqCallBack),
        spAuthReq);
}
```

The last line in Listing 12.2 calls the `BeginGetRequestStream()` method to start the service call. This calls the following code to build the body of the message being posted to the authentication.asmx service. The first thing is to create the SOAP envelope. The envelope defines the method called, the `Login()` method, and the parameters being passed, the `username` and `password`. Add the code from Listing 12.3 to your `MainPage` class.

LISTING 12.3: Handling the Authentication Request Callback

```
private void spAuthReqCallBack(IAsyncResult asyncResult)
{
    string envelope =
        @"<?xml version=""1.0"" encoding=""utf-8""?>
        <soap:Envelope xmlns:xsi=""http://www.w3.org/2001/XMLSchema-instance""
xmlns:xsd=""http://www.w3.org/2001/XMLSchema"" xmlns:soap=""http://schemas.xml-
soap.org/soap/envelope/"">
            <soap:Body>
            <Login xmlns=""http://schemas.microsoft.com/sharepoint/soap/"">
                <username>{0}</username>
                <password>{1}</password>
            </Login>
            </soap:Body>
            </soap:Envelope>";

    UTF8Encoding encoding = new UTF8Encoding();
    HttpWebRequest request = (HttpWebRequest)asyncResult.AsyncState;
    Stream _body = request.EndGetRequestStream(asyncResult);
    envelope = string.Format(envelope, userName, userPassword);
    byte[] formBytes = encoding.GetBytes(envelope);

    _body.Write(formBytes, 0, formBytes.Length);
    _body.Close();

    request.BeginGetResponse(new AsyncCallback(ResponseCallback),
        request);
}
```

The last line of the previous code posts the SOAP message to the web service and defines a method to callback when the method is completed, the ResponseCallback() method. The ResponseCallBack() method just verifies that the authentication completed successfully and fires the OnAuthenticated event. Add the code from Listing 12.4 to your MainPage class.

LISTING 12.4: Handling the Authentication Response Callback

```
private void ResponseCallback(IAsyncResult asyncResult)
{
    HttpWebRequest request =
        (HttpWebRequest)asyncResult.AsyncState;
    HttpWebResponse response =
        (HttpWebResponse)request.EndGetResponse(asyncResult);
    Stream content = response.GetResponseStream();

    if (request != null && response != null)
```

```
    {
        if (response.StatusCode == HttpStatusCode.OK)
        {
            using (StreamReader reader = new StreamReader(content))
            {
                //Put debugging code here
                string _responseString = reader.ReadToEnd();
                reader.Close();
            }
        }
    }

    //authentication complete
    OnAuthenticated(null, null);
}
```

You can also examine the response from the authentication method to verify everything is good. The ErrorCode will be NoError if there was a successful login and PasswordNotMatch if the username or password were incorrect. Listing 12.5 shows an example of a good response message in the _responseString variable from the code in Listing 12.4.

LISTING 12.5: Successful Authentication Response Message

```
<?xml version="1.0" encoding="utf-8"?>
<soap:Envelope
  xmlns:soap="http://schemas.xmlsoap.org/soap/envelope/"
  xmlns:xsi="http://www.w3.org/2001/XMLSchema-instance"
  xmlns:xsd="http://www.w3.org/2001/XMLSchema">
  <soap:Body>
    <LoginResponse
      xmlns="http://schemas.microsoft.com/sharepoint/soap/">
      <LoginResult>
        <CookieName>FedAuth</CookieName>
        <ErrorCode>NoError</ErrorCode>
        <TimeoutSeconds>1800</TimeoutSeconds>
      </LoginResult>
    </LoginResponse>
  </soap:Body>
</soap:Envelope>
```

When the user is authenticated, you can get the tasks from SharePoint. At this point the CookieContainer contains the FedAuth SAML token, and as long as you still have a reference to this object, you can pass it to every service call without authenticating again. Add the code from Listing 12.6 to your MainPage class:

LISTING 12.6: OnAuthenticated Event Handler

```
void MainPage_OnAuthenticated(object sender, EventArgs e)
{
    GetTasks();
}
```

There is one last thing you need to change to support using the CookieContainer. You must add the enableHttpCookieContainer attribute in the binding node of the clientconfig file and set it to a value of true. Listing 12.7 shows an example of where you add the enableHttpCookieContainer attribute for the ListsSoap binding node.

LISTING 12.7: Clientconfig Change to Support CookieContainer

```
<configuration>
    <system.serviceModel>
        <bindings>
            <basicHttpBinding>
                <binding name="ListsSoap"
                        enableHttpCookieContainer="true"
                        maxBufferSize="2147483647"
                        maxReceivedMessageSize="2147483647">
                    <security mode="None" />
                </binding>
            </basicHttpBinding>
        </bindings>
        <client>
            <endpoint address="http://Phone.contoso.com/_vti_bin/lists.asmx"
                    binding="basicHttpBinding"
                    bindingConfiguration="ListsSoap"
                    contract="ListsService.ListsSoap"
                    name="ListsSoap" />
        </client>
    </system.serviceModel>
</configuration>
```

You are ready to call the list web service to retrieve the List items. You already have the CookieContainer with the FedAuth security token from the authentication process; just attach the instance to the CookieContainer property of the `ListsSoapClient` object. Then the rest of the code in List-ing 12.8 is just a set of standard web service calls to SharePoint.

LISTING 12.8: Retrieving Data with SharePoint Web Services

```
private void GetTasksFBA()
{
    ListsService.ListsSoapClient lists =
        new ListsService.ListsSoapClient();

    // Attach the cookies to the call
    lists.CookieContainer = cookieJar;

    //Callback when call returns from SharePoint
    lists.GetListItemsCompleted +=
        new EventHandler<ListsService.GetListItemsCompletedEventArgs>
            (lists_GetListItemsCompleted);

    lists.GetListItemsAsync(
        "Tasks",                // listName
        String.Empty,           // viewName
        null,                   // query
        null,                   // viewFields
        null,                   // rowLimit
        null,                   // queryOptions
        null);                  // webID
}
```

Before you see how to handle the Task list return, the next section looks at an example of how to authenticate using the Unified Access Gateway (UAG) as an alternative to forms-based authentication.

ForeFront Unified Access Gateway

UAG is a Microsoft server product that enables you to access SharePoint from the Internet across the firewall. It also can act as the login form to log in to a SharePoint site that might or might not be secured using FBA. You can learn how to set up and configure UAG for SharePoint from a Microsoft whitepaper titled "Building Windows Phone 7 applications with Share-Point 2010 Products and Unified Access Gateway (UAG)" located at http://bit.ly/SPSL_UAG. The UAG whitepaper walks you through step-by-step on how to get UAG up and running. Figure 12.8 shows an exam-ple of the UAG configuration screen.

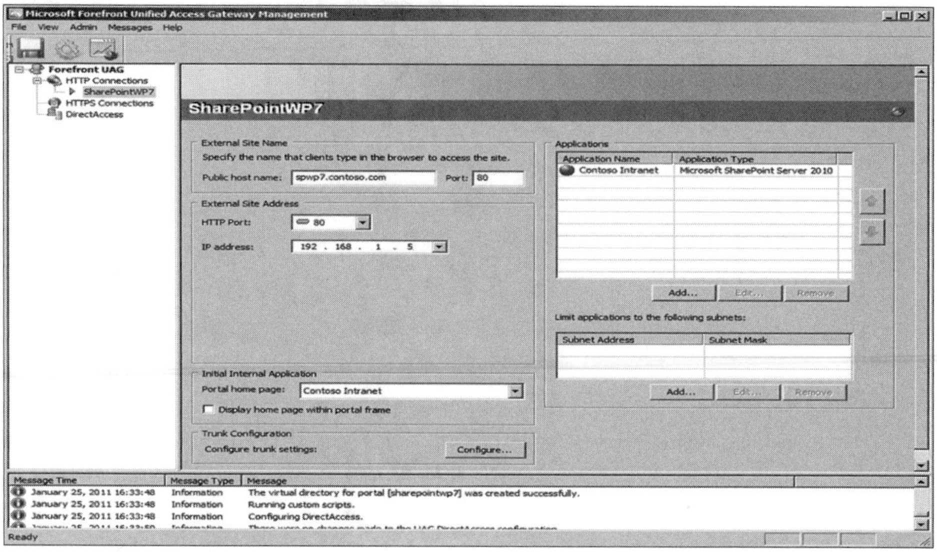

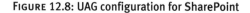

FIGURE 12.8: UAG configuration for SharePoint

When you have UAG configured and running, you can test it using Internet Explorer to browse to the address that you created, which maps to your internal SharePoint site. UAG presents you with a forms-based login screen, as shown in Figure 12.9. On this form, enter the same credentials you would use to log in to the SharePoint site itself.

Using UAG to authenticate against a SharePoint server is a little more straightforward than using FBA. This is not well documented anywhere, but in order to authenticate to UAG from the phone, you need to pass a couple of header parameters for each call. Consider the code in Listing 12.9, which uses UAG to pull List items from the Task list in SharePoint. This starts off the same as a normal SOAP call to SharePoint using the client proxy generated by the Visual Studio Add Reference command. The key is creating an `OperationContextScope` from the `InnerChannel` property of the `ListSoapClient` object. After you have established the `Operation ContextScope` you can create two headers for the `Authorization` and `UserAgent` properties.

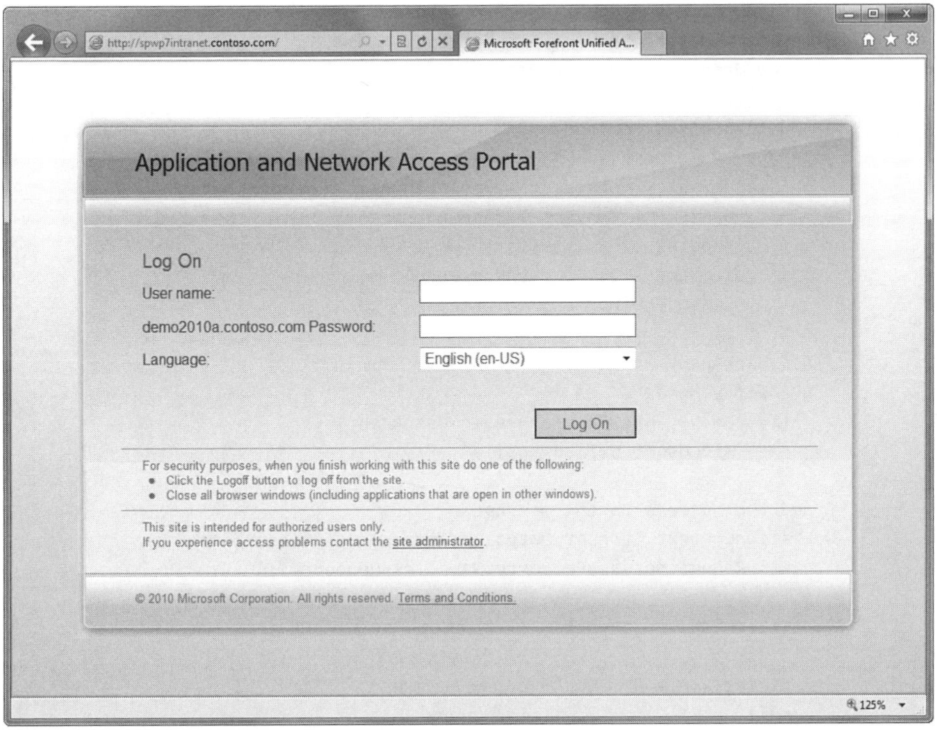

FIGURE 12.9: UAG login form

LISTING 12.9: Reading List Data Through a Unified Access Gateway

```
private void GetTasksUAG()
{
    ListsService.ListsSoapClient lists =
        new ListsService.ListsSoapClient();

    // TODO:Ask the user for these
    string userName = "Danj";
    string userPassword = "pass@word1";

    //Callback when call returns from SharePoint
    lists.GetListItemsCompleted +=
        new EventHandler<ListsService.GetListItemsCompletedEventArgs>
            (lists_GetListItemsCompleted);

    //Add the credentials to the message header
    using (OperationContextScope OCScope =
        new OperationContextScope(lists.InnerChannel))
    {
```

```
        //Create the Request Message Property
        HttpRequestMessageProperty msgProperty =
            new HttpRequestMessageProperty();

        //Add Authorization Property
        msgProperty.Headers
            [System.Net.HttpRequestHeader.Authorization] =
                "Basic " + Convert.ToBase64String(
                Encoding.UTF8.GetBytes(
                userName + ":" + userPassword)) +
                System.Environment.NewLine;

        //Add UserAgent Property
        msgProperty.Headers
            [System.Net.HttpRequestHeader.UserAgent] =
                "Microsoft Office Mobile";

        //Add the headers to the message
        OperationContext.Current.OutgoingMessageProperties.Add(
            HttpRequestMessageProperty.Name, msgProperty);

        lists.GetListItemsAsync(
            "Tasks",                // listName
            String.Empty,           // viewName
            null,                   // query
            null,                   // viewFields
            null,                   // rowLimit
            null,                   // queryOptions
            null);                  // webID
    }
}
```

In the previous code, the Authorization property is a Base64 encoded colon delimited username and password preceded with the type, which is Basic. For example Danj:pass@word1 becomes Basic RGFuajp-wYXNzQHdvcmQx. The UserAgent is Microsoft Office Mobile. This is important as it tells UAG how to handle the incoming request. If, for example, you didn't set this, UAG would assume you are calling from a browser and would try to send you additional information such as an ActiveX control, which your app can't handle.

You can learn more about UAG from the Microsoft UAG site at http://www.microsoft.com/forefront/unified-access-gateway/en/us/default.aspx.

Databinding to the Task List

You have seen how to authenticate against SharePoint using FBA and via UAG. When you have authenticated and called the Task list, handing the results is the same for both FBA and UAG. In this example, you use Silverlight data binding to bind the List items to the List box.

First you need to create a List box to bind the items to, as shown in Listing 12.10. Open the MainPage.xaml file and add the following code. This adds a `ListBox` control named `listBox1`. It also defines an item template called `ItemTemplate`.

LISTING 12.10: ListBox to Display Tasks

```
<Grid x:Name="ContentPanel" Grid.Row="1" Margin="12,0,12,0">
    <ListBox  ItemTemplate="{StaticResource ItemTemplate}"
              Name="listBox1" />
</Grid>
```

The item template defines what the List items will look like in the list. Add the code from Listing 12.11 to define an item template with three text blocks. The first text block has a font size of 32 and is bold. The text for all three is mapped to the field names in the collection of List items that you bind to the `ListBox`.

LISTING 12.11: ItemTemplate for Task Items

```
<phone:PhoneApplicationPage.Resources>
    <DataTemplate x:Key="ItemTemplate">
        <StackPanel>
            <TextBlock Text="{Binding Title}" FontSize="32"
                       FontWeight="Bold"/>
            <TextBlock Text="{Binding Priority}"/>
            <TextBlock Text="{Binding Status}"/>
        </StackPanel>
    </DataTemplate>
</phcne:PhoneApplicationPage.Resources>
```

Next you handle the return call from the `GetListItemsAsync()` method that you called with either FBA or UAG. The first thing to do is to get the results into an `XElement` object within which you access the data rows.

When you have the collections of data rows, you can use LINQ to convert them to a new collection of `Task` objects. Set the new collection of `Task` objects as the `ItemsSource` of the `ListBox`. This creates the List items to bind to the `ListBox`. Listing 12.12 shows how to handle the callback.

LISTING 12.12: Binding SharePoint Data to a ListBox on Windows Phone 7

```
void lists_GetListItemsCompleted(object sender,
        ListsService.GetListItemsCompletedEventArgs e)
{
    XElement listItems = e.Result;

    IEnumerable<XElement> rows = e.Result.Descendants(XName.Get("row",
"#RowsetSchema"));

    // Create a new collection of Task objects.
    IEnumerable<Task> tasks = from element in rows
                              select new Task
                              {
                                  Title =
(string)element.Attribute("ows_LinkTitle"),
                                  Status =
(string)element.Attribute("ows_Status"),
                                  Priority =
(string)element.Attribute("ows_Priority")
                              };

    // Data Bind the list items
    listBox1.ItemsSource = tasks;
}

// Task data structure
public class Task
{
    public string Title { get; set; }
    public string Status { get; set; }
    public string Priority { get; set; }
}
```

Press F5 to run the application. With everything set up correctly, you see the List items from the task list on your phone emulator, as shown in Figure 12.10.

FIGURE 12.10: SharePoint task list on the phone

You can see in Figure 12.11 what the task list looks like in SharePoint. For this example you have only used three fields from the list; Title, Priority, and Status. But you can easily expand this sample to use any of the fields from the list.

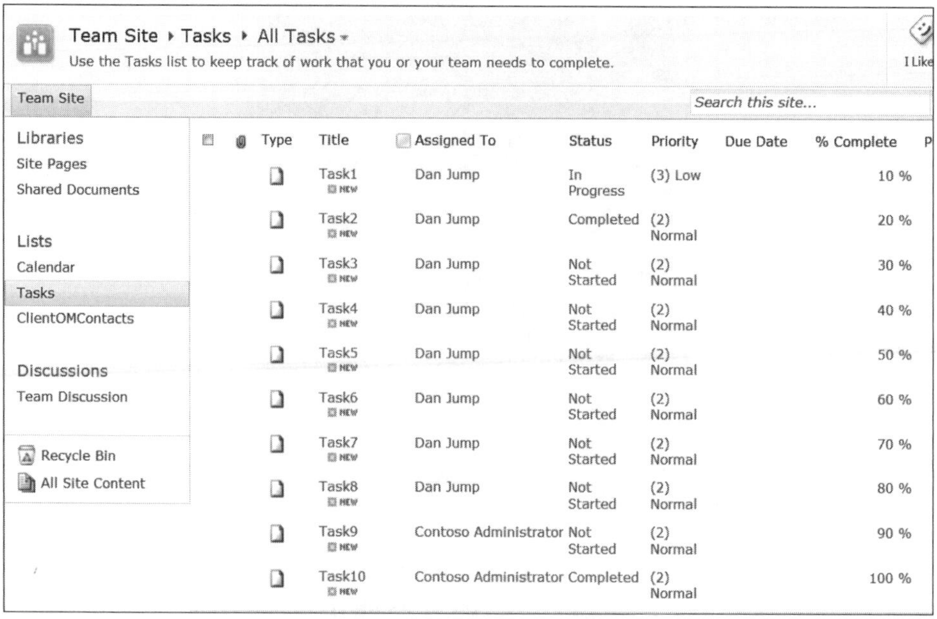

FIGURE 12.11: SharePoint task list in the browser

You have seen how to code the phone application, but what does it take to get a development environment up and running? In the next section, you see various patterns for setting up your developer machines.

Development Environment

One of the most difficult tasks in developing SharePoint applications is setting up your developer machines. When you add the phone environment and UAG into the mix, things can get complicated quickly. What you learn in this section is about some of the options when configuring your development environment.

Single Machine

This setup shown in Figure 12.12 uses a single machine with 64-bit Windows 7 installed. You then install SharePoint, Visual Studio, and the Windows Phone tools onto the machine. Everything is running natively and gives you the best performance. This is good if you have a limited amount of memory; 8GB or less. This also works well if you are not able to run a server operating system or Hyper-V. The best way to set up this environment is to use the SharePoint Easy Setup Script, located on MSDN at http://bit.ly/SPSL_EasySetup. The Easy Setup Script is a PowerShell script that automates the entire process of downloading and setup of everything you need to start building SharePoint solutions.

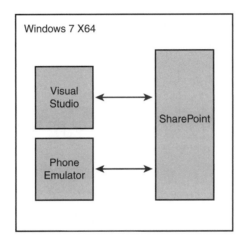

FIGURE 12.12: SharePoint task list in the browser

Multi-Machine

Using multiple machines is another common setup. This enables you to split the SharePoint image from the Visual Studio Phone tools. In this setup you can install SharePoint on a VHD or natively. You can also download the SharePoint Information Worker VHD from MSDN from http://bit.ly/SPSL_SharePoint2010VHD. The networking setup is shown in Figure 12.13. The SharePoint VHD is configured with two virtual switches, both on 192.168.150.xx. The first virtual switch is created as an internal-only switch with a static IP of 192.168.150.10. The network card on the SharePoint VHD that is connected to this switch is 192.168.150.1. It is a good practice to always set up your SharePoint VHD using this pattern even if you are not doing phone development. This provides a static endpoint for you to use the Remote Desktop Connection to access the VHD. The Remote Desktop Connection enables full screen, cut and paste between host and VHD, and drive access to host drives. Next, you connect your external Windows 7 development machine using the static IPs shown in Figure 12.13.

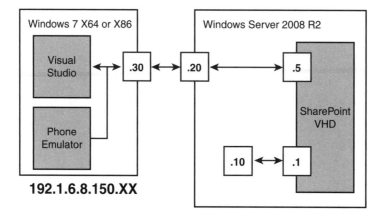

FIGURE 12.13: SharePoint task list in the browser

> **▪▪ TIP**
>
> The easiest way to connect your two developer machines together is to use a normal network cable and plug them directly into each other. Most modern network cards have the ability to automatically switch to support a crossover without a special crossover cable. If this does not work, you can always fall back to using a switch between the two machines.

Multi-Machine with UAG

This setup is the same as the previous setup except that you have added UAG to the server machine. This also requires splitting the network into two subnets, 192.168.1.xx and 192.168.150.xx. UAG does the mapping between these two subnets. Follow the diagram in Figure 12.14 below to set up the networking. This setup works well for testing building applications that need to use UAG, but you don't have enough resources to run everything on a single machine.

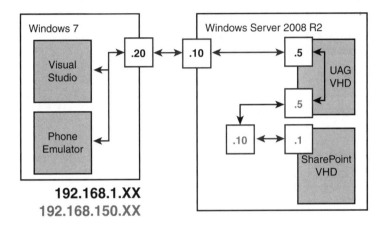

FIGURE 12.14: Multi-machine setup using UAG

Single Machine with UAG

The setup shown in Figure 12.15 is similar to the previous setup except that you are not using a second machine to run Visual Studio and the phone tools. In this scenario you install Visual Studio directly on the host machine. The key to making this setup work is that you need a physical phone device. You cannot use the emulator on the same machine running Hyper-V because this causes the machine to instantly crash. To get around this, set Visual Studio to deploy to the phone device attached to the machine through the Zune software installed on the host.

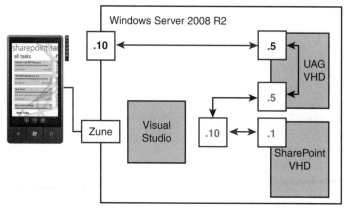

192.168.1.XX
192.168.150.XX

FIGURE 12.15: Single machine setup using UAG

Single Machine with Hyper-V

This setup is the preferred setup if you have enough resources to run three VHDs. This puts everything on a single machine, greatly simplifying the portability of the environment, and is a combination of a couple of the previous patterns. The key to this setup is that the Visual Studio phone tools and emulator must be installed on a Windows 7 32-bit VHD. In spite of what the SDK may say, at the time of this writing any other operating system including 64-bit Windows 7 will not work and causes the VHD or the host machine to crash. In the configuration shown in Figure 12.16, you have a Windows 7 client machine connected to both the UAG network and directly to the SharePoint network. This enables you to build and test applications that can use FBA or UAG without reconfiguring your machine.

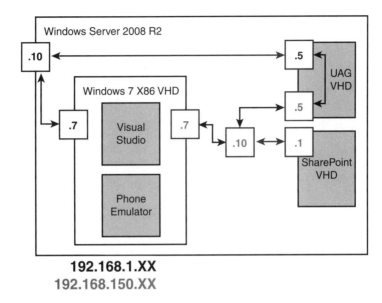

FIGURE 12.16: Single machine setup with Hyper-V

There are a number of different ways to configure your developer machines. The one you choose depends on the hardware you have available and the goal of your development. Other factors such as the ability to snapshot, install, rollback, and share instances all need to be considered when building your perfect setup.

Publishing an Application

After you have built your SharePoint phone application, you then need to deploy it to the marketplace. Visit the phone marketplace at http://create.msdn.com. The phone marketplace does not allow you to publish private applications. This means that any application you create will be visible to everyone on the marketplace. This is a challenge for business applications because many contain private information for a company. You need to consider this when designing your applications. There are many techniques to handle this situation such as obfuscation and activation keys. Although this is an advanced topic and beyond the scope of this book, you should be aware of the issue and think about the approach that best fits your company's policies and concerns.

When you are ready to publish the application you should follow the steps in the help page titled "App Hub Application Submission Walk-through" located at http://go.microsoft.com/fwlink/?LinkId=216139. There are five basic steps—upload, description, artwork, pricing, and submit. Figure 12.17 shows an example of the app submission page on App Hub.

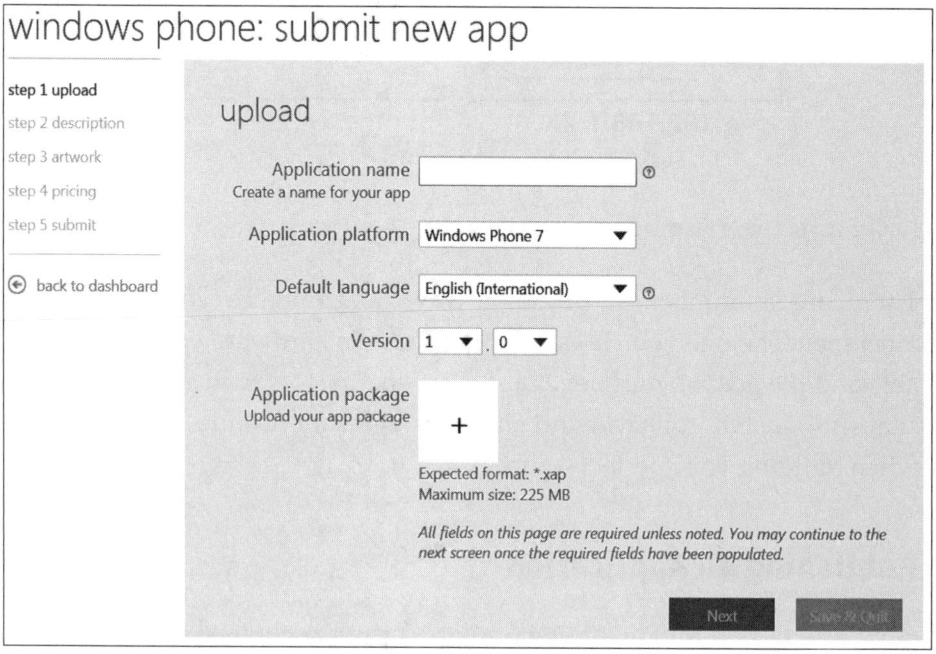

FIGURE 12.17: Submit your phone application

The Microsoft App Hub is a great resource for Windows Phone developers. On the site you can find many articles and whitepapers on building and publishing phone applications.

Summary

In this chapter you learned how to build phone applications that can leverage the SharePoint platform for data and services. Building phone applications using Silverlight against SharePoint is the next growth wave for SharePoint developers. As more companies move to SharePoint and as everyone depends on mobile applications for most business processes, phone developers who understand SharePoint will be in high demand. You also saw how you can leverage UAG to not only provide access across the firewall, but you can use UAG to provide authentication without changing your SharePoint site.

Building a great development environment for building SharePoint and Windows Phone applications can be a challenge. Although there is not one answer for everyone, you saw a number of ways that you could build out an environment that works for you and your company. You saw that you could build a setup that includes everyone on the client or everything on the server or a mix of the two environments.

The last consideration when building a phone application is how to deploy it to the marketplace for your users to install on their phones. There are unique considerations for a SharePoint application because the phone marketplace doesn't support private application submissions. But with a little planning, you can create an application that can only be accessed and used by authorized users.

■ 13 ■

Creating Silverlight Navigation

S HAREPOINT 2010 INCLUDES A BUILT-IN NAVIGATION SYSTEM that greatly simplifies managing SharePoint site collections and sites. In this chapter you learn how SharePoint navigation works, how to change the links rendered by navigation, and most importantly, how to use Silverlight to render the navigation for end users.

Out-of-the-Box Navigation

First of all, it's important to note that although SharePoint generates navigation dynamically based on sites, lists, and pages, it always does this within a single site collection. Navigation outside of a site collection must be configured manually by adding links to the navigation structure or by building a custom site map provider, as explained in the next section.

There are many kinds of sites available in SharePoint, and they often handle navigation in unique ways. The commonly used site definition is a "Team Site" that is designed for general collaboration; it is provided in all the SharePoint products including SharePoint Foundation 2010. This chapter refers to *team site* as a general category of site that includes the supplied Team Site as well as other sites derived from the same site definition. Examples of this are a blank site or a user's personal My Site.

In contrast to team sites, there are specialized publishing sites based on the Publishing Portal site definition provided in SharePoint Server 2010 (standard or enterprise edition). Publishing sites are intended for web publishing and include a number of extra features for managing, approving, and summarizing web content in a publishing scenario. Where a team site is intended for many-to-many collaboration, a publishing site is optimized for few-to-many web publishing.

The distinction between team and publishing sites is important in this chapter because they each handle navigation slightly differently.

Figure 13.1 shows standard Team Site navigation. Notice that navigation is shown in two areas of the page. Global navigation is shown at the top of the page, and by default it shows the current site and its children. It might inherit global navigation from its parent, so it shows a higher-level site and its children. For example, if a child site inherits its parent's global navigation, it shows the parent site and its peers, thus providing general navigation among this group of sites.

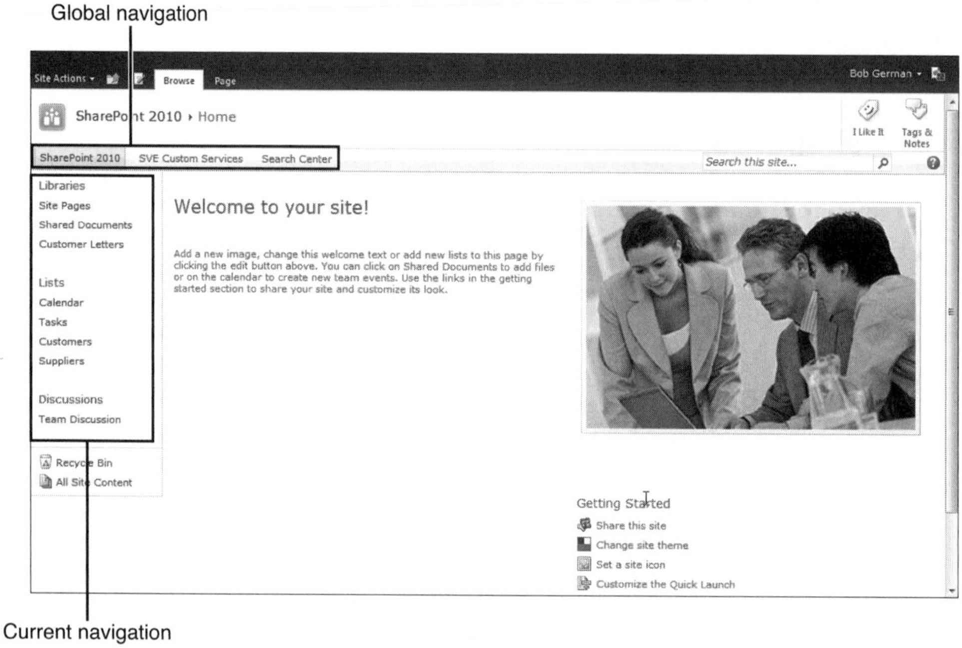

FIGURE 13.1: Navigation in a SharePoint 2010 Team Site

In the case of a team site, current navigation shows the lists and libraries in the site. This is also called the Quick Launch bar, and each list or library can be shown or hidden in current navigation by changing the Display This List on the Quick Launch option in list settings under the Title, Description, and Icon link.

Team Site settings include a section to control Look and Feel, as shown in Figure 13.2. Three of the settings control navigation.

FIGURE 13.2: Team Site Look and Feel settings

The Top Link Bar link leads to an administrative screen to manage the navigation bar at the top of every SharePoint page, as shown in Figure 13.3.

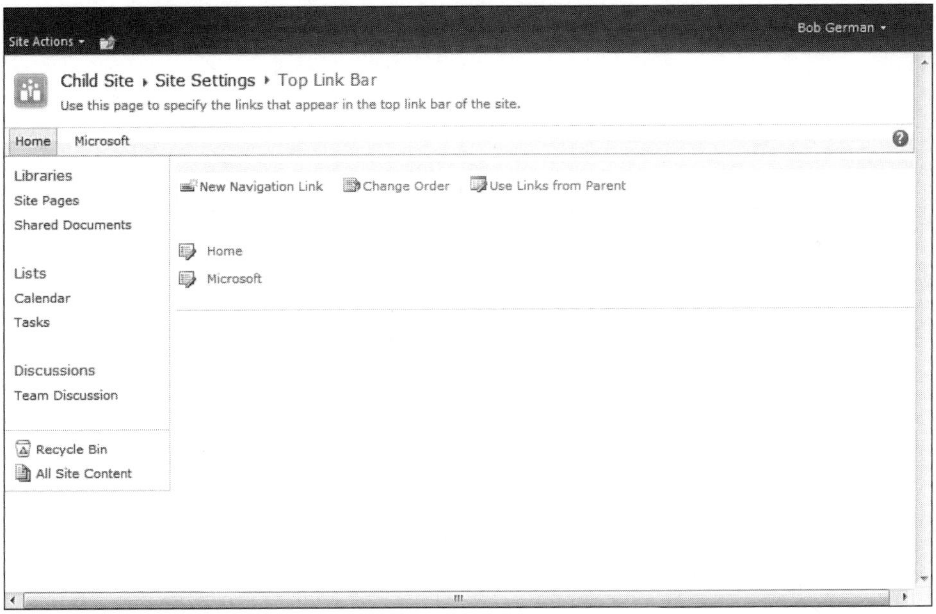

FIGURE 13.3: Top navigation settings in a SharePoint Team Site

SharePoint automatically generates top navigation links for Home (the current site, or its answer if Use Links from Parent is enabled) and its child sites. Administrators can add, edit, and rearrange the links and delete them as well under the edit icon to the left of each link on the navigation settings.

Quick Launch navigation, normally shown on the left side, shows the lists and libraries in the current site. There is no option to inherit links from a parent site; this restriction is removed with publishing sites. The lists and libraries are presented with headings such as Libraries, Lists, and Discussions, and these headings can be edited along with the links using the Quick Launch settings as shown in Figure 13.4.

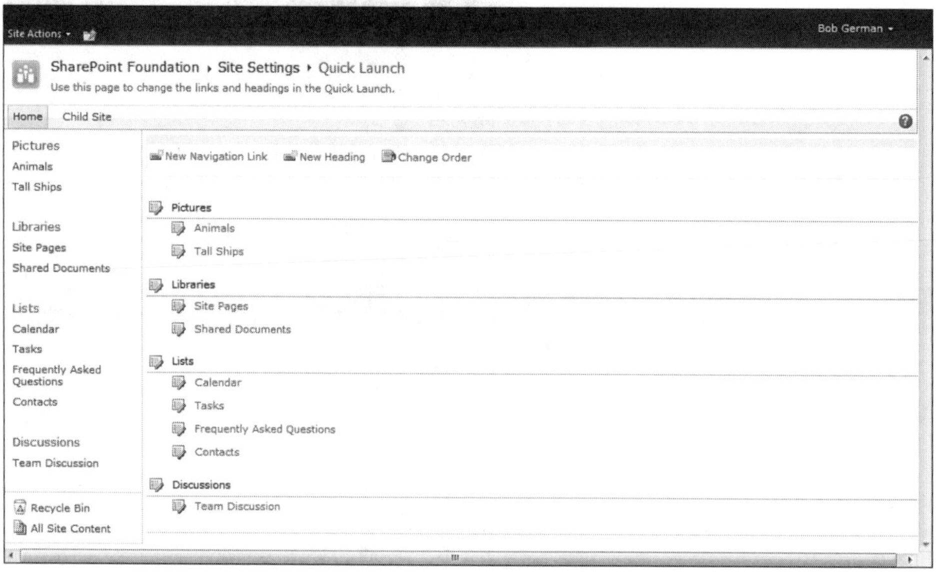

FIGURE 13.4: Quick Launch settings in a SharePoint Team Site

The Quick Launch bar can be replaced with a Tree View showing the lists and libraries of the current site using the Tree View settings page. Without programming, the Team Site is only capable of automatically generating navigation for one site and its children (in the top navigation) and the current site's lists and libraries (in Quick Launch or the Tree View).

Publishing sites are considerably more flexible. In a publishing site, both the top and side navigation are hierarchical, with the potential to show multiple site levels. Figure 13.5 shows a publishing site with its navigation. The "top" navigation in publishing sites is called *global navigation*. In this case, global navigation shows the parent site called English and its immediate children, based on the current site inheriting its global navigation from its parent. Pages and child sites within each of these sites appear in a drop-down menu. On the side of the site, we see *current navigation*, which shows the children of the parent, again because inheritance is enabled.

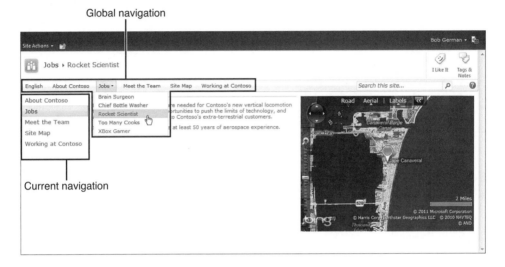

FIGURE 13.5: Navigation in a SharePoint 2010 publishing site

There are fewer Look and Feel options in publishing sites, as seen in Figure 13.6; however visiting the Navigation page, shown in Figure 13.7, reveals a much more extensive group of settings for both global and current navigation.

FIGURE 13.6: Team Site Look and Feel settings

FIGURE 13.7: Navigation settings in a SharePoint publishing site

Notice that global and current navigation can be controlled independently, and each can be set to inherit navigation items from the parent site. Each can also be set to show child sites, publishing pages, or both, and if they are selected, then child sites and pages are automatically added to the navigation hierarchy.

Both global and current navigation can be edited using a browser-based editor. The editor allows hiding the automatically created child site and publishing page links and also allows the manual creation of new links.

The more advanced navigation in a publishing site makes it much easier to organize information in a potentially large collection of sites.

Site Map Providers

Whatever you do, don't go building a new navigation system based on the SharePoint API. It might seem tempting to remove the out-of-the-box navigation controls from your master page and replace them with web controls that build a navigation structure using SharePoint API calls. It turns out that SharePoint's built-in navigation is orders of magnitude faster than the server APIs. It's worth paying attention to that overhead given that navigation is rendered multiple times on every SharePoint page for navigation controls including bread crumbs. The overhead from the client APIs would be even higher because they use the server APIs under the covers and also have to marshal requests over the network.

At this point you might think, "I'll outsmart him, I'll just cache the navigation structure and more than compensate for the performance difference!" This might be OK, as long as you take SharePoint's built-in security trimming system into account. Security trimming means that when any navigation is rendered in SharePoint, users can only see things they have permission to access. Thus, the navigation complies with SharePoint's built-in security system, and users don't discover things they shouldn't. Because the SharePoint APIs also respect security trimming, custom navigation controls based on the APIs would be security trimmed, but the cache would need to have a copy of the site hierarchy for each user to account for their potentially unique security access.

The beauty of SharePoint's navigation system is it caches the navigation structure and enough access control information to dynamically security trim the navigation hierarchy each user sees. End users expect this to work. There are many ways to gain (or deny) access to an item in SharePoint, so it's best to let SharePoint implement this for consistent access control.

SharePoint didn't invent its own navigation system from scratch; instead it built on the system already in ASP.NET, which defines a provider model for navigation. In this model, *site map providers* provide a hierarchy of *site map nodes* that represent some navigation structure. *Data source* objects consume the site map, and *navigation controls* bind to them and render the user interface.

This provider model allows navigation controls and site map providers to be interchanged for greater flexibility and code reuse. In the next section you learn how to create your own site map provider that can be consumed by SharePoint's out-of-the-box navigation system.

SharePoint provides a site map provider class called `PortalSiteMapProvider` for publishing sites; team sites are similar, except that they offer an `SPContentMapProvider` instead. Both inherit from ASP.NET's `System.Web.SiteMapProvider` class, and both provide a hierarchy of `SiteMapNode` objects that represent a site's navigation. Figure 13.8 shows the site map providers used in a SharePoint publishing site.

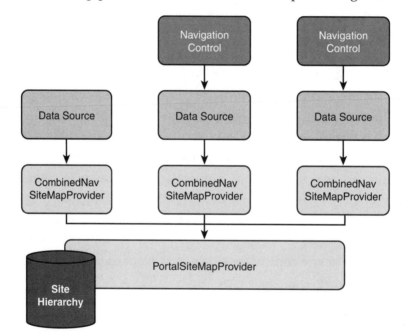

FIGURE 13.8: Site map provider hierarchy in publishing site

Site map providers can be stacked on top of one another, with one site map provider consuming the hierarchy from another and providing an altered site map to its consumers. SharePoint publishing sites do just this, as shown in Figure 13.8.

The `PortalSiteMapProvider` provides the site hierarchy as it currently exists, with security trimming applied. `CombinedNavSiteMapProvider` objects consume this hierarchy and alter it to create the Global and Current site maps and to account for editing performed in the site settings. Data source objects on the master page consume the `CombinedNavSiteMap-Providers` and are bound to the navigation controls we see in the Share-Point user interface.

SharePoint's built-in navigation controls, by the way, are very flexible and can be greatly customized by setting properties and using cascading style sheets.

Building a Site Map Provider

The navigation editor in Site Settings is nice, but it's no way to manage navigation across a large site collection. If you want to control SharePoint's navigation structure, the trick is to write your own site map provider that consumes one of the site map providers that ships with SharePoint, and then alter the structure before handing it on. Some potential uses include

- Adding or hiding links to aid navigation or enforce policy
- Stitching together multiple sites or site collections
- Adding links for business entities obtained from a database

Just remember to consider securely caching any external data you want to add.

> **■ TIP**
>
> The sample code for this chapter is for a publishing site. To use it, you need SharePoint Server 2010, Standard or Enterprise edition. Be sure you create your test site using the Publishing Portal template. Share-Point Foundation 2010 does not support publishing sites.

Writing a site map provider is as easy as inheriting from one, such as `PortalSiteMapProvider`, and overriding its `GetChildNodes` method. List-ing 13.1 shows a simple site map provider that adds a new heading called

Sample and links to the Microsoft Technology Center and SharePoint web sites .

LISTING 13.1: Custom Navigation Provider

```
public class NavigationProvider : PortalSiteMapProvider
{
    public override SiteMapNodeCollection
GetChildNodes(System.Web.SiteMapNode node)
    {
        if (node is PortalSiteMapNode &&
            (node == this.RootNode || node.Title == "English"))
        {
            PortalSiteMapNode portalNode = node as PortalSiteMapNode;
            SiteMapNodeCollection nodeCollection =
                base.GetChildNodes(portalNode);

            PortalSiteMapNode childNode = new
                PortalSiteMapNode(portalNode.WebNode,
                "Sample", NodeTypes.Heading,
                "http://www.microsoft.com/", "Sample",
                "Sample Links for You");
            nodeCollection.Add(childNode);

            childNode.ChildNodes = new SiteMapNodeCollection();

            PortalSiteMapNode grandchildNode = new
                PortalSiteMapNode(portalNode.WebNode,
                "MTC", NodeTypes.AuthoredLink,
                "http://www.microsoft.com/MTC/", "MTC",
                "Microsoft Technology Centers");
            childNode.ChildNodes.Add(grandchildNode);

            grandchildNode = new
                PortalSiteMapNode(portalNode.WebNode,
                "SharePoint", NodeTypes.AuthoredLink,
                "http://www.microsoft.com/sharepoint/", "SharePoint",
                "SharePoint Product Site");
            childNode.ChildNodes.Add(grandchildNode);

            return nodeCollection;
        }
        else
        {
            return base.GetChildNodes(node);
        }
    }
}
```

After the site map provider is written, the next challenge is to deploy it. This calls for a Farm solution. The code itself is installed as a .dll in the bin directory of each web application or in the global assembly cache. But SharePoint won't see the new site map provider without a change to ASP.NET's dreaded web.config file, where all site map providers are configured. Specifically, a line needs to be added to the `<providers>` element under the `<siteMap>` element:

```
<add name="SampleNavProvider" description="Sample provider"
     type="Chapter13.NavigationProvider, Chapter13, Version=1.0.0.0,
Culture=neutral, PublicKeyToken=d238a824d583ebab"
     NavigationType="Global" EncodeOutput="true" />
```

Fortunately, SharePoint provides a way to consistently manage web.config across all its web servers. The trick is to define a feature receiver that adds the entry to web.config when the feature is activated and removes it upon deactivation. SharePoint provides the `SPWebConfigModification` class for this purpose.

The sample code is written as a Farm solution with a farm-level feature for the navigation provider. This means it updates all web applications in the farm; if you want to affect only one web application, a web application feature would make more sense. The farm feature includes a receiver to manage web.config, as shown in Listing 13.2.

LISTING 13.2: Feature Receiver to Update web.config

```
public class Navigation_ProviderEventReceiver : SPFeatureReceiver
{
    // When the feature is activated, add the entry into web.config
    public override void FeatureActivated
                          (SPFeatureReceiverProperties properties)
    {
        SPWebConfigModification modification =
            new SPWebConfigModification();
        modification.Path = "configuration/system.web/siteMap/providers";
        modification.Name = "add[@name='SampleNavProvider']";
        modification.Sequence = 0;
        modification.Owner = "SampleNavProvider";
        modification.Type =
    SPWebConfigModification.SPWebConfigModificationType.EnsureChildNode;
        modification.Value = "<add name=\"SampleNavProvider\"
description=\"Sample navigation provider adds heading with links\" type=\"" +
```

```
                typeof(NavigationProvider).AssemblyQualifiedName +
                "\" NavigationType=\"Global\" EncodeOutput=\"true\" />";

        SPWebService contentService = SPWebService.ContentService;
        contentService.WebConfigModifications.Add(modification);
        contentService.Update();
        contentService.ApplyWebConfigModifications();
    }

    public override void FeatureDeactivating
                            (SPFeatureReceiverProperties properties)
    {
        SPWebConfigModification configModFound = null;

        SPWebService contentService = SPWebService.ContentService;
        Collection<SPWebConfigModification> modsCollection =
            contentService.WebConfigModifications;

        // Find the most recent modification of a specified owner
        int modsCount1 = modsCollection.Count;
        for (int i = modsCount1 - 1; i > -1; i--)
        {
            if (modsCollection[i].Owner == "SampleNavProvider")
            {
                configModFound = modsCollection[i];
            }
        }

        // Remove it and save the change to the configuration database
        modsCollection.Remove(configModFound);
        contentService.Update();
        contentService.ApplyWebConfigModifications();
    }
}
```

In the FeatureActivated method, a new SPWebConfigModification is
created, and its path property is set to the path where the modification is
to be performed. The name property specifies the XML element to be added
("add") and an attribute ("name") and its value. The Owner property is set
to a unique value that is needed to remove the modification at a later point.
Finally, the type property is set to the full type name of the new site map
provider. Notice that this can be done using .NET reflection to avoid having to deal with the long assembly name string.

When the `SPWebConfigModification` object is filled in, it is added to the `WebConfigModifications` collection in SharePoint's content service. The content service is updated to register the change in SharePoint's content database, and the modifications are applied to actually edit web.config on each web server.

To reverse the action in the `FeatureDeactivating` method, go back to SharePoint's content service and obtain the `WebConfigModifications` collection. Then loop through the collection and look for the modification with the same Owner property used when the modification was registered and remove it.

At this point, the new navigation can be rendered by SharePoint's out-of-the-box navigation controls, as shown in Figure 13.9. To make this work, you need to modify the master page to reference `SampleNavProvider` instead of `GlobalNavSiteMapProvider` and/or `CurrentNavigation`. Listing 13.3 shows a snippet of the out-of-the-box "v4.master" master page with global navigation switched to use `SampleNavProvider`. The `<SharePoint:AspMenu>` element is SharePoint's navigation control, and the `<PublishingNavigation:PortalSiteMapDataSource>` element is the data source object that connects to the `SampleNavProvider` site map provider.

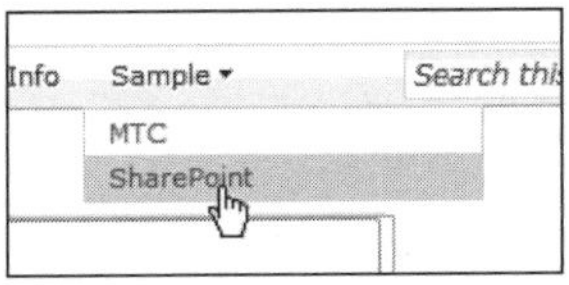

FIGURE 13.9: The sample navigation provider has added links to global navigation.

LISTING 13.3: Referencing the Site Map Provider in a SharePoint Master Page

```
<SharePoint:AspMenu
    ID="TopNavigationMenuV4"
    Runat="server"
    EnableViewState="false"
    DataSourceID="topSiteMap1"
    AccessKey="<%$Resources:wss,navigation_accesskey%>"
    UseSimpleRendering="true"
    UseSeparateCss="false"
    Orientation="Horizontal"
    StaticDisplayLevels="2"
```

```
    MaximumDynamicDisplayLevels="3"
    SkipLinkText=""
    CssClass="s4-tn"/>
<PublishingNavigation:PortalSiteMapDataSource
    ID="topsitemap1"
    Runat="server"
    SiteMapProvider="SampleNavProvider"
    EnableViewState="false"
    EnableInheritance="true"
    StartFromCurrentNode="false"
    ShowStartingNode="true"
    TreatStartingNodeAsCurrent="true"/>
```

This change can be made using SharePoint Designer, or updated master pages can be deployed along with the solution. The code sample includes three master pages in a module called MasterPage, as shown in Table 13.1. To see the `SampleNavProvider` in action, simply go to Site Settings and under Look and Feel, click Master Page and select the v4-SampleNav.master page.

TABLE 13.1: Master Pages Included in the Navigation Code Sample

File Name	Description
V4-SampleNav.master	This is the out-of-the-box v4.master file, except that the `SampleNavProvider` replaces the normal site map providers.
V4-TreeNav.master	This is the out-of-the-box v4.master file, except that the current navigation control (on the left) has been replaced with the Silverlight tree navigation control (explained later in this chapter).
V4-SampleTreeNav.master	This is the out-of-the-box v4.master file in which the site map providers have been switched to use `SampleNavProvider` and the current navigation control has been replaced with the Silverlight tree navigation control, explained later in this chapter

Building a Navigation Web Part

To work on a navigation control, begin by building something more familiar: a simple web part. This will be a Navigation Web Part that shows the site hierarchy viewed through any of the available site map providers. This web part is useful in its own right as a site map display, and also allows you to easily view any site map provider by simply editing the web part.

Figure 13.10 shows the Navigation Web Part. It uses an out-of-the-box Silverlight tree control to show the site hierarchy. The tree automatically expands to show the current site or page and highlights the current location.

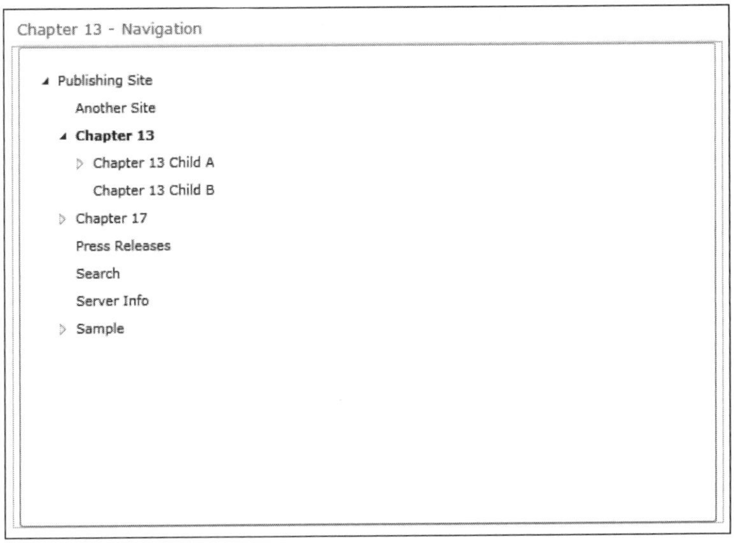

FIGURE 13.10: Navigation Web Part

Figure 13.11 shows the Navigation Web Part's editing experience. A custom editor part allows the user to select the site map provider to display from a list of available providers.

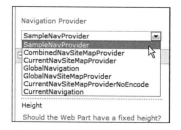

FIGURE 13.11: Editing the Navigation Web Part

Take a moment to examine the editing experience itself. The web part is in a single class called `NavigationWP.cs`, which includes a property to hold the site map provider name and declares an editor part to edit this property. This is shown in Listing 13.4.

LISTING 13.4: Setting up the Editor Part for the Site Map Web Part

```
// Property to hold navigation provider name
[Personalizable(PersonalizationScope.Shared)]
[WebBrowsable(false)]
public string NavProvider { get; set; }

// Set up custom Editor Part
public override EditorPartCollection CreateEditorParts()
{
    ArrayList editorPartArray = new ArrayList();

    NavigationEP editorPart = new NavigationEP();
    editorPart.ID = this.ID + "_editorPart";
    editorPartArray.Add(editorPart);
    return new EditorPartCollection(editorPartArray);
}
```

Notice that the property's `WebBrowsable` attribute is set to false, so SharePoint won't create a text box to edit this string. Instead, the override of `CreateEditorParts()` is used to instantiate a custom editor part called `NavigationEP`, and pass it back as part of an `EditorPartCollection`.

The editor part itself is a simple composite control that uses an ASP.NET DropDownList to display the available site map providers. This list is initialized in `CreateChildControls()` as shown in Listing 13.5. The list of available providers is readily available from the `System.Web.SiteMap` class by way of a static property called `Providers`.

LISTING 13.5: Populating the Editor Part with a List of Site Map Providers

```
DropDownList navProviderDropDownList = new DropDownList();

protected override void CreateChildControls()
{
    base.CreateChildControls();

    this.Controls.Add(new LiteralControl("<p>Navigation Provider</p>"));
    if (navProviderDropDownList.Items.Count == 0)
    {
        foreach (SiteMapProvider p in SiteMap.Providers)
        {
            if (p is PortalSiteMapProvider)
            {
                navProviderDropDownList.Items.Add
                            (new ListItem (p.Name));
            }
        }
    }
    this.Controls.Add(navProviderDropDownList);

    this.Controls.Add(new LiteralControl("<br /><br />"));
}
```

The editor part also includes the standard overrides SyncChanges() and
ApplyChanges() update the editor part controls with the current property
value and update the property value from the editor part controls during
editing. These are shown in Listing 13.6.

LISTING 13.6: SyncChanges() and ApplyChanges() in the Editor Part

```
// SyncChanges - Override to update the EditorPart controls
// with the latest web part properties
public override void SyncChanges()
{
    this.EnsureChildControls();

    if (this.WebPartToEdit is NavigationWP)
    {
        NavigationWP webPart = this.WebPartToEdit as NavigationWP;
        navProviderDropDownList.Text = webPart.NavProvider;
    }
}

// ApplyChanges - Override to update the web part with the
// latest EditorPart control values
```

```
public override bool ApplyChanges()
{
    if (this.WebPartToEdit is NavigationWP)
    {
        NavigationWP webPart = this.WebPartToEdit as NavigationWP;
        webPart.NavProvider = navProviderDropDownList.Text;
    }
    return true;
}
```

The web part itself passes the entire site map to Silverlight for rendering. In this way, the Silverlight application can be programmed to show as much of the navigation hierarchy as desired, interacting with the user as she explores the options, without any need to go back to the SharePoint server for more information. The site map is passed using the same serialization technique explained in Chapter 10, "Accessing SharePoint with Web Services."

The solution contains a class in `NavigationNode.cs` that is used to serialize a simplified version of the site map to Silverlight. This class is included in both the SharePoint and Silverlight projects.

A `NavigationNode` object can be a single node or the parent of a whole hierarchy. The node contains string properties for `Title` and `Url`, plus boolean properties `IsExpanded` (to tell Silverlight to expand the node on rendering) and `IsCurrent` (to tell Silverlight to highlight the node as the current one). It also includes a property called `Children` of type `List <NavigationNode>`; this allows the node to be part of a hierarchy. An entire hierarchy of `NavigationNode` objects can be serialized and deserialized using the `Serialize()` and `Load()` methods, exactly the same as in Chapter 10.

In addition, the `NavigationNode` class includes a method called `Get NavigationNode()`, which fills in the node from a site map provider, and `GetNavigationNodeCollection()`, which fills in a collection of child nodes. These are recursive methods that fill in the entire hierarchy with a single call to `GetNavigationNode()`. Listing 13.7 shows the `NavigationNode` class, including these methods, and its serializable properties. It uses a base class, `SerializableObject`, to fill in the `Serialize()` and `Load()` methods.

LISTING 13.7: NavigationNode Class Used to Pass Navigation Information to Silverlight

```
[DataContract]
public class NavigationNode : Utility.SerializableObject<NavigationNode>
{
    [DataMember]
    public string Title { get; set; }
    [DataMember]
    public string Url { get; set; }
    [DataMember]
    public bool IsExpanded { get; set; }
    [DataMember]
    public bool IsCurrent { get; set; }
    [DataMember]
    public List<NavigationNode> Children { get; set; }

    public static NavigationNode GetNavigationNode
                    (SiteMapProvider provider, SiteMapNode node)
    {
        NavigationNode result = new NavigationNode();
        bool expandThis = false;

        result.Title = node.Title;
        result.Url = node.Url;
        result.Children = GetNavigationNodeCollection(provider,
            node.ChildNodes, out expandThis);
        result.IsCurrent = (node == provider.CurrentNode);
        result.IsExpanded = expandThis || (node == provider.CurrentNode);

        return result;
    }

    private static List<NavigationNode>
            GetNavigationNodeCollection(SiteMapProvider provider,
            SiteMapNodeCollection nodeCollection, out bool expandParent)
    {
        bool expandThis = false;

        List<NavigationNode> result =
            (from SiteMapNode childNode in nodeCollection
             select new NavigationNode()
             {
                 Title = childNode.Title,
                 Url = childNode.Url,
                 Children = GetNavigationNodeCollection(provider,
                         childNode.ChildNodes, out expandThis),
                 IsCurrent = (childNode == provider.CurrentNode),
                 IsExpanded = expandThis ||
```

```
                                (childNode == provider.CurrentNode)
            }).ToList();

        expandParent = (from NavigationNode n in result
                        where n.IsExpanded
                        select true).Any<bool>();

        return result;
    }
}
```

An initial call to GetNavigationNode() passes in a SiteMapProvider and its root SiteMapNode:

```
NavigationNode navRoot = NavigationNode.GetNavigationNode
                    (siteMapProvider, siteMapProvider.RootNode);
```

This fills in a new NavigationNode object with the information from the root node and calls GetNavigationNodeCollection() to fill in the children. GetNavigationNodeCollection() uses a LINQ query to build a list of children and calls itself recursively to fill in any grandchildren and other descendants.

The web part itself creates a hidden field to hold the serialized NavigationNode tree and a Silverlight plugin control to render the Silverlight application that displays it. This is performed in CreateChild Controls, as shown in Listing 13.8. Then the OnPreRender() method is overridden to actually populate the hidden field with the NavigationNode tree. This is because during web part editing, the user's new selected site map provider won't be available until after ViewState processing, and by the time OnPreRender() runs, it will definitely be there.

LISTING 13.8: Navigation Web Part

```
private HtmlInputHidden navInfoField;
private SilverlightPlugin silverlightPlugin;

protected override void CreateChildControls()
{
    base.CreateChildControls();
```

```
    navInfoField = new HtmlInputHidden();
    this.Controls.Add(navInfoField);

    silverlightPlugin = new SilverlightPlugin();
    string siteCollectionUrl = SPContext.Current.Site.Url;
    silverlightPlugin.Source = ((siteCollectionUrl == "/") ? "" :
                                siteCollectionUrl) +
                                "/ClientBin/NavigationSL.xap";
    this.Controls.Add(silverlightPlugin);
}

protected override void OnPreRender(EventArgs e)
{
    base.OnPreRender(e);
    try
    {
        SiteMapProvider siteMapProvider =
            (SiteMapProvider)SiteMap.Providers[this.NavProvider];

        // Set up hidden field with serialized navigation tree
        NavigationNode navRoot =
            NavigationNode.GetNavigationNode(siteMapProvider,
            siteMapProvider.RootNode);
        navInfoField.Value = navRoot.Serialize();

        // Set up Silverlight object
        silverlightPlugin.InitParameters = "NavInfoFieldId=" +
            navInfoField.ClientID;
    }
    catch (Exception ex)
    {
        this.Controls.Clear();
        this.Controls.Add(new LiteralControl
            (HttpUtility.HtmlEncode(ex.Message)));
    }
}
```

The code for this chapter includes a Silverlight application called NavigationSL that knows how to consume the `NavigationNode` hierarchy and bind it to a Silverlight `TreeView` control. For the purposes of this book, the `TreeView` control has the advantage that it's included for free with Silverlight and is capable of hierarchical data binding. You can choose a fancier rendering, but the approach is the same.

As before, the work begins with the `Application_Startup` event in the Silverlight App.xaml.cs file, shown in Listing 13.9. The event handler looks for the hidden form field's client ID in `InitParams`, and if it finds it, it uses the HTML Bridge to read the field's content and load it into a `Navigation Node` hierarchy.

LISTING 13.9: Silverlight Application Startup Event Handler

```
private void Application_Startup(object sender, StartupEventArgs e)
{
    if (e.InitParams.ContainsKey("NavInfoFieldId"))
    {
        HtmlDocument doc = HtmlPage.Document;
        HtmlElement element =
            doc.GetElementById(e.InitParams["NavInfoFieldId"]);
        if (element != null && element.GetAttribute("value") != null)
        {
            string jsonString = element.GetAttribute("value").ToString();
            if (jsonString != "")
            {
                Chapter13.NavigationNode navRoot =
                    Chapter13.NavigationNode.Load(jsonString);
                UIElement p = new MainPage(navRoot);
                this.RootVisual = p;
            }
        }
    }
}
```

The application startup event passes the `NavigationNode` tree to the `MainPage` class in its constructor, which is shown in Listing 13.10. The Tree-View control expects to be bound to a hierarchical collection (that is, a collection of hierarchies, rather than a single tree root). To accommodate this, the root `NavigationNode` is placed in a new `List<NavigationNode>` as its sole member, which is then bound to the `TreeView` control.

LISTING 13.10: The MainPage Constructor Binds the Navigation Hierarchy to a TreeView Control

```
public MainPage(Chapter13.NavigationNode navRoot)
{
    InitializeComponent();
```

```
    this.navRoot = navRoot;

    // The TreeView expects to be bound to a collection, so make the root
    // be a collection of one
    List<Chapter13.NavigationNode> l = new
        List<Chapter13.NavigationNode>();
    l.Add(navRoot);

    // Bind the hierarchy
    navigationTreeView.ItemsSource = l;

    // Expand the tree to show the current page
    Dispatcher.BeginInvoke(() =>
    {
        ExpandTree(navigationTreeView);
    });
}
```

The tricky part of this is getting the tree to expand to show the current page. This is done using the IsExpanded and IsCurrent properties of each NavigationNode. Unfortunately, the TreeView doesn't have bindings to support the expanded state of a node, so this needs to be done in code. Further, this code can't be run in the MainPage constructor because the data binding runs in the background; the TreeView can't be expanded in the MainPage constructor because its nodes aren't filled in yet. This is easily fixed by using Dispatcher.BeginInvoke() to expand the tree after the background processing is complete.

The ExpandTree() code is shown in Listing 13.11. There are two signatures for this method; the first begins at the top of the TreeView and expands its root node. From there, the second method is used to recursively expand nodes as specified in the NavigationNode properties.

LISTING 13.11: Code to Expand the TreeView to Show the Current Page

```
private void ExpandTree(TreeView tv)
{
    TreeViewItem tvi =
        navigationTreeView.ItemContainerGenerator.ContainerFromIndex(0)
        as TreeViewItem;
    if (tvi != null)
    {
        ExpandTree(navRoot, tvi);
```

```
        }
    }

private void ExpandTree(Chapter13.NavigationNode node, TreeViewItem tvi)
{
    // Attach the correct style based on whether this is the current node
    if (node.IsCurrent)
    {
        tvi.Style = (Style)this.Resources["CurrentTreeViewItem"];
    }
    else
    {
        tvi.Style = (Style)this.Resources["NotCurrentTreeViewItem"];
    }

    // If the node should be expanded but the TreeViewItem isn't, then
    // expand it and dispatch another call to process the children
    if (node.IsExpanded && !tvi.IsExpanded)
    {
        tvi.IsExpanded = true;
        tvi.Dispatcher.BeginInvoke(() => { ExpandTree(node, tvi); });
    }
    else
    {
        // OK, this node is all set. Process any children next.
        foreach (object o in tvi.Items)
        {
            Chapter13.NavigationNode childNode =
                o as Chapter13.NavigationNode;
            TreeViewItem childTvi =
                tvi.ItemContainerGenerator.ContainerFromItem(childNode)
                as TreeViewItem;
            if (childTvi != null)
            {
                ExpandTree(childNode, childTvi);
            }
        }
    }
}
```

Silverlight styles are used to highlight the current node. Then a check is made to see if the node needs to be expanded; if so, another call to ExpandTree must be dispatched. As you might suspect, the TreeView is creating its child controls only as its branches are expanded, so you need to keep using the Dispatcher to allow the background processing to happen.

When a `TreeViewItem` is finally expanded, the `foreach` loop at the bottom of the method loops through its children to expand them as needed.

The only remaining task is to make the `TreeView` respond to a user clicking its nodes and then navigating the web browser to the corresponding page. This is done by hooking the `SelectedItemChanged` event on the `TreeView`. The event handler is quite simple, as shown in Listing 13.12.

LISTING 13.12: SelectedItemChanged Event Handler

```
private void navigationTreeView_SelectedItemChanged
            (object sender, RoutedPropertyChangedEventArgs<object> e)
{
    if (e.NewValue is Chapter13.NavigationNode)
    {
        Chapter13.NavigationNode selectedNode =
            e.NewValue as Chapter13.NavigationNode;
        System.Windows.Browser.HtmlPage.Window.Navigate(
            new Uri(selectedNode.Url, UriKind.RelativeOrAbsolute));
    }
}
```

The HTML Bridge makes it easy to navigate to the user's destination, and the Site Map Web Part is complete.

Building a Navigation Control

There isn't a huge difference between the Navigation Web Part and a navigation control. Both are ASP.NET composite controls, so the code is nearly identical. The code download for this chapter includes a navigation control called NavigationAspMenu.cs. Instead of being derived from an ASP.NET web part, it's derived from `System.Web.UI.WebControls.Menu`, the same class that SharePoint's out-of-the-box global and current navigation controls are derived from. Other than that, the only difference is that we need to go to the data source to obtain the site map provider, as shown in Listing 13.13.

LISTING 13.13: Navigation Control Reads from the Data Source Object

```
protected override void OnPreRender(EventArgs e)
{
    try
    {
        SiteMapDataSource dataSource =
            this.GetDataSource() as SiteMapDataSource;

        if (dataSource != null)
        {
            SiteMapProvider siteMapProvider = dataSource.Provider;

            // From here on, the method is the same as in the
            // Navigation web part
            // . . .
        }
    }
}
```

Rendering a Navigation Control on a SharePoint Master Page

At this point, you're almost ready to use the navigation control; however, if you put it on a SharePoint page now, you would get the dreaded error telling you that the control is not marked as safe. To do this, you need to add a *safe control entry* to web.config. Because safe controls come up all the time, this is much easier than adding the site map provider earlier in this chapter; rather than manually manipulating web.config, you can simply add an entry to the Safe Controls Entries in one of the SharePoint items in Visual Studio 2010. In the code sample, it's in the ClientBin module. In the SharePoint project, click the ClientBin module and open its properties view. Scroll down to the Safe Control Entries collection and click the ellipsis (…). This displays the Safe Control Entries dialog box. In this case, there's a defined safe control entry for the entire namespace, as shown in Figure 13.12.

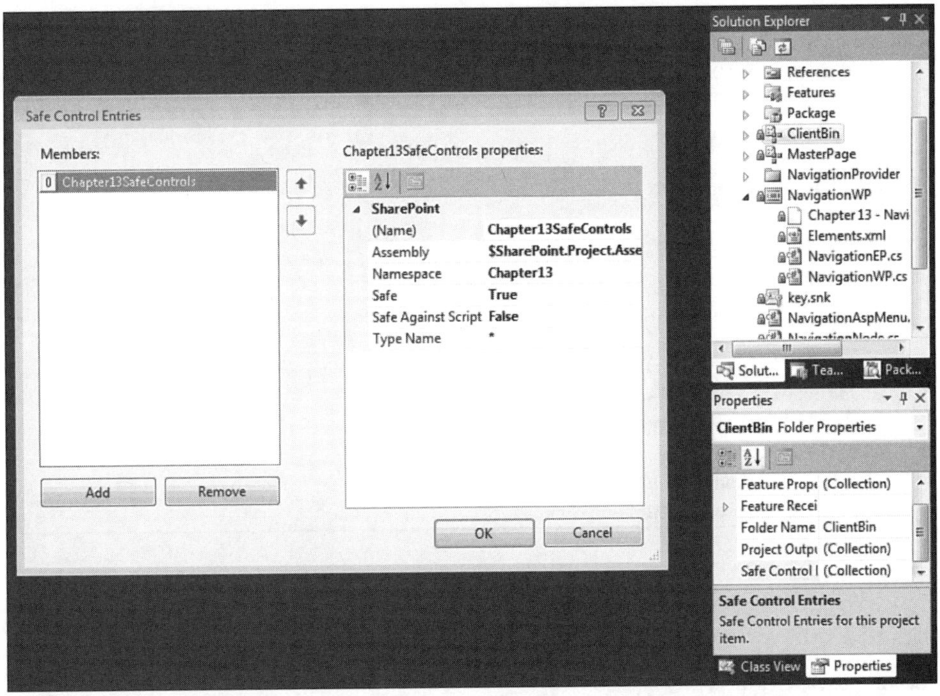

FIGURE 13.12: Adding a safe controls entry to allow the navigation control to run

Finally, you can change the master page to use the new navigation control. This is provided in two of the master pages that are included in the code download: v4-TreeNav.master replaces the context navigation with the new navigation tree, and v4-SampleTreeNav.master makes the same replacement and also switches from the standard `CurrentNavigation` site map provider to the sample site map provider from earlier in this chapter. Listing 13.14 shows the relevant lines in v4-SampleTreeNav.master.

LISTING 13.14: Referencing the New Navigation Control and Site Map Provider in a Master Page

```
<Chapter13:NavigationAspMenu
    ID="Chapter13NavigationMenu"
    Runat="server"
    EnableViewState="false"
    DataSourceID="topSiteMap2"
    AccessKey="<%$Resources:wss,navigation_accesskey%>"
    UseSimpleRendering="true"
    UseSeparateCss="false"
```

```
    Orientation="Horizontal"
    StaticDisplayLevels="2"
    MaximumDynamicDisplayLevels="3"
    SkipLinkText=""
    Height="600"
    Width="153"
    CssClass="s4-tn"/>

<!-- Data Source for Nav Control -->
<PublishingNavigation:PortalSiteMapDataSource
    ID="topsitemap2"
    Runat="server"
    SiteMapProvider="SampleNavProvider"
    EnableViewState="false"
    EnableInheritance="true"
    StartFromCurrentNode="false"
    ShowStartingNode="true"
    TreatStartingNodeAsCurrent="true"/>
```

The result, as shown in Figure 13.13, is the same navigation tree rendered as the side navigation in a SharePoint page.

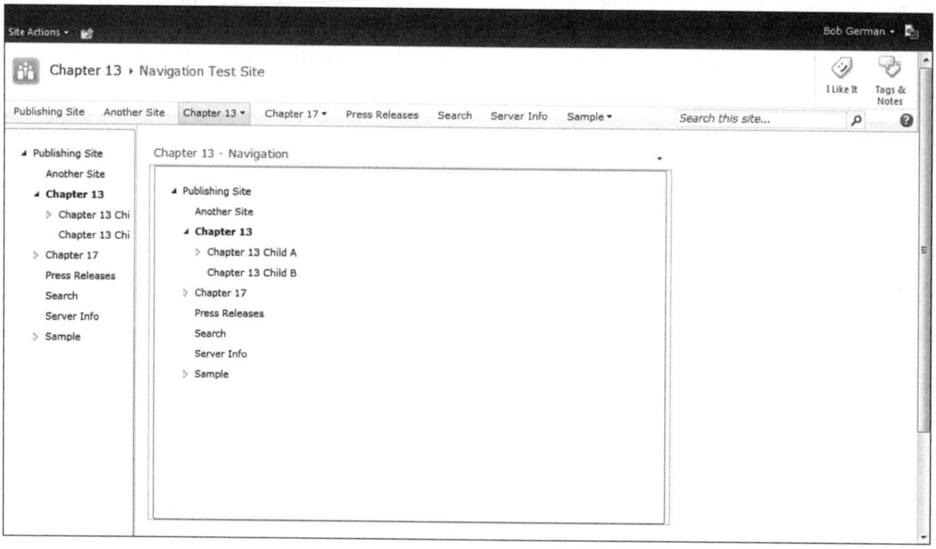

FIGURE 13.13: The navigation control and Navigation Web Part in use

Summary

In this chapter, you have seen how the out-of-the-box navigation works and how you can augment it with your own site map provider. You know better than to try and craft a new navigation system due to the complexities of SharePoint security trimming and the need for low overhead given that navigation is rendered in multiple places on every SharePoint page. And you learned to make a new navigation control using Silverlight, which can provide a richer experience for the end user.

It should also be clear by now that by working with the ASP.NET navigation system, you can mix and match your Silverlight navigation with SharePoint's out-of-the-box navigation and any third-party ASP.NET navigation controls you might choose to add to your toolkit. Overall, SharePoint and ASP.NET provide a highly flexible and extensible platform to build your own site navigation experience.

■ 14 ■

SharePoint and Silverlight in the Cloud

S O FAR IN THIS BOOK, you've worked through many Silverlight solutions for SharePoint, and getting to this point is an achievement. This chapter builds on what you've learned and shows you how to integrate Silverlight into SharePoint Online as a service within Office 365.

The Microsoft Office365 product offering consists of three relatively distinct parts:

1. Communications—Instant Messaging, Voice and Video calls, and web conferencing
2. Email with Outlook 2010 and Outlook Web Access
3. Collaboration with SharePoint Online

A great way to think of SharePoint Online is the same as SharePoint 2010—a web portal through which individuals can store and exchange documents, as well as other information such as Tasks and Calendars—but in this case "it's in the cloud." (To be clear what the cloud is in this case, it's a public multi-tenant Software as a Service infrastructure located in Microsoft datacenters.) SharePoint Online (SPO) delivers most of the same site collection level developer features as in the on-premise Microsoft SharePoint 2010 product line.

Why then is there a special chapter on SPO? Although SPO offers developers the ability to upload custom applications, there are caveats in how to accomplish this task. To know why this important, you need only to understand that SPO is a multitenant environment. This means customers "share" resources like CPU and RAM—but do not share their data. This fact must be kept in mind when building applications. As discussed throughout this book, SharePoint Sandboxed Solutions is the feature that allows developers to run custom code in multitenant environments without administrators worrying about the stability of servers running SharePoint Online. Most importantly, when SPO is combined with Sandboxed Solutions to host Silverlight applications, developers can create custom Visual Studio 2010 solutions that can be immediately uploaded to SharePoint Online.

In fact, there are many types of customizations to SPO. In this chapter you focus on Silverlight external data connectivity to SharePoint Online; building custom web parts in Visual Studio 2010; and adding a Ribbon group, buttons, and building several Silverlight applications to connect to SharePoint data sources. The purpose is to show how to mesh Silverlight into the SharePoint Online to enable rich solutions that can connect to sources beyond the reach of the Sandbox in accordance with good practical use for the SharePoint Client Object Model. After reading this chapter, you'll have a good idea how to apply the knowledge from other parts of this book to SharePoint Online as well.

Let's take a look at a custom project for SharePoint Online to get a better idea of these concepts. Figure 14.1 shows a Silverlight application embedded into a SharePoint Sandboxed Web Part and deployed with a Ribbon customization to Office365 SharePoint Online. You've used these models before in this book, but the implementation and deployment differs enough for us to spend time exploring in SharePoint Online. Additionally, the goal of many cloud applications is data integration—what better way than to build a project in Office365 accessing data from Azure, Microsoft's cloud-based application environment.

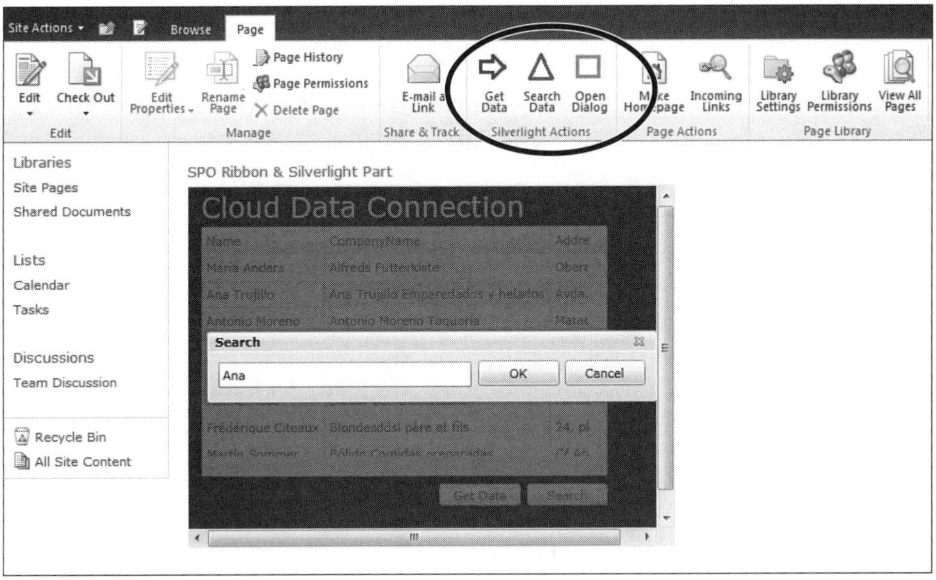

FIGURE 14.1: Office365 SharePoint Online Silverlight Web Part connected to Azure

SharePoint Online Sandboxed Solutions, Development Environment, and Deployment

As mentioned previously, custom development packages with SharePoint Online will be SharePoint 2010 Sandboxed Solutions and Silverlight Solutions in Visual Studio 2010. With SPO, our development environment is a local instance of SharePoint 2010 Foundation or Enterprise Server and is the same development environment as suggested in this book. Although not necessary, testing should occur on local servers before publishing to SPO.

The Visual Studio solution types have been covered in previous chapters, but let's go over them briefly. In this chapter, three types of projects are mixed together to create integrated solutions:

- Visual Studio Silverlight Solutions
- Visual Studio SharePoint Sandboxed Solutions
- Visual Studio SharePoint Ribbon Solutions (declarative SharePoint Ribbon markup for customization)

Sometimes when working with more complex SharePoint projects, dependent artifacts, such as lists, images, or content types, might not be represented in our production SPO site. Perhaps the data required is absent or external service references are not available. For these reasons when planning for SPO with Sandbox Solutions, also plan to incorporate other artifacts, like images, into the Visual Studio SharePoint deployment packages; it's recommended to deploy them to the Site Assets library. This way, the main code and all related pieces can be published and tested as a single unit. The strategy is especially useful when deploying to remote and external platforms. Alternatively, images can be included in the Silverlight .xap file for deployment. In most cases, inclusion in the .xap file makes its size larger, and downloading and executing the application takes more time. If the images are deployed to the Site Assets library in Sandbox Solutions, the .xap size stays smaller, and the images can be changed without your needing to recompile the .xap file.

In general, the deployment model features local and remote environments for testing and production (SharePoint Online). The deployment packages are deployable to all environments. Figure 14.2 shows an example of local test and remote production environments.

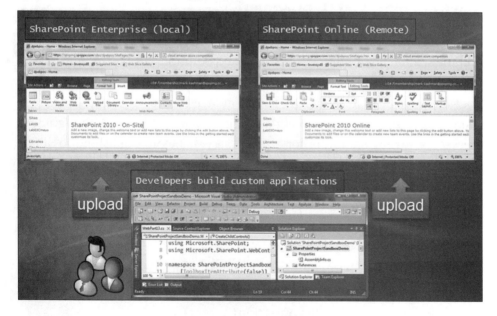

FIGURE 14.2: Example: Local test and remote production environments

Deployment packages can contain a couple of web parts or modules. With a basic Silverlight application for SharePoint, there is only one file—the Silverlight .xap application file and, commonly, the .xap file is uploaded manually to the Site Assets list in SharePoint Online. When uploaded, take the URL reference to the file in the Site Assets list (as shown in Figure 14.3) and reference when adding an out-of-the-box Silverlight Web Part to a SharePoint page.

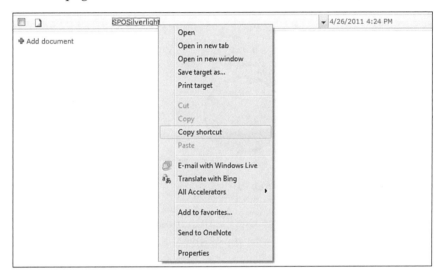

FIGURE 14.3: Copying a shortcut to a Silverlight .xap file

In Figure 14.4, adding a new out-of-the-box Silverlight Web Part in SharePoint Online is slightly different than SharePoint Foundation.

- The More Web Parts button contains the Silverlight Web Part.
- The parts are in the Media and Content category.
- Select the Silverlight Web Part and click Add.
- You are prompted, "No Silverlight Application (.xap) is specified […]"
  - Open the Tool Pane and configure.
  - Use the .xap URL from the Site Assets list.

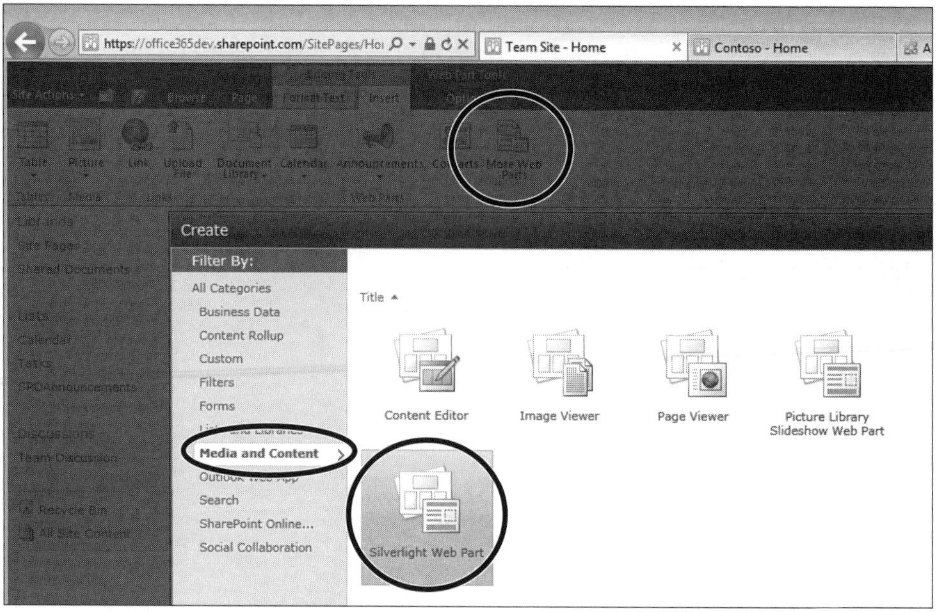

FIGURE 14.4: Adding the Silverlight Web Part

A developer can upload the .xap file into most lists. The "Site Assets" list provides a common place to hold these files, as well as images or .css files.

The following list contains the basic steps in the process of creating, deploying, and activating a sandboxed solution in SharePoint Online:

1. **Develop and test the solution.** Create a solution on a local computer where SharePoint Foundation 2010 is installed.

   - Develop a Silverlight Application and deploy to the SharePoint Silverlight Web Part.
   - Develop a sandboxed solution and embed the Silverlight Application.

2. **Deploy and activate the solution.** After you create and debug your solution on the local computer, upload the solution package (.wsp) file to the Solution Gallery for activation.

3. **Assign resources for the site collection's sandboxed solutions.**

   Ensure sandboxed solutions resources have been allocated to the site collection (see Figure 14.5).

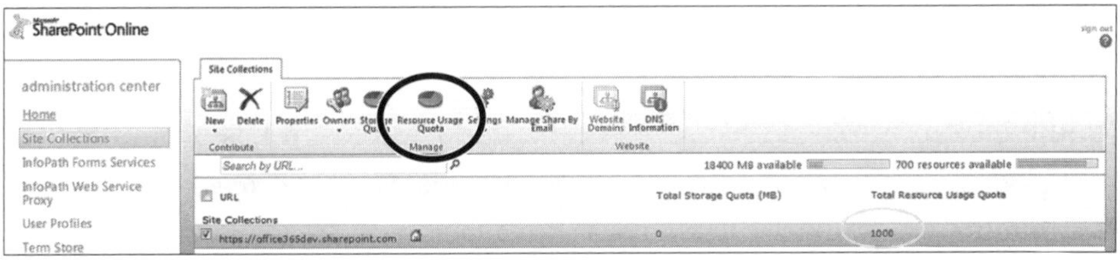

FIGURE 14.5: Setting a resource quota in SharePoint Online

To explain the Resource Usage Quota a little more, in the Office365 Dashboard for SharePoint, ensure site collections using sandboxed web parts have a Resource Allocation value (also referred to as *resource points*). With a value of zero, sandboxed solutions do not activate. In the example shown in Figure 14.5, 1000 resource points are allocated. However, 300 points is a good value to begin with because each Office365 account has overall point apportionment (a small Office365 account point allotment is 6000), and you distribute points to each site as needed. Later, if an Administrator judges more points are needed, she can update the value in the Administrator dashboard, and alerts can be sent to the site collection Administrator based on a percentage of resource allocation usage. The dashboard is located off the SharePoint Online Administrator Center under Manage SharePoint Online.

■ NOTE

Each customer can get to his SharePoint Online Administration Center by typing https://YourDomain-admin.sharepoint.com where you replace Your-Domain with the company name you signed up with for Office365.

Web Services in SharePoint Online

Web services are interesting in SPO…and sandboxed solutions do not allow external connections. However, Silverlight can access SharePoint data via Client Side Object Model and external data services directly.

Deciding which data access method to use is a design choice based on authentication, ease of access, or other criteria. Microsoft has committed to supporting direct access to external data via web services. SharePoint Online plans to support those core components of Business Connectivity Services (BCS) for direct access to external data via web services. For example, if the Administrator connects SPO to an external service and grants access to users, then Silverlight clients can easily integrate the SharePoint (external list) data with the Client API and do not need to carry service references or authenticate remotely—this is a strong point because SPO can centrally manage security and service references. In a different scenario, the application could be independent of SharePoint Online to manage its service connections and authentication. There are benefits to either solution, but it's good to point out the choices.

SharePoint Online Client Object Models

SPO uses the same Client APIs available in SharePoint on-premise and mentioned previously in this book. This book sticks with the Silverlight SharePoint Client API to retrieve data in its examples, but it is important to note SPO has the same access to the SharePoint List REST interface, as well as the Excel Services REST interface. The Excel API lets developers open workbooks through a URL and display or update data.

WCF and ASP.NET Web Services

Although SharePoint web services and other external data connections are not available for use in sandboxed solutions, you can access them through Silverlight applications. These types of data sources are external sources like Azure or On-Premise WCF solutions. For details on connecting to external data sources, see Chapter 11, "Accessing External Data," which explains how to wire up Silverlight to display the data of your choosing.

SharePoint Online Debugging

Debugging sandboxed solutions in SharePoint Online can be very challenging. In SPO, developers have no access to server resources or counters, cannot log errors to a file, and can't attach a debugger to SharePoint Online IIS process or sandboxed solution process. Additionally, even if a SharePoint correlation error is shown to the user, the developer can't research logs to find the cause.

However, in a much more positive light, Silverlight allows you to attach to the browser process running the SharePoint Online site to directly debug and hit breakpoints in the Silverlight code. The interesting conundrum comes with the question of how you might log information or errors with the SPO restrictions. Also, how might you debug the mix of Silverlight and SharePoint Online to receive useful information as the application runs? In simple applications, where the code might just be Silverlight, the issue is easier, of course. However, many applications will also be running a full set of sandboxed code coupled with a Silverlight client; in those situations, retrieving debug data at all levels is helpful. Here are some helpful hints:

- Use the Developer Dashboard to see if the issue is in your web part. This is the icon enabled on the far upper right corner of the browser.
- Pull the suspected web part back to your local environment and commence debugging and testing with Visual Studio 2010. Use the local debugger to set breakpoints and evaluate values and errors.
- Look for missing artifacts on the SharePoint Online site, such as Lists or Images.
- Put your code in try-catch-blocks in the catch statement.
  - Use a Textbox to output error messages.
  - Use a SPList to log error messages. Be sure to also create a function to remove entries in the list. If the list grows too large, site performance may be degraded.

In Figure 14.6, the Developer Dashboard is enabled by clicking the icon in the upper left corner. Importantly, when enabled, the dashboard has sections describing the load times for the sandboxed web part to inform the developer how the parts are loading. For example, if a developer puts code in the sandbox solution server side OnLoad() or OnPrerender() methods, the load time could be very slow, perhaps indicating the issue is not within the Silverlight client but within the sandboxed code accompanying it. Figure 14.6 shows an example of the web part initialization, load, and render times.

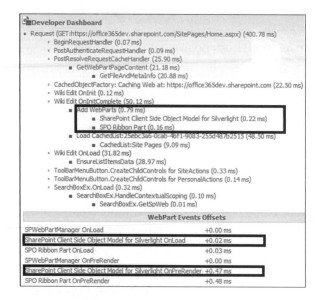

FIGURE 14.6: Developer Dashboard

Customization of the Developer Dashboard with the SharePoint SP MonitoredScope class is not supported in sandboxed solutions. Fortunately, the default output of dashboard is helpful to gain insight on coding issues.

SharePoint Online API "Additional" Restrictions for Sandboxed Solutions

SharePoint Online has additional restrictions in the Microsoft.SharePoint namespace in addition to the default set of restrictions for standard SharePoint sandboxed solutions. (Full details can be found on MSDN at http://bit.ly/SPSL_SandboxedAPI.) The best strategy is installing Visual Studio Service Pack 1 that contains compiler instructions to throw an error if restricted types are used when the SharePoint sandboxed solution project attribute is true and the project is compiled. However, additionally blocked items for SPO will not be covered in VS2010 SP1, so they are listed here. If you accidentally try to use one, the sandboxed solution throws a runtime error stating that there has been a security exception, which assists in uncovering the root of the problem.

The additionally blocked namespaces for SharePoint Online are

- `microsoft.sqlserver`

- `microsoft.win32`

- `system.array.createinstance`

- `system.data.sql`

- `system.data.sqlclient`

- `system.data.sqltypes`

- `system.delegates`

- `system.io.pipes`

- `system.io.ports`

- `system.reflection`

- `system.runtime.interopservices`

- `system.runtime.remoting`

- `system.threading`

- `system.type.gettype`

- `system.type.invokemember`

There are a few targeted exceptions to this block, however. The following types and members from the previous list of blocked namespaces can be used in a sandbox solution in SPO:

- `system.runtime.interopservices.layoutkind`

- `system.reflection.fieldinfo.getvalue`

- `system.reflection.memberinfo.get_name`

- `system.reflection.memberinfo.getcustomattributes`

- `system.reflection.propertyinfo.get_propertytype`

- `system.reflection.propertyinfo.getvalue`

- system.reflection.propertyinfo.setvalue

- system.threading.monitor.enter

- system.threading.monitor.exit

- system.threading.thread.get_managedthreadid

- system.threading.thread.get_currentthread

SharePoint Online Silverlight "Client Side Object Model" Data Project

Now that you've reviewed most of the information for SharePoint Online developers, let's build a common project using the SharePoint Client Side Object Model for Silverlight and publish to SPO. If you've read Chapter 8, you should be familiar with the SharePoint Client Side Object Model for Silverlight (CSOM).

Let's step through a project, and although you've done this before, the publishing aspect at the end is different. In brief, you create a Silverlight application in Visual Studio 2010, then add code to the default Page.xaml.cs file. Next, you build and upload the project's application package (.xap) file to a document library. Then insert a Silverlight Web Part into a web parts page and point the URL source of the web part to the .xap file's path location in a document library.

You need to add a reference to the Microsoft.SharePoint.Client. Silverlight and Runtime DLLs to use the SharePoint Client Object Model (CSOM). Use the DLLs found on the local SharePoint machine in the .. \14\TEMPLATE\LAYOUTS\ClientBin directory. In Figure 14.7, the project deploys the files with the Silverlight .xap file.

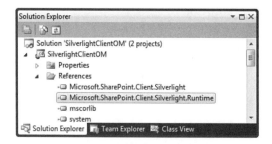

FIGURE 14.7: Client Object Model assemblies for Silverlight

There are a number of ways to accomplish the task of publishing a Silverlight application to SharePoint. In fact, several of them are covered in this book. However, for this sample, you want to use a simple way to build and manually publish to understand the publishing process.

Let's build the project shown in Figure 14.8.

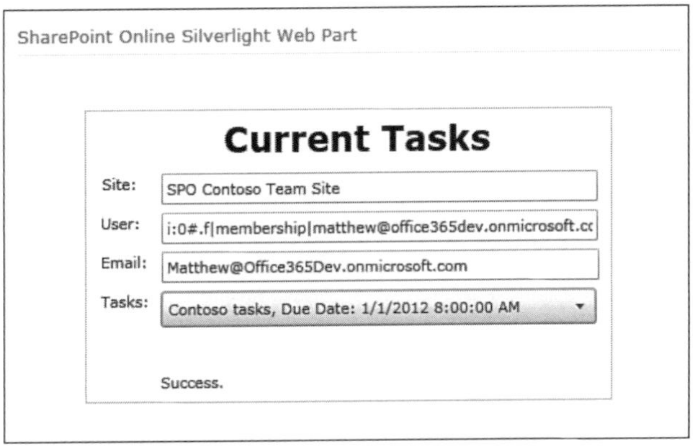

FIGURE 14.8: Client Object Model example in SharePoint Online

Create a new Silverlight Application and name it SilverlightClientOM, as shown in Figure 14.9.

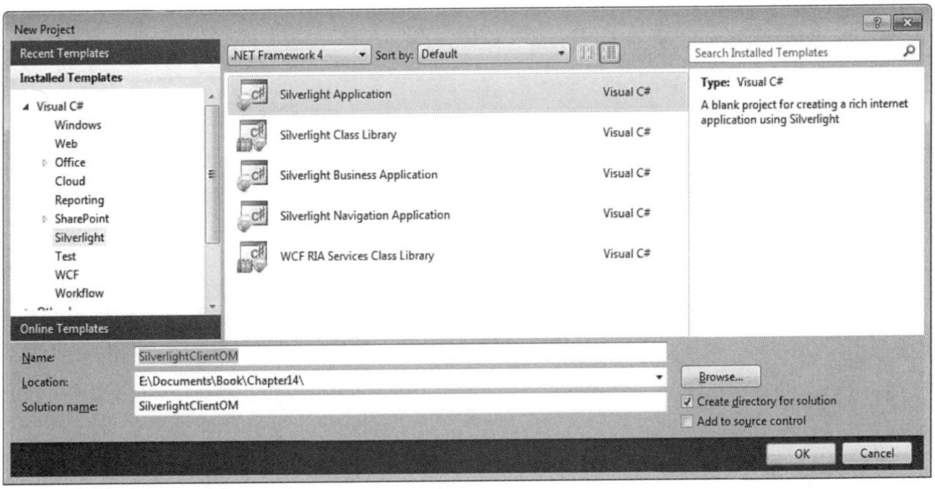

FIGURE 14.9: Creating the Silverlight project for the client OM example

Accept the default Silverlight Application type and click OK, and you are presented with the dialog box shown in Figure 14.10.

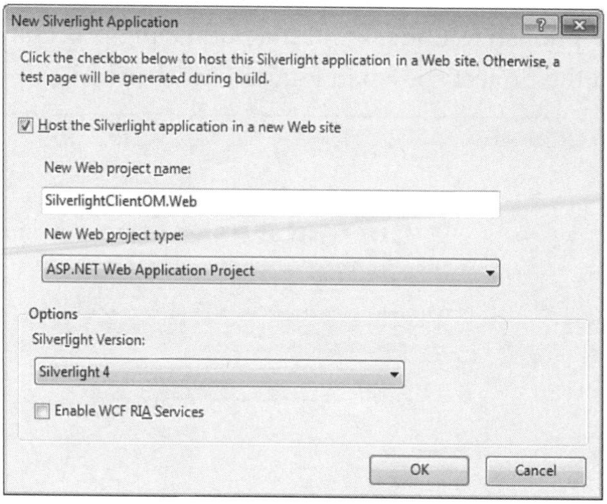

FIGURE 14.10: Selecting the Silverlight project type

Navigate to SharePoint ..\14\TEMPLATE\LAYOUTS\ClientBin and copy Microsoft.SharePoint.Client.Silverlight.dll and Microsoft.Share-Point.Client.Runtime.dll to your local Visual Studio project folder, as shown in Figure 14.11.

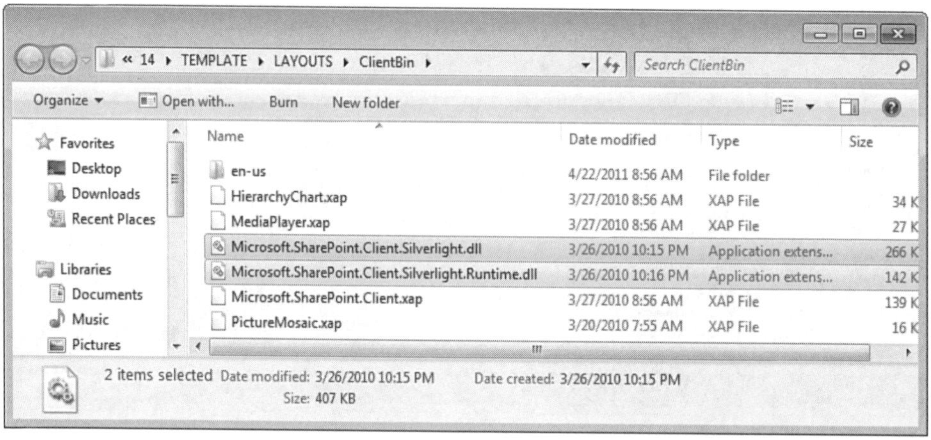

FIGURE 14.11: Copying the Client Object Model .dll files from the ClientBin directory

After pasting, the Visual Studio Project folder now contains the assemblies, as shown in Figure 14.12.

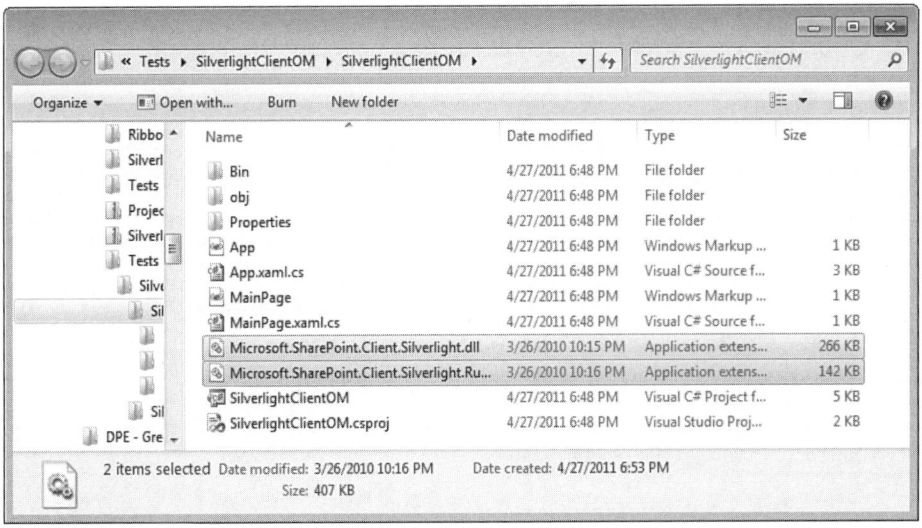

FIGURE 14.12: Copying the Client Object Model .dll files to the local project directory

In Visual Studio Silverlight project, right-click the project and select Add Reference; then add the two assemblies copied into your Silverlight ClientOM project folder as shown in Figure 14.13.

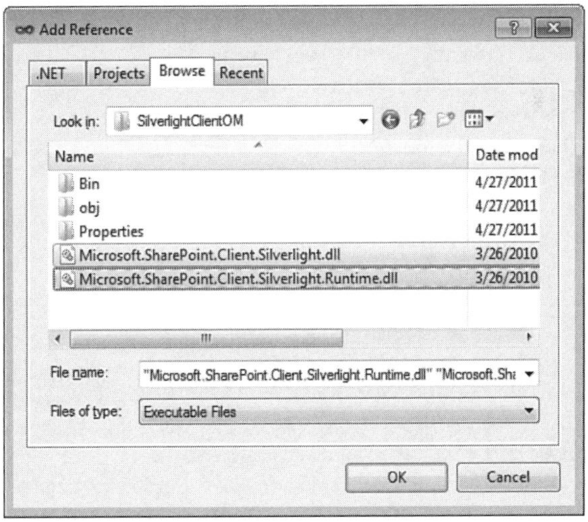

FIGURE 14.13: Adding references to the Client Object Model

Next add a reference to the Silverlight SDK Client Libraries. On the .NET tab in Add Reference locate and select the System.Windows.Controls.Data. Input assembly to add it to the project.

Open the MainPage.xaml.cs file and add a using statement:

```
using Microsoft.SharePoint.Client;
```

At this point, you have the necessary references to construct and deploy a Silverlight CSOM project. Next add code to build a custom UI with Silverlight.

Open the MainPage.xaml file and replace the UserControl XAML with the XAML shown in Listing 14.1. Note the reference to xmlns:sdk allowing the use of the sdk labels in the project.

LISTING 14.1: XAML for Client OM Example

```
<UserControl x:Class="SilverlightClientOM.MainPage"
    xmlns="http://schemas.microsoft.com/winfx/2006/xaml/presentation"
    xmlns:x="http://schemas.microsoft.com/winfx/2006/xaml"
    xmlns:d="http://schemas.microsoft.com/expression/blend/2008"
    xmlns:mc="http://schemas.openxmlformats.org/markup-compatibility/2006"
    mc:Ignorable="d"
    d:DesignHeight="294" d:DesignWidth="434"
xmlns:sdk="http://schemas.microsoft.com/winfx/2006/xaml/presentation/sdk">

<Grid x:Name="LayoutRoot" Background="White" Height="218" Width="401">
        <Border BorderBrush="Silver" BorderThickness="1" Height="217"
          HorizontalAlignment="Left" Name="border1"
          VerticalAlignment="Top" Width="400" />
        <TextBox Height="23" HorizontalAlignment="Left"
          Margin="58,76,0,0" Name="UserText" VerticalAlignment="Top"
          Width="331" />
        <sdk:Label Height="23" HorizontalAlignment="Left"
          Margin="12,76,0,0" Name="label2" VerticalAlignment="Top"
          Width="39" Content="User:" />
        <sdk:Label Height="22" HorizontalAlignment="Left"
          Margin="12,105,0,0" Name="label1" VerticalAlignment="Top"
          Width="39" Content="Email:" />
        <TextBox Height="23" Margin="58,105,11,0" Name="EmailText"
          VerticalAlignment="Top" />
        <ComboBox Height="27" HorizontalAlignment="Left"
          Margin="57,134,0,0" Name="TaskComboBox" VerticalAlignment="Top"
          Width="331" />
        <sdk:Label Height="27" HorizontalAlignment="Left"
          Margin="12,134,0,0" Name="label3" VerticalAlignment="Top"
```

```
         Width="36" Content="Tasks:" />
        <sdk:Label Height="35" HorizontalAlignment="Center"
         Margin="18,6,6,0" Name="label4" VerticalAlignment="Top"
         Width="378" Content="Current Tasks" FontSize="26"
         FontFamily="Verdana" FontStretch="Expanded" FontWeight="Bold" />
        <TextBlock Height="23" HorizontalAlignment="Left"
         Margin="57,194,0,0" Name="ErrorMessage" Text="TextBlock"
         VerticalAlignment="Top" Width="333" />
        <sdk:Label Height="28" HorizontalAlignment="Left"
         Margin="13,47,0,0" Name="label5" VerticalAlignment="Top"
         Width="36" Content="Site:" />
        <TextBox Height="23" HorizontalAlignment="Left"
         Margin="58,47,0,0" Name="UserSite" VerticalAlignment="Top"
         Width="331" />
    </Grid>
</UserControl>
```

Return to the MainPage.xaml.cs file and add `FilterTasksByUser()` method and call it in the MainPage constructor as shown in Listing 14.2.

LISTING 14.2: Button Click Event Handler for Client OM Example

```
public partial class MainPage : UserControl {
        private Site site;
        private Web web;
        private User user;
        private List list;
        private ListItemCollection listItems;
        private ClientContext SPContext;

        public MainPage() {
            InitializeComponent();
            FilterTasksByUser();
        }

        private void FilterTasksByUser() {
            ErrorMessage.Text = string.Empty;
            try {
                //SPContext = new
ClientContext("https://MySPOSite.sharepoint.com");
                SPContext = new ClientContext("http://contoso");

                site = SPContext.Site;
                web = site.RootWeb;
                user = web.CurrentUser;
                list = web.Lists.GetByTitle("Tasks");

                SPContext.Load(site);
```

```
        SPContext.Load(web);
        SPContext.Load(list);
        SPContext.Load(user);

        SPContext.ExecuteQueryAsync(Succeeded, Failed);

    } catch (Exception x) {
        ErrorMessage.Text = x.Message;
    }
}
```

Add the methods shown in Listing 14.3 to capture the asynchronous response.

LISTING 14.3: Client Object Model Response Handlers

```
private void Succeeded(object sender, ClientRequestSucceededEventArgs args) {
        this.Dispatcher.BeginInvoke(delegate()
        {
            ComboBoxItem CItem;

            UserText.Text = user.LoginName.ToString();
            EmailText.Text = user.Email.ToString();
            UserSite.Text = web.Title.ToString();

            if (listItems == null) {

                CamlQuery camlQuery = new CamlQuery();
                string query =
                    (@"<View><Query><Where>
                            <Eq>
                              <FieldRef Name='AssignedTo'/>
                                <Value Type='User'>{0}</Value>
                            </Eq>
                        </Where></Query>
                      <RowLimit>100</RowLimit>
                    </View>");
                camlQuery.ViewXml = string.Format(query, UserText.Text);

                listItems = list.GetItems(camlQuery);
                SPContext.Load(listItems);
                SPContext.ExecuteQueryAsync(Succeeded, Failed);

            } else {
                foreach (var item in listItems) {
                    CItem = new ComboBoxItem();
```

```
                    CItem.Content = Convert.ToString(item["Title"]) + ",
Due Date: " + Convert.ToString(item["DueDate"]);   //avoid null exceptions in
return values.
                    TaskComboBox.Items.Add(CItem);
                }
            }

            ErrorMessage.Text = "Success.";
        }
        );
    }

    public void Failed(object sender, ClientRequestFailedEventArgs args) {
        this.Dispatcher.BeginInvoke(delegate()
        {
            ErrorMessage.Text += "Call Failed.";
        }
        );
    }
}
```

Modify the URL string parameter to reference the SPO site collection URL; likely it's HTTPS protocol. (The purpose of hardcoding the value of the URL in this example is to explicitly demonstrate how the value is used. The value can be parameterized later to dynamically select the correct URL string.)

Right-click the solution and build the application. To deploy to SharePoint Online:

1. Log in to SharePoint Online as Administrator.
2. Navigate to the Site Assets Library.
3. Click Add Item and choose the location of your current Silverlight project.
4. Locate the SilverlightClientOM.xap file located in the BIN\Debug\ folder.
5. Upload the file to SharePoint Online.
6. After uploading, right-click the item link and copy shortcut. (Keep it handy!)

Add a Silverlight Web Part as shown in Figure 14.14:

1. Go to the SharePoint page where you want to web part to be loaded.
2. Click the Page tab and then the Edit button.
3. Click the More Web Parts button to view available web parts.
4. Select the Media and Content category.
5. Select the Silverlight Web Part and click Add.
6. When prompted,
   a. "No Silverlight Application (.xap) is specified [...] open the Tool Pane and Configure."
   b. Open the tool pane and use the .xap Shortcut URL from the Site Assets list item.

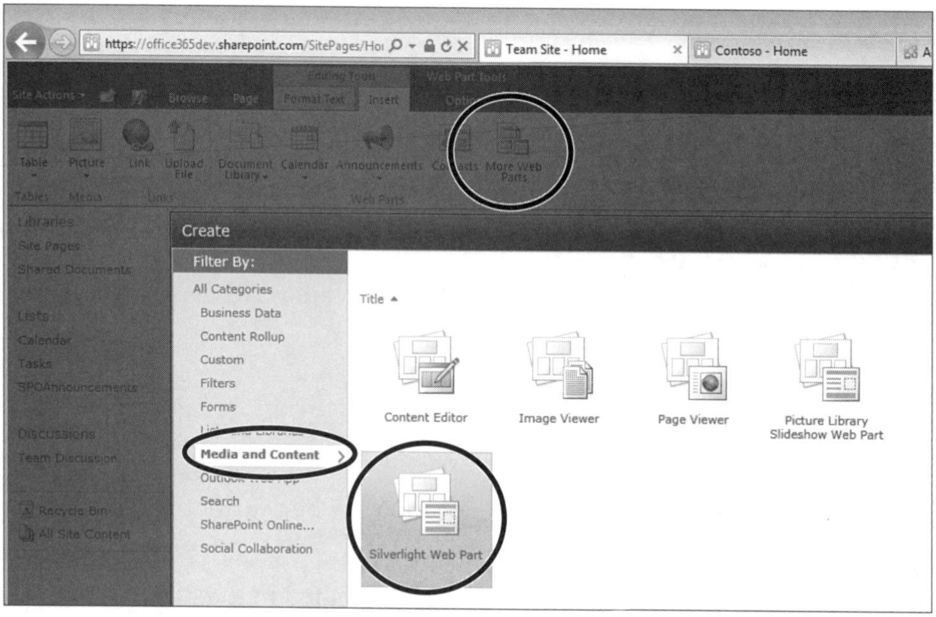

FIGURE 14.14: Adding a Silverlight Web Part

7. Click OK, and the Silverlight application loads.

   a. Optionally, manage the Height, Width, and other properties in Web Part Properties page. If so, select Apply and watch for formatting errors to fix.

8. Click the Save and Close button in the SharePoint Ribbon.

At this point, the project is complete. You can test the project by adding tasks assigned to you. Review the values in the Silverlight Combo Box against the assigned tasks. Try changing the URL value in code and deploy to your local instance of SharePoint. What differences are there?

SharePoint Online Silverlight REST Data Project

In this project, shown in Figure 14.15, you connect to SharePoint Online List REST service to extract data and demonstrate using the REST protocol in SPO.

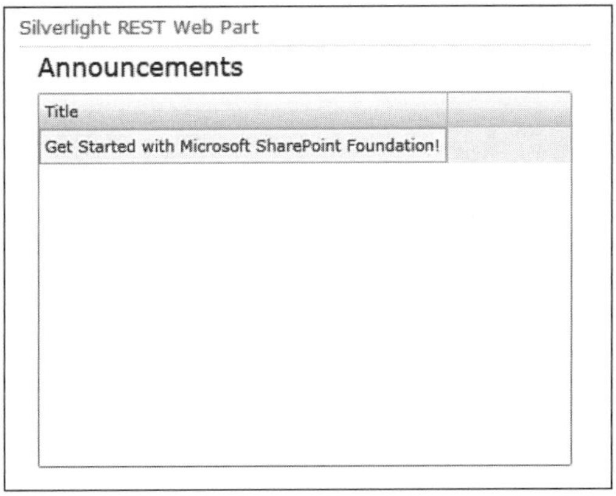

FIGURE 14.15: REST data protocol example

Create a new Silverlight Application, and name it SilverlightREST, as shown in Figure 14.16.

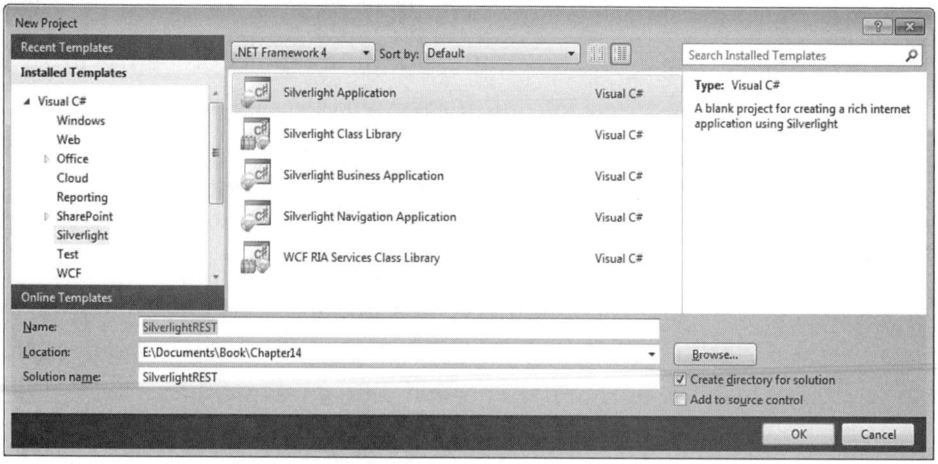

FIGURE 14.16: Adding the SilverlightREST project

Accept the default Silverlight Application type, as shown in Figure 14.17.

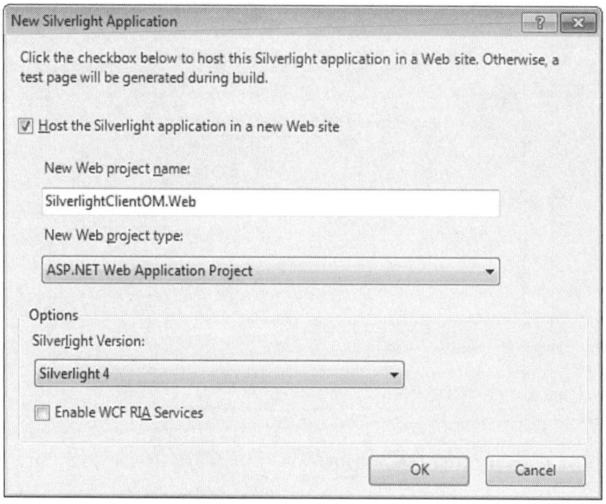

FIGURE 14.17: Selecting the Silverlight project type

Generate a web service proxy to the local SharePoint REST service (*local* is the installation of SharePoint running on your local machine). This is shown in Figure 14.18.

1. Add a reference to the /_vti_bin/listdata.svc.

2. Update the Namespace to ListSvc.

3. Click OK.

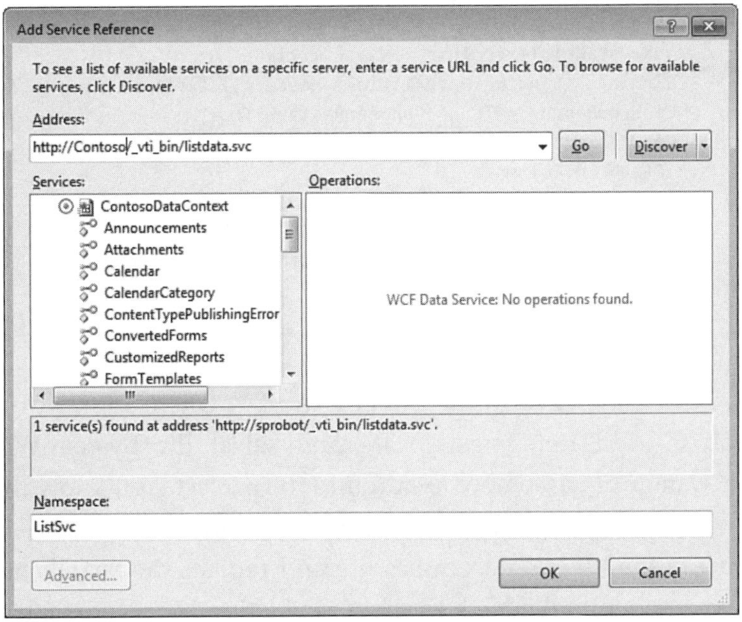

FIGURE 14.18: Adding a service reference to the local REST service

It's important to understand that you use the *local* reference to the list-data.svc service to generate the service proxy; then hardcode the local URI into the service instance to test locally. Finally, when you're ready to publish to SharePoint Online, you modify the URI to your SharePoint Online site collection URI + /_vti_bin/listdata.svc.

Using the hardcoded values is only a strategy to step through the process of understanding the REST service reference. After completing the project, use the Silverlight Context object to dynamically reference the URI (for example: SPContext.Current.Site.Url).

Here, you want to add a `DataGrid` and bind one column to demonstrate pulling that data and presenting in the UI. To accomplish this quickly, open the MainPage.xaml file and replace the Grid control with the XAML shown in Listing 14.4:

LISTING 14.4: XAML for REST Example

```
<Grid x:Name="LayoutRoot" Background="White">
    <sdk:DataGrid AutoGenerateColumns="False" Height="257"
      HorizontalAlignment="Left" Margin="12,31,0,0" Name="dataGrid1"
      VerticalAlignment="Top" Width="376">
        <sdk:DataGrid.Columns>
            <sdk:DataGridTextColumn x:Name="Title"
              Binding="{Binding Path=Title}" Header="Title"
              CanUserReorder="True" CanUserResize="True"
              CanUserSort="True" Width="Auto" />
        </sdk:DataGrid.Columns>
    </sdk:DataGrid>
    <sdk:Label Height="28" HorizontalAlignment="Left" Margin="12,0,0,0"
      Name="label1" VerticalAlignment="Top" Width="181"
      Content="Announcements" FontSize="18" />
</Grid>
```

Next add a reference to the Silverlight SDK Client Libraries. On the
.NET tab in Add Reference, locate and select the System.Windows.
Controls.Data.Input assembly to add it to the project. You know the refer-
ence is needed if the `sdk:DataGrid` does not compile.

Return to the MainPage.xaml.cs file and replace the `MainPage()` constructor method with the method shown in Listing 14.5. Note that, as mentioned, you need to change the URI when publishing to SharePoint Online.

The REST service reference uses the `ListSvc` namespace. If a different
value was used, locate the data context by referring to the site `Name` +
`DataContext`. In the example here, `Contoso` site name plus `DataContext`
equals `ListSvc.ContosoDataContext` as the proper reference.

LISTING 14.5: Methods to Retrieve Data from ListData.svc

```
public MainPage()
{
    InitializeComponent();

    //ListSvc.ContosoDataContext ctx = new ListSvc.ContosoDataContext(new
Uri("https://MySharePointOnlineSite.sharepoint.com/_vti_bin/listdata.svc"));
    ListSvc.ContosoDataContext ctx = new ListSvc.ContosoDataContext(new
Uri("http://contoso/_vti_bin/listdata.svc"));

    // Instantiate the collection
    System.Data.Services.Client.DataServiceCollection
        <ListSvc.AnnouncementsItem> AnnouncementsCollection =
```

```
new DataServiceCollection<ListSvc.AnnouncementsItem>();

// Register a event handler
AnnouncementsCollection.LoadCompleted +=
    new EventHandler<LoadCompletedEventArgs>
    (AnnouncementsCollection_LoadCompleted);

//Query that returns all announcements
DataServiceQuery<ListSvc.AnnouncementsItem> query =
    ctx.Announcements;

// Execute the query.
AnnouncementsCollection.LoadAsync(query);

}
```

Add the method in Listing 14.6 to capture the asynchronous response.

LISTING 14. 6: Method to Handle REST Response

```
private void AnnouncementsCollection_LoadCompleted
                (object sender, LoadCompletedEventArgs e)
{
    // Get the  collection that executed the query.
    var binding = (DataServiceCollection<ListSvc.AnnouncementsItem>)
        sender;
    dataGrid1.ItemsSource = binding;
}
```

Right-click the solution and build the application. When it's working locally, it's time to deploy to SharePoint Online:

1. Log in to SharePoint Online as Administrator.

2. Navigate to the Site Assets list.

3. Click Add Item and choose the location of your current Silverlight project.

4. Locate the SilverlightREST.xap file located in the BIN\Debug\ folder.

5. Upload the file to SharePoint Online.

6. After uploading, right-click the item link and copy shortcut.

Add a SharePoint Silverlight Web Part to host the Silverlight Application:

1. Open the Web Part Tools Pane and add the reference URL to the .xap file.
2. Click OK, and the Silverlight application loads. Optionally, manage the Height, Width, and other properties in the web part's Properties page.
3. Click the Save and Close button on the SharePoint Ribbon.
4. The project is complete.

SharePoint Online Azure Project

In this project you use SQL Azure to access a public OData data source. The data source has anonymous access so you can easily build and test a solution for use in SharePoint Online. You also integrate the application into the SharePoint Ribbon to enhance the UI application cohesiveness between Silverlight and SharePoint Online.

The ability to access resources regardless of the application topology is an important aspect of data availability. Combined with Office365, companies will have ways to provide custom data applications directly into SharePoint Online. In this type of scenario, the Information Worker using Office365 could simply have access to multiple external resources in one location. Examples could be a simple weather service or useful line of business applications such as Shipping and Tracking, Supply Chain Management, Sales Contacts, or Video Training. Developers can combine cloud and on-premise data to create integrated solutions providing access to business functions.

SharePoint Online, SQL Azure, and Silverlight

In this project, you create a sandboxed solution, add a web part embedding the Silverlight Object, and then add an XML element to define Ribbon buttons. The Silverlight Application contains a web service OData reference to

SQL Azure, a Silverlight Grid to display data and a Search interface. The JavaScript on the Ribbon uses the HTML Bridge to call Silverlight methods.

A note about security, as in this example, you specifically use an anonymous connection to SQL Azure to demonstrate data access. In reality, authenticated connections are almost always used. SQL Azure can be opened in conjunction with Azure Web Services and Azure ACS (Access Control Services) or directly with a Live ID session or Secret Key issued by SQL Azure. A review of the security methods for Silverlight access is beyond the scope of this chapter; however, "Security for Windows Azure" guidance can be found at http://msdn.microsoft.com/en-us/library/ff934690.aspx.

To get started, you add a couple of Visual Studio projects to the solution:

1. Create a new Empty SharePoint Project solution named Ribbon Prototype.

2. Accept Sandboxed Solution project type.

3. In RibbonPrototype project, add an assembly reference to System.ServiceModel.dll.

4. Add a web part (do not add a Visual Web Part) called RibbonPart.

5. Add an Empty Element part named GroupRibbonElement.

6. Add a Module named stylelibrary.

7. Add a new Visual Studio Silverlight Project to the RibbonPrototype Solution and name the project SPOSilverlight.

8. Add a Silverlight child window called Activity to the SPOSilverlight project.

9. Add a service reference to the SPOSilverlight project and call the namespace NorthwindCatalog. Add a reference to https://odata.sqlazurelabs.com/OData.svc/v0.1/hqd7p8y6cy/Northwind/ and click OK.

All the components are in place to add code, and the VS Explorer resembles what you see in Figure 14.19:

FIGURE 14.19: Solution Explorer for the Azure project

In the SharePoint RibbonPrototype Project

While you are adding the declarative SharePoint Ribbon markup to the project, take a minute to examine the structure of the Ribbon component being added. Note specifically the `Location` value—it tells SharePoint where the buttons will be visible. Also review the `CommandUIHandler` for `SelectExecuteCommand`; it is the call to the HTML Bridge for JavaScript to call into the Silverlight application methods executing code.

Open the Features folder and right-click on the RibbonPart.Feature to view it in the Feature Designer. Update the Title to "SharePoint Online Ribbon Prototype." Then open GroupRibbonElement\Elements.xml and add the XML shown in Listing 14.7. This code tells SharePoint to display three new buttons in the Ribbon and defines a Javascript command for each of them.

LISTING 14.7: Elements.xml for the GroupRibbonElement Module

```xml
<?xml version="1.0" encoding="utf-8"?>
<Elements xmlns="http://schemas.microsoft.com/sharepoint/">
  <CustomAction
    Id="Ribbon.WikiPageTab.CustomGroup"
    Location="CommandUI.Ribbon">
    <CommandUIExtension>
      <CommandUIDefinitions>
        <CommandUIDefinition
          Location="Ribbon.WikiPageTab.Groups._children">
          <Group
            Id="Ribbon.WikiPageTab.CustomGroup"
            Sequence="55"
            Description="Silverlight Actions"
            Title="Silverlight Actions"
            Command="EnableCustomGroup"
            Template="Ribbon.Templates.Flexible2">
            <Controls Id="Ribbon.WikiPageTab.CustomGroup.Controls">
              <Button
                Id="Ribbon.WikiPageTab.CustomGroup.CustomGroupExecute"
                Command="SelectExecuteCommand"
                Image16by16="/Style Library/stylelibrary/16x16Placeholder.png"
                Image32by32="/Style Library/stylelibrary/32x32SPOArrow.jpg"
                LabelText="Get Data"
                TemplateAlias="o2"
                Sequence="15" />
              <Button
                Id="Ribbon.WikiPageTab.CustomGroup.CustomGroupWindow"
                Command="SelectCommandOpenChildWindow"
                Image16by16="/Style Library/stylelibrary/16x16Placeholder.png"
                Image32by32="/Style Library/stylelibrary/32x32SPOTriangle.jpg"
                LabelText="Search Data"
                TemplateAlias="o2"
                Sequence="18" />
              <Button
                Id="Ribbon.WikiPageTab.CustomGroup.CustomGroupOther"
                Command="OpenDialogCommand"
                Image16by16="/Style Library/stylelibrary/16x16Placeholder.png"
                Image32by32="/Style Library/stylelibrary/32x32SPOSquare.jpg"
```

```
                    LabelText="Open Dialog"
                    TemplateAlias="o2"
                    Sequence="19" />
              </Controls>
           </Group>
        </CommandUIDefinition>
        <CommandUIDefinition
          Location="Ribbon.WikiPageTab.Scaling._children">
           <MaxSize
             Id="Ribbon.WikiPageTab.Scaling.CustomGroup.MaxSize"
             Sequence="15"
             GroupId="Ribbon.WikiPageTab.CustomGroup"
             Size="LargeLarge" />
        </CommandUIDefinition>
      </CommandUIDefinitions>
      <CommandUIHandlers>
        <CommandUIHandler
          Command="EnableCustomGroup"
          CommandAction="javascript:return true;" />
        <CommandUIHandler Command="SelectExecuteCommand"
          CommandAction="javascript:
                             function cmdExecuteCommand()
                             {
                                var mySilverlightObject = document.getElement-
ById('sponline');

                                if (mySilverlightObject != null)
mySilverlightObject.Content.SPOSilverlight.ExecuteCommand();
                             }

                         cmdExecuteCommand();
                           "/>


        <CommandUIHandler Command="SelectCommandOpenChildWindow"
                          CommandAction="javascript:
                             function cmdOpenChildWindow()
                             {
                                var mySilverlightObject = document.getElement-
ById('sponline');

                                if (mySilverlightObject != null)
mySilverlightObject.Content.SPOSilverlight.ActivateChildWindow();
                             }

                         cmdOpenChildWindow();
                           "/>


        <CommandUIHandler Command="OpenDialogCommand"
                          CommandAction="javascript:
                             var dialogOptions = {
```

```
                                    url: 'http://www.microsoft.com/en-
us/office365/online-software.aspx',
                                    title: 'Office365',
                                    allowMaximize: false,
                                    showClose: true,
                                    width:700,
                                    height:600
                                };
                                SP.UI.ModalDialog.showModalDialog(dialogOptions);
    " />

        <CommandUIHandler Command="SelectCommandServerPostback"
                          CommandAction="javascript: alert('My Postback');
__doPostBack('RibbonizedWebPartPostback','My Postback');" />


        <CommandUIHandler Command="MakeAlert"
                          CommandAction="javascript: alert('Hello World');" />
      </CommandUIHandlers>
    </CommandUIExtension>
  </CustomAction>
</Elements>
```

Now open the RibbonPart\Elements.xml file and modify the Group
property value to SharePoint Online Ribbon Silverlight Web Part. Then
open the RibbonPart\RibbonPart.webpart file and change its Title property to SPO Ribbon Part. Finally, open RibbonPart\RibbonPart.cs and
replace all the code and using statements with the code in Listing 14.8.

Note that the code writes out the Silverlight control in a literal control.
There are other ways to do this in SharePoint, but this is an example where
you can also change the .xap file reference in code.

It's important to explicitly label the embedded object ID sponline. The
out-of-the-box SharePoint Web Part gives the Silverlight application a random ID, and you can't hook the HTML Bridge Javascript calls. This is a key
component to wiring up the SharePoint Javascript to Silverlight.

LISTING 14.8: Web Part Code in RibbonPart.cs

```
using System;
using System.ComponentModel;
using System.Web;
using System.Web.UI;
using System.Web.UI.WebControls;
```

```csharp
using System.Web.UI.WebControls.WebParts;
using Microsoft.SharePoint;
using Microsoft.SharePoint.WebControls;
using System.Collections.Generic;
using System.Linq;
using System.Web.UI.HtmlControls;
using System.Xml.Linq;
using System.ServiceModel;

namespace RibbonPrototype.RibbonPart {
    [ToolboxItemAttribute(false)]
    public class RibbonPart : WebPart {
        // Constants
        private string POSTBACK_EVENT = "RibbonizedWebPartPostback";

        protected override void CreateChildControls() {
            // Handle postback from ribbon or dialogs.
            HandleRibbonPostback();

            //Add Controls
            Literal ctrl = new Literal();
            string outString =
                "<div id=\"MySilverlightControlHost\" >" + "\n" +
                "<object id=\"sponline\" data=\"data:application/x-silverlight-
2,\" type=\"application/x-silverlight-2\" width=\"100%\" height=\"100%\">" +
"\n" +
                "<param name=\"source\" value=\"" + SPContext.Current.Site.Url +
"/SiteAssets/SPOSilverlight.xap\"/>" + "\n" +
                "<param name=\"onError\" value=\"onSilverlightError\" />" +
"\n" +
                "<param name=\"background\" value=\"white\" />" + "\n" +
                "<param name=\"minRuntimeVersion\" value=\"4.0.50826.0\" />" +
"\n" +
                "<param name=\"autoUpgrade\" value=\"true\" />" + "\n" +
                "<a
href=\"http://go.microsoft.com/fwlink/?LinkID=149156&v=4.0.50826.0\"
style=\"text-decoration:none\">" + "\n" +
                "<img src=\"http://go.microsoft.com/fwlink/?LinkId=161376\"
alt=\"Get Microsoft Silverlight\" style=\"border-style:none\"/></a>" + "\n" +
                "</object></div>";

            ctrl.Text = outString;
            this.Controls.Add(ctrl);
        }

        private void HandleRibbonPostback() {
            if (this.Page.Request["__EVENTTARGET"] == POSTBACK_EVENT) {
                string passedArgument =
                    this.Page.Request.Params.Get("__EVENTARGUMENT");
```

```
                //Each Ribbon event can be parsed and executed.
                if (passedArgument == "value") {
                    // do something interesting
                }
            }
        }
    }

    protected override void OnPreRender(EventArgs e) {
        LoadAndActivateRibbonContextualTab();
        base.OnPreRender(e);
    }

    private void LoadAndActivateRibbonContextualTab() {

    }
  }
}
```

Now open the StyleLibrary\Elements.xml and add the XML in Listing
14.9. This is how you get the project images packaged for use in SharePoint
Online. It is good to review the declarative markup and then after package
deployment find them using a web browser to confirm the URL and location. The project functions without button images, but you can copy or create new images as needed. Learning the URL paths and XML properties for
the StyleLibrary is important; however, images might also be copied into
the Visual Studio project, and the XML updates as needed.

LISTING 14.9: Code to Deploy Images to SharePoint Online

```
<?xml version="1.0" encoding="utf-8"?>
<Elements xmlns="http://schemas.microsoft.com/sharepoint/">
  <Module Name="stylelibrary" Url="Style Library"
xmlns="http://schemas.microsoft.com/sharepoint/">
    <File Path="stylelibrary\32x32SPOSquare.jpg"
Url="stylelibrary/32x32SPOSquare.jpg"  Type="GhostableInLibrary" />
    <File Path="stylelibrary\32x32SPOArrow.jpg"
Url="stylelibrary/32x32SPOArrow.jpg"  Type="GhostableInLibrary" />
    <File Path="stylelibrary\32x32SPO.jpg"
Url="stylelibrary/32x32SPO.jpg"  Type="GhostableInLibrary" />
    <File Path="stylelibrary\32x32Placeholder.png"
Url="stylelibrary/32x32Placeholder.png"  Type="GhostableInLibrary" />
    <File Path="stylelibrary\16x16SPO.jpg"
Url="stylelibrary/16x16SPO.jpg"  Type="GhostableInLibrary" />
    <File Path="stylelibrary\32x32SPOTriangle.jpg"
Url="stylelibrary/32x32SPOTriangle.jpg"  Type="GhostableInLibrary" />
```

```
    <File Path="stylelibrary\16x16Placeholder.png"
Url="stylelibrary/16x16Placeholder.png"  Type="GhostableInLibrary" />
  </Module>
</Elements>
```

Open the SPOSilverlight Silverlight Project.

Add references to the Silverlight WCF RIA Service SDK and Silverlight Client SDK. You might notice if you're pasting the code into a new project that not all the references resolve because the SDKs are not added. Managing the SDK references can be complex, so be sure to compare the completed Visual Studio project RibbonPrototype to match the references.

Create the search window as a Silverlight child window named Activity.xaml. Open the SPOSilverlight\Activity.xaml file and replace the XAML with the markup shown in Listing 14.10.

LISTING 14.10: XAML Markup for Search ChildWindow

```
<controls:ChildWindow x:Class="SPOSilverlight.Activity"
xmlns="http://schemas.microsoft.com/winfx/2006/xaml/presentation"
           xmlns:x="http://schemas.microsoft.com/winfx/2006/xaml"
           xmlns:controls="clr-namespace:System.Windows.Controls;
assembly=System.Windows.Controls"
           Width="417" Height="65"
           Title="Activity">
    <Grid x:Name="LayoutRoot" Margin="2">
        <Grid.RowDefinitions>
            <RowDefinition />
            <RowDefinition Height="Auto" />
        </Grid.RowDefinitions>

        <Button x:Name="CancelButton" Content="Cancel"
         Click="CancelButton_Click" Width="75" Height="23"
         HorizontalAlignment="Right" Margin="0,-1,0,4" />
        <Button x:Name="OKButton" Content="OK" Click="OKButton_Click"
         Width="75" Height="23" HorizontalAlignment="Right"
         Margin="0,-1,80,4" />
        <TextBox Height="23" HorizontalAlignment="Left" Name="textBox1"
         VerticalAlignment="Top" Width="234" Grid.RowSpan="2" />
    </Grid>
</controls:ChildWindow>
```

Open SPOSilverlight\Activity.xaml.cs file and make sure the functions shown in Listing 14.11 are present:

LISTING 14.11: Button Click Events for Child Window

```
private void OKButton_Click(object sender, RoutedEventArgs e)
{
    this.DialogResult = true;
}

private void CancelButton_Click(object sender, RoutedEventArgs e)
{
    this.DialogResult = false;
}
```

Open the MainPage.xaml file and replace the all the XAML with the markup shown in Listing 14.12.

LISTING 14.12: XAML Markup for MainPage User Control

```
<UserControl x:Class="SPOSilverlight.MainPage"
   xmlns="http://schemas.microsoft.com/winfx/2006/xaml/presentation"
    xmlns:x="http://schemas.microsoft.com/winfx/2006/xaml"
    xmlns:d="http://schemas.microsoft.com/expression/blend/2008"
    xmlns:mc="http://schemas.openxmlformats.org/markup-compatibility/2006"
    mc:Ignorable="d"
    d:DesignHeight="300" d:DesignWidth="400"
xmlns:sdk="http://schemas.microsoft.com/winfx/2006/xaml/presentation/sdk">

    <Grid x:Name="LayoutRoot" Background="#FF2A34B7">
        <sdk:DataGrid AutoGenerateColumns="False" Height="225"
         HorizontalAlignment="Left" Margin="12,36,0,0" Name="dataGrid1"
         VerticalAlignment="Top" Width="376">
        <sdk:DataGrid.Columns>
            <sdk:DataGridTextColumn x:Name="ContactName"
             Binding="{Binding Path=ContactName}" Header="Name"
             CanUserReorder="True" CanUserResize="True"
             CanUserSort="True" Width="Auto" />
            <sdk:DataGridTextColumn x:Name="CompanyName"
             Binding="{Binding Path=CompanyName}" Header="CompanyName"
             CanUserResize="True" CanUserSort="True" Width="Auto" />
            <sdk:DataGridTextColumn x:Name="Address"
             Binding="{Binding Path=Address}" Header="Address"
             CanUserReorder="True" CanUserResize="True"
             CanUserSort="True" Width="Auto" />
        </sdk:DataGrid.Columns>
        </sdk:DataGrid>
```

```
        <Button Content="Search" Height="20" HorizontalAlignment="Left"
         Margin="313,268,0,0" Name="button1" VerticalAlignment="Top"
         Width="75" Click="button1_Click" />
        <sdk:Label Height="28" HorizontalAlignment="Left"
         Margin="12,0,0,0" Name="label1" VerticalAlignment="Top"
         Width="314" Foreground="White" FontSize="26"
         Content="Cloud Data Connection" />
        <Button Content="Get Data" Height="20" HorizontalAlignment="Left"
         Margin="232,268,0,0" Name="button2" VerticalAlignment="Top"
         Width="75" Click="button2_Click" />
    </Grid>
</UserControl>
```

In the code that follows, a generic query statement from the Customers Context is used to demonstrate accessing the customer collection. It is important to know the `customerBindingCollection.LoadAsync(query)` method takes a `DataServiceQuery` type. Here is how the example queries the data:

```
DataServiceQuery<NorthwindCatalog.Customer> query = ctx.Customers;
```

To upgrade the query to use LINQ in future projects, explicitly cast the LINQ query as `DataServiceQuery`. This is shown in Listing 14.13.

LISTING 14.13: Casting the LINQ Query to DataServiceQuery

```
System.Data.Services.Client.DataServiceQuery
    <NorthwindCatalog.Customer> query;
query = (DataServiceQuery<NorthwindCatalog.Customer>)
        from customers in ctx.Customers
        where  customers.ContactName.Contains("value")
        select customers;
```

In this code, you also add the Search method to highlight the found item. The implementation accesses the `DataGrid` item collection as shown in Listing 14.14.

LISTING 14.14: Retrieving the Customer Collection

```
//Cast the Collection so we can enumerate it
DataServiceCollection<NorthwindCatalog.Customer> Customers =
(DataServiceCollection<NorthwindCatalog.Customer>)dataGrid1.ItemsSource;
```

Build the select statement to query the Customers collection to return items meeting the search criteria. Then the item is simply added to the SelectedItems collection to highlight, as shown in Listing 14.15.

LISTING 14.15: Code to Highlight the Customers the User Searched For

```
//Query the Collection
var query = from c in Customers
            where c.ContactName.Contains(sw.textBox1.Text)
            select c;
//Add Selected Items
foreach (var item in query)
{
    dataGrid1.SelectedItems.Add(item);
}
```

Return to the MainPage.xaml.cs file and replace all the code with the code in Listing 14.16. Note the use of the [ScriptableType] attribute to mark the MainPage class as visible to Javascript, and the [Scriptable MemberAttribute] to allow the methods to be seen in script. The call RegisterScriptableObject completes the process, making the Silverlight class accessible from Javascript.

LISTING 14.16: MainPage to Display Data from SQL Azure

```
using System;
using System.Collections.Generic;
using System.Linq;
using System.Net;
using System.Windows;
using System.Windows.Controls;
using System.Windows.Documents;
using System.Windows.Input;
using System.Windows.Media;
using System.Windows.Media.Animation;
using System.Windows.Shapes;
using System.Data.Services.Client;
using System.ComponentModel;

namespace SPOSilverlight
{
    [System.Windows.Browser.ScriptableType()]
    public partial class MainPage : UserControl
    {
        private NorthwindCatalog.Northwind ctx;
```

```
    public MainPage()
    {
        InitializeComponent();
        System.Windows.Browser.HtmlPage.RegisterScriptableObject
            ("SPOSilverlight", this);
        button1.IsEnabled = false;
    }

    [System.Windows.Browser.ScriptableMember()]
    public void ExecuteCommand()
    {
        // Instantiate the context based on the data service URI.
        ctx = new NorthwindCatalog.Northwind(new
Uri(https://odata.sqlazurelabs.com/OData.svc/v0.1/hqd7p8y6cy/Northwind/
        ));

        // Instantiate the binding collection.
        System.Data.Services.Client.DataServiceCollection
          <NorthwindCatalog.Customer>
          customerBindingCollection = new
          DataServiceCollection<NorthwindCatalog.Customer>();

        // Register a handler for the LoadCompleted event.
        customerBindingCollection.LoadCompleted += new
          EventHandler<LoadCompletedEventArgs>
          (customerBindingCollection_LoadCompleted);

        // Define a query that returns all customers.
        DataServiceQuery<NorthwindCatalog.Customer> query =
          ctx.Customers;

        // Execute the query.
        customerBindingCollection.LoadAsync(query);
    }

    [System.Windows.Browser.ScriptableMember()]
    public void ActivateChildWindow()
    {
        Activity myWindow = new Activity();
        myWindow.Title = "Search";
        myWindow.Closed += new EventHandler(myWindow_Closed);
        myWindow.Show();
    }

    void myWindow_Closed(object sender, EventArgs e)
    {
        Activity sw = (Activity)sender;
```

```csharp
    if (sw.DialogResult == true &&
        sw.textBox1.Text != string.Empty)
    {
        dataGrid1.SelectedItems.Clear();

        //Cast the Collection so we can enumerate it
        DataServiceCollection<NorthwindCatalog.Customer>
          Customers =
          (DataServiceCollection<NorthwindCatalog.Customer>)
          dataGrid1.ItemsSource;

        //Query the Collection
        var query = from c in Customers
                    where c.ContactName.Contains(sw.textBox1.Text)
                    select c;

        //Add Selected Items
        foreach (var item in query)
        {
            dataGrid1.SelectedItems.Add(item);
        }
    }
    else if (sw.DialogResult == false)
    {
        //MessageBox.Show("Cancelled");
    }
}

private void customerBindingCollection_LoadCompleted
    (object sender, LoadCompletedEventArgs e)
{
    // Get the binding collection that executed the query.

    var binding =
      (DataServiceCollection<NorthwindCatalog.Customer>) sender;

    if (e.Error == null)
    {
        // Consume a data feed that contains paged results.
        if (binding.Continuation != null)
        {
            // If there is a continuation token,
            // load the next page of results.
            binding.LoadNextPartialSetAsync();
        }
        else
        {
            // Since there are no remaining results pages,
            // bind the collection to the view source.
```

```
                    // in propeties bind to ElementName, DataContext
                    dataGrid1.ItemsSource = binding;
                    button1.IsEnabled = true;
                }
            }
            else
            {
                // Display the error returned by the data service.
                MessageBox.Show(string.Format
                    ("An error has occured: {0}", e.Error.Message));
            }
        }

        private void button1_Click(object sender, RoutedEventArgs e)
        {
            ActivateChildWindow();
        }

        private void button2_Click(object sender, RoutedEventArgs e)
        {
            ExecuteCommand();
        }
    }
}
```

Right-click the solution and Build All and then right-click the SharePoint project and select Package. Deploy the solution to SharePoint Online as follows:

1. Log in to SharePoint Online as Administrator.
2. Navigate to the Site Assets list. This location is referenced in the SharePoint Web Part file. If uploading to another list, modify the source location in the Silverlight embedded object.
3. Click Add Item and choose the location of your current Silverlight project.
4. Locate the SPOSilverlight.xap file located in the BIN\Debug\ folder.
5. Upload the file to SharePoint Online
6. After uploading, right-click the item link and copy shortcut.

Add a sandboxed web part to SharePoint Online:

1. Go to Site Actions Menu and click Site Settings.
2. Click the Solutions Link under Galleries.
3. Click Solutions Tab.
4. Click Update Solution.
5. Locate the RibbonPrototype.wsp file and upload, as shown in Figure 14.20.
6. Activate the solution (click the Activate button).

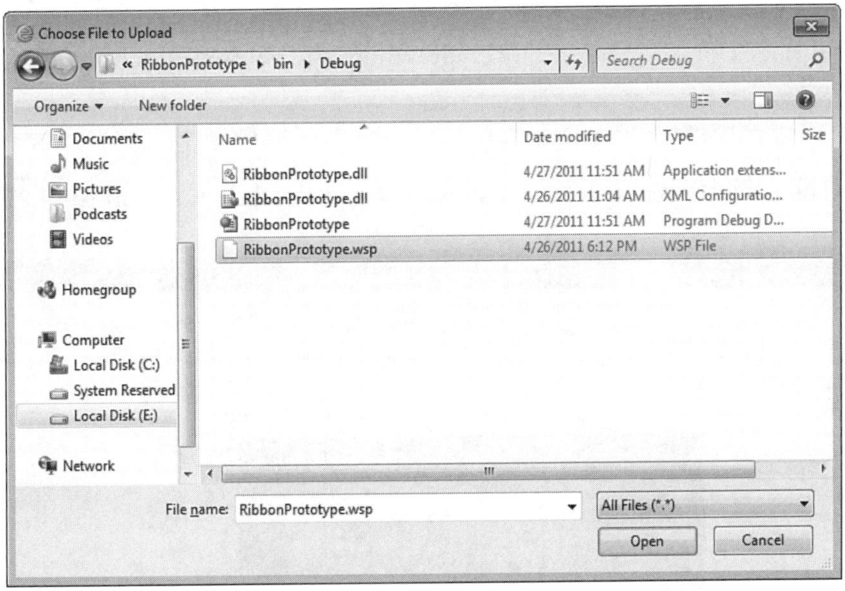

FIGURE 14.20: Uploading the .wsp file to the SPO Solutions Gallery

7. Return to the SharePoint page where you want to add the web part.
8. Click the Page tab and then the Edit button.
9. Click the Insert tab.
10. Click the More Web Parts button to view available web parts.
11. Select the SharePoint Online Ribbon Silverlight Web Part category.
12. Add the SPO Ribbon Part.

13. Save and close the SharePoint page.

14. The Silverlight application loads. Optionally, manage the Height, Width, and other properties in the Web Part Properties page. After completing the project, the scrollbars might be modified with the Silverlight embedded object properties in code.

15. Test the Ribbon button to call the Silverlight methods

> ■ **NOTE**
>
> The Ribbon functions are deployed to the root site collection, and the SPO Ribbon Part, which contains the Silverlight Application, should be placed on the SharePoint page where the Ribbon functionality is present.

16. The project is complete and should appear as shown in Figure 14.21.

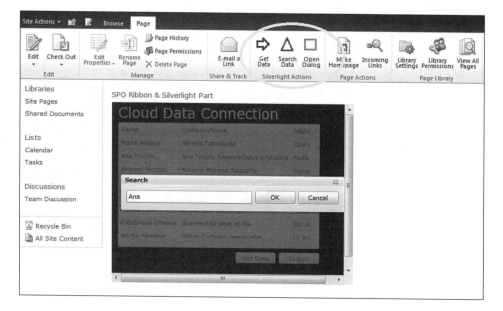

FIGURE 14.21: Completed Azure project

Authentication in Managed Client Object Models

For most SharePoint Online Silverlight projects, the application runs in the context of the current user, and by default the Silverlight Client Object Models authenticate users by using their SharePoint Online credentials.

Related Authentication Topics

A topic of interest would be how to authenticate and get data from Share-Point Online (SPO) in a client application, perhaps a Silverlight Out-of-Browser or Windows application. With an Interactive User solution, developers might pop up a browser in a dialog window where the user could enter their Office365 credentials, and the developer attaches the authentication cookies Office365 issued to the SharePoint Client Side Object Model to query your SPO site. Microsoft has published a whitepaper on how to accomplish this task (http://msdn.microsoft.com/en-us/library/hh147177.aspx) and provided sample code (http://code.msdn.microsoft.com/Remote-Authentication-in-b7b6f43c).

This solution works well, but it's not a good solution if your client code is a service or another application where a user isn't present. To deal with this scenario the code needs to effectively log in on the user's behalf. To do this the developer queries the Office365 Secure Token Service (STS) directly using Windows Identity Foundation (WIF) and a user's credentials. WIF helps with managing the security tokens and requests to the STS.

■ TIP

To do this you need to have the WIF runtime installed and, in brief, you need to:

- Use WIF to log in with the Office365 STS
- Extract the Authentication Cookies from the response
- Construct a CookieContainer with those cookies
- Attach the CookieContainer to the Client Object Model web request
- Call the SPO site and return information from the site

External Authentication

Accessing remote resources in Azure or On-Premise via a web service might also require authentication, and using the context of the current user does not work. Authentication can be accomplished with an Office365 Federated User in SharePoint Online. However, in many cases, Office365 Federation is unavailable to many users, and there are a couple of alternate solutions. For example, within the Silverlight application, a dialog can be presented asking for user credentials for remote service access on application initialization. This solution might not be as seamless as sometimes expected from applications, but it does promote a direct request for credentials that the user must enter to gain access. Another solution, returning to the first example in this chapter, might involve accessing the user login name paired with email address as well as evaluating the HTTP Header Referrer values, then sending the values to the web service for evaluation before granting access. In a variation of these two solutions, the customer might also be given a secret key—often a GUID—and asked to put the key in a known SPO list location after securely logging into the site. The Silverlight application could then present the key to a remote service during the service call to gain access. Many customers opt for granting access based on other requirements—for example, ease of access (a weather service may provide anonymous access to data). In all scenarios, if the data requires a highly secure environment, then perhaps sharing it via public web service, regardless of authentication, is not a viable solution for the specific implementation. Whichever solution is ultimately selected, Office365 Federation is often selected as default authentication, but there are options and choices that depend on the authentication requirements.

Summary

Cloud computing is becoming increasingly popular as customers seek to lower the cost and effort of deploying complex software solutions on premises. SharePoint Online, a part of the Microsoft Office365 suite, is such a solution and provides a good amount of SharePoint capabilities in the cloud. Silverlight is a natural way to add custom web parts and other extensions to SharePoint Online because it runs in the client, outside of the restricted cloud environment.

15.

Creating a Silverlight Field Control

SHAREPOINT PROVIDES quite a number of *field types* for use throughout the product to define the data representation in every column of every list in SharePoint. These begin with the basics, such as text, numbers, and dates and get more advanced, including field types for rich, multiline text, as well as person, choice, and lookup fields. If you want to see the fields available on a SharePoint site, go to Site Settings and, under Galleries, view the Site Columns Gallery; all of these fields are based on out-of-the-box field types.

In this chapter, you learn to add your own field types in SharePoint. Each field knows how to store its data in SharePoint's content system and how to render itself for viewing or editing. Naturally, this viewing and editing will use Silverlight. Figure 15.1 shows the finished field being edited in a SharePoint publishing site. The field remembers all the map settings and respects them when the page is viewed.

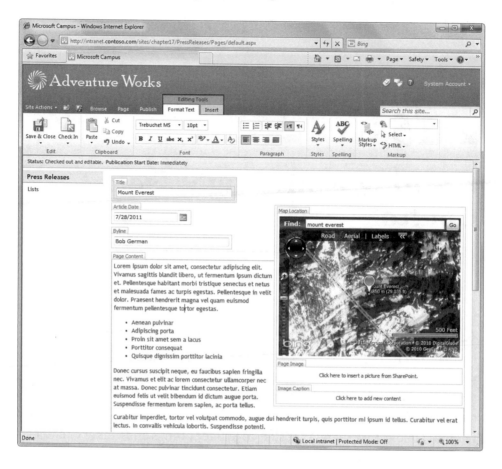

FIGURE 15.1: A Map field control on a SharePoint publishing page

The programming example in this chapter adds a location field type, which uses Bing Maps to display and edit the location. When installed, any list in SharePoint can be geo-coded and mapped by simply adding a location column. In addition, you learn to add a site column using the new field type and to add that column to a *page layout* for use in SharePoint publishing sites. This allows for web pages in which the map is edited as a field on the page, rather than as a web part. Along the way, you learn a bit about SharePoint's web publishing system.

You can notice some parallels between this chapter and Chapter 7, "Accessing SharePoint Using the HTML Bridge," because both use the HTML Bridge to communicate between SharePoint and Silverlight in a hidden input field. In this case, the location information is serialized and placed in the field as a simple string, which can be readily accessed by Silverlight as well as the page logic. In this case, using the HTML Bridge is important since you really want to post back the location along with the other fields on the page or dialog box, where they are saved or abandoned depending on whether the user presses the Save button or does some other post-back on the page. Directly saving the data via the Client Object Model would save the data prematurely and ignore the user's wishes to back out the change if she presses the Cancel button.

It might be easier to follow this chapter if you download the code sample and follow along in a working project. The code sample includes a SharePoint project called Chapter15.sln and a pair of Silverlight applications, MapViewSL and MapEditSL, for viewing and editing the maps. In the SharePoint project, a module called ClientBin uses project output references to deploy the two .xap files.

To make the project work, you need to download and install the Bing Maps Silverlight Control and to obtain a Bing Maps application ID. For information on downloading the control, see http://bit.ly/SPSL_BingMapsSLControl; to obtain an application ID, see http://bit.ly/SPSL_BingMapsAppId. In addition, be aware that because the solution includes SharePoint publishing page layout, it requires SharePoint Server 2010 Standard or Enterprise Edition (not SharePoint Foundation 2010); however, if you pare back the solution, the field type itself can be used in SharePoint Foundation 2010 to geo-code general list and library content.

Defining the Bing Maps Field Type

Although the SharePoint user interface can be used to create new *fields*, or site columns as they're called in the UI, creating a new field type is a developer task. This requires a SharePoint farm solution, given the field needs to be defined in an XML file that lives on the file system of every SharePoint server, and this is forbidden in a sandboxed solution. At a minimum, this includes a new field class, derived from one of the built-in SharePoint field types and an XML file that declares the field in SharePoint.

There is no Visual Studio project template or item for a field type; if you were starting from scratch, you'd need to create it yourself. The approach is to begin with an empty SharePoint project, create a class file, and derive it from one of the out-of-the-box field types. In this case, the field in Map-Field.Field.cs is derived from `SPFieldText`, which is already defined in SharePoint as a text field. The new class stores its content in a SharePoint text field, and you serialize the location information into that text field using the `DataContractJsonSerializer`, just as in Chapter 7. This makes it easy to store and pass around simple strings, and it can be used both on the SharePoint server and in Silverlight.

Listing 15.1 shows the code for the new field type, which is included in the code download under the MapLocationFieldType folder in a file called MapField.Field.cs.

LISTING 15.1: SharePoint Field Type Class

```
public class MapFieldControlField : SPFieldText
{
    public MapFieldControlField(SPFieldCollection fields,
            string fieldName) : base(fields, fieldName)
    {
    }

    public MapFieldControlField(SPFieldCollection fields,
            string typeName, string displayName)
            : base(fields, typeName, displayName)
    {
    }

    public override BaseFieldControl FieldRenderingControl
    {
        // Override the control for rendering this SPField
        [SharePointPermission(SecurityAction.LinkDemand,
         ObjectModel = true)]
        get
        {
            BaseFieldControl fieldControl = new MapFieldControl();
            fieldControl.FieldName = this.InternalName;
            return fieldControl;
        }
    }
}
```

There's not much here, really; the only thing the derived class does is to override the SPTextField's `FieldRenderingControl` property, which tells SharePoint which web control to use when rendering the field. That's where all the magic happens to turn a text field into a location field.

When the solution is deployed, SharePoint installs this class on every server in the SharePoint farm. The next step is to add an .xml file that will tell SharePoint about the new field type and refer it to the `MapField ControlField` class. To do this, add a SharePoint mapped folder to your project and navigate to TEMPLATE\XML as the folder to map to. Anything placed in this folder in your Visual Studio project is deployed to the TEMPLATE\XML folder on every SharePoint server, under the SharePoint root in the file system.

To tell SharePoint about our field, the .xml file must be named following the pattern fldtypes*.xml; in the code download, the file is called fldtypes_MapFieldControl.xml. SharePoint reads this file to learn about the new field type and class. The declaration for the Bing Maps field type is shown in Listing 15.2.

LISTING 15.2: XML Declaration of a Field Type

```
<?xml version="1.0" encoding="utf-8"?>
<FieldTypes>
  <FieldType>
    <Field Name="TypeName">MapViewField</Field>
    <Field Name="TypeDisplayName">Map View</Field>
    <Field Name="TypeShortDescription">Bing Maps location</Field>
    <Field Name="ParentType">Text</Field>
    <Field Name="UserCreatable">TRUE</Field>
    <Field Name="FieldTypeClass">Chapter17.MapFieldControlField,
$SharePoint.Project.AssemblyFullName$</Field>
  </FieldType>
</FieldTypes>
```

The contents of this file are pretty self-explanatory. The new field type is given internal and display names as well as a description and reference to the parent field type. The `Field` attribute named `FieldTypeClass` contains the class and full assembly name, which Visual Studio conveniently fills in for you in place of the `$SharePoint.Project.AssemblyFullName$` token.

The solution won't compile yet, of course, because we haven't created the `MapFieldControl` class that we used in the `FieldType`. This is covered in the next section.

Building a Silverlight Field Control

A SharePoint Field Control is similar to a conventional web part or web control, except that it has more than one *mode*, so it can present a different user interface depending on whether it's in Display, Edit, New, or Invalid mode. This allows one control to present the field in display, edit, and new dialog boxes and pages throughout SharePoint.

A field control must be derived from SharePoint's `BaseFieldControl` class and must implement a `Value` property that allows access to the field's value. Listing 15.3 shows the somewhat elaborate `Value` property implementation for the field control. Notice that the property is aware of the control's mode, and when it's in an Edit mode, stores the value directly as a web control (`MapSelectControl`) to get or set the value directly from Silverlight in a hidden input control. It also reads and updates SharePoint's stored version of the field value, which is stored in the `base.ItemField-Value` property.

LISTING 15.3: Field Control Value Property

```
// We always have a MapSelectControl in the wings to hold the
// current selection
private MapSelectControl mapEditControl = new MapSelectControl();

public override object Value
{
    get
    {
        if (ControlMode == SPControlMode.New ||
            ControlMode == SPControlMode.Edit)
        {
            // If we are editing a new or existing item,
            // then the control's value is in the editing
            // control
            if (mapEditControl != null &&
                mapEditControl.SerializedMapLocation != null)
            {
                return mapEditControl.SerializedMapLocation;
```

```
                }
                else
                {
                    return String.Empty;
                }
            }
            else
            {
                // If we are viewing the item, then the control's
                // value is the field value from SharePoint
                if (base.ItemFieldValue != null)
                {
                    return base.ItemFieldValue;
                }
                else
                {
                    return String.Empty;
                }
            }
        }
        set
        {
            // Set the value in SharePoint and in the map editing control
            base.ItemFieldValue = value;
            if (value != null)
            {
                mapEditControl.SerializedMapLocation = value.ToString();
            }
            else
            {
                mapEditControl.SerializedMapLocation = String.Empty;
            }
        }
    }
}
```

Field controls are still ASP.NET controls and still have a CreateChild
Controls() method you can use to create child controls that render the user
interface. Listing 15.4 shows CreateChildControls() for the location field
control.

LISTING 15.4: CreateChildControls()

```
private bool errorSet = false;
private string errorMessage = "";

protected override void CreateChildControls()
{
```

```
    base.CreateChildControls();

    try
    {
        if (this.ControlMode == SPControlMode.Display)
        {
            CreateDisplayModeChildControls();
        }
        else
        {
            CreateEditModeChildControls();
        }
    }
    catch (Exception ex)
    {
        errorSet = true;
        errorMessage = ex.Message;
    }
}
```

As you can see, it's not doing much yet; it simply calls other methods depending on the display mode and sets up a bit of exception handling.

Listing 15.5 shows the display mode controls creation and an override of the display mode render method. Notice that now you're dealing with another kind of display mode: the design mode. Design mode is derived from the great-grandparent of all controls, the Control object, and is a boolean that tells you if the control is on a design surface (such as Share-Point Designer) or not. If it is, you won't try to render the Silverlight control but will stick to a simple gray box. This shows up when you add the field to a page layout in SharePoint Designer.

Also notice that you're passing all the information needed to render a map down to Silverlight. You dig into how the location is stored in the next section; for now, just notice that you're passing some of the location properties via `InitParams` to Silverlight. You're also passing in an application ID; that's required by Bing Maps to ensure you've got a valid Bing Maps account. The application ID is stored in the top-level site's property bag; this is covered later in the chapter as well.

LISTING 15.5: Display Mode Rendering

```
private SilverlightPlugin sl;

private void CreateDisplayModeChildControls()
{
    string applicationId = "";

    SPWeb web = SPContext.Current.Site.RootWeb;

    if (web.Properties.ContainsKey(Constants.ApplicationIdPropertyKey))
    {
        applicationId =
            web.Properties[Constants.ApplicationIdPropertyKey].ToString();
    }

    if (!this.DesignMode)
    {
        BingMapsLocation location;
        if (Value.ToString() != "")
        {
            // There is a location - reconstitute it
            location = BingMapsLocation.Load(Value.ToString());
        }
        else
        {
            // There never was a location - make an empty one
            location = new BingMapsLocation();
        }


        if (location.IsValid)
        {
            // Set up the Silverlight control, passing
            // the field value as the video URL to play
            sl = new SilverlightPlugin();
            sl.Source = SPContext.Current.Site.Url +
                "/ClientBin/MapViewSL.xap";
            sl.InitParameters = "latitude=" +
                location.Latitude.ToString() +
                ",longitude=" + location.Longitude.ToString() +
                ",zoomlevel=" + location.ZoomLevel.ToString() +
                ",mode=" + location.Mode.ToString().ToLower() +
                ",applicationid=" + applicationId;

            this.Controls.Add(sl);
        }
        else
        {
```

```
                errorSet = true;
                errorMessage = "No valid location to map - please set ";
            }
        }
    }


// Render the Silverlight control in a <div> so it will
// be the right dimensions on the page (Note SharePoint does this
// automatically for web parts ...)
protected override void RenderFieldForDisplay
                            (System.Web.UI.HtmlTextWriter output)
{
    output.Write("<div style=\"height:" +
                    Height.ToString() + "px;width:" +
                    Width.ToString() +
                    "px;color:white;background-color:CornflowerBlue;"+
                    "text-align:center;\">");
    if (this.DesignMode)
    {
        // Very simple rendering in SharePoint Designer
        output.Write("<b>*** MAP HERE ***</b>");
    }
    else if (this.ControlMode == SPControlMode.Display)
    {
        // OK we're in display mode, render the child controls
        // with exception handling
        if (!errorSet && sl != null)
        {
            try
            {
                sl.RenderControl(output);
            }
            catch (Exception ex)
            {
                output.Write("Error rendering map field: " +
                    ex.Message);
            }
        }
        else
        {
            output.Write("Error displaying map: " + errorMessage);
        }
    }
    output.Write("</div>");
}
```

A later section explains how the map actually gets displayed in Silverlight. This section focuses on the field control for now and examines the server-side Edit mode rendering. For modularity, the Edit mode is handled by a second web control, `MapSelectControl`. The field control always creates one of these as a handy place to store the field's value and is capable of editing the field. Listing 15.6 shows the Edit mode rendering.

LISTING 15.6: Edit Mode Rendering

```
// We always have a MapSelectControl in the wings to hold the
// current selection
private MapSelectControl mapEditControl = new MapSelectControl();

// Create child controls for edit mode
private void CreateEditModeChildControls()
{
    if (this.ControlMode != SPControlMode.Display)
    {
        // Handle the possibility that someone registered a Bing Map
        // Location selector in an (ASCX) template file
        MapSelectControl mapSelectorInTemplate =
            this.TemplateContainer.FindControl(this.TemplateName)
            as MapSelectControl;
        if (mapSelectorInTemplate == null)
        {
            // No Bing Map Location selector was found in the control
            // template ASCX files.
            // Add the default selector.
             this.Controls.Add(this.mapEditControl);
        }
        else
        {
            // Swap in the Bing Map Location selector from the control
            // template ASCX file
            mapSelectorInTemplate.SerializedMapLocation =
                this.mapEditControl.SerializedMapLocation;
            this.mapEditControl = mapSelectorInTemplate;
        }
    }
}
```

There is some logic here for rendering a *template file*; this is an ASP.NET user control that can be used to override a field's editing experience. The code supports such a file, but it's easier to use a real server control, so that's what you create by default. You could probably omit this logic and simply add the editing control, but this is the best practice because it allows adding a template file later.

Listing 15.7 shows the MapSelectControl class. It places the MapEditSL Silverlight application on the page and will pass in two InitParams: the application ID and the client ID of a hidden input control that contains the serialized location. This allows the Silverlight application to place a new location in the field for posting back to the server.

LISTING 15.7: MapSelectControl Class Handles Field Input

```
public class MapSelectControl : WebControl
{
    // Fields to hold child controls
    private Label messageLabel;
    private HiddenField locationHiddenField;
    private SilverlightPlugin silverlightPlugin;

    // Fields for exception handling
    private bool errorSet = false;
    private string errorMessage = "";

    public string SerializedMapLocation
    {
        get
        {
            EnsureChildControls();
            return this.locationHiddenField.Value;
        }
        set
        {
            EnsureChildControls();
            this.locationHiddenField.Value = value;
        }
    }

    protected override void OnInit(EventArgs e)
    {
        base.OnInit(e);

        // This ensures that the child control receives its postback.
        EnsureChildControls();
    }

    protected override void CreateChildControls()
    {
        base.CreateChildControls();
```

```
        messageLabel = new Label();
        this.Controls.Add(messageLabel);

        locationHiddenField = new HiddenField();
        this.Controls.Add(locationHiddenField);
    }

    protected override void OnPreRender(EventArgs e)
    {
        base.OnPreRender(e);

        try
        {
            string applicationId = "";
            SPWeb web = SPContext.Current.Site.RootWeb;

            if (web.Properties.ContainsKey
                (Constants.ApplicationIdPropertyKey))
            {
                applicationId =
            web.Properties[Constants.ApplicationIdPropertyKey].ToString();
            }

            silverlightPlugin = new SilverlightPlugin();
            silverlightPlugin.Source = SPContext.Current.Site.Url +
                "/ClientBin/MapEditSL.xap";

            silverlightPlugin.InitParameters = "locationControlId=" +
                this.locationHiddenField.ClientID +
                ",applicationId=" + applicationId;

            this.Controls.Add(silverlightPlugin);

        }
        catch (Exception ex)
        {
            messageLabel.Text = "Error launching location editor: " +
                ex.Message;
            locationHiddenField.Visible = true;
        }
    }

    protected override void Render(HtmlTextWriter writer)
    {
        if (!errorSet)
        {
            writer.Write("<div style=\"width:400px; height:300px;\">");
            base.Render(writer);
            writer.Write("</div>");
```

```
        }
        else
        {
            writer.Write(errorMessage);
        }
    }
}
```

Notice the calls to `EnsureChildControls()`; this is called to ensure that `CreateChildControls()` has been run and that the child controls are created and ready to go. When the `SerializedMapLocation` property is changed, the change is immediately written to the underlying hidden input control. To allow this, you need to call `EnsureChildControls()` from the property getter and setter so the hidden input control will always be there.

Over the next three sections, you complete the field control by filling in your own serializable class for holding a location, the strategy for storing the Bing Maps application ID, and the Silverlight applications to display and edit maps.

Serializing a Bing Maps Location

The `SPTextField` stores text, but this solution needs to store a location and not just any location, but a location for use with Bing Maps, which includes settings for the map viewer such as the zoom level and whether to show street or aerial maps. To easily do this, and do it in a way in which Silverlight as well as SharePoint can get at the data, you can use the `DataContractJsonSerializer` just as you did in Chapter 7. Please refer to that chapter for the details; this section focuses on the location data itself.

Listing 15.8 shows a portion of the `BingMapsLocation` class, omitting the `Load()` and `Serialize()` methods, which are the same as they were in Chapter 7.

LISTING 15.8: BingMapsLocation Class

```
[DataContract]
public class BingMapsLocation
{
    [DataMember]
    public double Latitude { get; set; }
```

```
[DataMember]
public double Longitude { get; set; }
[DataMember]
public double Altitude { get; set; }
[DataMember]
public double ZoomLevel { get; set; }
[DataMember]
public MapMode Mode { get; set; }
[DataMember]
public string ErrorMessage { get; set; }
[DataMember]
public string StreetAddress { get; set; }
[DataMember]
public DateTime GeoCodeTime { get; set; }
[DataMember]
public bool IsValid { get; set; }

public enum MapMode { Road, Aerial }

public BingMapsLocation()
{
    this.Latitude = 0.0;
    this.Longitude = 0.0;
    this.Altitude = 0.0;
    this.ZoomLevel = 10.0;
    this.Mode = MapMode.Road;
    this.ErrorMessage = "Location not set";
    this.StreetAddress = "";
    this.IsValid = false;
}
```

The properties begin with the obvious latitude and longitude, as well as altitude, though that's not currently used. Bing Maps allows zoom levels from 1 (the widest view) to 21 by default (this can vary based on location and is the most zoomed-in view). The object stores the zoom level and map mode, which can be set to show a road map or aerial view.

To allow more efficient geo-coding, you also store the most recently geo-coded address, the time, and any error that might have been returned when geo-coding. This allows the code to check to see if the same street address was already geo-coded, to avoid doing it again unnecessarily.

All the geo-coding is done on the Silverlight side, though it could be done on the server if that were needed for some reason. This is covered in the section Displaying and Editing Maps in Silverlight, next.

The other methods of the `BingMapsLocation` class allow a location to be transformed into a string using the `Serialize()` method and a string to be transformed into a location object using the `Load()` method. This is the same technique described in Chapter 7. Listing 15.9 shows how the `Serialize()` and `Load()` methods are used.

LISTING 15.9: Using the Serialize() and Load() Methods

```
BingMapsLocation location = BingMapsLocation.Load(locationString);
// do something to the location
locationString = location.Serialze();
```

Getting Started with Bing Maps

Bing Maps provides a Silverlight control and SDK for rendering and interacting with maps and a set of web services for interacting with the Bing Maps service. For information and download instructions, see http://bit.ly/SPSL_BingMapsSLControl. You need to install the Silverlight control on your development machine and add references to `Microsoft.Maps.MapControl.dll` and `Microsoft.Maps.MapControl.Common`.

To use the Bing Maps control and web services, you need an application ID. This can easily be obtained at http://bit.ly/SPSL_BingMapsAppId, and in most cases there is no charge. (See terms of use for details.)

This application ID is needed in your Silverlight applications to access the Bing Maps service. It's simple enough to pass it from SharePoint to Silverlight via using `InitParams`, but the question is where to store it in SharePoint. A Bing Maps web part might store the application ID in a web part setting, but this doesn't help the field control, which might be used in any number of pages or list items and should only need to be set once. The solution is to store it in a SharePoint *property bag* and allow the user to set the property in Site Settings. Every SharePoint web and site contains a property bag that can store name-value pairs; the sample stores the application ID in the property bag of the top-level site of the site collection where it is installed.

If you install the sample code for this chapter, you should see a new link under Site Collection Administration, under Site Settings for the top-level site of your site collection. The link is called Chapter 15—MapView Settings and leads to the page shown in Figure 15.2.

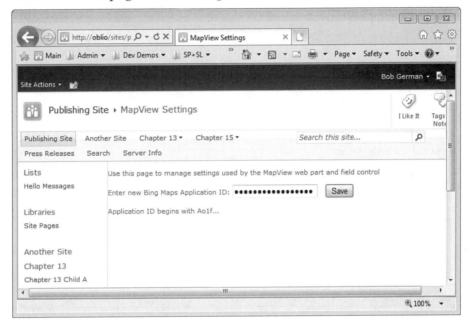

Figure 15.2: Setting the Application ID

This is a SharePoint *layouts page*, as indicated by the fact that the URL contains the _layouts folder following the site URL. To add this to Visual Studio, right-click the SharePoint project and click Add; then on the fly-out menu, click SharePoint Layouts Mapped Folder. Visual Studio creates a folder in your project that is mapped to SharePoint's TEMPLATE\ LAYOUTS folder under the SharePoint root, so anything you place in the Visual Studio folder is deployed to TEMPLATE\LAYOUTS and is accessible under any SharePoint site's _layouts folder. In this case, there is an ordinary folder called Chapter15—MapView within the Layouts folder to isolate our new page and avoid naming conflicts. Within that folder, right-click to add a new item and select a SharePoint 2010 Application Page. This puts an ordinary .aspx page in your project, which you can use however you wish.

The page in this case is called MapSettings.aspx, and contains a few simple ASP.NET controls to capture the application ID. The full page contains a number of directives and content placeholders so it will work within SharePoint's master page system; these are created by Visual Studio for you, so all you need to do is fill in the "Main" placeholder as shown in Listing 15.10.

LISTING 15.10: MapSettings.aspx Page to Save Application ID

```
<asp:Content ID="Main" ContentPlaceHolderID="PlaceHolderMain"
 runat="server">
    <br />
    Use this page to manage settings used by the MapView web part and
    field control<br />
    <br />
    Enter new Bing Maps Application ID:
    <asp:TextBox ID="ApplicationIdTextBox" Text="" runat="server"
     TextMode="Password" />  
    <asp:Button ID="SaveButton" runat="server" Text="Save"
     OnClick="SaveButton_Click" /><br />
    <br />
    <asp:Label ID="MessageLabel" runat="server" Text=""
     EnableViewState="false" />
</asp:Content>
```

Listing 15.11 shows the code-behind. It retrieves the application ID to show part of it to the user and updates the application ID if the user saves a new one.

LISTING 15.11: Saving the Application ID in the Web Property Bag

```
public partial class MapSettings : LayoutsPageBase
{
    protected void Page_Load(object sender, EventArgs e)
    {
        EnsureChildControls();
        if (!IsPostBack)
        {
            SPWeb web = SPContext.Current.Site.RootWeb;
            if (web.Properties.ContainsKey
                            (Constants.ApplicationIdPropertyKey))
            {
                string applicationId =
            web.Properties[Constants.ApplicationIdPropertyKey].ToString();
```

```
                ApplicationIdTextBox.Text = applicationId;
        }
        else
        {
            MessageLabel.Text = "No application ID is defined.";
        }
    }
}

protected void SaveButton_Click(object sender, EventArgs e)
{
    SPContext.Current.Site.RootWeb.Properties
        [Constants.ApplicationIdPropertyKey] =
        ApplicationIdTextBox.Text;
    SPContext.Current.Site.RootWeb.Properties.Update();
}

protected override void OnPreRender(EventArgs e)
{
    base.OnPreRender(e);
    if (ApplicationIdTextBox.Text.Length > 5)
    {
        MessageLabel.Text = "Application ID begins with " +
            ApplicationIdTextBox.Text.Substring(0, 5) + "...";
    }
    else
    {
        MessageLabel.Text = "No application ID is defined.";
    }
}
}
}
```

This allows the field control, or any of the server code, to easily retrieve the application ID from the site collection property bag.

Although this is enough to get the page working, you still need to add it to the Site Collection Administration page. This can be done by adding a custom action to an Elements.xml file in the project; in this case you add it to the Elements.xml file already under the ClientBin folder in the project, which is being used to deploy the .xap files. Listing 15.12 shows the complete Elements.xml file. As you can see, the <CustomAction> tag adds the action to site settings; any page can be linked to from settings (or other menus in SharePoint) using this tag.

LISTING 15.12: Adding the Site Settings Page to Elements.xml

```xml
<?xml version="1.0" encoding="utf-8"?>
<Elements xmlns="http://schemas.microsoft.com/sharepoint/">
  <Module Name="ClientBin">
    <File Path="ClientBin\MapViewSL.xap" Url="ClientBin/MapViewSL.xap" />
    <File Path="ClientBin\MapEditSL.xap" Url="ClientBin/MapEditSL.xap" />
  </Module>
  <CustomAction Id="MapView.SettingsAction"
   GroupId="SiteCollectionAdmin"
   Location="Microsoft.SharePoint.SiteSettings"
   Sequence="1000"
   Title="Chapter 17 - MapView Settings">
      <UrlAction Url="_layouts/Chapter17-MapView/MapSettings.aspx"/>
  </CustomAction>
</Elements>
```

Displaying and Editing Maps in Silverlight

The MapViewSL Silverlight application is responsible for displaying a mapped location, and it's really pretty simple. First, in the `Application_Startup()` method under App.xaml.cs, you extract the Init-Params containing all the information needed to render the map and pass them to the `MainPage` via its constructor. This is shown in Listing 15.13.

LISTING 15.13: Application_Startup for the MapViewSL Application

```csharp
private void Application_Startup(object sender, StartupEventArgs e)
{
    double latitude = 0.0;
    double longitude = 0.0;
    double zoomLevel = 1.0;
    string mode = "aerial";

    string applicationId = "";

    if (e.InitParams.ContainsKey("latitude") &&
        e.InitParams.ContainsKey("longitude") &&
        e.InitParams.ContainsKey("zoomlevel") &&
        e.InitParams.ContainsKey("mode") &&
        e.InitParams.ContainsKey("applicationid"))
    {
        Double.TryParse(e.InitParams["latitude"].ToString(),
            out latitude);
        Double.TryParse(e.InitParams["longitude"].ToString(),
```

```
        out longitude);
    Double.TryParse(e.InitParams["zoomlevel"].ToString(),
        out zoomLevel);
    mode = e.InitParams["mode"].ToLower();
    applicationId = e.InitParams["applicationid"];
}

this.RootVisual = new MainPage(latitude, longitude, zoomLevel,
                        mode, applicationId);
}
```

The MainPage XAML is exceedingly simple, containing just the Bing Maps control as shown in Listing 15.14.

LISTING 15.14: Main Page XAML for MapViewSL Application

```
<Grid x:Name="LayoutRoot" Background="White">
    <m:Map x:Name="myMapControl" />
</Grid>
```

The code behind isn't much more complex than that. The Bing Maps control makes it really easy, as shown in Listing 15.15.

LISTING 15.15: Main Page Code for MapViewSL Application

```
public MainPage(double latitude, double longitude,
            double zoomLevel, string mode, string applicationId)
{
    InitializeComponent();

    myMapControl.CredentialsProvider =
        new ApplicationIdCredentialsProvider(applicationId);

    if (mode == "aerial")
    {
        myMapControl.Mode = new AerialMode(true);
    }
    else
    {
        myMapControl.Mode = new RoadMode();
    }

    myMapControl.SetView(new Location(latitude, longitude), zoomLevel);

    Pushpin p = new Pushpin();
    p.Location = new Location(latitude, longitude);
    myMapControl.Children.Add(p);
}
```

When rendered, the map display looks like the image in Figure 15.3, shown here with an aerial view of Boston's historic Fenway Park. As you can see, the map is centered on the chosen location, which is also marked with a pushpin.

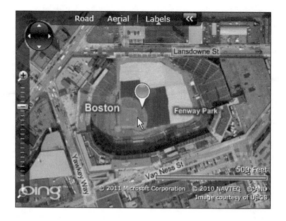

FIGURE 15.3: MapViewSL display

The MapEditorSL application is more interesting. Figure 15.4 shows the user interface. A text box and button have been added to allow geo-coding, and the map can also be moved using the mouse and zoom control to refine the location.

FIGURE 15.4: Geocoding with the MapEditSL application

The `Application_Startup` method is simpler in this case, in that it passes in the application ID (of course) and the client ID of a hidden input field containing the serialized location. This allows you to push a new location into the hidden field so it is posted back to the host along with the rest of the New or Edit form.

Listing 15.16 shows the MapEditSL Main Page XAML. Notice that in addition to adding a text box and button for geo-coding, the map control now has event handlers for `MouseClick` and `ViewChangeOnFrame`. These fire when the user clicks the mouse or changes the view frame, such as zooming or changing from road to aerial view. Note that clicking the view frame centers the view and the pushpin on the location clicked.

LISTING 15.16: MapEditSL XAML

```
<Grid x:Name="LayoutRoot" Background="White">
  <Grid.RowDefinitions>
    <RowDefinition Height="30"/>
    <RowDefinition/>
  </Grid.RowDefinitions>
  <Grid>
    <Grid.Background>
      <LinearGradientBrush EndPoint="0.5,1" StartPoint="0.5,0">
        <GradientStop Color="#D80C0B0B" Offset="0"/>
        <GradientStop Color="#D8000000" Offset="1"/>
        <GradientStop Color="#D8726666" Offset="0.689"/>
        <GradientStop Color="#FF453C3C" Offset="0.307"/>
        <GradientStop Color="#D82B2626" Offset="0.164"/>
      </LinearGradientBrush>
    </Grid.Background>
    <Grid.ColumnDefinitions>
      <ColumnDefinition Width="0.132*"/>
      <ColumnDefinition Width="0.781*"/>
      <ColumnDefinition Width="0.087*"/>
    </Grid.ColumnDefinitions>
    <TextBlock d:LayoutOverrides="Height" Text="Find:" Margin="10,5,0,0"
      FontSize="13.333" FontWeight="Bold" Foreground="White" />
    <TextBox x:Name="StreetAddressTextBox" Margin="5,5,0,5"
      d:LayoutOverrides="Height" Grid.Column="1" />
    <Button Content="Go" Click="Button_Click" d:LayoutOverrides="Height"
      Grid.Column="2" Margin="3" />
  </Grid>
  <m:Map x:Name="myMapControl" MouseClick="myMapControl_MouseClick"
    ViewChangeOnFrame="myMapControl_ViewChangeOnFrame" Margin="0"
    Grid.Row="1" />
</Grid>
```

Listing 15.17 shows the `MainPage` constructor. It uses the same technique shown in Chapter 10 to read the location from the hidden input field using the HTML Bridge. If the field contains a valid location, it's loaded into a new `BingMapsLocation` object; if not, you make a new `BingMapsLocation` object (which points to a location with latitude and longitude of zero). Then the location is mapped using much the same code you saw in the MapViewSL application.

LISTING 15.17: MainPage Constructor for MapEditSL Application

```
string locationControlId;
BingMapsLocation location;
string applicationId;
Pushpin currentLocationPushpin = new Pushpin();

public MainPage(string locationControlId, string applicationId)
{
    InitializeComponent();

    // Save away the location control and Bing Maps application ID
    this.locationControlId = locationControlId;
    this.applicationId = applicationId;

    // Get credentials provider for this app ID
    myMapControl.CredentialsProvider =
        new ApplicationIdCredentialsProvider(this.applicationId);

    // Get the location from the location control
    HtmlDocument doc = HtmlPage.Document;
    HtmlElement hiddenField = doc.GetElementById(locationControlId);
    if (hiddenField.GetAttribute("value") == null)
    {
        // If no location is provided, make a new one
        this.location = new BingMapsLocation();
    }
    else
    {
        // If we have a location, load it as a BingMapsLocation object
        string locationString =
            hiddenField.GetAttribute("value").ToString();
        this.location = BingMapsLocation.Load(locationString);

        StreetAddressTextBox.Text = this.location.StreetAddress;
```

```
        // Point map to the location, and set the mode (road vs. aerial)
        myMapControl.SetView(new Location(this.location.Latitude,
            this.location.Longitude), this.location.ZoomLevel);
        if (this.location.Mode == BingMapsLocation.MapMode.Road)
        {
            myMapControl.Mode = new RoadMode();
        }
        else
        {
            myMapControl.Mode = new AerialMode(true);
        }
    }

    // Now set a pushpin on the location
    currentLocationPushpin.Location =
        new Location(this.location.Latitude, this.location.Longitude);
    myMapControl.Children.Add(currentLocationPushpin);
}
```

Things start to get interesting in the event handlers. The MouseClick event fires when the user clicks on the map. It centers the map and pushpin on the point where he clicked. Listing 15.18 shows the code. Note that the Location object class is part of the Bing Maps SDK, but this.location refers to your own BingMapsLocation field.

LISTING 15.18: MouseClick Event Handler

```
private void myMapControl_MouseClick(object sender, MapMouseEventArgs e)
{
    // User clicked on the map, center on the clicked location
    Location l = myMapControl.ViewportPointToLocation(e.ViewportPoint);
    myMapControl.SetView(l, this.location.ZoomLevel);
    currentLocationPushpin.Location = l;

    StreetAddressTextBox.Text = "";

    // Now remember the location and update the location control so it
    // will get posted back
    this.location.StreetAddress = "";
    this.location.Latitude = l.Latitude;
    this.location.Longitude = l.Longitude;
    this.location.Altitude = l.Altitude;
    this.location.IsValid = true;
    UpdateLocationField();
}
```

```
private void UpdateLocationField()
{
    // Now push back to the host!
    string locationString = this.location.Serialize();
    HtmlDocument doc = HtmlPage.Document;
    HtmlElement hiddenField = doc.GetElementById(locationControlId);
    hiddenField.SetAttribute("value", locationString);
}
```

The UpdateLocationField() method is used to update the hidden field when the user makes other changes. For example, Listing 15.19 shows the ViewChangedOnFrame event handler, which saves changes to the display mode and zoom level.

LISTING 15.19: ViewChangedOnFrame Event Handler

```
private void myMapControl_ViewChangeOnFrame
                            (object sender, MapEventArgs e)
{
    // User changed mode or zoom level, so save it in the location and
    // update the location control so it will get posted back
    this.location.ZoomLevel = myMapControl.ZoomLevel;
    if (myMapControl.Mode is AerialMode)
    {
        this.location.Mode = BingMapsLocation.MapMode.Aerial;
    }
    else
    {
        this.location.Mode = BingMapsLocation.MapMode.Road;
    }
    UpdateLocationField();
}
```

When the user clicks the button, the address in the text box is geo-coded. This is shown in Listing 15.20. For development purposes, you need to add a reference to the staging environment in Bing Maps at http://staging. dev.virtualearth.net/webservices/v1/metadata/geocodeservice/geocode service.wsdl. Call the service GeoCodeService.

Notice that the code checks to see if the street address in the Bing MapsLocation is the same as the one being geo-coded so it can skip the web services call if it's the same location again. The geo-code service allows setting of a confidence filter; this code is optimistic and uses a low-confidence filter, which is likely to return results more often, even if they're not as sure to be accurate.

Listing 15.20: Geo-Coding with Bing Maps

```csharp
private void Button_Click(object sender, RoutedEventArgs e)
{
    // User clicked the button, so geocode the address they typed
    GeoCode(this.StreetAddressTextBox.Text, applicationId);
}

// Return true if a new location will be loaded
private bool GeoCode(string streetAddress, string applicationId)
{
    if (streetAddress == this.location.StreetAddress)
    {
        // Location did not change
        return false;
    }

    // OK we're going to try to look up the address
    // No matter what we'll want to indicate to our caller that the
    // location has changed. Mark the location as not valid until we
    // get a new geocode
    bool locationWillChange = true;
    this.location.StreetAddress = streetAddress;
    this.location.IsValid = false;

    try
    {
        BasicHttpBinding binding = new BasicHttpBinding();
        EndpointAddress endpoint = new EndpointAddress
("http://dev.virtualearth.net/webservices/v1/GeocodeService/GeocodeService.svc"
);

        GeocodeService.GeocodeRequest request =
            new GeocodeService.GeocodeRequest();
        request.Query = location.StreetAddress;
        request.Options = new GeocodeService.GeocodeOptions();
        request.Options.Filters =
            new ObservableCollection<GeocodeService.FilterBase>();

        GeocodeService.ConfidenceFilter filter =
            new GeocodeService.ConfidenceFilter();
        filter.MinimumConfidence = GeocodeService.Confidence.Low;
        request.Options.Filters.Add(filter);
```

```
            request.Credentials =
                new Microsoft.Maps.MapControl.Credentials();
            request.Credentials.ApplicationId = applicationId;

            GeocodeService.GeocodeServiceClient client =
                new GeocodeService.GeocodeServiceClient(binding, endpoint);
            client.GeocodeCompleted += new
                EventHandler<GeocodeService.GeocodeCompletedEventArgs>
                (client_GeocodeCompleted);
            client.GeocodeAsync(request);
        }
        catch (Exception ex)
        {
            this.location.ErrorMessage = ex.Message;
            this.location.IsValid = false;
        };

        return (locationWillChange);
    }


    void client_GeocodeCompleted(object sender,
                            GeocodeService.GeocodeCompletedEventArgs e)
    {
        if (e.Result.ResponseSummary.StatusCode ==
                            GeocodeService.ResponseStatusCode.Success)
        {
            if (e.Result.Results.Count > 0)
            {
                GeocodeService.GeocodeResult result = e.Result.Results[0];
                this.location.Latitude = result.Locations[0].Latitude;
                this.location.Longitude = result.Locations[0].Longitude;
                this.location.Altitude = result.Locations[0].Altitude;
                this.location.ErrorMessage = "";
                this.location.GeoCodeTime = DateTime.Now;
                this.location.IsValid = true;

                myMapControl.SetView(
                    new Location(this.location.Latitude,
                                this.location.Longitude), 10);
                currentLocationPushpin.Location =
                    new Location(this.location.Latitude,
                                this.location.Longitude);
```

```
            UpdateLocationField();
        }
        else
        {
            this.location.ErrorMessage = "Address not found";
            this.location.IsValid = false;
        }
    }
    else
    {
        this.location.ErrorMessage = e.Error.Message;
        this.location.IsValid = false;
    }
}
```

You might be pleased to find that the geo-coding feature is very flexible and can find landmarks as well as street addresses. Try looking for "Statue of Liberty," "Pyramids at Giza," or "Hollywood Sign."

Using the Location Field

If you stopped at this point, you should be able to deploy the solution as it is and add one or more Bing Maps Location fields to any list in SharePoint. For example, Figure 15.5 shows how to add a location to a contacts list, allowing you to show a map for each contact in the list.

The user can find addresses and landmarks, fine-tune the location by clicking, and adjust the view by zooming and selecting road or aerial rendering. If he clicks Save, then the map is saved right in the contact list item. Figure 15.7 shows a view of the map in a contact. Note that the map has no relation to the Address and City fields in the contact, but to the map location selected when the contact is edited.

Once the new Location column is added, we can simply edit any contact in the list to edit its map view and location, as shown in Figure 15.6.

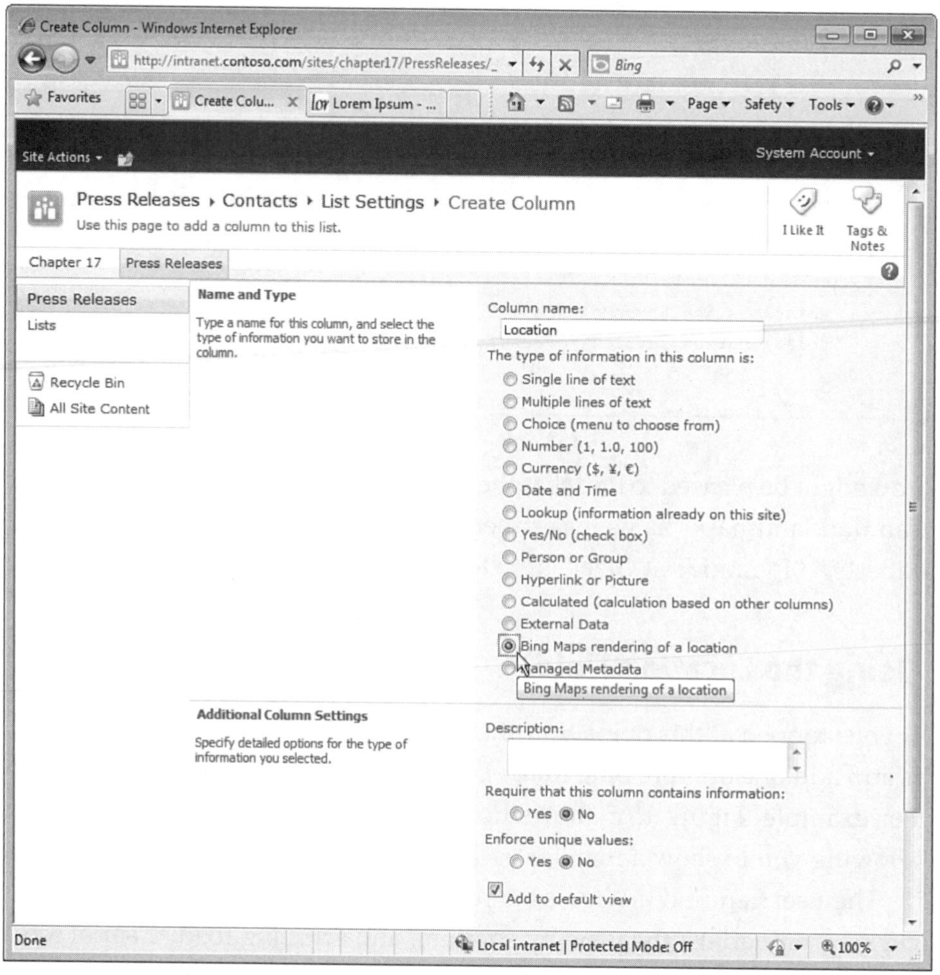

FIGURE 15.5: Adding a location field to a contacts list

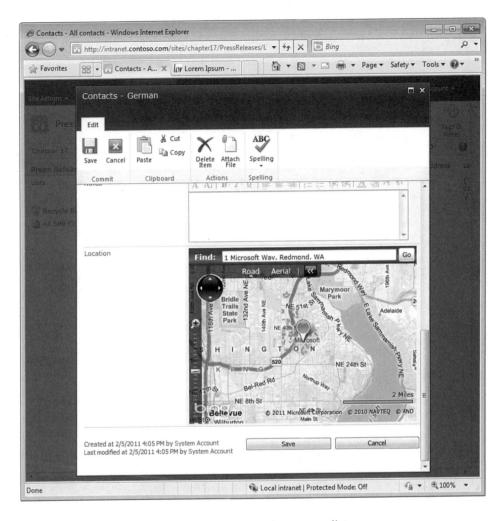

FIGURE 15.6: Editing a location field in a SharePoint contacts list

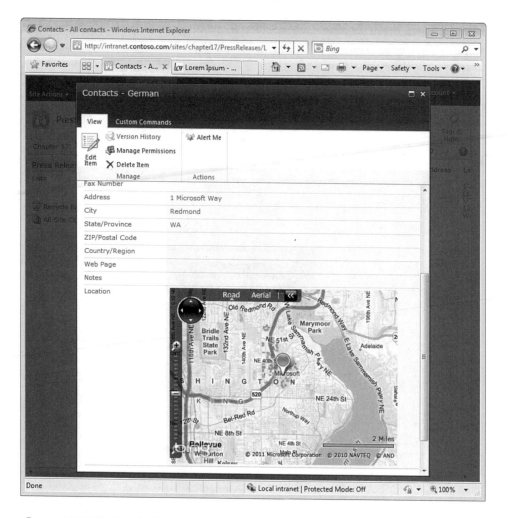

FIGURE 15.7: Viewing the location of a contact

This is pretty cool on its own because now you can geo-code anything in SharePoint by simply adding a Bing Maps Location field to a list or library. To take it to the next step, you connect it with SharePoint's web publishing system to allow maps to be first-class fields on pages, with a full editing workflow, page versioning and approval and all the other Web Content Management features in SharePoint.

Field Controls and Publishing Sites

When publishing a web site, different people have different responsibilities that extend to each web page. For example, a marketing specialist chooses the site branding and works with graphic artists and web developers to implement the brand and basic page structure. An information architect can determine the navigation structure and the fields that appear on different page layouts. And authors and editors can directly edit page content and manage media files and other site content.

SharePoint Server 2010 solves these problems by adding publishing sites to the more basic sites provided in SharePoint Foundation. To make use of them, it's best to create a site collection with the "Publishing Portal" template. This sets up your site collection to host pages in /Pages libraries, with editable fields and page navigation.

Figure 15.8 shows the rendering of a page in a SharePoint publishing site. The master page provides the basic page structure and branding, and the page layout places field controls on the page. This provides a consistent structure for, say, a news article or a catalog listing. Each field control renders and edits a field in the Pages library. For example, the Title field in the Pages Library is rendered by a text field control. This allows the Pages library to manage page content with all the features of any SharePoint library: versioning, approval, workflow, and so on.

When someone requests a publishing page, such as http://myserver/Pages/Article123.aspx, SharePoint reads the Pages library and obtains its page layout, which is a special field indicating the .aspx page that renders the page. This is a real .aspx page in SharePoint's content system, in the Master Page Gallery. SharePoint renders the page layout using the currently selected master page. The field controls then show each field, including, soon, your map field. This is shown in more detail in Figure 15.9.

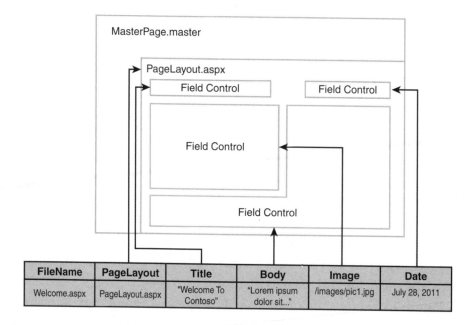

FIGURE 15.8: Rendering a SharePoint publishing page

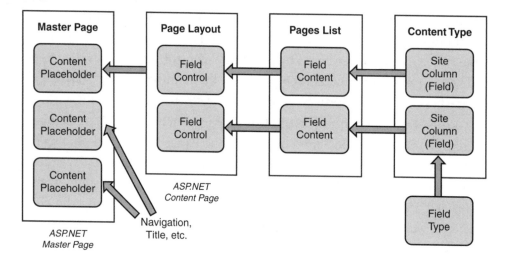

FIGURE 15.9: Content flow in a SharePoint publishing page

Looking at Figure 15.9, begin in the lower right corner, with your field type. The field type can be used to instantiate one or more site columns. Site columns are called *fields* in the SharePoint object model. Content types, oddly named consistently between the programming and user interfaces, organize the site columns into reusable sets. A Pages list supports the Page content type and can hold any other content types derived from Page. In this case the derived content type includes a location site column.

To render the new page content type, you need to associate one or more page layouts with it. The page layout contains the actual field controls to render and edit content, and it binds the field controls to the page's underlying fields. The page layout itself shows through a Content Placeholder in the master page, generally the largest one on the page. Other Content Placeholders might display the title, navigation, and other page features that are part of SharePoint or the branding treatment.

Defining a Bing Maps Column and Content Type

Columns (or fields) can exist at multiple levels in SharePoint. A column can be added to a list, or a site column can be defined. To view site columns, go to Site Settings and select Site Columns under the Galleries heading. If a site column is defined in the top-level site of a site collection, it can be used in lists and libraries throughout the site collection.

Site columns allow SharePoint to match a column across lists or content types—for example, a shoe size and a temperature might both be numbers in SharePoint, but when they're called "shoe size" or "temperature" they are created as columns either in the list or as a site column.

In similar fashion, content types can exist in lists, or in the Site Content Types Gallery at the site or site collection level. Content types define, well, types of content, such as tasks, contacts, documents, or pages. Each content type contains a set of site columns and can inherit from other content types; for example an Article Page (a web page intended for a news article) is derived from the Page content type.

■ TIP

Content types are normally limited to a single site collection, but they can be distributed to many site collections using the Content Type Hub in the SharePoint Managed Metadata Service. For more information, see http://bit.ly/SPSL_CTHub.

In this section, you learn how to create a site column for the location field type and an Article Page with Layout content type that's derived from Article Page.

An easy way to create the site column would be to go to the Site Columns Gallery and create the column directly. If your field type is defined and working, that will get you going. However, it's not packaged, and the site column needs to be manually created, which throws a wrench into the ability to test and deploy the solution. The same is true for the content type.

To create the site column and content type in Visual Studio and include them in your solution, begin by right-clicking the SharePoint project and adding a new item; select Content Type under the SharePoint 2010 templates as shown in Figure 15.10.

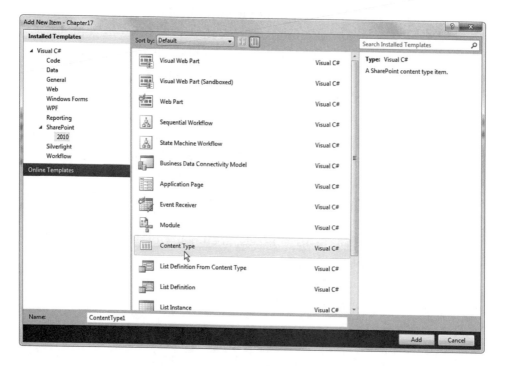

FIGURE 15.10: Creating a content type in Visual Studio

You now have an opportunity to choose the Parent content type, as shown in Figure 15.11.

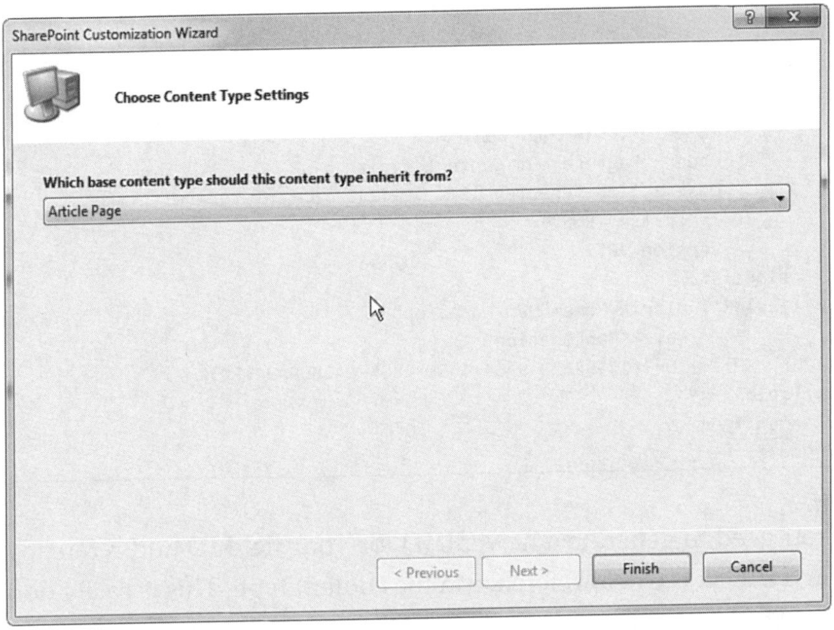

FIGURE 15.11: Choosing the Parent content type

You are rewarded with an elements.xml file containing a new content type with the trickiest part, the long compound ID, all figured out for you. Content type IDs are concatenations of GUIDs, with each derived content type adding its GUID to the end. Just ensure that the Parent content type is available wherever you deploy the solution.

It is necessary to manually edit the XML to declare the site column and a reference to it in the content type. Listing 15.21 shows the complete Elements.xml file, which is included in the solution download in the Chapter15 project under MapLocationField.

LISTING 15.21: Declaring a Site Column and Content Type

```
<?xml version="1.0" encoding="utf-8"?>
<Elements xmlns="http://schemas.microsoft.com/sharepoint/">

  <Field ID="{12595A28-9364-465E-AB07-2A2B6BAD91E9}"
         Name="MapLocation"
         DisplayName="Map Location"
         Type="MapViewField"
         Required="FALSE"
         Group="Custom Columns"
```

```
            />

<!-- Parent ContentType: Article Page (0x010100...) -->
<ContentType ID="0x010100..."
             Name="Article Page with Map"
             Group="Page Layout Content Types"
             Description="Chapter 17 - Article content type with map"
             Inherits="TRUE"
             Version="0">
    <FieldRefs>
      <FieldRef DisplayName="Map Location"
                Name="MapLocation"
                ID="{12595A28-9364-465E-AB07-2A2B6BAD91E9}" />
    </FieldRefs>
  </ContentType>
</Elements>
```

You need to generate a new GUID for your field ID and reference the same GUID in the field reference in the content type. This is easily done in Visual Studio by selecting Create GUID on the Tools menu and pasting the GUID into your XML file.

The full schema reference for Elements.xml is available at http://bit.ly/SPSL_ElementsSchema.

Defining a Page Layout

The easiest way by far to create a page layout in SharePoint is to use SharePoint designer. The Article Page with Map page layout that's included in the code download was made by editing the ArticleRight.aspx page layout that's included with SharePoint.

To do this yourself, begin by downloading and installing SharePoint Designer from http://bit.ly/SPSL_DownloadSPD2010. Start SharePoint Designer and open your development site; then click the Page Layouts link on the left. You see all the page layouts in the site, as shown in Figure 15.12. Right-click the page layout you wish to copy and copy it, paste it, and rename it to your liking.

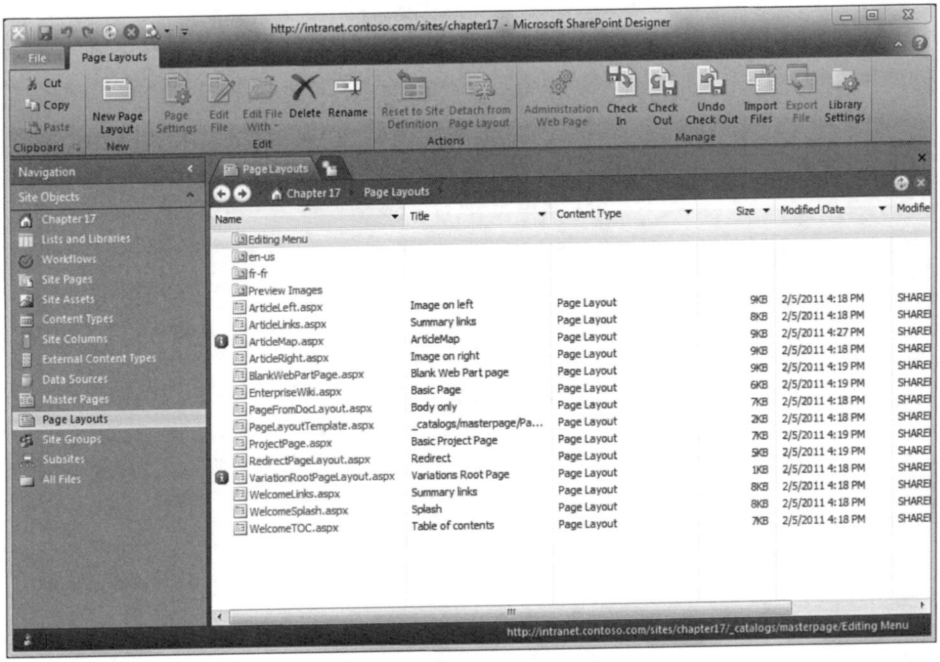

Figure 15.12: Opening a Page Layout in SharePoint Designer

Now click your new page layout to open its Settings page, as shown in Figure 15.13.

On the settings page, under Customization, click Manage All File Properties in the Browser, and the browser opens, allowing you to view the properties of the page layout in its gallery. Click Edit Item and change the Associated Content Type to your new content type, as shown in Figure 15.14.

Save your changes and close the web browser, returning to SharePoint Designer. Now click Edit File to edit the page layout's markup, and add the map field control. You might be prompted to edit in Advanced Mode; go ahead and do this.

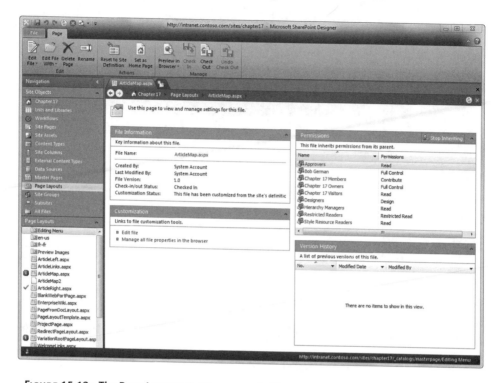

FIGURE 15.13: The Page Layouts Settings page in SharePoint Designer

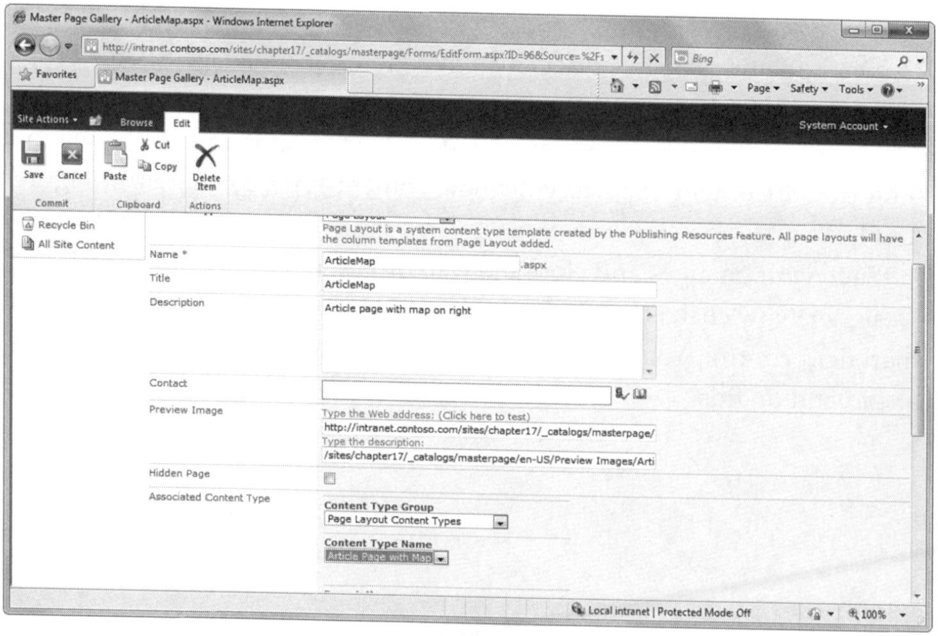

FIGURE 15.14: Changing the Associated Content Type of a Page Layout

When the page is open, you can choose to edit it in Design or Code mode, or a split view. When you're ready to place your new field on the page layout, click the Insert tab and open the SharePoint drop-down on the Ribbon. It might take a while for all the choices to populate; when they do, scroll down, and at the bottom you can see all the available fields on the page based on the associated content type, as shown in Figure 15.15. Select the Map Location field and drag it onto the page.

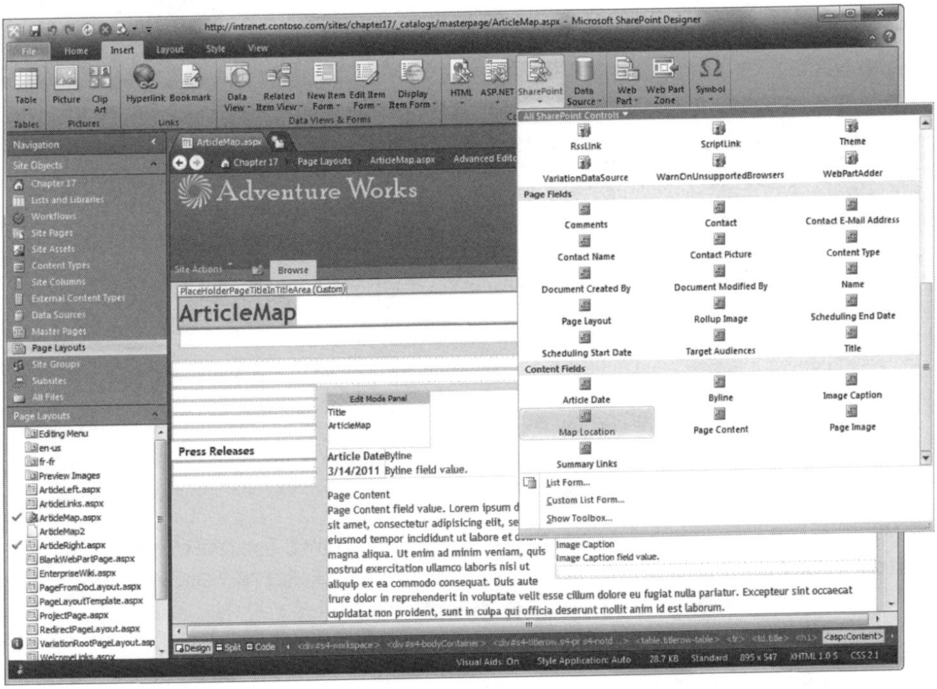

FIGURE 15.15: Adding a field to a Page Layout in SharePoint Designer

At this point, you could check in and approve your page layout, but only on your development web site. Indeed, it's a good idea to test the page layout and adjust the details while it's in SharePoint Designer. However, to package the page layout for deployment along with the new field control, you need to bring it into our Visual Studio project.

This is a simple matter of copy and paste. In SharePoint Designer, click the Code tab to display all the markup for the page layout. Select all of it and copy it to the clipboard.

Next, return to Visual Studio and create a new module called Master-Page. Even though SharePoint Designer gives the illusion of a separate library for page layouts, they live in the Master Page Gallery along with the master pages. Inside the module, create a new item and add a Code File item with the filename of your page layout, in this case, ArticleMap.aspx. Simply paste the markup into this file.

Even though Visual Studio created an Elements.xml file for you, you need to add some properties to correctly mark the file as a page layout and to mark its associated content type. Listing 15.22 shows the Elements.xml file.

LISTING 15.22: Elements.xml for a Page Layout

```xml
<?xml version="1.0" encoding="utf-8"?>
<Elements xmlns="http://schemas.microsoft.com/sharepoint/">
  <Module Name="MasterPage" Url="_catalogs/masterPage">
    <File Path="MasterPage\ArticleMap.aspx" Url="ArticleMap.aspx"
          Type="GhostableInLibrary">
      <Property Name="Title" Value="ArticleMap"/>
      <Property Name="MasterPageDescription" Value="Article page with map on
right"/>
      <Property Name="ContentType"
               Value ="$Resources:cmscore,contenttype_pagelayout_name;"/>
      <Property Name="PublishingAssociatedContentType" Value=";#Article Page
with
Map;#0x010100C568DB52D9D0A14D9B2FDCC96666E9F2007948130EC3DB064584E219954237AF39
00242457EFB8B24247815D688C526CD44D0052bc7cfd01064eb996b3225d0963bf69;#" />
      <Property Name="PublishingPreviewImage"
Value="~SiteCollection/_catalogs/masterpage/$Resources:core,Culture;/Preview
Images/ArticleLeft.png,
~SiteCollection/_catalogs/masterpage/$Resources:core,Culture;/Preview
Images/ArticleLeft.png"/>
    </File>
  </Module>
</Elements>
```

Notice that the file is marked as GhostableInLibrary; this indicates that it is an item in a SharePoint library that can be further edited and versioned, which is exactly the case for the Master Page Gallery. In addition, a ContentType property is provided for the page layout itself; for this you can use a $Resources token, which Visual Studio converts into the content type for a page layout. The associated content type in the PublishingAssociated ContentType property must be specified in full; this contains the long compound GUID from the content type's Elements.xml file. You can also optionally provide a preview image to display to users when they are selecting a page layout.

Using the Location Field in a Publishing Site

At this point the solution contains everything that's needed to publish web pages including maps. The field type knows how to represent a map location as a data type in SharePoint, and the field control knows how to render and edit the maps using Silverlight. An instance of the field and a content type are provided for use in page authoring, as is a page layout to hold it all. You can now begin to create web pages with map fields.

To do this, go to your publishing site and, on the Site Actions menu, select New Page. Give the page a name and click Create. You get the default page layout; to change it, click the Page tab, open the Page Layout dropdown, and select your new page layout as shown in Figure 15.16.

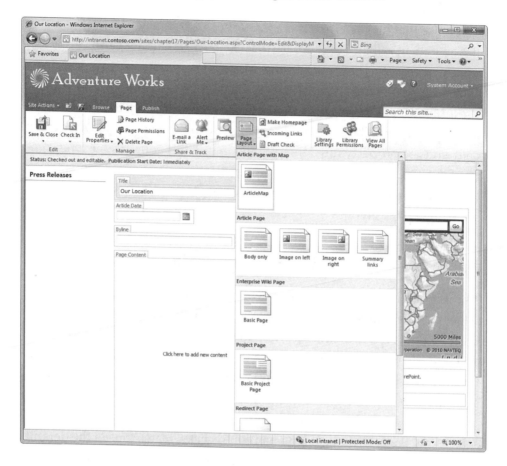

FIGURE 15.16: Using the New Page Layout

The editing experience is much as it was when the field was in a contacts list, except now it's on a publishing page surrounded with other fields and is part of a rich web site editing experience, as shown in Figure 15.17. The map will be approved and versioned along with all the other fields on the page, providing a consistent editing and publishing experience.

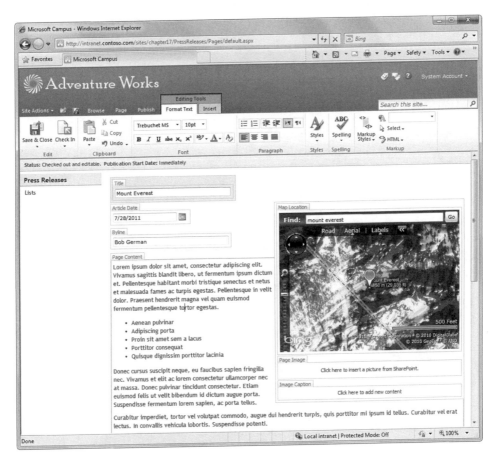

FIGURE 15.17: Editing the Page with Map

Summary

This chapter demonstrates a number of key concepts that allow you to make powerful changes in SharePoint. It shows you how to add new kinds of data, to display them in any list, and then how to integrate them into the SharePoint web publishing system. The map could as easily be a stock ticker, a molecule, or a musical chord. With the ability to create new field types, you can add almost anything to SharePoint's content system.

Index

X-Y-Z

informIT.com

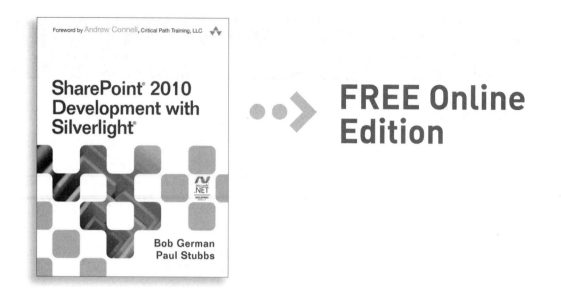

FREE Online Edition

Your purchase of **SharePoint 2010 Development with Silverlight** includes access to a free online edition for 45 days through the Safari Books Online subscription service. Nearly every Addison-Wesley Professional book is available online through Safari Books Online, along with more than 5,000 other technical books and videos from publishers such as Cisco Press, Exam Cram, IBM Press, O'Reilly, Prentice Hall, Que, and Sams.

SAFARI BOOKS ONLINE allows you to search for a specific answer, cut and paste code, download chapters, and stay current with emerging technologies.

Activate your FREE Online Edition at www.informit.com/safarifree

> **STEP 1:** Enter the coupon code: ZAZRWBI.

> **STEP 2:** New Safari users, complete the brief registration form. Safari subscribers, just log in.

If you have difficulty registering on Safari or accessing the online edition, please e-mail customer-service@safaribooksonline.com